ADVERTISING WORKS 8

ADVERTISING WORKS 8

Papers from the IPA Advertising Effectiveness Awards

Institute of Practitioners in Advertising, 1994

Edited and introduced by

Chris Baker

NTC PUBLICATIONS LIMITED

First published 1995 by **NTC Publications Limited**
Farm Road, Henley-on-Thames, Oxfordshire, RG9 1EJ, United Kingdom
Telephone: 01491 574671

British Library Cataloguing in Publication Data
Advertising Works 8: papers from the IPA Advertising Effectiveness Awards 1994.
  1. Great Britain. Advertising
  I. Baker, Chris   II. Institute of Practitioners in Advertising
  659.111

ISBN 1–870562–99–2

Typeset by NTC Publications Ltd
Printed and bound in Great Britain
by Biddles Ltd, Guildford and King's Lynn

Contents

CONTENTS

IPA
Advertising Effectiveness Awards
1994

This book is the 'volume of record' of the eighth biennial IPA Advertising Effectiveness Awards Scheme. *Advertising Works 8* follows its seven predecessors by documenting the winning entries to the latest competition. The 20 case histories from 1994 published here add to the over 140 already made available via previous Advertising Works volumes. All previous entries to the awards – almost 600 in total – are now available via the newly established IPA Advertising Effectiveness Data Bank[1].

The aims of the IPA Advertising Effectiveness Awards remain the same as when they were first set up on 1980:

1. To generate a collection of case histories which demonstrate that, properly used, advertising can make a measurable contribution to business success.

2. To encourage advertising agencies (and their clients) to develop ever-improving standards of advertising evaluation (and, in the process, a better understanding of the ways in which advertising works).

The format and judging criteria remain fundamentally the same, but there has been significant evolution as well, most notably via the introduction of the longer term, 'brand effects' category in 1990, and a rationalisation of the category structure in 1994.

Collectively the assembled case histories again deliver strongly against the Awards' primary objective, providing ample evidence that – when used and executed in the right way – advertising remains a cost-effective and accountable business tool. In changing and ever more challenging market conditions, advertising *still* works.

However, in many ways the real value of this book resides in the specific and very practical insights the case histories provide into *how to* plan and execute advertising that works, and then evaluate it.

The case histories which follow are detailed. With minor editing changes (eg some technical appendices have been omitted), what is published is the same as that originally submitted to the judges. All provide background to the business context and strategic thinking behind the advertising concerned, a description of the advertising itself, as well as necessarily a detailed analysis isolating the contribution made by advertising to overall business success. As a result, this is not the kind of book to be read 'cover to cover'. Rather it is a reference book to be dipped into, to be informed and stimulated by those case histories which are of relevance and interest at a given point of time. To help in this respect, there is a short guide to the 20 case histories at the end of this introductory section.

Before this there is a fuller background on 'the competition' plus some broader observations about the state of the art – in advertising, its evaluation, and brand marketing generally – that can be drawn from the 'class of '94'.

THE COMPETITION

Prior to 1980 there was virtually no case history material demonstrating advertising effectiveness, anywhere in the world, which was both published and sufficiently rigorous in its analysis and presentation of data to be convincing. This was a major barrier to both justifying the industry's services to its customers, and the promotion of best practice and a more accountable culture within advertising.

These Awards were designed to help fill this vacuum and have done so very successfully since 1980, producing a fresh tranche of effectiveness cases every two years. The demands for proof are considerably more rigorous than those made by effectiveness awards in the USA and in continental Europe. Elsewhere, the Advertising Federation of Australia (from 1990) and Canadian Congress of Advertising (from 1992) have based their awards on the UK IPA format.

Entries to the Awards must be in the form of written papers, up to 4,000 words in length (6,000 for multi-country entries), not counting appendices and charts. Each entry form must be countersigned by the agency's chief executive and by a competent representative of the client, by which act copyright is passed to the IPA.

The criteria on which entries are judged are perhaps best explained by quoting from the actual instructions given to judges. These are substantially the same as those formalised by Paul Feldwick, my predecessor as Convenor of Judges.

Notes for Judges

1. The main criterion for judging is simple: *how convincing is the case put for the specific contribution of advertising to business success?* The onus is on the author to anticipate questions and counter-arguments. Papers fail because they do not consider all the relevant facts, or present data in an obfuscatory way (on purpose or through carelessness). If you – as a sceptical but not necessarily 'expert' reader – feel reasonably convinced that it was indeed the advertising that produced the results claimed for it, then the paper is a contender.

2. However, when you read the papers you will find it not quite so simple. In some cases it is almost absurdly easy to demonstrate the advertising effect (eg for a 'partwork' magazine or direct response-based cases). In other cases, isolating the effect can be fiendishly difficult: car campaigns are a good example. Clearly it would be absurd and contrary to the spirit of the awards only to reward simple and obvious entries. We therefore find in practice we have to judge the arguments relative to the difficulties they have faced, both in terms of the advertising task and the evaluation of its effects.

3. Effectiveness in these awards is defined as contribution to *the business*. This does not mean that measures such as awareness or brand image are irrelevant – far from it, they are often vital – but there needs to be some sort of argument which links those to business objectives, ultimately in terms of sales or profitability. We also need to be careful that we do not only reward short term paybacks – the long term competitiveness, resilience and leverage of the brand can be at least as important. (This is especially true, of course, in the 'Long term' category.)

4. Papers will obviously be less likely to convince if they are poorly written or presented. Good clear English, clarity of argument, and good presentation of data all help. You should expect to see a clear exposition of the background to the campaign, the development of the strategy, and a clear statement of what was actually done and when (creative work and media plans), as well as the review of the performance.

5. You are not expected to be an expert in statistical modelling. Papers which use such techniques still have a duty to be intelligible to the general reader. Authors who make vague claims about models without presenting sufficient detail and technical evidence do not help their case.

6. You should not be influenced by whether you personally liked or hated the advertising, or whether it was 'creative' or not; you should judge the argument objectively. An author may as part of the case show that 'creativity' contributed to the effectiveness: that is a different matter.

7. 'Bonus points' should certainly be added for papers which add something new to our knowledge, or make an original point. They must of course conform to the basic criteria as well.

These criteria show the difference between these awards and other advertising industry awards (which generally focus on the recognition of original thinking and craft skills); ie their single-minded focus on the demonstration of effectiveness. This difference is reinforced the fact that, as in previous years, the majority of the judging panel was drawn from *outside* the advertising industry.

The entry – by category

The 1994 entry was again excellent both in terms of quantity and quality. 73 case histories were submitted by 29 advertising agencies for some of Britain's biggest advertisers – including British Airways, British Telecom, Cadbury, Procter & Gamble, Unilever and Whitbread – as well as many with smaller budgets. Virtually all of these made a good case that the advertiser's money had been well spent. The 20 cases, from 11 agencies, which emerged as Award or Special Prize winners represent real excellence in terms of the judging criteria laid down.

1994 saw a rationalisation of the number of categories. This did not change overall eligibility to enter or the total number of Awards available, but removed anomalies and provided a more coherent basis for judging. The six categories in 1992 (New brands; Established; 'Longer and Broader'; Small budgets; European; Special including financial) have now become three, structured in terms of the three main *roles* of advertising: to *launch* a new brand, to *change* the position of an established brand, or to *build or sustain* a brand over the longer term. The three categories are thus as follows:

1. **New brands/advertisers,** to include established brands with no significant previous advertising (21 entries).

2. **New campaigns** for previously advertised brands, resulting in significant short term changes in their business performance (36 entries).

3. **Advertising over the long term,** showing a benefit to a brand or business over several years (16 entries).

The standard of papers was good across all three categories and the judges chose to distribute Awards broadly in line with the number of entries to each category. The rationalisation of categories does not seem to have disadvantaged any given type of paper or changed the overall character of winners. Of the 1994 winners, five would have qualified for the now-defunct Small Budgets category (under £500,000pa), three for 'Special' and one for European. This is broadly similar to the 1992 profile.

A second change in 1994 was the introduction of Special Prizes, to be given over and above category awards, designed to recognise particular types or aspects of entry the judges wish to encourage. Six Special Prizes were awarded, for:

- Integration with other marketing tools.
- Direct response.
- Limited budgets.
- Best use of media planning.
- European (multi-country) campaigns.
- Innovative thinking.

Five of the Special Prizes winners in 1994 also won a category award, the other was commended.

BROADER OBSERVATIONS AND LESSONS FROM 1994

The 20 case histories which emerged as Award or Special Prize winners – all published here – represent excellence in one or more of the following criteria: the sheer scale of the effect achieved; originality in thinking and/or execution; telling us something new about how advertising works; overcoming an intrinsically difficult advertising or evaluation task.

A number of hurdles stand between an effective piece of advertising and a successful Award entry: adequate data, the time and ability to assemble a well-argued case, and a client who will give permission to enter. Nevertheless, the winning entries represent a widely drawn sample of 'effective advertising' – and indeed successful brand marketing – in recent times. They provide a unique 'window' on the state of the art in advertising and its evaluation, and brand marketing generally.

The individual cases which follow will repay detailed inspection. My fellow judge Terry Prue has already demonstrated some of their richness in his 'frameworkish' analysis of the 1994 awards entries[2]. From my own perspective some overall observations emerge, largely complementary to the views he developed.

'Joined up thinking'

Although not their primary objective, these cases provide insight into the processes associated with successful advertising and what it is that advertising agencies do for their money. This could be characterised as 'joined up thinking' across several stages: *Information, Analysis, Understanding, Insight, Ideas, Advertisements, Media implementation, Exploitation* (eg PR, promotions, distribution leverage), *Evaluation*, and *Resulting next steps*.

Case histories are inevitably somewhat simplified, sanitised and revisionist in their treatment of what actually happened. 'Insider experience' of the process suggests that it would be wrong to regard the above as discrete, and so potentially 'unbundlable', stages. Rather they tend to blur one into another, with multiple feedback loops. The separation of creation from strategy neglects the fact that strategy is often informed by creation. The separation of evaluation from subsequent strategic thinking can also result in a loss of quality and sensitivity. Another of my fellow judges, Jeremy Bullmore, described this way of working – which he regards as central to the value agencies add to their clients' businesses – in a recent speech now published by the IPA:

> *"In real life, as we well know, it's a seemingly endless and circuitous sequence of gathering knowledge, generating hypotheses, finding an expression for them, getting reactions to them, interpreting rather than accepting those reactions, modifying, rejecting, starting again, inviting intuition, guesswork, luck, regrouping, re-introducing discipline, checking again against real people.*
>
> *Scientists lie about this process at least as disgracefully as advertising people because it doesn't sound either scientific or manly. In fact, of course, it's both. Those of us with a fondness for long words know this way of working*

to be called hypothetico-deductive; but it's almost never overtly apparent in the advertising it inspires – any more than a sound knowledge of anatomy will be overtly apparent in a good life drawing."[3]

The Boddingtons case history is an excellent example of both the process and value of 'joined up thinking'. Boddingtons had three marketing objectives which could easily point in three very different directions: the creation of a major national take-home brand; the creation of a major national pub brand; the protection of its regional heartland. To realise these objectives so completely with, in effect, a single campaign is no mean feat – it required considerable strategic and creative insight, and a *holistic* view of the overall task. It is difficult to see how the Boddingtons solution could have been achieved without a multi-skilled team of people working very closely together. Of course this does not necessarily mean that all these people have to work for the same company, but the 'advertising agency concept' certainly provides an environment where these kinds of results are more likely to happen.

Peperami is another argument against 'unbundling'. From the outside success could be assumed just to be the result of a stroke of creative brilliance. The case history makes it clear that there was much more to it than that. Insights from semiotic analysis and 'confessional interviews' with users put the Creatives into the right area. Creative input to strategic development research then helped refine strategy. Subsequent pre-testing gave the client confidence to run the very bold work that went on to produce such dramatic results in the marketplace. Media planning – which led to the advertisements developed being placed into programming where they would most stand out (as well as effectively reaching their target audience) – was also a key factor. This helped deliver advertising awareness – in this case the main driver of sales – that was the highest in the broader 'snack' market with, in competitive terms, a relatively limited budget of £800,000.

'Integrated media thinking' – rather than just 'efficient media buying' – was also a central factor in Boddingtons, Nissan Micra, Cadbury's Boost, and Wonderbra case histories.

Diversity and evaluation

The winners remind us that advertising can play different roles, which mean timescales for success can also be very different. Cases such as Peperami and Boddingtons relate to dynamic change and rapid payback as a result of advertising. For others such as BMW, British Airways, and Cadbury's Roses a longer term perspective makes the power of advertising most vividly apparent. The AIDS case history perhaps puts this into sharpest relief – early and continued commitment to communicating about this issue has much to do with the UK in 1994 being a 'low AIDS prevalence' country (compared to other European countries which chose 'not to talk about it').

If any further evidence is required to undermine the value of simplistic, standardised uni-dimensional approaches to advertising research, then the reader will find it from inspection of this latest batch of case histories. They remind us that successful advertising can work in a number of ways – in Terry Prue's terms[2] *persuasion, involvement,* or *salience,* or indeed across two or even all three of these models. Each of these models can be 'supercharged' by exceptionally high advertising awareness or retarded by low advertising awareness.

In 1994 Award winners also show diversity in terms of ease of measurement. In some cases the contribution of advertising can be measured relatively easily and immediately. For Peperami advertising was the only significant variable (other factors such as distribution could easily be dealt with), the sales effect dramatic and immediate, with strong corroborative evidence in the form of exceptional levels of advertising awareness and popularity.

But in others (the majority) demonstration of the commercial impact of advertising is considerably harder, particularly in the short term. This is inconvenient but unsurprising. Increasingly marketing success is driven by factors which conspire to make the evaluation of advertising more difficult: high levels of *integration* and resulting interaction across the mix, making it harder to isolate what's doing what; *consistent* relationship building (albeit frequently refreshed by innovation or other 'new news'), which is harder to measure in the short term than variability; *new thinking* which challenges the conventional roles of the game, rendering established norms less useful.

Nevertheless, as in previous Awards, many of these cases show that 'hard to measure' doesn't mean 'can't measure'. Most use some form of 'argument by elimination': ie examine the overall performance of the brand over time (sales and profitability); dispose or otherwise take account of all potential influential factors both 'internal' to the brand and contextual (eg price, distribution, weather); advertising effects can then be inferred from the residual, with 'corroborative' evidence provided by consumer research measures such as awareness, image and usage. The accumulated weight of evidence can produce a solid, but still ultimately circumstantial, measure of advertising effectiveness.

This of course begs the question of the 'base level assumption' – *what would have happened without advertising?* Any evaluation needs to understand the underlying trend of the brand, which is rarely simply to stand still. The 1992 Milkman IPA case history[4] was based on reducing the rate of sales decline rather than sales growth. The Arthur's catfood case history[5] – not a winner in the 1994 IPA Awards, but nevertheless instructive – is similarly based on the maintenance of equilibrium via advertising in a situation where competitive factors were against the brand. Making realistic 'base level of assumptions' often means looking *outside* the brand to develop external competitive benchmarks. The BMW, British Airways and AIDS case histories were particularly good examples of this, comparing their performance with that of close competitors (BMW, British Airways) and/or the same 'product' in different countries (BMW, AIDS).

'Only advertising can do this'

We live in a world of multiplying marketing and communications possibilities, and increasing 'cohabitation' of advertising with other marketing techniques within integrated campaigns. It is easy to overlook advertising's unique properties, and the fact that other marketing techniques are rarely a true alternative to it. Advertising can of course often be justified simply in 'cost per thousand' terms (ie the cost of delivering the desired message to a given audience), but its real uniqueness stems from two related factors: (i) its power to grab people's attention, excite their interest and capture their imagination; (ii) its ability to create an atmosphere in which other elements of the mix become more effective, and it simply becomes easier to do business. The 1994 Award Winners put advertising's unique properties in high relief. Here are five of the most striking examples where it would be hard to disagree that 'only advertising can do this':

1. BMWs are excellent and innovative cars. In the car market the car itself – allied to value for money – is the most potent element of the marketing mix. Despite being relatively expensive in the UK, BMW's long term sales and image growth in the UK greatly outstripped its performance in other European markets where it has not enjoyed the same quality and consistency of advertising support. This was evident both in absolute terms and benchmarked against its closest competitor, Mercedes.

2. The Wonderbra is a highly individual product which had been on sale in the UK for 26 years. In early 1994 its new owner, Playtex, faced the threat of a me-too competitor launched by the old licensee, Gossard (the Ultrabra). Despite this sales have almost doubled, due to a cleverly deployed £330,000 advertising spend which has generated directly related PR with a notional value of £18,000,000.

3. In 1984 British Airways had the image of a 'run of the mill' nationalised industry. Since then its fortunes have been transformed, both in terms of profitability and perception. The product has been re-engineered, but research shows that competitive service standards have improved to. If British Airways had not shouted their ambition to become 'The World's Favourite Airline' loud and wide would customers have noticed the change, and would staff have responded to deliver it?

4. Boddingtons' Draughtflow device was a wonderful idea – at last bitter drinkers could get the same experience at home as in the pub. But Boddingtons also sell cans without this device and these have increased their sales as well. And pub sales have increased dramatically to, well above that which can be explained by distribution gains.

5. Halls Soothers' success doubled total Halls sales in two years in a very competitive market. It did this by redefining medicated confectionery to include indulgence values, thus creating a positive difference versus less medicinal brands such as Tunes and avoiding cannibalisation of the original Halls Mentho-Lyptus line. Only advertising could have established these indulgence values.

Innovation, creativity and brands

The evidence of these awards run counter to the pessimism in some quarters about the future of brands and advertising. But it also confirms that ever more competitive market conditions set more exacting standards for brand and advertising success – in particular, a greater commitment to innovation, creativity and continuing to offer your customers real value. It is those who lack commitment to this more dynamic concept of the brand that tend to fall by the wayside.

With the benefit of hindsight, in the hedonistic '80s the concept of 'adding value' via advertising and other marketing action often lost touch with reality. As another of my fellow IPA judges, David Hearn of KP, once observed, 'adding value' had become synonymous with sticking gold stripes on your packaging and charging more for your product.

In the more realistic '90s it is perhaps not surprising that a high proportion of the most successful advertising appears to be founded more on the communication of *'integral values'*, rather than simply 'added values'. Advertising based on the communication of *fundamental product truths* – albeit in a very creative way – has come much more to the fore.

These 'product truths' may be based upon product innovation and ongoing product improvement – BMW, British Airways, Boddingtons, and John Smith's Bitter are exemplars of this. Alternatively they may come from extracting the full value from existing, but under-exploited, appeals of highly individual products: for instance, Peperami, Wonderbra and Marston's Pedigree.

This does not make the 'added' emotional values which differentiate powerful brands from good products any less important. However, today success tends to be even more dependent than previously on these 'added values' being associated with a good and innovative product, and ideally strongly *integrated* with (not just attached to) this product.

Despite this refocussing on product truths, creative advertising remains very much an integral part of brand innovation, not just a messenger of it. Indeed, despite being judged on the criterion of commercial effectiveness, a high degree of creativity is a consistent ingredient in this year's winners. They highlight amongst other things something that smart advertisers have long known – that 'creative' advertising does not just add value, *it saves you money*. Successes such as Peperami, Wonderbra, and the Nissan Micra come from advertising spends which, in a broader competitive context, are relatively low.

The high level of creativity witnessed in the 1994 Award Winners continues a long term trend observable over the eight competitions – judged on the same criteria in essentially the same way – since 1980. For most of the '80s the majority of winning cases were characterised by well planned strategies, and 'on strategy' but fairly average advertisements. The more sophisticated and challenging conditions of the '90s tend to demand rather more: not just well planned strategies and 'efficient' execution, but also a high degree of creativity.

'Effective creativity' in 1994 has come to mean much more than just creative *advertisements*. It embraces creative thinking on a broader front about strategy, the use of media and other ways in which a product or service can be communicated to its target market.

Four factors for effectiveness

Advertising effectiveness is now very much the product of several factors, each of which increasingly depend on creative thinking to deliver their full contribution:

- Strategic impact.
- Executional impact.
- Media impact.
- 'Integration leverage'.

'Strategic Impact' is about more than just an efficient strategy which positions a brand clearly against the pre-existing psychology and needs of the market. It can be increased by innovation and creative thinking which anticipates consumer needs and redefines how they look at your brand and the market generally (thus changing the rules of the game to your advantage). Some of the cases already mentioned – such as Boddingtons, Peperami, BA and Wonderbra – have a particularly high level of 'strategic impact'. Others include The Edinburgh Club, whose success was based on the targeting of core non-users (the unfit and overweight) rather than the conventional stereotype for fitness clubs of beautiful people with beautiful bodies; the Nissan Micra, which chose to focus on developing a real personality for the car, rather than product or user image; The Co-operative Bank, which has prospered since it stopped trying to compete head-on with other, bigger banks, and adopted a totally different strategy based upon an 'ethical' positioning.

'Executional Impact' is about more than just delivering the message in an efficient way. It can be maximised by creativity which helps messages stand out, capture consumers' imaginations, and live on in their minds *as well*. As Terry Prue[2] has pointed out, several of the 1994 winners are characterised by exceptional levels of advertising awareness.

'Media Impact' is about more than just reaching the right people in a cost-efficient way. It can be further enhanced by deploying media in a relevant but unexpected way to make a creative message stand out even more than its intrinsic creativity merits. Wonderbra gained much more word of mouth and PR because it used an unexpectedly public medium (posters). Boddingtons led with magazines in a market where TV was the norm. The Nissan Micra (innovative use of press), Cadbury's Boost (radio rather than the TV norm) and Peperami (innovative time buying) case histories also demonstrate enhanced effectiveness due to creative, not just efficient, media planning.

'Integration Leverage' means the active exploitation of advertising as part of an overall integrated plan. Wonderbra is an example of extremely high 'integration leverage', with advertising very deliberately planned for PR exploitation and to help force distribution. Several other 1994 winners are examples of high integration leverage, with BMW, BA and The Co-operative Bank amongst the most notable.

'Joined up thinking' can make these four effectiveness factors *multiplicative* rather than just additive. High scores on each individually help drive success, low scores on any tend to hinder it. Increasingly success will demand high scores on two or more of these – the very best amongst the 1994 Awards winners tend to score well on all four.

'New News' versus 'Consistent Theme Advertising'

This subject was initially explored – in the context of the sample of effective advertising provided by the Awards – in my Introduction to *Advertising Works 7*[4].

The trend noted then continues. A large and increasing proportion of cases of effective advertising have a significant component of 'new news'. As already observed above, this 'new news' increasingly – although by no means always – relates to tangible product innovation (or under appreciated product truths).

However, as also noted in *Advertising Works 7*, we should not regard 'new news' and consistency (or at least continuity) as being alternatives or in opposition. In many of the most successful advertising campaigns (and indeed brands) they co-exist. This is something that Sir Michael Perry recognised in his recent 'state of the nation' address about brand marketing:

> *"In a dynamic economy, brands are not only a guarantee of quality and replicability – they are the vehicle whereby the manufacturer can turn around innovation, in its widest sense to the customer... Advertising is at its best, and most effective, when it communicates new information that consumers actually want to hear – and when its impact is cumulative and coherent."* [6]

Further reassurance that innovation and consistency are not incompatible comes from an inspection of human needs. Two of our most fundamental drives are the need for *security* – the familiar, comfortable and reassuring – and the need for *change* – the new, the different and exciting. That these two needs can co-exist in the same person at the same time lends support that innovation and consistency can – indeed should – co-exist in advertising campaigns and brands.

Many of the consistent, long term campaigns awarded in 1994 are in fact also vehicles for 'new news': BMW and British Airways are prime examples. The case for John Smith's Bitter is particularly interesting in this context: by using the established Jack Dee 'No nonsense' campaign (initially developed in the context of the draught pint) to deliver the news about the 'widget' in its canned variant, sales of the *whole* brand have benefited, not just the featured product variant.

Other new campaigns awarded look likely to become consistent, longer-term campaigns. For instance Peperami, Boddingtons and Wonderbra have developed their campaigns on the same theme since their cases were submitted in June 1994; in the case of Wonderbra, also to communicate new product news within its established format.

As noted in 1992, the overall balance between 'new news' and consistency will vary across the marketing cycle. The ability to be consistent presupposes that you have a unique and ownable territory to develop and protect in the first place. Virtually all consistent long term campaigns can be tracked back to time when they did something new and different to 'disrupt' the then conventions of the marketplace to claim such a territory via a unique and ownable creative theme. Examples from previous Awards include Andrex, PG Tips, Oxo and indeed Levis: they may seem part of the furniture now but they were very much 'new creative news' when the respective campaigns broke. The same is true for now well-established campaigns awarded in 1994: BMW, when it first became 'the ultimate driving machine' in 1979; BA when it became 'The World's Favourite

Airline' in 1983; Cadbury's Roses when it claimed the informal gift 'Thank you' role in 1979; and more recently Boddingtons, when it claimed its territory of creaminess in 1991.

In Conclusion

Overall this year's Award winners are a testimony to the value of *thinking beyond convention* – not just in execution, but across the whole brand mix: whether product, strategy, use of media or the way advertising is integrated (and exploited) within the total plan. In the area of advertising evaluation there is a lot of 'best practice' to learn from and copy. When it comes to producing effective advertising in the first place, we can perhaps learn as much from the 'mindset' of the winners as from what they actually did. As John Hegarty commented on the recent launch of the IPA's new Advertising Effectiveness Case History Data Bank:

> "*It's always good to learn about how others have been successful – even if it's only to learn how to do it differently*".

References

1. The IPA Advertising Effectiveness Data Bank; comprises the almost 600 case histories entered to the Awards since 1980; further information, and details on how to access it, contact:
   Institute of Practitioners in Advertising, 44 Belgrave Square, London, SW1X 8QS
   Tel: 0171 235 7020   Fax: 0171 245 9904.
2. Prue, T, 'The 1994 IPA Advertising Effectiveness Awards', *Admap*, November 1994.
3. Bullmore, J, 'Advertising costs half as much as you think it does: but do you know which half?', published by the IPA, December 1994.
4. *Advertising Works 7*, Ed. Baker, C, NTC Publications 1992.
5. Weavers, H, 'Arthur's – stability in a world of change', *Admap*, November 1994.
6. Perry, Sir M, 'The Brand – Vehicle for value in a changing marketplace', *Advertising Association 1994 President's Lecture*, Advertising Association.

A SHORT GUIDE TO THE CASE HISTORIES

Advertising over the longer term

BMW 1979–1994   (pp3–23)

Coverage: How consistent creative advertising has capitalised on BMW's consistent ethos, as well as communicating product innovation, to generate sales and profit growth well ahead of competitive and international benchmarks. Greatly increased sales were achieved without undermining BMW's exclusive image and premium price position.

Period: 1979–94

Media: Primarily Press (also TV, Posters)

The Judges' View: BMW fought off strong competition to win the Grand Prix, most notably from Boddingtons. Both are major marketing successes in which the decisive role of advertising has been clearly demonstrated. Both were also characterised by a high degree of originality (strategy and execution) in the conception of the advertising involved. BMW won the day due to sustained success and consistent implementation over some 15 years, added to the way that the case faced up to a particularly difficult evaluation challenge presented by the car market (where multiple factors which impact strongly upon consumer choice, not least the product itself).

The nature and consistency of BMW advertising was only made possible by excellent products and a consistent company ethos (quality, performance, engineering excellence and technological advance). One of the most telling points in this case was indeed how the impact of product excellence and innovation was taken into account in isolating the contribution made by advertising. This involved international comparisons of both sales and image, for BMW in isolation and in comparison with key competitors, most notably Mercedes. The cars and the ethos are the same everywhere, but BMW's competitive standing has advanced much more in the UK than elsewhere.

Overall this is a supreme example of how advertising can add value to (or rather *extract value from*) an already excellent product, to create a brand which commands a high price premium and retains considerable exclusivity. This despite the fact there are six times more BMWs on the road now (the majority of them 'bottom of the range' models) than there were in 1980.

BA – The World's Favourite Airline (pp25–50)

Coverage: How advertising helped to transform British Airways from a loss-making nationalised industry to the World's most successful airline. This paper takes a global perspective, producing evidence of success on routes all over the World (over and above that which could be explained simply by operational improvements).

Period: 1983–94

Media: Primarily TV (also all other media)

The Judges' View: In 1983 British Airways set a new corporate vision which was very different from the then reality: '*to become the best and most successful international airline in the World*'. Ten years on this has been realised, both in terms of profitability and perception. Other factors have played their part, but it is hard to see how this transformation could have been achieved without advertising which communicated this vision loud and wide.

The BA product has improved considerably over this period, but so has much of the competition. The most telling points of this case, in addition to the sheer scale of the success, relate to the way that image versus its key competitors has improved much more than improvements in service delivery alone would suggest; how market share has grown on established routes where a 'level competitive playing field' exists; and how BA's image has shifted consistently in line with the advertising *around the World*.

This case is an inspiring example of advertising in its brand-building role (rather than simply as an effective sales generator). The transformation of BA from a 'run of the mill' national carrier to a successful global brand in so short a period would not have been possible without advertising. The cost of that advertising was small relative to the value it created in terms of extra passengers, improved margins and making it a desirable business partner for strategic alliances.

Health Education Authority – HIV/AIDS Prevention Campaign (pp51–79)

Coverage: How advertising has successfully been used to supplement other means of communication: specifically to keep the AIDS message in front of the public at times when media interest was flagging, and to develop specific messages to specific target groups. This is a case of a long-running campaign which has necessarily had frequent changes in executional approach.

Period: 1988–93

Media: TV, Press, Radio, Posters

The Judges' View: This case is very much a testimony to the power of communication generally, and the value of 'paid-for' communication in particular. Clearly this is an issue which has received vast amounts of 'unpaid' media attention, but the media have a short attention span, tend to treat the issue in a rather one-dimensional way, and AIDS is anyway something that most people would rather not think about. This case is based on analysis which shows that without advertising the perceived threat of AIDS would have diminished amongst 'low risk' groups such as young heterosexuals, resulting in less condom usage.

Whilst specific linkages are made between advertising, awareness and behaviour, perhaps the most telling point is that the UK is a 'low AIDS prevalence' country. The UK's commitment to communicating about this issue – including advertising – is belatedly being adopted by several other European countries who have only latterly recognised that 'not talking about it' will not make the problem go away.

Cadbury's Roses – "Thank You Very Much"   (pp81–101)

Coverage: How accurate repositioning, consistently implemented and creatively refreshed, has helped Roses overtake the once-dominant brand leader, Quality Street.

Period: 1979–93

Media: TV

The Judges' View: This is a clear demonstration of the power of advertising as a positioning tool. When the memorable, but strategically vacuous, Norman Vaughan 'Roses Grow On You' campaign failed to make an impact on the then dominant brand leader, Quality Street, a strategic review identified a *tangible role* that Roses could play – that of 'the best informal gift'.

The clarity and emotional status that the strategy has given the brand has provided the basis for consistent implementation of the 'Thank You' campaign since 1979. This long-running campaign has been largely responsible for Roses overtaking Quality Street to claim brand leadership, despite lower average advertising spend, whilst also promoting growth of the overall 'twistwrap' sector.

Roses demonstrates both the value of consistent strategy *and* 'creative refreshment'. Consistent focus on the 'informal gift' positioning has led to ownership of the 'Thank You' territory, which is so strong that when Quality Street tried to reflect it in their advertising it only served to benefit Roses. 'Creative refreshment' came in the form of new executions of the same strategy when BBH took over the account from Y&R in 1989; long term sales growth, which had plateaued, was resumed.

The Home Office – Smoke Alarms: "Every Home Should Have One" (pp103–126)

Coverage: How advertising very cost-effectively created awareness and action to achieve the desired end-result in the majority of UK households.

Period: 1987–94

Media: TV

The Judges' View: This is a very clear case in which advertising has been used essentially to manage a market: first effectively to create a market, then to focus on particular vulnerable groups who had been slow to adopt smoke alarms, and finally to encourage 'aftercare' and maintenance of alarms installed.

        The scale of effects is impressive – in seven years penetration of smoke alarms has risen from 5% to 70%, and many lives have been saved. This is an excellent example of what can be achieved with a relatively small media spend when you have a potent underlying message, and advertising is intelligently deployed.

New brands or advertisers

Boddingtons – "By 'eck"   (pp129–160)

Coverage: How advertising helped transform Boddingtons from a regional brand to a leading national bitter in both pub and take-home sectors.

Period: 1991–94

Media: Press and TV (also Posters)

The Judges' View: Boddingtons is an object lesson in the value of thinking beyond convention. Mainstream bitters – and Boddingtons *is* a mainstream bitter – tend to focus on sociability and user imagery in their advertising; Boddingtons focused single-mindedly on a product attribute. Mainstream bitters tend to reflect 'mainstream' values; Boddingtons adopted an aspirational premium positioning. For bitters the 'pub pint' is the highest form of product delivery; Boddingtons led with cans (though the majority of their volume comes from draught). Mainstream bitters lead with TV; Boddingtons led with press.

        This case is also notable for the breadth of the marketing challenge Boddingtons faced: to become a national brand whilst keeping faith with its regional heartland, and to develop both pub and take-home business. The strategy of focusing on a product attribute – smoothness, as evidenced by a creamy head and golden colour – not only led to executions which stood out and made people want to buy it, it also bridged some very different target audiences. Whoever you are, whatever you drink, the product truth remains the same.

Overall then Boddingtons is not just commendable for the results achieved (which were excellent) but also the *way* they were achieved. It demonstrates how focus and simplicity is often the best solution to what may look a complicated and multi-faceted marketing problem.

Marston's Pedigree (pp161–177)

Coverage: How the first major foray into advertising for a long-established brand has helped turn decline into growth in challenging market conditions.

Period: 1992–94

Media: TV

The Judges' View: Marston's Pedigree is an excellent product with a strong 'word of mouth' reputation, at least within its immediate heartland. It had not previously received significant advertising support. Received wisdom might be that such a product *should not need* advertising and indeed advertising might undermine its reputation (by suggesting a 'sell out').

This case is a straightforward demonstration of how this reasoning need not apply – if you've got a good product, tell people about it. Well-judged advertising, capturing the essence of the brand, has helped manage 'word of mouth' and accelerate the spread of its reputation to considerable commercial advantage.

Sales increases are more notable because they have been achieved in the considerably more competitive situation following the introduction of the Government's Beer Orders. The 'spin-off' benefits of the advertising on overall pub traffic and company profile/morale are also of note.

The Launch of the Nissan Micra (pp179–193)

Coverage: How an unconventional approach to car advertising successfully launched the premium-priced replacement to the old 'value for money' Micra. This case is particularly notable for *innovative media planning*, for which it won a Special Prize.

Period: 1992/93

Media: Press, Posters and TV

The Judges' View: Another excellent example of the value of thinking beyond convention in a market where the offering seems to be becoming increasingly uniform, from product to promotion. The new Micra also marked Nissan's desire to move from a positioning which had essentially been based on value for money, to one based on cars that people actively *wanted* to own.

The Micra launch was radical both creatively and in its related use of media. It succeeded because it got noticed (despite high competitive noise) and developed an attractive personality for the car (based on its distinctive styling, but difficult to capture via 2D photography).

To the advertising sceptic perhaps the most compelling argument for 'creative advertising' is that *it saves you money*. In the final analysis this is the story of a successful launch achieved with a lower spend than competitors who tend to rely more on 'aerial bombardment' techniques.

Clarks Shoes – The Launch of CICA (pp195–216)

Coverage: How advertising helped develop a profitable niche for Clarks in the 'trainer' market. By well-targeted advertising it transformed an own-label product line into an added value brand.

Period: 1992/93

Media: TV

The Judges' View: This is a classic example of how advertising can add value. From a consumer perspective this meant adding a measure of credibility in a sector in which Clarks had little; from a commercial perspective it meant supporting a price premium over 'own brand' product.

Against strong competition CICA's success was really down to focus in targeting and media planning. It realised that is was pointless trying to take on the likes of Nike and Reebok in 'young male' market and instead focused on boys and girls under 12, and adults over 25 (principally their parents). These were people who could be converted. By concentrating on this target a relatively small budget delivered volume growth *and* a price premium of 20% over own brand product (which was almost identical in product terms).

The Launch of Halls Soothers (pp217–233)

Coverage: How advertising helped create a new positioning in the medicated confectionery market with particular appeal to young females.

Period: 1992–94

Media: TV

The Judges' View: This case is based upon a strategy which could only fully be delivered via advertising: to redefine medicated confectionery to include indulgence. The new product, brand name and packaging all helped to position Halls Soothers at the milder, better-tasting end of the medicated confectionery spectrum, but only advertising could establish the indulgence values to create a positive difference versus such brands as Tunes.

The advertising connected strongly with a real consumer need to be the main factor in a highly successful launch. Halls' volumes have doubled in two years, Soothers' volume being totally additive to that of the long established, more medicinal Halls Mentho-Lyptus line.

New campaigns for previously advertised brands

Peperami – The Consequences of Unleashing a Beast   (pp237–261)

Coverage: How advertising extracted the full value of a unique and idiosyncratic product to dramatic effect.

Period: 1993/94

Media: TV

The Judges' View: The exceptional impact of a new campaign, on both sales and awareness, made this case the unanimous selection for Gold.

But this case is also notable for *how* these effects were achieved. The brand was, almost literally, put on the psychiatrists' couch to reveal the inner workings and full possibilities of its personality. Semiotic analysis and 'confessional' interviews with users played an important part. The confident decision to talk direct to the end consumers (mainly young males), rather than accommodate the purchaser (usually Mum, who was looking for something a little more 'well behaved' in terms of advertising), was well justified by research. Peperami was a winner in the recent Account Planning Group Awards and overall this case demonstrates the contribution that the account planning discipline, as well as innovative media planning, can make.

The value of unbridled creative advertising is evidenced by two further facts. First, all this was achieved with a spend of just £800,000. Second, the success of Peperami caused both Sainsbury and Tesco to delist their own label Salami sticks.

Playtex – The Wonderbra   (pp263–278)

Coverage: How famous advertising has made the 26 year old Wonderbra famous too. This case won the Special Prize for *integration with other marketing tools* for the way a small advertising budget was deployed to generate vast amounts of directly related PR coverage.

Period: 1994

Media: Posters and Press

The Judges' View: Wonderbra is most notable for two things. First, the immense amount of publicity generated from a relatively small advertising spend (£330,000). Second, the fact that this has translated to a near doubling of sales when, with the launch of the me-too Gossard Ultrabra, the opposite may have been the case.

However, this is also a prime example of the value of being true to your product and its benefits. Wonderbra is a confident, upfront kind of product and has succeeded because it has been advertised in a confident, upfront (but not crude or crass) kind of way. The UK convention (unlike say France) has been to advertise underwear in a coy, 'private' way and Wonderbra has benefited from its ability to break this convention, particularly via the selection of 'public' media.

Cadbury's Boost – "Why Work and Rest When You Can Play?" (pp279–307)

Coverage:	How advertising helped Boost make headway against a dominant brand leader by doing it differently, in terms of message, medium and overall 'attitude'.
Period:	1991–93
Media:	Radio (plus some TV)
The Judges' View:	The lesson of not playing the game to the rules of a brand leader may not be new, but is nevertheless one that is often ignored.

In these terms a major virtue of this case is not just that a change of strategy worked in commercial terms, but *how* these results were achieved. Rather than trying to compete head-to-head with Mars, the long-established dominant brand leader in the 'Gutfill' or 'Energy' sector, Boost chose to play the game by its own rules.

This change of thinking resulted in a strategy based upon 'youth appeal' – Mars was relatively weak in this respect and Boost additionally had a young user profile. Consumer research provided an insight into what young male consumers want from an 'Energy' bar – *'Why work and rest when you can play?'*. This led to a different advertising 'attitude' and the selection of radio as a main medium (both because it had the right attitude, and was a medium Boost could own).

The Edinburgh Club – Turning Fatties into Fitties (pp309–327)

Coverage:	How advertising succeeded in attracting considerable new custom in a competitive market by positioning The Edinburgh Club as being for a very different target market than conventional health clubs. This case shows what can be done in a local arena with a very small budget.
Period:	1991–94
Media:	Press (also Posters)
The Judges View:	This is a compelling example of how the quality of thinking behind your advertising can be more important than the size of

your budget. Further it demonstrates that the evaluation of advertising effect does not necessarily need a lorryload of tracking survey reports and retail audit data.

At the root of the success was the bold but solidly-based strategy to target 'core non-users' of health clubs, on the basis that they presented a large part of the population who nobody was trying to appeal to. It also shows the difference that a little wit and quality in execution can make in the generally dismal world of local advertising.

The Co-operative Bank – "Profit with Principles" (pp329–352)

Coverage: The successful repositioning of The Co-operative Bank, based on a fundamental but unexploited truth which differentiates it from other Banks: its 'ethical' approach to the investments it makes. Advertising has played an important part, but this case won the Special Prize for *innovative thinking* for the way this strategy has guided all the Bank's communications and actions.

Period: 1992–94

Media: Press and TV

The Judges' View: This case is really about how an advertising agency helped give its Client a clear *vision,* which was then communicated to immediate effect via advertising and all other elements of the mix.

The previous strategy, based on product innovation, was neither financially sustainable nor delivering the right sorts of customers. It was further hampered by the Bank's image problem. Before this campaign The Co-operative Bank seemed inevitably to be going the way of the Co-operative grocer.

The Co-operative Bank lacked the resource to fight head-on with the major Banks, and was not really like them anyway. The 'capture' and reframing of a core truth about the Bank provided the key to a new, positively differentiated, 'ethical' positioning. This is not relevant to everyone, but can be made relevant and motivating to enough people to give the Bank a secure future. Innovative thinking has led to what is probably the first major example of 'ethical advertising' in the UK.

John Smith's Bitter – "A Widget We Have Got" (pp353–373)

Coverage: How good advertising helped John Smith's respond to competitive innovation. Though focused upon the canned variant it shows how the whole brand benefited.

Period: 1993/94

Media: TV

The Judges' View: A good brand with good advertising it may be, but John Smith's has suffered in the take home trade as a result of competitive product innovation, most notably from Boddingtons. This case gives hope to brands facing successful new competitors – all is not lost.

Me-too technology and good advertising has rapidly recovered the situation for John Smith's, not just in terms of sales but also in terms of a relevant brand property – the 'widget' – to give it a place in consumer's minds alongside Boddingtons' 'cream'.

This case is another example of how focusing on 'new news' in one area of the product mix – in this case using the established 'No nonsense' Jack Dee campaign theme – can benefit the whole brand. Although all last Winter's advertising focused on the 'widget', the advertising also stimulated pub sales as well.

How Advertising Helped Strepsils   (pp375–399)

Coverage: How advertising successfully gave Strepsils throat lozenges a more efficacious positioning in the face of new competition.

Period: 1990–94

Media: TV

The Judges' View: This advertising worked as it was intended, both in terms of commercial return and giving Strepsils a more efficacious positioning to help counter new competitors with more medicinal identities.

Advertising regulations in this sector prevented talking about Strepsils' active ingredients in advertising so the task was more down to 'form' than 'content'. If the received wisdom is that advertising that people like tends to work best, then this is one of the exceptions to that rule. This advertising was successful in large part *because* it was not particularly likeable and dissonant with established cosy image. It successfully challenged consumers to re-evaluate the brand and use it for the more 'serious' usage the product is designed to cope with.

Health Education Board for Scotland – Smoking: Sticks and Carrots   (pp401–418)

Coverage: How advertising was deployed very effectively to help Scottish smokers give the habit up. It shows how it was the *combination* of negative and positive elements of the message that drove the exceptionally high levels of response to the offer of counselling via Smokeline. (This case won the Special Prize for *Direct Response*).

Period: 1992/93

Media: TV (also Posters)

The Judges' View: On an effectiveness level this case is most notable for the scale of response achieved – 6% of all regular smokers in Scotland contacted Smokeline in its first year.

On a broader level the 'stick and carrot' approach which produced this response has a lot to commend it. This campaign was so successful because it didn't depend *solely* on negative messages (which tend to be rejected to avoid anxiety) or positive messages (which tend to be accepted but not initiate action). It was the combination of moving evocations of the negatives with the offer of helping hand *in the same message* which proved so effective.

National Dairy Council – The Riddle of Twin Peaks (pp419–439)

Coverage: How advertising has successfully promoted milk to children. This case includes invaluable general learning for anyone engaged in marketing to children.

Period: 1990–93

Media: TV

The Judges' View: This case makes a convincing argument for the cost-effective use of advertising in stimulating consumption of milk amongst 2–15 year olds.

The analysis of *how* the advertising has worked is particularly innovative and will be of interest to anyone targeting children. An understanding of the way in which 'crazes' are created and then percolate down from older children to younger children has implications for the type of copy, the need for frequent copy refreshment (to avoid otherwise rapid wear-out) and targeting.

British Diabetic Association – Increasing Awareness of Diabetes Symptoms
(pp441–449)

Coverage: This campaign provided potential diabetes sufferers with information to help diagnose themselves. A well-planned, cleverly monitored test (using panels of doctors) was conducted in Wolverhampton and Basingstoke. The results of this small-scale test led to funding to extend the campaign nationally in 1994.

Period: 1993

Media: Posters and Press

The Judges View: The paper was ingenious both in strategy (self-diagnosis) and the evaluation of a smallscale test. It shows how much can be done with limited resources, which made it the unanimous choice for the Special Prize for *limited budget* cases.

IPA ADVERTISING EFFECTIVENESS EXECUTIVE COMMITTEE

Chairman: Hamish Pringle – Chairman, CME.KHBB

Chris Baker – Planning Director, Bainsfair Sharkey Trott

Gary Duckworth – Chairman, Duckworth Finn Grubb Waters

Paul Feldwick – Executive Director of Planning, BMP DDB Needham

Steve Gatfield – Managing Director and Chief Executive, Leo Burnett

Tessa Gooding – Communications Manager, IPA

Janet Hull – Director of Advertising Effectiveness, IPA

Nigel Maile – Financial Director, Bartle Bogle Hegarty

Simon Marquis – Editorial Director, Marketing

Sue Pedley – Planning Consultant, Euro RSCG

Nick Phillips – Director General, IPA

Dominic Proctor – Chief Executive, J Walter Thompson

Andrew Robertson – Chief Executive, WCRS

Mark Robinson – Business Development Director, Publicis

1994 IPA ADVERTISING EFFECTIVENESS AWARDS JUDGING PANEL

Chairman: Sir Michael Angus, President of the CBI (1992-1994) and Chairman of Whitbread PLC

Convenor of Judges: Chris Baker, Planning Director, Bainsfair Sharkey Trott

David Bell, Chief Executive, The Financial Times

John Brady, Director, McKinsey & Co

Jeremy Bullmore, Non Executive Director, WPP

David Cowan, Business Strategy Consultant, David Cowan Associates

Gary Duckworth, Chairman, Duckworth Finn Grubb Waters

David Hearn, Group Managing Director, KP Foods

Caroline Marland, Deputy Managing Director and Advertising Director, The Guardian and The Observer

Peter Mitchell, President of the WFA and Strategic Affairs Director, Guinness PLC

Terry Prue, Partner, HPI Research Group

Professor Ken Simmonds, Professor of Marketing and International Business, London Business School

ACKNOWLEDGEMENTS

The success of the 1994 IPA Advertising Effectiveness Awards owes a great deal to *Marketing Magazine* for being the principal sponsor of the Awards presentation, for producing and distributing the awards supplement in their own, their sister publication *Campaign* and the *Financial Times* and for supplying free advertising space.

The IPA would also like to thank the following companies whose support helped make the presentation possible:

Bartle Bogle Hegarty

BMP DDB Needham

Channel 4 Television

ITV Network Centre

J Walter Thompson Co Limited

KPMG Peat Marwick

Millward Brown

Mirror Group Newspapers

The Marketing Forum

Many people worked hard to make the awards a success, especially Hamish Pringle, chairman of the Advertising Effectiveness Committee, Chris Baker Convenor of Judges and, Nick Kendall whose agency, BBH devised the advertising campaign. From the IPA, particular thanks are due to Tessa Gooding, Janet Hull, Lynne Robinson, Jean Aligorgi, Amelia Gains and Elly McDonald.

Prizes

Advertising campaigns which benefited a business by maintaining or strengthening a brand over a longer period

GRAND PRIX

BMW – How 15 years of consistent advertising helped BMW treble sales without losing prestige
Tim Broadbent
  WCRS for BMW (GB) Ltd

GOLD (THE CHARLES CHANNON AWARD)

10 years of the World's favourite advertising – But how much did it have to do with the World's most profitable airline?
Fiona MacGill and Kara Gnodde
  Saatchi and Saatchi Advertising for British Airways

SILVER

HEA AIDS Advertising – The effective use of mass media advertising to meet the challenge of AIDS
Louise Whittet
  BMP DDB Needham for the Health Education Authority

Cadbury's Roses – "Thank You Very Much"
Liz Watts & Cindy Gallop
  Bartle Bogle Hegarty for Cadbury

BRONZE

Smoke Alarms – "Every home should have one"
Andrew Crosthwaite
  Euro RSCG for the Home Office

CERTIFICATE OF COMMENDATION

Daz – Ladies talk about Daz
Ros King and Vanessa Morrison
  Leo Burnett for *Procter & Gamble*

Clerical Medical 1990-1994 – Branding the truth
Lorna Young
  Butterfield Day Devito Hockney for *Clerical Medical Investment Group*

Anchor Butter – Until the cows came home
Sally Marsden
  Saatchi & Saatchi for *Anchor Foods Limited*

Products or services which are new, or have no significant history of advertising

GOLD

Boddingtons – "By 'eck"
Guy Murphy
  Bartle Bogle Hegarty for *the Whitbread Beer Company*

SILVER

Marston's Pedigree – How Victorian values strengthened a brand
Alan Cooper
  Simons Palmer Denton Clemmow and Johnson for *Marston's*

BRONZE

Nissan Micra
Paul Mayes
  TBWA for *Nissan Motor (GB) Ltd*

The launch of CICA – How advertising helped Clarks gain entry into the premium trainer market
Colin Mitchell
  BMP DDB Needham for *Clark Shoes*

The launch of Halls Soothers – "It started with a kiss"
Rachael Duckett
  McCann-Erickson for *Warner Lambert Confectionery*

CERTIFICATE OF COMMENDATION

Pepsi Max – Advertising to the Max
Jeremy Williams and Russell Seekins
  Abbott Mead Vickers: BBDO for *Pepsi Cola International*

The launch of Jeep Cherokee in the UK
Fran Foster
  DFSD Bozell for *Chrysler Jeep Imports UK*

Child Road Safety – For the sake of children
Sally Ford-Hutchinson
  DMB & B for *the COI/Department of Transport*

The launch of Heineken Export or how to smooth talk your way to success
Jon Howard
  Lowe Howard-Spink for *the Whitbread Beer Company*

Chicken Tonight – Advertising that dares to come out of the closet
John Stuart
  J Walter Thompson for *Brooke Bond Foods Ltd*

New campaigns from previously advertised brands, which resulted in significant short term effects on sales or behaviour

GOLD

Peperami – The consequences of unleashing a beast
Justin Kent
  SP: Lintas for *Van Den Bergh Foods*

SILVER

The Wonderbra – How thinking big ensured the survival of the fittest
Susanna Hailstone
  TBWA for *Playtex*

Cadbury's Boost – "Why work and rest when you can play?"
Derek Robson
  Bartle Bogle Hegarty for *Cadbury*

The Edinburgh Club – Turning fatties into fitties
Mark Gorman
  The Leith Agency for *The Edinburgh Club*

BRONZE

The Co-operative Bank – "Profit with principles"
Sarah Ryder
  Butterfield Day Devito Hockney for *The Co-operative Bank*

"A widget we have got" – How advertising helped John Smith's Bitter to break into an established market
Dean Webb and Richard Butterworth
  BMP DDB Needham for *Courage Limited*

How Advertising helped Strepsils to grab a market by the throat
Malcolm White
  BMP DDB Needham for *Crookes Healthcare Limited*

Health Education Board for Scotland – Smoking: sticks and carrots
Charlie Robertson
  The Leith Agency for *the Health Education Board for Scotland*

National Dairy Council – The riddle of twin peaks
Rachel Hatton
  BMP DDB Needham for *the National Dairy Council*

CERTIFICATE OF COMMENDATION

How the awareness of the symptoms of Diabetes was increased
Julian English and Jeremy Prescot
  Kilmartin Baker for *the British Diabetic Association*

BT – How "we want your business" proved invaluable to BT's business
Geraldine Knee
  Butterfield Day Devito Hockney for *BT*

The free guide to Fruit-ella's number 1 success with children
Rachael Duckett
  McCann-Erickson for *Warner Lambert Confectionery*

Birds Eye Crispy Chicken – The success of going "completely cuckoo"
Nick Jones
  Ogilvy & Mather for *Bird's Eye Walls Ltd*

Making Batchelors eligible again
Keir Cooper
  SP: Lintas for *Brooke Bond Foods*

Carlings – No wonder it's No. 1
John Carter
  WCRS for *Bass Brewers*

SPECIAL PRIZES

INTEGRATION WITH OTHER MARKETING TOOLS

The Wonderbra – How thinking big ensured the survival of the fittest
Susanna Hailstone
   TBWA for *Playtex*

DIRECT RESPONSE

Health Education Board for Scotland – Smoking: sticks and carrots
Charlie Robertson
   The Leith Agency for *the Health Education Board for Scotland*

EUROPEAN

10 years of the World's favourite advertising – But how much did it have to do with the World's most profitable airline?
Fiona MacGill and Kara Gnodde
   Saatchi and Saatchi Advertising for *British Airways*

LIMITED ADVERTISING/RESEARCH FUNDS

How the awareness of the symptoms of Diabetes was increased
Julian English and Jeremy Prescot
   Kilmartin Baker for *the British Diabetic Association*

MEDIA PLANNING

Nissan Micra
Paul Mayes
   TBWA for *Nissan Motor (GB) Ltd*

THE MARKETING AWARD FOR INNOVATION

The Co-operative Bank – "Profit with principles"
Sarah Ryder
   Butterfield Day Devito Hockney for *The Co-operative Bank*

Section One

Advertising over the longer term

1

BMW

How 15 years of consistent advertising helped BMW treble sales without losing prestige

INTRODUCTION

An objective of these awards is "better understanding of how advertising works". This case shows advertising working in a different way from all previous car-related entries: it shows how consistent advertising for BMW over a long period of time has built an exceptionally strong brand.

All previous car cases have shown the effects of *new* advertising campaigns, reflecting *changes* of strategy.

This may be because new advertising can give a sudden twitch to the needles of research dials, which makes it easier to demonstrate how changes in consumer attitudes coincide with changes in sale.

However, even if campaign zigzags can make *demonstrations* easier, they don't have a monopoly of advertising *effectiveness*.

This is because all brands, including car brands, are inanimate objects which have been given a personality.

Creating the perception of a strong personality requires consistency.

We say that a person whose behaviour is *inconsistent* from day to day (one day jolly, but the next day sad; one day confident, but the next day insecure) has a *disturbed* personality.

But we say a person whose behaviour is *consistent* day in and day out has a *strong* personality.

It follows that consistent advertising campaigns are more likely to build strong brand personalities in reality, even if the research deck is stacked against demonstrations of their effectiveness.

This case also suggests that the so-called "death of brands" which has excited some commentators has been greatly exaggerated. It shows that high consumer demand for the BMW brand helped BMW (GB) and its dealers to sell more cars, at high margins, than would be expected.

BMW'S BUSINESS OBJECTIVES

BMW (GB) was established in 1979 as a wholly-owned subsidiary of BMW (AG). It replaced a distributor which also sold other 'performance' marques such as Maserati.

Its objective was to treble volume sales by 1990 (from 13,000 new cars a year to 40,000) while maintaining high profit margins.

ADVERTISING OBJECTIVES

WCRS was appointed in 1979 and began the "ultimate driving machine" campaign which is still running.

A primary advertising objective was to create a richer brand image. BMWs were mainly known as performance cars, reflecting the models imported in the 1970s. It was necessary to reach beyond the 'enthusiast' consumer segment in order to achieve the sales target.

A secondary objective was to improve BMW's reputation as prestige cars, even though people would see more of the less exclusive models on the road as sales grew.

THE ADVERTISING STRATEGY WHICH MET THESE OBJECTIVES

BMW's strategy has been shaped by four concepts: core brand values, sniper strategy, centre of gravity and BMW tone of voice.

Core Brand Values

Research indicates that the BMW brand is selected before individual models.

The brand was, in the past, very demanding of its driver as he was expected to share the potency of its performance imagery. Broadening its image allowed more types of drivers to desire BMW and rationalise its high price.

Increasing the brand's prestige helped sell more affordable models; as a younger marque than Mercedes or Jaguar, BMW at that point lacked the prestige conferred by heritage.

> "A BMW doesn't give me any prestige to arrive outside the Polygon Hotel in, I'll be honest. The BMW is not – well, the mechanics are brilliant, but it does nothing for me."

> "I, rightly or wrongly, regard that Mercedes have had a quality motor car for a good while, and BMW are trying very hard to catch up the Mercedes image. But they are a younger company who are coming along, if you like, behind a position that Mercedes have been in for a while."

> "I don't think they're in that (Mercedes/Jaguar) club yet."

Car clinic qualitative research,
Communications Research Ltd, July 1980.

Consumer research and 'product interrogation' with BMW engineers in Germany ("interrogating the product until it confesses to its strengths" is a cornerstone in the WCRS strategic process) identified four core brand values:

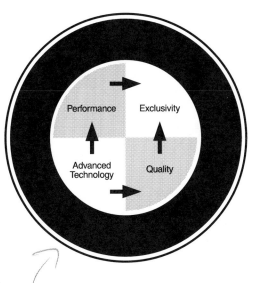

Figure 1. *BMW core brand values*

These values shape all BMW communications, though their expression in advertising has evolved in response to social, economic, environmental and competitive changes.

Performance

Has evolved from "cars which go faster" to "cars which are rewarding to drive", as pure 0-60mph acceleration has become less relevant (and socially acceptable) in today's driving conditions.

Figure 2. *'Performance' advertising*

Quality

Has evolved from "cars which are well made" to "quality which permeates every aspect of BMW ownership, from initial design through to servicing", as standards of car construction have risen among all manufacturers.

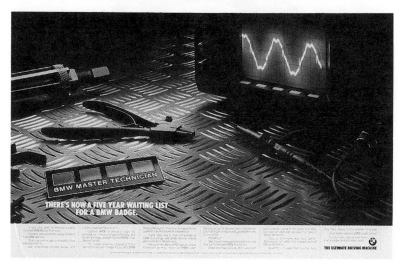

Figure 3. *'Quality' advertising beyond the car's construction*

Advanced technology

Has evolved from "the latest technology" to "the most relevant and thoughtful technology", as other manufacturers – particularly Japanese – have packed their cars with hi-tech gizmos.

Figure 4. *'Advanced technology' advertising*

Exclusivity
The product of these values, has evolved from "rarity and snob value" to "values not available elsewhere – only BMW could make a car like this", as the number of BMWs seen on the road has increased.

ENOUGH SAID.

Figure 5. *'Exclusivity' advertising*

The evolution of core values ensured that BMW, the ultimate yuppy driving machine of the 1980s, remains a relevant and socially acceptable brand in the recessionary 1990s.

Sniper Strategy

BMW advertising in Britain is notable for the production of a large number of different advertisements every year.

Each ad shows a different aspect of core brand values, aimed at a particular group in the marketplace, hence the term 'sniper' strategy.

Research is used to identify particular groups of prospective customers and establish which attributes are most important to them. For example, an ad about quality would help sell a 3 Series to an older man who values this attribute most, while an ad about 3 Series performance would be more attractive to a successful young executive.

Since 1979, 253 colour advertisements in leisure and weekend magazines, and – more recently – 24 television commercials, all reflecting core values, have created a richer image for BMW in Britain than elsewhere.

This approach is different from other car advertisers, who make fewer advertisements and show each one more often. But BMW cars are not mass-produced, so neither are BMW advertisements.

Centre of Gravity

This concept recognises that the BMW brand is made up of many models varying dramatically in price and performance but sharing a driving experience that can be identified as 'BMW'.

Placing greater advertising emphasis than sales warrant on more advanced models raises the centre (average perception) of the brand higher.

This benefits the less expensive models in the range by adding to the intangible desirability of owning a BMW; it militates against hardnosed comparisons of price/specification/performance with 'ordinary' cars. For example, a BMW 316i buyer would currently have to spend an extra £2,000 to match competitive specification, and he could easily choose a faster car at the price – but then he would not own 'a BMW'.

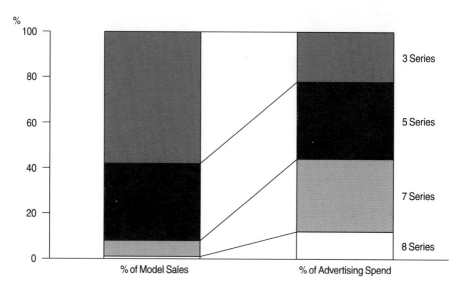

Figure 6.   *Raising the brand's centre of gravity*
Base: *1990, a typical year which had no major new car launches.*

Many ads have stressed the similarities between the less expensive and more expensive models in the range (see Figure 7).

BMW Tone of Voice

The BMW advertising produced over the years by WCRS looks and feels remarkably similar because of its consistent tone of voice.

The 'BMW world' is not warm.

There are few humans or signs of humans, because humanity can suggest fallibility, *whereas BMWs are shown as precise, cold, technical icons with jewel-like perfection.*

The car is the master of each ad. The advertising idea is based on facts about the car.

Figure 7. *Advertising stressing the similarities between the less expensive and more expensive models in the range.*

The art direction is a neutral frame in which the idea exists. There are no contrivances to add superficial glamour, such as stately homes, sunsets, or glamorous blondes.

Assumptive wit is used to puncture pomposity and create a feeling of belonging to the 'BMW club' amongst those who enjoy the joke:

Figure 8. *Assumptive wit rewards the reader*

These values have been consistent across *all* BMW communications, creating a campaign that is better known than would be predicted from BMW's relatively modest advertising budget. Since 1980, BMW has spent £91m on advertising (at MEAL prices), which is a modest sum against sales of £6.3bn.

Summary of BMW's Advertising Strategy Since 1979

BMW (GB) approached the challenge of trebling sales volume at high margins by using advertising to *build the BMW brand*. It changed the perception of BMWs from performance cars to a richer view of the brand.

This was achieved by advertising additional 'core brand values', and by the 'sniper' strategy of communicating many aspects of BMW values in a large number of advertisements.

The marque's prestige was enhanced by raising the brand's 'centre of gravity': associating the values of top-end BMWs with more affordable models.

Its consistent tone of voice harnessed the energy of all BMW communications to the overall brand.

The question is, did this strategy work?

In the following sections we show that it worked superbly.

BMW'S BUSINESS SUCCESS

BMW (GB) set out to treble sales. This has been achieved. Market share has almost trebled too, as BMW sales outperformed the market.

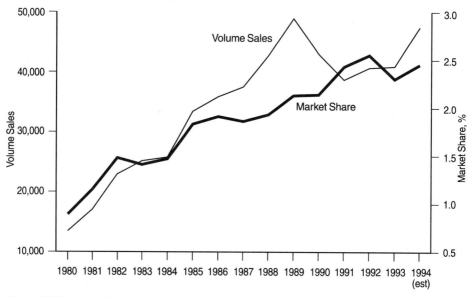

Figure 9. *BMW sales and market share*
Note: *1994 estimate based on percentage increase in year to April 1994 vs 1993; market share to April 1994*
Source: BMW, SMMT

BMW (GB) set out to achieve growth *with* high profit margins. This has been achieved.

BMW (GB) has made profits every single year since 1980. Annual profits depend on the prevailing Sterling/Deutschmark exchange rate; however, total company profits since 1980 amount to just under £400m (source: BMW company reports).

What are the causes of BMW's exceptional sales success?

To answer this question, we shall first show that price, distribution and improved products *could not* be solely responsible for BMW's sales success; then we shall show that richer brand imagery has created exceptionally strong consumer demand.

FACTORS WHICH COULD *NOT* EXPLAIN BMW'S SALES SUCCESS

Price

One might expect that BMW's sales trebled because of lower prices. But German cars have become more expensive in Britain as the Deutschmark has risen over Sterling.

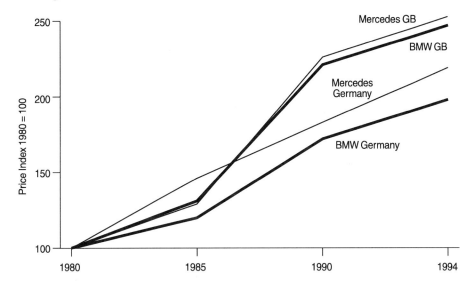

Figure 10. *German car price rises in Britain vs Germany, 1980-94 – Examples: BMW 5 and Mercedes 200/300*
Source: *Auto Motor und Sport* (Germany), *What Car?* (Britain)

The strength of the brand allowed BMW price increases even during the recession, unlike the market as a whole.

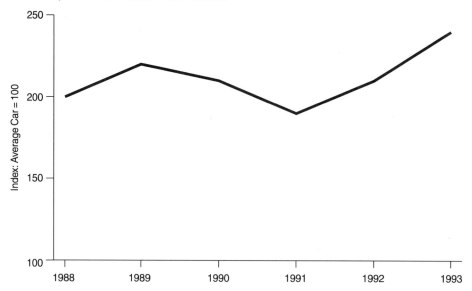

Figure 11. *Price of average BMW vs price of average car*
Base: *New car registrations value divided by volume.*
Source: SMMT, Mintel, BMW

BMW's price increases were *not* due to selling a higher proportion of expensive models. Prices have risen even though BMW is selling proportionately more of its least expensive models.

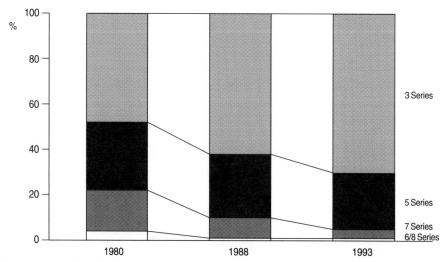

Figure 12. *BMW's sales mix by volume*
Source: BMW

It is clear that BMW's sales success is *not* due to lower prices. BMW prices have risen by more than the market, even though BMW sells proportionately fewer expensive models.

Distribution

One might expect that BMW's sales trebled because distribution trebled. But the number of BMW dealers has increased only a little (though the *quality* of BMW dealerships has continually improved).

However, BMW's rate of sale has overtaken the market average rate of sale, reflecting growing consumer demand for BMWs.

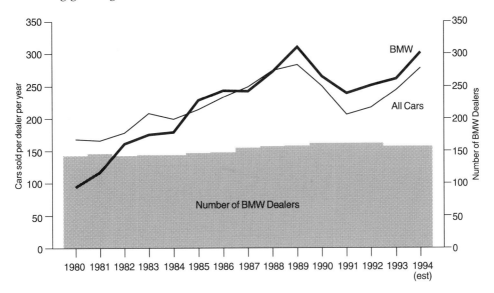

Figure 13. *BMW dealership numbers and BMW's rate of sale vs all cars*
Source: BMW, Sewells International 1993, SMMT

It is clear that BMW's sales success is *not* due to increased distribution. The number of BMW dealers has grown by 10%, while sales have trebled.

Improved Products

One might expect that BMW sales trebled because the products improved. (It has been shown in previous IPA papers that better cars sell more[1].) But although the *same* improved BMWs are on sale throughout Europe, BMW's sales growth in Britain has outperformed BMW's sales growth in Germany, France, and Italy.

In 1980, Britain was the fourth largest market for BMWs in Europe (after Germany, France and Italy); by 1993, the British market was second only to Germany.

---

1. See for example the Volkswagen Golf paper in the 1992 IPA awards.

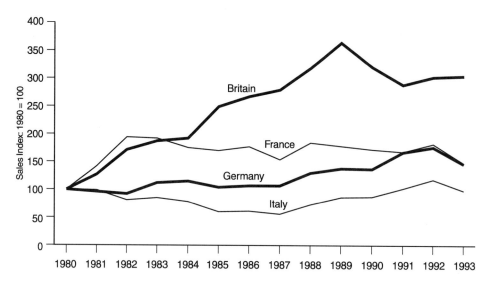

Figure 14. *BMW sales in Germany, Britain, France and Italy*
Source: BMW (AG).

It is clear that BMW's sales success is *not* just due to better products, because the *same* cars have sold better in Britain than in other countries.

THE STRENGTH OF THE BMW BRAND IN BRITAIN

The total number of BMWs on the road has increased from 81,000 in 1980 to 455,000 in 1993. The BMW 3 Series *alone* now sells more than all Audi and Saab *combined.*[2]

One would expect that as BMW lost exclusivity in reality it would come to be seen as a more ordinary car.

However, BMW imagery has improved and it has become perhaps the strongest marque in Britain.

A dedicated tracking study shows that now BMW has the strongest overall image of any major car brand, stronger even than Mercedes on key attributes.

---

2. It also outsells previous IPA winners such as the Mazda range, the Renault 19 and the Mini.

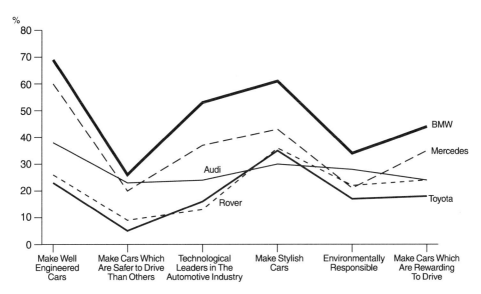

Figure 15. *BMW's brand image strengths*
Source: Harris Research, April 1994

An international image study commissioned by BMW (AG) shows that Britain is the *only* market in which BMW is more highly regarded than Mercedes.

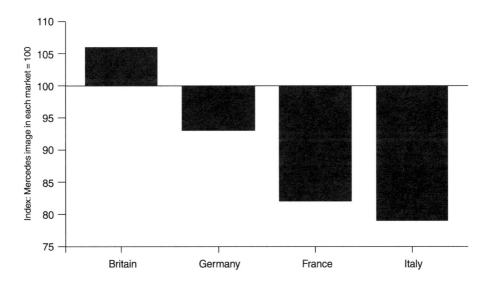

Figure 16. *BMW imagery vs Mercedes, 1992/93*
Base: *Average of 18 product image dimensions. See appendix for details.*
Source: International BMW Image Study 1992/93, Dr Salcher Team GmbH

The following graph shows that BMW exceeds Mercedes on image dimensions such as 'acceleration' and 'sportiness' in all markets, but in Britain alone BMW also exceeds Mercedes on other key dimensions: the brand's imagery has become richer in Britain than elsewhere.

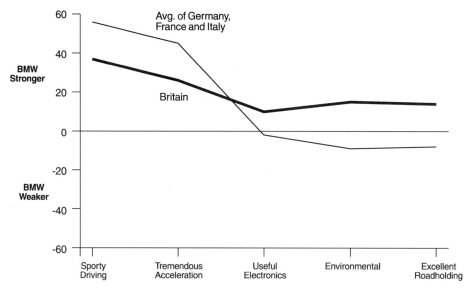

Figure 17. *BMW's richer brand imagery in Britain. Differences between BMW and Mercedes image ratings.*

BMW's richer image in Britain has been achieved although the profile of model sales is very similar to that in France and Italy:

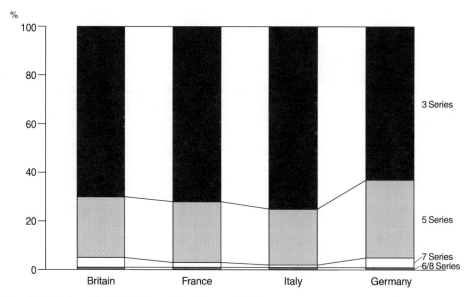

Figure 18. *BMW sales profiles in Britain, France, Italy and Germany in 1993*

This survey can be compared with a similar survey from 1979 to show how BMW's imagery has improved over the long term (though this did not include competitive marques, and the image statements differ).

In 1979, BMW in Britain had weaker imagery than BMW in Germany (the home market is invariably stronger). But by 1992/93 BMW imagery in Britain at least matched BMW in Germany, while BMW's imagery in other markets has fallen relatively further behind BMW's imagery in Germany.

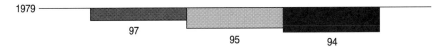

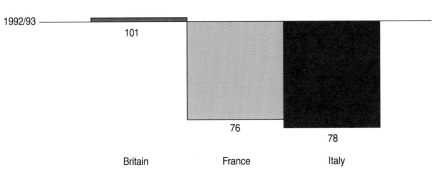

Figure 19. *BMW's imagery vs its imagery in Germany – Index: BMW in Germany = 100*
Base: *As above, and average of 16 product image dimensions in 1979. See appendix for details.*
Source: As above, and International BMW Image Study 1979, Enmid-Institut GmbH.

Consumer demand for BMW has become stronger than its market share would suggest; research shows it is second only to Vauxhall.

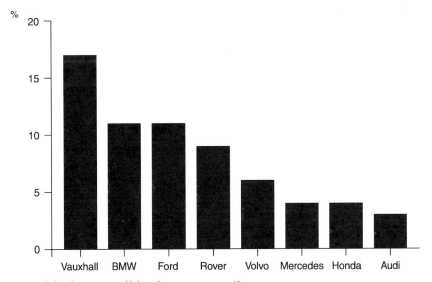

Figure 20. *Q. "Which make are you most likely to choose as your next car?"*
Source: Harris Research, April 1994

The strength of the brand has created exceptional consumer loyalty. For example, BMWs and Audis are almost equally reliable cars, yet BMW owners are much more likely to repurchase than Audi owners.

TABLE 1: CUSTOMER LOYALTY VS PROBLEMS WITH CAR

	BMW	Audi
Average number of problems per owner	1.02	1.03
Previous car was same make	58%	37%

Source: 1993 New Car Buyers' Survey

Qualitative research explains how the brand helps BMW owners 'forgive' any problems with their cars:

"If I'd had these experiences with a Rover, I'd think "Typical". As it's a BMW, I think I'm unlucky."

Cragg Ross Dawson, The BMW Brand, March 1994

Qualitative research shows BMWs are so desirable because BMW is seen as unique:

"Within the set of enviable cars (BMW, Mercedes, Jaguar, Lexus), BMW alone offers youthfulness."

Ockwell Associates, BMW advertising research, March 1994

BMWs have become symbols of success, not just sportiness. This gives new models a flying start in consumer appeal, as motoring journalists know:

(Of the new BMW Compact)

"The Golf has a 10 bhp advantage and it's also better specified, with a standard electric sunroof, trip computer and a decent stereo – but it doesn't have BMW's coveted 'spinning prop' badge."

Top Gear, April 1994

"It says, "Hey, look – we've made it" a lot more convincingly than a Citroën ZX or a Volkswagen Golf."

What Car?, May 1994

"Go on Rupert and Camilla, you know it makes sense."

What Car?, June 1994

Dealers now believe BMW is simply the best franchise to have in the whole market (see Figure 21).

In conclusion, price, distribution, and better products *could not* explain how BMW trebled sales in Britain. It is the exceptional *richness of the brand* that has created exceptionally strong consumer demand.

The next question is how advertising *consistency* helped create such a strong brand.

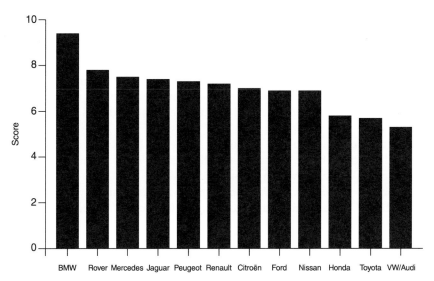

Figure 21. *Q. "Compared with all other franchises, how would you rate the value of holding your franchise, on a score of 1-10?"*
Source: Retail Motor Industry Federation, 1993/94

HOW ADVERTISING CONSISTENCY CREATED AN EXCEPTIONALLY STRONG BRAND

A minor benefit of advertising consistency is that the campaign becomes known; BMW's advertising is much better known than would be expected on its relatively modest budget (smaller than Proton's, for example).

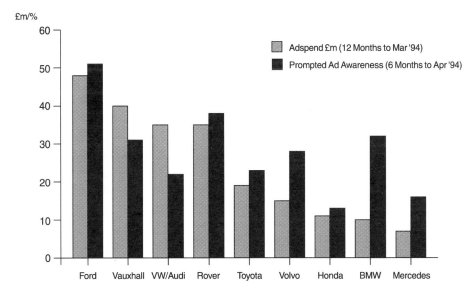

Figure 22. *BMW's high adverting awareness vs expenditure*

The fundamental benefit is what the *fact* of consistency signals to consumers about the company which is responsible for the cars and how they are advertised.

It signals that BMWs are made by a group of people who have "a distinctive philosophy", "a certain mindset", "a certain way of doing things to achieve a certain goal". It signals that BMW has a view of *how quality cars ought to be*.

Consumers believe that BMWs are good because BMW single-mindedly sets out to make good cars; that BMW unswervingly follows its vision of what a good car is; that BMW puts the manufacture of what it sees as good cars above all other considerations.

In research, no other car manufacturer, not even Mercedes, comes across as being so dedicated to the art of making really desirable cars. (Source: Cragg Ross Dawson, The BMW Brand, March 1994.)

This impression of *dedicated determination* has been created by the *consistency* with which BMW has advertised the excellence of its cars for 15 years.

THE VALUE OF THE BMW BRAND

"You pay £9,000 for the car and £5,000 for the badge."

Competitive car owner, 1990

It has been shown that since 1979

—   BMW prices rose higher than market prices;
—   BMW's distribution rose by only 10%;
—   and yet sales trebled, which is a much higher rate of growth than other European markets which sold the same cars.

It has also been shown that the BMW brand in Britain

—   is stronger than it was in 1979;
—   is now stronger than other leading marques such as Mercedes;
—   that Britain is the only market in which BMW is stronger than Mercedes;
—   and that Britain is the only market in which the brand has become as strong as it is in Germany, if not stronger.

The only reasonable explanation for BMW's sales success in Britain is that the exceptional strength of the brand has created exceptionally strong consumer demand; and it has been explained how the consistency of BMW's advertising has created the impression of a company dedicated to the manufacture of good cars.

The remaining issues are to try to place a cash value on the extra strength of the brand in Britain, and then to relate this value to the cost of the advertising which helped create the extra brand strength.

There are two empirical methods of estimating how much of BMW's sales are due to the strength of the brand.

First, suppose that BMW had average rate of sale increases – the same as the market rate of sale increases over 1980-93.

Second, suppose that BMW sales in Britain had grown at the same rate as they did in Germany, France and Italy over 1980-93.

Calculating BMW's hypothetical sales under *both* these suppositions eliminates some of the variables which would mask how much influence the stronger brand has had on sales. The effect of product improvements is eliminated in the comparison between other countries and Britain, because all markets received the same improved products. The effect of economic recession hitting European car markets at different times is eliminated in the average market rate of sale comparison, because the recession in Britain hit BMW at the same time as other marques.

The following two graphs show what volume sales *would* have been under both suppositions, compared to *actual* volume sales.

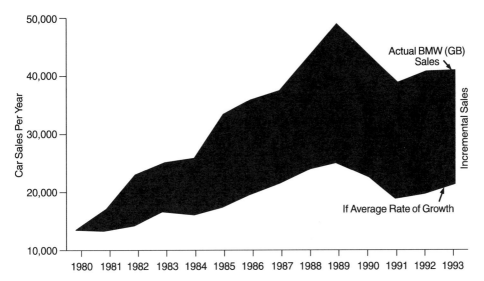

Figure 23. *If BMW's rate of sale had grown at same rate as market rate of sale*

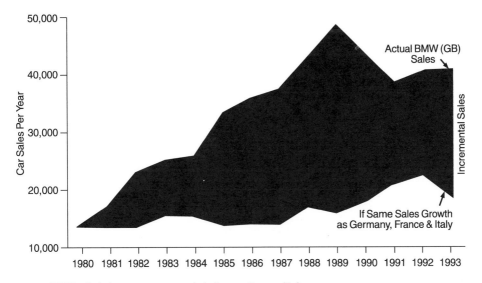

Figure 24. *If BMW's sales had grown at same rate as sales in Germany, France and Italy*

It can be seen that in both cases sales would have been significantly lower. The following table shows how much sales revenue would have been lost.

	Actual sales 1980-93	If... BMW's rate of sale increased at the same rate as all cars' rate of sale	If... BMW had same sales growth as in Germany, France and Italy
TABLE 2: SALES REVENUE			
Sales volume	466,327	263,989	255,440
Sales value*	£6.3bn	£3.6bn	£3.1bn
Actual sales higher by...	n/a	£2.7bn	£3.2bn

Note: * Total sales value 1980-93 divided by total sales volume gives the average BMW car price over this period: £13,521.

It can be seen that extra strength of the BMW brand has probably been worth around £2.7bn – £3.2bn in extra sales over the past 15 years.

These numbers are so large and surprising it may be worth repeating that only two reasonable assumptions have been tested: that BMW could have had *average rate of sale increases*, or that BMW could have had the *same sales growth* as in other major European markets.

What these calculations do not allow for is improvements in dealer *quality*. There is no way to quantify dealer quality over time and across markets, therefore it can only be assumed to be a constant for these calculations.

However, improvements in dealer quality generally relate to better conversions of prospects to sales. What advertising does is deliver new prospects in the first place. In 1993, for example, BMW's advertising created 35,000 enquiries, nearly all from non-customers, which helped dealers sell to the 14,600 new customers won last year. So far this year (to 20 May 1994) advertising has been responsible for 99% of dealers' 'hot' and 'medium' prospects.

IN CONCLUSION

It has been demonstrated in all previous IPA car cases that a sudden twitch to the needles of research dials coincided with changes in sales. However, the research deck is stacked against a similar demonstration here.

What it is possible to show is that BMW's advertising set out to enrich the brand's appeal, and that this has happened, and this has only happened in Britain, and that only in Britain have sales trebled.

BMW's advertising expenditure through WCRS has been £91m. As this has helped create brand values worth some £3bn in extra sales, the value of BMW's brand-building campaign seems beyond question.

APPENDIX – BRAND IMAGE DIMENSIONS

The 1979 study included the following image dimensions:

Comfortable	Elegant	Technically perfect
Economical	Roomy	Modern
Fast	Reliable	High performance
Safe	Quiet	Well made
Easy to handle	Good roadholding	Sporty
Good styling		

Respondents rated BMW with marks up to 100. The results were:

AVERAGE IMAGE ATTRIBUTION

	%
Germany	85.6
Britain	82.8
Italy	81.5
France	80.3

The 1992/93 study included the following image dimensions:

Reliable	Acceleration	Safety
Equipment	Engine	Quality
Technology	Comfortable	Styling
Low noise	Spacious	Consumption
Roadholding	Environmental	Useful electronics
Sporty	Roadholding (winter)	

Respondents were asked which marque each statement applied to. They could name more than one marque per statement. The results for BMW and Mercedes were:

AVERAGE IMAGE ATTRIBUTION

	BMW %	Mercedes %
Germany	49.9	53.4
Britain	50.4	47.6
Italy	38.7	48.9
France	38.1	46.4

2
10 Years of the World's Favourite Advertising
But how much did it have to do with the world's most profitable airline?

"The problem for BA is that it only makes a profit if we sell seats at the highest possible price... it's very easy to fill the plane and lose money".

John Watson, British Airways' Director of Regions and Sales, *Financial Times*, January 1991.

We will demonstrate that BA have indeed been able to sell more than enough seats at the 'highest possible prices'. And, that they've been able to do this because from a shabby, run-down state industry they have built the most valued and valuable brand in the airline business.

Obviously, products, service improvements, convenient schedules and pricing have all been important in building and maintaining that brand. In the words of a customer:

"They haven't just painted the 'planes and made beautiful commercials. The people have changed, too. They've delivered the goods".

However, the main point of this case is to show that 10 years of distinctive advertising that has constantly built the right expectations, often surprised, thrilled, charmed, and captured the mood of the times around the world, (even made grown men cry), has made a major difference, and has been instrumental in building and magnifying the values of the British Airways brand to give it its enviable status. In fact, we will argue that it has been the main sustainable competitive advantage.

It is impossible to do *full* justice to 10 years and over 60 countries in the space permitted. Furthermore, for reasons of history, and often sheer feasibility, we don't have many of the usual 'fmcg' type audits (eg switching data). We also have frustrating gaps and inconsistencies in data sources, and re-analysis that we might otherwise have done (eg further analysis of the image data) has been impossible to do.

We have produced a long term view, and gone for weight of evidence in the 'big picture' of the British Airways story. This is because the complexity of the airline business, and inevitable short term 'incidents' in it, means that close inspection of the business in concentrated bursts often gives a distorted view (eg how do you *really* legislate for the fact that during the Gulf War many people chose to fly Swiss Air, believing it to be safer because Switzerland was 'neutral'?).

Also, a view of the long term effect more accurately reflects the nature of the emotional and financial *investment* that British Airways has made in its communication over time.

IN THE BEGINNING…, IT WAS B AWFUL

In 1982, Lord King and Sir Colin Marshall were brought in to turn around British Airways in preparation for privatisation.

The city point of view…

They inherited a company that was running a loss of £541m in '81/'82, and as far as investors in the city were concerned, was an unattractive investment prospect. A MORI study of investor attitudes in 1982 showed that BA was rated as the least attractive investment of all the possible privatisation targets at that time.

The staff perception…

British Airways staff had nothing to be proud of in 1982. Demoralising staff cuts (50,000 to 37,000) added to the feeling of demotivation.

> "Morale was on the floor after the redundancies and losses."
>
> Lord King, *Sunday Times* 27/4/1990

The ramifications of a demoralised workforce were felt not only internally in terms of lack of efficiency and progress, but very importantly, externally by passengers.

From the consumer perspective…

The consumer perception of BA in the UK was that it was a shambling bureaucracy, lacking in imagination, aloof and disinterested in its passengers. The airline was not felt to live up to the advertising claim 'We'll take more care of you'.

> "Never been seen to hold a conversation with anybody – unlike their ads"
> "It's the British syndrome of 'Why should I do more than I'm paid for?'"
>
> CRAM Qualitative Research 1983

Outside the UK, BA was generally recognised as having a worldwide network, but it was perceived nonetheless to be Anglo-centric rather than international. The product offering was seen as run-of-the-mill, nothing special.

The quotes below are from qualitative research carried out in July/August 1982 in UK/France US/Germany/Hong Kong.

> "Few airlines appear to have established any particular cachet and most have in fact not transcended the positive/negative images of their country of origin. This is true of British Airways"
>
> (Extract from summary)

In France BA is associated with:

"recent aristocratic or colonial celebrities", "gin", "dirty old planes".

In the US BA was:

"proper, stiff, and middle-aged"

(Consumer quotes)

SETTING OUT TO BE THE BEST AND MOST SUCCESSFUL AIRLINE IN THE WORLD...

To turn British Airways into a financially successful company, the corporate vision was to become *"the best and most successful international airline in the world"*.

Management looked at three key areas to implement change: service (ie customer care); product (ie facilities on the ground and on board); and advertising.

1. *In service...*

   Qualitative and quantitative research from 1982 confirmed the new management's firm belief that service to the customer was key. The findings suggested that interaction with staff was twice as important as 'hard' product factors (eg comfort of seat, quality of meal) in affecting a positive assessment of an airline, and even more influential in affecting a negative assessment.

   BA therefore set in motion a customer care programme that would take two years to complete. 'Putting People First' involved taking every single member of staff through a two day seminar designed to underline the importance of customer care and motivate employees. Refresher programmes have been repeated regularly.

2. *In product...*

   Whilst product was recognised as not being as influential on customer satisfaction as service, if the airline was really to meet its business requirement of attracting more people willing to pay more, it clearly needed to ensure that the product was *competitive* versus other airlines. Again, a long-term programme was put into place and over the last 10 years BA has endeavoured to ensure product enhancements are in-line with passenger needs and expectations.

3. *Then, in inspiring people about it with new advertising...*

   The new management at BA recognised that the old advertising was a waste because it was not true. 'We'll take more care of you' was an overclaim and incredible to consumers. 'Fly the Flag' was re-enforcing the Anglo-centric image of the airline and working against its aim to be seen as an international airline.

Saatchi and Saatchi were appointed in the summer of 1982 to help develop a new campaign for the airline. The brief was for advertising that could capture the management's stated aim of being 'the best international airline in the world' and then to be capable of attracting consumers willing to pay that little bit more.

"I needed to grab attention, to persuade people, our own staff, that this was different from a
nationalised industry. When we changed the agency people said 'This management must be serious.'"

Lord King, *Sunday Times* May 1990

THE BIRTH AND DEVELOPMENT OF 'THE WORLD'S
FAVOURITE AIRLINE'

As we have discussed, in 1982 BA's actual offering to the consumer did not at all
support that it was the best international airline in the world. In line with Lord
King's words, however, it was felt important to begin to shift people's expectations
and parochial view of BA in advance of product and service improvements.

The initial strategy that was developed exploited BA's key strength, its large
international network. A quantified study conducted across five countries (UK, US,
Germany, France and Hong Kong) in the summer of 1982 confirmed that being
perceived to be the world's largest airline was a good thing. The most important
advantages were associations with 'good service' (28%), 'convenient flight times'
(25%), 'reliability of departures' (24%) and 'safety' (20%). All of these factors
were recognised (and have subsequently been frequently confirmed) as being key
drivers of choice.

'The World's Favourite Airline' translated the corporate goal of being the best
into an advertising line that uniquely positioned British Airways as an airline that
more people around the world choose to fly. With this line, the airline could begin
to develop the notion that BA was somehow more desirable, even though at this
time 'favourite' ('preferred above others', Oxford definition) was not a word
naturally associated with BA. Whilst a surprising fact to many (and intentionally
so) it was grounded in hard fact – BA really could claim to carry more passengers
internationally than any other airline.

In the long-term of advertising development *'Masterbrand'* advertising would
represent the global face of BA to all flyers, and was designed to claim the high
ground which would then be supported by product experience. *'Sub-brand'* (eg
Club World) and tactical advertising would later harness the values of Masterbrand
(ie would feed off and play into the values such as prestige and status), whilst
communicating the more specific benefits for individual consumer segments.

Masterbrand Advertising

Over the years, the Masterbrand advertising has been developed through three key
stages:

1. *1983 – 1985*
    The first stage (eg 'Manhattan') was designed to establish the new line,
    focusing predominantly on impressing upon the consumer the size, stature, and
    internationalism of British Airways. It aimed to signal that there was change at
    BA and to associate the company with success, using the surprising fact of size.

2. *1985 – 1987*
    By 1985, the airline was ready to tell consumers overtly about the service
    changes they had made. The Supercare campaign provided now credible

support for 'the World's Favourite Airline' in the form of excellent customer care. The commercials dramatised the extent staff would go to for customers on a grander, bigger scale than the standard airline service ad did. The larger-than-life Superman theme was designed to be impactful and impressive whilst humorous enough to give the commercials warmth.

3. *1989 – present*
    Following the privatisation (1987) and the launch of Club World (1988), the Masterbrand strategy moved into an important new stage. After a spell focused on the city and businessmen, it was time to re-focus on the wider customer base. There were also many countries around the world whose image of BA was still shaped by attitudes to Britain. These varied by country from the quaint Burberry Englishman in the States to the dominating imperialist in Australia. The common requirement to encourage this spectrum of flyers to continue to value BA, was to re-affirm the impressive size of the airline's international network whilst bringing more warmth and humanity to the brand personality. 'Global' and subsequently 'Feeling Good' aimed to do this by turning the straight fact that BA carries more passengers internationally into an involving emotional message: "We bring 24 million people to other people all round the world every year". It reflected the real end benefit of flying – that people fly to meet other people.

Sub-brand Advertising

Alongside the Masterbrand advertising, the sub-brand advertising, for Club World, Club Europe, Concorde, Super Shuttle and First Class, has been much more tightly focused on specific consumer targets. Bearing in mind the overall aim of getting more people to travel at a higher price, advertising business brands has been an important part of the mix.

A notable example, 'Boardroom', launched the first sub-brand Club World, capturing a totally new perspective on business travel. Most airline advertising talks about the service and latest on-board features. It is almost impossible to outdo other airlines in this respect. Competitive advantages tend to be short-lived. Instead, 'Boardroom' exploited the end benefit of good service – delivering the businessman ready to do business, and accurately captured for BA the mood of the moment in the business world – the sexiness of 'dog-eat-dog'. The recent relaunch, 'Up on the Roof', touched a new nerve on the businessperson's needs in the '90s – presenting a long haul flight as a time to escape from all the stresses of business and recharge.

A SUMMARY OF THE KEY ADVERTISING OBJECTIVES

At different times in the 'World's Favourite Airline' advertising history, the specific objectives and requirements have changed. However, looking at the overall picture, the core advertising objectives have remained constant.

The aim has been to develop advertising that *adds value* to the brand:
—   The intention has always been that the advertising should make a virtue of its size, giving the brand a unique and valuable sense of *prestige* and *status*.

'FLYING CITY'

SOUND: *Location effects to end.*
MALE: Roger Manhattan

Continue descent to flight level eight
zero.
2ND MALE: Roger Heathrow.

MALE: Manhattan that's correct
contact radar director on one two
zero decimal four.

Roger Manhattan continue to 2,000
feet, reduce speed to 170 knots.

3RD MALE: Every year more
people ...

... choose to fly with British
Airways ...

... to more countries than with any
other airline. In fact, every year we
bring ...

... more people across the atlantic
than the entire population of
Manhattan.

MALE: Manhattan you are cleared
to land.

3RD MALE: British Airways, the
World's favourite airline.

'SWIMMERS/LIPS/EYES/EARS/FACE'

SOUND: *Music and singing in background to end.*

 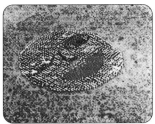 

MALE: Every year …   … the World's favourite airline …   … brings twenty four million people together.

'CLUB CLASS'

MALE: So two years in New York and he thinks he can tell us how to run things.

2ND MALE: It's alright I've fixed things.

He's travelling overnight on the Red Eye.

3RD MALE: And he won't have had time to incorporate those new figures I sent him in his report.

He'll be tired.

2ND MALE: I've arranged for the chaffeur to bring him straight here.

4TH MALE: Morning

5TH MALE: New Club World delivers the businessman ready to do business.

MALE: Pleasant trip?

4TH MALE: Yes thank you.

5TH MALE: New Club World ...

... from the World's favourite airline.

— It has been recognised that 'big' could mean 'cold' and that it is therefore key to try to be impressive in a way that reflects that the airline understands and *cares* about its customers.

Overall, the advertising has tried to make the brand that little bit more desirable and valued by customers, so that when there are two flights leaving about the same time, the choice will be BA, even though it may be slightly more expensive.

To sum up...

We have set out the development and implementation of strategies drawn up in 1982 designed to improve the product, service and advertising. We will now turn to the remarkable achievements of the airline against the goals it set itself, before looking at how this success was achieved.

AND THE VISION CAME TRUE

Getting people to pay more...

Over the last ten years, British Airways has successfully driven a premium versus the market.

Since on any one flight airline prices may vary dramatically, the best measure of price paid in this market is 'yield per revenue passenger kilometre' (y/rpk). This is the average revenue earned for a kilometre that a paying passenger flies. Published fares would not be a reasonable measure as they do not take into account promotional discounts and consolidator offers (ie they are not the actual prices paid).

In Figure 1, BA's y/rpk is compared over time to its key competitors. Average A includes all the biggest players in the market as a comparison. To include a broader

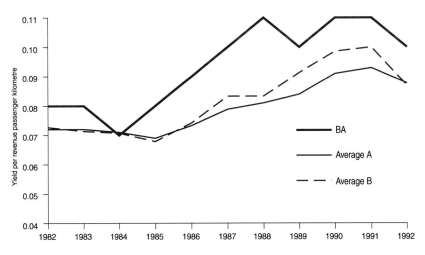

Figure 1. *BA yield per revenue passenger kilometre vs average of competitors*
Note: ***Average A:*** *All airlines with over 35,000m rpks ie American, Continental, Delta, Pan Am, JAL, Singapore, TWA, United, Air France, Lufthansa.* ***Average B:*** *is average A plus KLM, Alitalia, Iberia, Qantas, Air Canada (20,000m + rpks)*
Source: ICAO

selection of airlines, Average B also incorporates several smaller airlines (considerably less than half the size of BA). The graph shows that BA has grown and sustained an advantage over the market – in 1992 this was a premium of approximately 15% (over $1billion).

We believe we have made a fair comparison by looking at an average of all the large international airlines. Even when including some of the smaller airlines, BA is clearly sustaining a premium. Furthermore, the airlines represent those competing on BA's most important routes. Flights to the Americas, for example, account for around 31% of the airline's operating profit (in 1992).

Attracting a greater share of passengers...

Further, in driving this increasing premium vs the market, BA has also succeeded in attracting comparatively more passengers. Their available capacity has been growing in line with market growth, but they have been relatively more successful in filling their planes which has resulted in a growth in their overall share of passengers.

A clear reflection of the fact that BA is succeeding in attracting customers (even at this generally higher price) is that its market share is *ahead* of its capacity share on its key routes ie its share of the number of passengers carried is ahead of its share of the seats it has available (Figure 2). The fact that BA's load factor (ie percentage of seats filled) is up versus the market also confirms this (Figure 3).

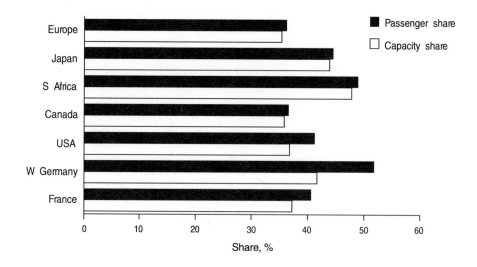

Figure 2. *BA capacity share versus passenger share*
Source: SCAMP

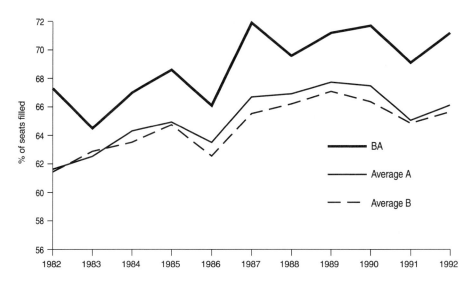

Figure 3. *BA Load factor vs average of competitors*
Note: **Average A:** *All airlines with over 35,000m rpks ie American, Continental, Delta, Pan Am, JAL, Singapore, TWA, United, Air France, Lufthansa.* **Average B:** *is average A plus KLM, Alitalia, Iberia, Qantas, Air Canada (20,000m + rpks).*
Source: ICAO

To finish painting the picture of success, looking at market share over the last 10 years, BA has invariably grown its share on key routes, often despite increased competition (notably on the US route). See Figure 4.

HOW AND WHY HAS BA MANAGED TO ACHIEVE THIS SUCCESS?

We will explore a number of possible factors: product and service improvements; schedule advantage; price control advantages; superior frequent flyer schemes. Our intention is to provide evidence to show that none of these factors could fully explain the achievements in driving superior consumer value. *The reason for this is that in none of these areas has BA grown a sustained advantage relative to competition.*

Was it down to product and service improvements?

Bearing in mind that long-term customer care and product enhancement projects were put into place in 1982, it would not be unreasonable to presume that superior product and/or service may have driven the success.

In order to look at the whole picture ie the trend and comparative picture on *hard product factors* (eg legroom) and *soft service factors* (attitude of staff), we have had to take data from three sources:
—   BA In-flight Survey for the hard product factor trend and a top-line feel for service factors since 1982.
—   BA Consumer Audit for a more sensitive picture of service (available only from '86/87).
—   IATA independent study which gives a *comparative* picture on hard and soft factors since 1989.

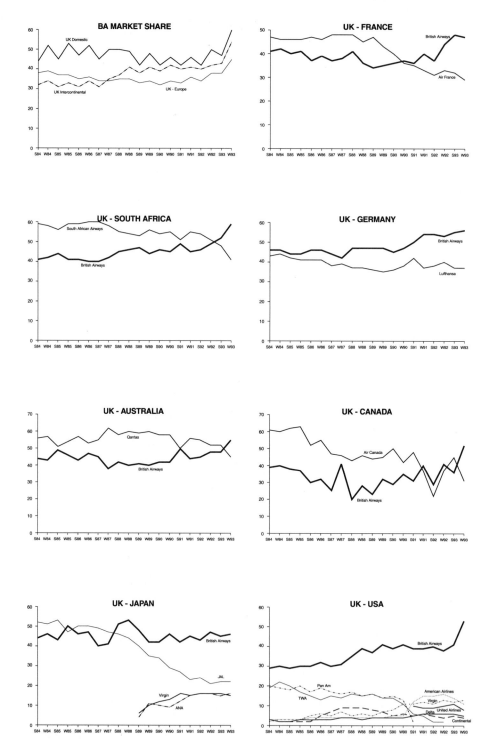

Figure 4. *BA market share on key routes, 1984-93*
Source: SCAMP

It is clearly not ideal that no single source is available that reveals the whole picture over time. However, all three sources get as close as is possible to an assessment of actual in-flight experience, as they are conducted during the journey (ie passengers can look down and see how much leg-room they've got, rather than simply being influenced by their impressions of the brand). Furthermore, they corroborate one another, giving us confidence in the data.

BA In-flight Survey

The BA In-flight Survey covers what have been consistently found to be the key hard product factors in affecting overall assessment. Figure 5 shows hard product ratings (scored on a scale of 1-5) for 5 key factors for short and long haul.

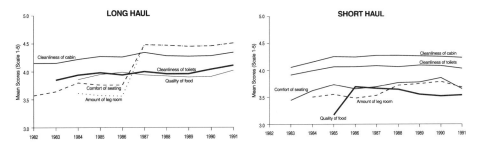

Figure 5. *BA In-flight survey hard product ratings*

In both charts we see an improvement across 1983–1985, after which the overall picture is flat. The lift on 'seating' on long haul is in line with the Club World relaunch.

The In-flight Survey focuses on assessing product rather than staff attitude. However, one statement regarding 'friendliness of crew' has consistently been included, as has an 'overall assessment of the in-flight service'. As we have mentioned before, the latter will be heavily influenced by staff attitude (twice as important as hard product factors according to CRAM research in 1983). Figure 6 shows that there was a slight improvement up until 1985 but that the long-term picture has been relatively flat.

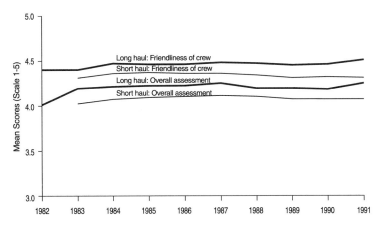

Figure 6. *BA In-flight Survey ratings*

Looking at detailed service data on a more sensitive rolling monthly scale, although there are short-term blips, the long term picture is essentially flat.

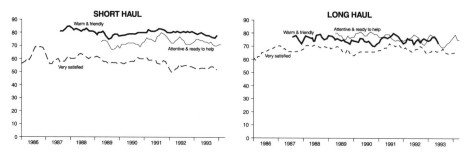

Figure 7. *BA Consumer Audit of staff service*

So it seems that initial programmes did lift consumer perceptions that BA have subsequently maintained.

The critical question is how this level of consumer satisfaction *compares to competition*, and whether it has driven a sustained advantage.

IATA Transatlantic Survey

An independent survey conducted by IATA gives us a fair competitive picture. This survey is conducted on-board transatlantic flights so allows us to compare BA vs many of its key competitors.

Figure 8 shows that between 1989 and 1991 BA was overall rated *behind* the market on product and service and has been roughly *on a par* since that time.

This data is entirely consistent with our qualitative assessment that BA's service offering, albeit improved, has not distanced itself from its competitors. The change in attitude from BA's staff was definitely picked up by consumers following 'Putting People First' and since then the service has been considered to be very good. Likewise, product improvements such as wider seats/more legroom have been noted and overall the product offering is considered to be good; indeed *amongst* the best in the market.

However, we should bear in mind that:

a) *a product advantage does not remain a competitive advantage for very long* (eg hot on the heels of the Club World launch, 35 other business classes were launched).

b) *consumers' expectations are constantly being raised* as everybody is improving, so long-term their level of satisfaction has not improved dramatically.

In the words of Sir Colin Marshall:

> "Every major airline in the world is flying aircraft of broadly similar quality – they all have to meet the same safety and noise requirements – some may boast that their service record is better, on the whole, there is not a huge difference."
>
> Sir Colin Marshall, *Sunday Times*, May 1990

Hence, although it would be ridiculous to deny its contribution, we cannot see that product and service alone could have been responsible for the remarkable success relative to competitors.

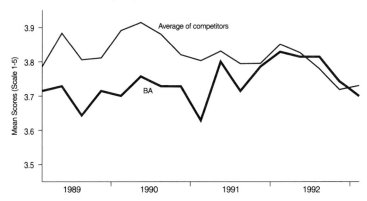

AVERAGE OF HARD PRODUCT RATINGS

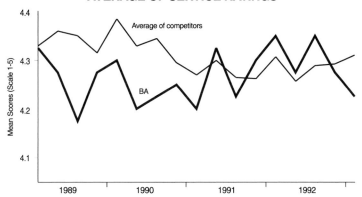

AVERAGE OF SERVICE RATINGS

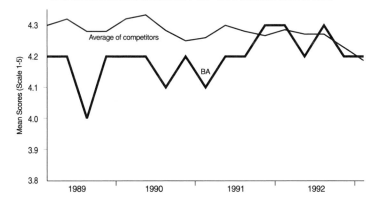

OVERALL ASSESSMENT OF IN-FLIGHT SERVICE

Figure 8. *BA vs average of competitors; hard product, service and in-flight service ratings*
Note: **Competitors averaged**
           American, Delta, KLM, Lufthansa, Virgin, United, US Air
           Statements averaged
           Service: *Speed of check-in, Courtesy of check-in staff, Efficiency of cabin crew, Courtesy, Friendliness of check-in staff*
           Product: *Comfort of seat, Amount of legroom, Storage space, Cleanliness of cabin, Cleanliness of washroom.*
Source: IATA Transatlantic Survey

Was it down to the network and schedule?

It would not be unreasonable to suggest that BA might have grown its advantage on schedule, and that this might account for its ability to attract more people and charge a premium. Convenience of schedule, whilst less important as a driver of choice for long haul, has consistently been found to be the key determinant on short haul for businessmen (source: MAI business travellers survey 1984–1993).

As one of the largest airlines in the world, and operating out of Heathrow, BA must clearly have some advantage vs many other airlines. However, this was also the case in 1982. It is difficult to assess precisely, but evidence shows that BA's competitive advantage hasn't grown, and indeed if anything, it has declined.

In overall terms, BA's capacity has only grown in line with market growth (see Figure 9), and as they have grown, they have moved to a greater proportion of larger planes. This would not suggest a *growth* in network advantage.

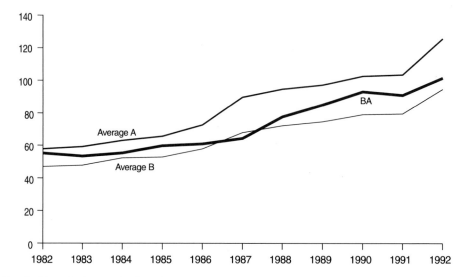

Figure 9. *BA capacity share growth vs the market*
Note: *For details of airlines included in Average A and B, see note to Figure 1*
Source: ICAO

Regarding timing of slots, BA tends to have an advantage in the UK, but the national carrier will have the advantage at the destination end. Heathrow is increasingly congested and Schipol is being marked as the central European airport for the next decade.

Evidence suggests that BA's actual schedule advantage has probably been eroded since 1982 because since that time, many of its key routes (eg transatlantic), have been de-regulated at both ends, resulting in fierce competition for slots. In comparison, some key competitors in Europe remain regulated, giving the national carrier a distinct advantage world-wide versus BA.

It does not appear feasible that BA's schedule accounts for the growth we have witnessed. In fact, in view of the increased competition, BA's success is all the more remarkable.

Was it just because they had an advantage in controlling prices?

Since the deregulation of the British air transport system, and the Americas, there has been a *decline* in relative competitive advantage – arguably, regulated European airlines can still inflate prices artificially.

As well as this decline in competitive advantage, we have seen that BA has driven its *share of passengers* as well as its premium, and this (market share growth) could not be the result of price controls.

Was it because of the frequent-flyer scheme?

Motivated by the incentive of accruing air-miles and privileges (eg preferential booking), customers may have been more loyal, and prepared to pay a premium.

In Britain, certainly some passengers will have flown BA (even at a slightly higher price) rather the competitor on offer, in order to accrue air-miles. However, BA only launched an independent frequent flyer scheme in 1991. By this time, 33% of BA's premium cabins were full with passengers who belonged to frequent flyer programmes of *other* airlines.

Frequent-flyer schemes have burgeoned world-wide, particularly in the States where the schemes originated, and are developing fast in Europe. Not only do most other airlines offer these schemes, but the air-mile rewards that BA offers are often less advantageous than some of the competitor offers eg the same international itinerary that would earn you two return economy tickets to Rome on Lufthansa (plus hotel nights and car rental), would only earn one economy return to Venice on BA (source: Lufthansa 'Miles and More' May 1994).

It appears that BA does not have an advantage with their frequent flyer scheme outside the UK. Indeed, BMRB tracking data shows that in markets where these schemes are developed, consumers do not rate BA very highly vs other available schemes.

TABLE 1: BA'S SCORE INDEXED VS COMPETITORS

	Canada	Germany	France	East Coast	West Coast
"Have a good frequent flyer scheme"	–29	–5	–1	–52	–54

Source: BMRB 1993

In conclusion...

Notwithstanding the great strides that British Airways has made in terms of customer service, product and incentives, we have shown that these factors cannot fully account for BA's success. We have shown that this is because they have not been able to deliver a sufficient or sustained competitive advantage.

SO, WHY *IS* BRITISH AIRWAYS THE WORLD'S FAVOURITE AIRLINE?

Having discounted these other factors we will now show that what *has* grown dramatically versus the market is BA's *brand strength* on key image dimensions.

Let us remind ourselves of how BA was perceived versus competition in 1984 (the earliest date for common data).

Figure 10 shows British Airways' profile versus key competitors in all the markets tracked by BMRB in 1984 (NB 1984 was after the launch of 'The World's Favourite Airline'). The charts demonstrate very clearly that BA was just one of the pack, with no clearly differentiated image profile.

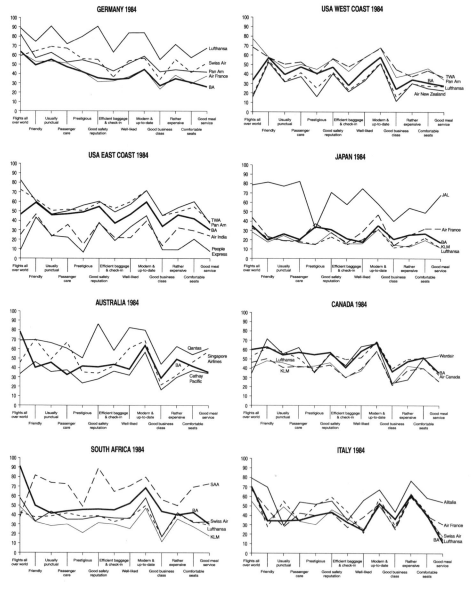

Figure 10. *British Airways profile vs key competitors by market in 1984*
Source: BMRB

How the image has changed...

In the following BMRB international tracking charts (Figures 11-14) the score attributed to BA is indexed vs the four/five competitors tracked in that country at that time. (Note that there are no significant variations in airline usage in any of the samples that would explain the shifts over time.)

In the UK, the tracking study changed in 1989 from the research company Millward Brown to BJM. However, because we have looked at the relative picture vs competition in the form of an index, we are showing an accurate measure of the shift in image. In both 1984 and 1994 BA is measured against the average of its eight key competitors for business in the UK.

1. *Prestige/status*

   British Airways now *owns* prestige in the minds of consumers world-wide. Figure 11 shows dramatic increases and significantly higher indices vs the market. (And we should note that Germany had no TV advertising until 1992, unlike all the other countries.)

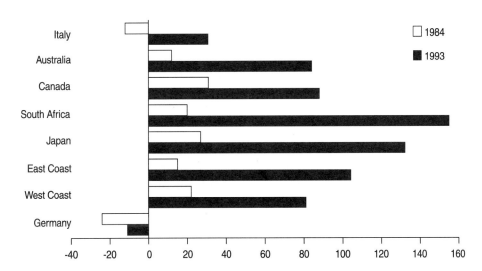

Figure 11. *'Prestigious' indexed vs competition*
Source: BMRB

   In the UK the index in 1984 was 158, versus 1994, 227 (where average of competitors = 0).

2. *Size/international*

   Is there an enhanced consumer perception of BA's key strength, its world-wide network?

   Even in countries like Canada, Australia and South Africa where BA was already recognised as a world-wide airline, there has been an increase in consumer perception of its world-wide network way beyond the reality of any improvement vs competition. (Remember, capacity has only grown in line with the market.) The UK index moved up from 133 to 194.

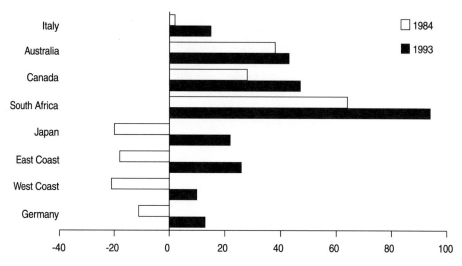

Figure 12. *'Flights all over the world' indexed vs competition*
Source: BMRB

3. *Understanding the consumer*

We have mentioned before that it was a corporate objective to associate the airline with status and scale, whilst being perceived to offer warm service to the consumer (ie 'big' should not mean 'uncaring'). The best dimension we have over time to assess the more caring side is 'friendly', although it is only one dimension of the closeness that BA has tried to develop with its customers.

The area of care and friendliness is always the hardest to influence, particularly versus the local airline. Especially when some airlines have *positioned* themselves as 'friendly' (eg Far-Eastern airlines and Virgin). We also know from qualitative research that the elements that make up 'friendliness' vary widely from country to country.

Figure 13 shows a general improvement around the world since 1984, apart from in Italy and Japan where, along with Australia, BA is not perceived as friendly versus competition. Amongst the Japanese and Australians, not surprisingly, Far Eastern airlines (and in Australia, Qantas) eclipse BA in this respect. But BA is seen to be more friendly than European or American airlines. The Italians do not regard BA as 'friendly', but they do think it is more 'caring' than Alitalia.

In the UK, BA's improvement on this measure has been countered recently by Virgin and Singapore whose nominal shares have improved dramatically. BA's dispute with Virgin may also have had a dampening effect. The index has moved down from 158 in 1984 to 91 (average = 0), in 1994.

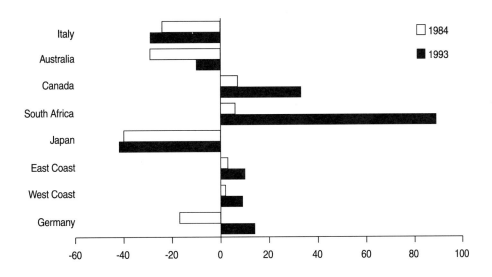

Figure 13. *'Friendly' indexed vs competition*
Source: BMRB

4. *Leader/ Innovator*
   BA has developed a profile that is more closely associated with being modern and ahead of the field than *equally* thrusting competitors.

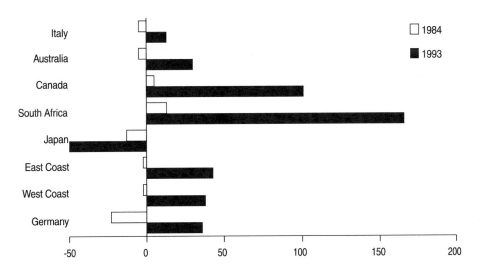

Figure 14. *'Modern and up-to-date/ahead of the field' indexed vs competition*
Note: *In 1984, the attribute tracked was 'modern and up-to-date'. This was later changed to 'ahead of the field' which was felt to be more appropriate.*
Source: BMRB

In the UK the index has also shown an improvement that further widens the gap from 81 to 115 (average of competitors = 0).

So, the one sustained competitive advantage...

From a position of parity in 1984, BA has distanced itself from the competition on certain motivating image dimensions. It is our contention that it is BA's advertising that has driven this important, long-term advantage over the competition by shaping, through its advertising, how people feel about the brand in their hearts and minds.

THE WORLD'S FAVOURITE AIRLINE CAMPAIGN AS A MAJOR ENGINE OF THE BRAND'S SUCCESS

The effect of the World's Favourite Line...

Nowadays, people spontaneously link 'The World's Favourite Airline' with British Airways.

> "The BACC ruled last week that the word 'favourite' was the property of BA"
>
> *Campaign* April 8, 1994

> "Oh no, I don't think they should change that... it's become their trademark"
>
> 'Smile' qualitative research, UK, USA, France and Italy; December 1991

Quantitative research amongst a general sample of prospective customers and amongst staff showed that by 1988:

73% of passengers and 94% of staff felt it had become part of the BA image;

87% of staff felt it represented all the things they were striving for.

The research also confirmed what has been consistent in qualitative learnings ie that the line has a number of important positive associations, namely;

"International, successful, confident, established, large, caring".

The effect of bringing the line alive in advertising...

British Airways has amongst the most talked about advertising in the world. There are advertising spoofs on BA advertising (Hotpoint, Phileas Phogg, Britain's Petite); in Australia the 'Global' ad was given free spots because it was felt to drive up ratings; in Turkey, 'Feeling Good' is used to introduce the evening news on television.

It is all very well to be talked about, but is this linked to BA's success? The advertising has been talked about for two key reasons:

— Dramatic, distinctive executions making a virtue of the airline's size.
— Bringing alive fresh consumer insight.

The net effect around the world has been to build the key dimensions of BA's image of status, prestige and consumer empathy.

Dramatic and distinctive in execution...

"BA's 'Global' ad scored the highest ever branded cut-through for a single execution on our stochastic monitor".

"Because of the consistency of the advertising and the number of memorable blockbusters, the BA TVR consistently delivers higher cut-through scores than other airlines".

BJM Research and Consultancy Ltd

"We have seen enough of aeroplanes in ads... this is different... it grabbed my attention".

Consumer research verbatim quote UK 1983

"British Airways' new commercial that puts a smile on everyone's face will be on air tonight at 21.30 during the European Championship League on Interstar. Don't miss it".

Sabah, 25/11/92, Turkey

"Towns stood still for $4.5m ad".
"The result is an ad that has won accolades for its originality and sheer entertainment value".

New Zealand Herald, 30/4/90)

"Corporate aspects of BA's image improved almost without exception during the course of the 'Manhattan' campaign. Modernity, importance, present success and contribution to the economy all became more strongly identified with the airline".

MORI, September 1983

Ahead in terms of consumer understanding...

"Warm, caring BA sells friendly skies. BA gets warm and real".

B&T, Sydney

"BA shows us a fresh and unexpected human face for the '90s. It's a wonderful idea, beautifully executed".

Adweek, January 1990

"BA is ahead of the game in its promotion of in-flight relaxation, but other airlines will inevitably follow... BA is reflecting what is happening in society generally".

Touche Ross

"What has made BA the World's favourite airline? It's the feeling it creates in 25 million people world-wide".

Daily News 'Weekend', 20/11/92

"Some say it's advertising's equivalent to man walking on the moon. Few would disagree".
Sunday Mail, Adelaide, 11/2/90

So, qualitatively, we are convinced that advertising has had a disproportionately positive effect on the development of consumer attraction to the brand. But can we make the link quantitatively?

Goodness of fit...

To demonstrate the link as conclusively as possible, we have plotted the average shift (1993 vs 1984) for the main dimensions (prestigious, flights all over the world, modern and up-to-date/ahead of the field, friendly) on the world-wide tracking study against a factored index of 'advertising appreciation' for BA vs competitors. The result is startling (Figure 15). Looking at the closeness of the profiles, there is clearly a link between appreciation of advertising and shift in image ie in those countries where advertising is most highly regarded eg South Africa, the shift in image is greatest.

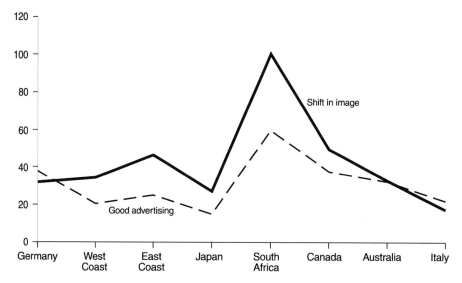

Figure 15. *Shift in image vs 'good advertising'*

BUT HAVE WE MISSED ANYTHING?

Is there anything other than the advertising that could have affected British Airways' image in this way? We have already discounted product and service on the basis that they do not offer a sustained advantage. The only other possibilities that seem feasible are powerful positive PR and the effect of the privatisation.

The privatisation

The successful privatisation may well in itself have had an impact on prestige and status, and given a lift to BA staff internally. However, we would assert that the advertising contributed to a successful privatisation in the first place by accelerating the improvement in image. In MORI surveys between 1985 and 1987, investors, analysts and captains of industry consistently refer to advertising/image as a key ingredient of BA's growing attractiveness.

Most importantly, we would argue that the successful privatisation of BA in the UK seven years ago could not have resulted in an image shift world-wide with such long-lasting consequences.

Positive PR

We have already indicated the extent to which advertising itself has generated favourable PR for British Airways. It is often the currency in which the media refers to the airline.

However, British Airways is certainly successful in the UK in creating PR opportunities which may contribute to its image as prestigious and innovative eg around product launches. Around the world, however, the local airline in each country is more likely to attract similar PR attention. And in the UK, particularly recently, BA has had to weather negative PR with regard to high profits and competitive disputes.

We would therefore discount PR generated by sources other than advertising as the driving force behind the shift in image.

THE STRONGEST AIRLINE BRAND IN THE WORLD

Interbrand valued the BA brand in 1992 and declared it the most powerful airline brand in the world.

They calculated that the percentage of British Airways' corporate assets accounted for by brand values had been steadily increasing, with the percentage in 1992 indexing 361 versus 1980. This is expected to continue to grow significantly, and by the year 2010, it is estimated that 46% of corporate assets will rely on brand values alone.

The value of 'The World's Favourite Airline' cannot be overestimated. To put it into a digestible context, the premium that BA has been able to command whilst growing its market share has been worth an estimated $7.8 billion over the last 10 years.

The weight of evidence indicates that advertising must have been a major contributor. The £400m spent on advertising world-wide has been an astute investment.

Finally, the brand as a business platform...

So, brand values allow British Airways to charge a premium. However, there are also many other ways that they are able to leverage the power of their brand to a business advantage. For instance:
— Launching and extending sub-brands – eg the 'Masterbrand' gives British Airways' Holidays credibility and Club World, prestige.
— Maximising responses from promotions – most recently, 'World Offers'.
— Lifting staff morale – "I tell people I work for the World's Favourite" (Cabin Crew research 1993).
— Trade – travel agents want to be associated with BA.
— Alliances – in the race to form the world's biggest global alliance, BA is the brand that can most credibly lead a truly global alliance (MBL Alliance research 1993).
— Generating positive PR from new ideas – in 1992, the interactive City-breaks cinema commercial generated an estimated £500,000 of PR world-wide.

—   Bouncing out of a difficult market environment: 'The World's Biggest Offer',
    which got the World flying again after the Gulf War, could only have been
    launched by a brand with bona fide international credentials.

TO CONCLUDE...

The superior value and values of the British Airways brand have been significantly
driven by distinctive and perceptive advertising over a ten year period.

The strength of the brand, and the 'highest possible prices' it is able to
command, gives British Airways an exceptionally powerful platform for further
profitable development world-wide over the next ten years.

3

HEA AIDS Advertising

The effective use of mass media advertising to meet the challenge of AIDS

INTRODUCTION

In the UK there is a new generation with different sexual behaviour because of the threat of HIV and AIDS.[1]

Partly as a result of this, the UK is now "a low prevalence country in a high prevalence world", its AIDS prevalence dropping from 93% of the twelve EC countries average rate in 1984, to 54% in 1993.[2]

This case will argue that this is at least partly a result of the government's mass media advertising through the Health Education Authority (HEA) around AIDS which achieved its two primary objectives:

i)   preventing HIV/AIDS slipping off the public agenda; and

ii) encouraging condom use among young heterosexuals.

We will evaluate the HIV/AIDS advertising developed by BMP DDB Needham on behalf of the HEA from December 1988 to December 1993.

The focus will be on the campaigns run in general public media. It excludes advertising targeted specifically at gay men which ran in gay clubs and press.[3]

---

1. Source: National Survey of Sexual Attitudes and Lifestyles ('National Survey') as published in: Johnson A, Wadsworth J, Wellings K, and Field J (1994) *Sexual Attitudes and Lifestyles* Blackwell Scientific Publications. (All subsequent references to the National Survey are from this publication.) The National Survey represents the first comprehensive survey of UKs sexual behaviour and attitudes. It interviewed a representative sample of 18,876 men and women aged 16-59. Interviewing took place from May 1990 to November 1991 (and hence overlapped with the largest period of HEA advertising activity).

2. Source: WHO European Centre for the Epidemiological Monitoring of AIDS. Quarterly report no.40 (31.12.93). Analysis: HEA.
Behaviour change among gay men and the success of needle exchange schemes have also kept AIDS prevalence in the UK low.

3. The advertising to gay men was designed for an audience at a very different stage of awareness and understanding about the risks of HIV. Moreover, promoting 'safer sex' to this audience primarily involved promoting non-penetrative sex. Only latterly (1992 onwards) has HEA advertising focussed on advice on condom use for gay men.

THE EARLY DAYS: 1986–1988

By the mid 1980s AIDS was seen by the government as one of the greatest threats to the UK's public health this century, and significant public education campaigns preceeded the work developed by BMP and the HEA.

In 1986 and 1987 the Department of Health (DOH) through TBWA dramatically announced the arrival of AIDS in the UK. The campaign, featuring apocalyptic images of tombstones and icebergs, stressed the seriousness of AIDS, and that everyone was at risk. The multi media advertising was supported by a leaflet distributed to all 23 million households in Britain.

The high level of awareness and anxiety generated by this campaign proved a double-edged sword. It was impossible for the government to continue publicity at this level. In fact there was a twelve month gap before further advertising appeared. But because publicity stopped, people believed the threat of AIDS had lessened.

The HEA was created in 1987, and took over responsibility for all aspects of AIDS public education[4].

Its first work (through TBWA) attempted to address some of the problems it had inherited. Swings in public concern from alarm to complacency needed replacing by more reasonable levels of concern amongst the relevant group, ie sexually active young heterosexuals. Two commercials ran in Spring 1988, 'Flat' and 'Disco'.

Tonally, however, the advertising remained sombre and threatening, echoing TBWA's earlier work.

By mid 1988 the HEA was seeking a more balanced and factual advertising approach. BMP were appointed in the autumn of 1988.

THE NEW APPROACH TO HIV/AIDS ADVERTISING

Autumn 1988 to December 1993

To prevent the transmission of HIV, the HEA wanted to encourage young sexually active heterosexuals (demographically 16-34 year olds with two or more sexual partners in the last 12 months) to use condoms.

The development of advertising strategies to achieve this was guided by behavioural models, notably the 'Health Belief Model'[5]. This states that to change their behaviour:

> "individuals must have sufficient concern about health issues and believe that:
> — they are susceptible to the illness and hence perceive a threat;
> — illness would be avoided with appropriate behaviour change;
> — behaviour can be changed at an acceptable cost."

---

4. With the exception of drugs, the responsibility for which remained with the DOH.

5. "Health Belief Model" (Rosenstock, Strecher and Becker) as quoted by McEwan R and Bhopal R (1991) *HIV/AIDS health promotion for young people: a review of theory, principles and practice* HEA AIDS Programme Paper No.12. See also Wellings K (1992) *Assessing AIDS Prevention in the General Population*. Report for the EC Concerted Action (I UMSP, Lausanne)

   It should be noted there are criticisms of this model, not least that it oversimplifies the social and psychological complexities around behaviour change (in much the same way as models of consumer purchasing behaviour in FMCG markets do).

Advertising therefore had to work on two levels.

a) To maintain 'sufficient concern' around HIV/AIDS, advertising needed *to prevent HIV/AIDS slipping off the public agenda*. The nature of HIV (its long incubation period and the inability to tell by sight if someone is infected) meant:
    — many were likely to be positive without knowing it;
    — thousands who had been diagnosed often chose not to disclose their HIV status for fear of being marginalised.
    These factors resulted in
    — no 'visible' evidence of AIDS for most of the general population;
    — generally 'low' official statistics exposed by the press.
    Advertising had to impress upon the general public:
    i)   AIDS was a serious ongoing threat;
    ii) it was an increasing problem relevant to heterosexuals;
    iii) the link between HIV and AIDS (to explain the apparent 'invisibility' of AIDS).

b) For 16-34 year olds with 2+ partners we needed to *encourage them to use condoms* by creating the conditions for behaviour change suggested by the Model. Thus advertising was used to:
    i)   encourage them to believe they personally could be at risk from HIV;
    ii) promote condoms as the primary means of prevention; and
    iii) reduce some of the 'barriers' around condom use, as a means of removing their emotional 'cost'.

Achieving both sets of objectives, particularly from 1989 to 1992, also involved targeting those with an influence upon the sexually active young. High profile, mass market media such as TV and national press were used for large parts of the campaign to reach beyond young heterosexuals to the broader public. (See Figure 1.)

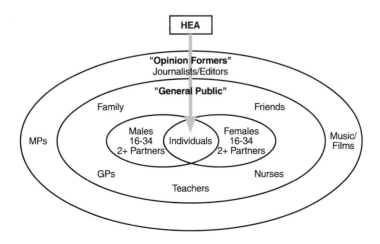

Figure 1.

CHRONOLOGY OF THE CAMPAIGN

Tables 1 & 2 provide a summary of the HEA's HIV/AIDS advertising in wider media from December 1988 to December 1993[6]. Broadly the advertising since 1988 can be grouped under three headings:
— keeping HIV/AIDS on public agenda and encouraging perceptions of risk among heterosexuals;
— reducing the barriers to condoms;
— safer sex on holiday.

TABLE 1: HIV/AIDS CAMPAIGN CHRONOLOGY: DECEMBER 1988 – DECEMBER 1993

Timing	Campaign Title	Target	Specific Objectives	Media	Spend
December 1988-March 1989	HIV Facts	General public 16-34s, 2+ partners	Keep HIV/AIDS on public agenda. Link HIV to AIDS.	National Press	£1.8m
Spring/Summer 1989	Empowerment	Young women	Help breakdown barriers to condom use	Women's Press	£179k
Summer 1989	Travel	Young holidaymakers	Reminder to use condoms on holiday	Poster/Tubecards	£171k
World AIDS Day 1 December 1989	WAD	General public 16-34s, 2+ partners	Keep HIV/AIDS on public agenda. Link HIV to AIDS.	National Press	£179k
February-March 1990	Experts	General public 16-34s, 2+ partners	Re-establish importance of AIDS. Reassert heterosexual risk.	TV National Press	£2.9m
Summer 1990	Travel	Young holidaymakers	Take condoms on holiday	Posters near airports Tubecards/Radio	£313k
Autumn 1990	'Hands'	Behaviourally bisexual men	Identify with HIV risk	Special interest male press	£47k
December 1990-March 1991	'Testimonies I'	General public 16-34s, 2+ partners	Keep HIV/AIDS on public agenda. Personalise risk for young heterosexuals and promote condoms	TV	£2.3m
December 1990-February 1991	Mrs Dawson	16-34s, 2+ partners	Normalise condoms	Cinema	£431k
July-August 1991	'Testimonies II'	General public 16-34s, 2+ partners	Keep HIV/AIDS on public agenda. Personalise risk for young heterosexuals and promote condoms	TV Radio	£1.58m
July-August 1991	Mrs Dawson	16-34s, 2+ partners	Normalise condoms	Cinema	£120k
Summer/Autumn 1991	'Hands'	Behaviourally bisexual men	Identify with HIV risk	Male Press/ Supplements	£95k
December 1991-February 1992	'Testimonies III'	General public 16-34s, 2+ partners	Keep HIV/AIDS on public agenda. Personalise risk for young heterosexuals and promote condoms		
	PLUS				
	Mrs Dawson	16-34s, 2+ partners	Normalise condoms	TV	£1.24m
December 1991-February 1992	Mr Brewster	16-34s, 2+ partners	Normalise condoms	Cinema	£167k
June-August 1992	Mr Brewster	16-34s, 2+ partners	Normalise condoms	Cinema	200k
August-October 1992	AIDS Can Affect Anyone	Black and minority ethnic groups	Raise profile of AIDS as issue for this target	Posters	£215k
July-December 1992	How Far	Young women	Help negotiate condom use	Womens Press	£110k
July-December 1992	Immortal	Pre-scene young gay men	Safer sex information	Youth Press	£131k
December 1992-March 1993	Mrs Dawson and Mr Brewster	16-34s, 2+ partners	Normalise condoms	TV	£2.6m
Summer 1993	Travel	Young holidaymakers	Take condoms on holiday	Posters near airports Airport washrooms Tubecards/Radio	£338k
Autumn 1993	How Far	Young women	Help negotiate condom use	Women's Press	£300k
				Total Gross Spend (incl VAT)	£15.4m

6. Targeting specific messages in wider media.
    At certain points in time advertisements have appeared which contained specific messages (usually different to the heterosexual/general public message) for specific target audiences, but which had to be placed in wider media in order to reach those audiences, and therefore will have been seen by the 'general public' and considered part of the overall campaign.

TABLE 2: HEA HIV/AIDS ADVERTISING APPEARING IN WIDER MEDIA
December 1988 – December 1994

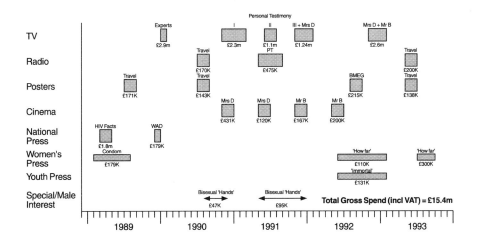

Keeping HIV/AIDS on public agenda and encouraging perceptions of risk among heterosexuals

'HIV Facts', 'Experts' and the 'Testimonies' advertising all used high profile mass media and were expected to reach each of the 'rings' described in figure 1.

'HIV Facts' was a national press campaign communicating the link between HIV and AIDS. It ran from December 1988 to March 1989.

Through 1989 and into 1990, however, public concern about HIV/AIDS waned, fuelled by press coverage of three issues which appeared to suggest there was no HIV risk for heterosexuals:

— a parliamentary question from Lord Kilbracken which highlighted the very low number of people known to have been infected via vaginal sex with partners with no other 'risk factor'[7]:

— The Sunday Times serialisation of Fumento's 'The Myth of Heterosexual AIDS'[8]:

— a government report revising downwards estimates and predictions of levels of HIV infection[9].

National press advertising ran in support of World AIDS Day in 1989 as a counter balance to the negative press coverage, and in February and March 1990 the 'Experts' campaign set the record straight. Leading experts reiterated the known

---

7. This received a great deal of news coverage – for example, the front page of the Daily Mail. The advertising always had to bridge the gap between current levels of infection and future potential of the epidemic.

8. Michael Fumento's book was originally published in the US in the autumn of 1989, and controversially rejected by UK publishers.

9. *Acquired Immune Deficiency Syndrome in England and Wales: Projections using data to end September 1989 (PHLS)* – also known as the 'Day Report'. Stood as the successor to a previous report, *Short Term Prediction of HIV Infection and AIDS in England and Wales 1988* ('Cox Report') which had predicted the number of people in Britain with HIV to be between 20,000 and 50,000.

facts around HIV and AIDS, emphasising the risks to heterosexuals. This advertising ran at peak times and high weights.

Having re-established on a factual level that HIV posed a risk to heterosexuals, the advertising from December 1990 to February 1992 used the testimonies of 'ordinary' people, infected with HIV to encourage people to believe "someone like me could become HIV positive"[10]. The testimonies concluded by promoting condoms as the means of protection. There were three stages to the campaign, each launched in high profile media, and then focussed on 16-34 year olds.

These three campaigns dominated the yearly advertising spend from 1989 to 1991, as their objectives of keeping HIV/AIDS on the agenda and stressing heterosexual risk were prioritised through that time.

Reducing the barriers to condoms

A range of work was developed to tackle the barriers to condom use.

Most notably, first in cinema, then on TV, 'Mrs Dawson' and 'Mr Brewster' were designed to reduce the embarrassment around condoms by positioning them as normal, everyday items ('condom normalisation'), and women's press advertising was used to help young women use condoms.

Through 1992 and 1993, once perceptions of risk had been considered to have been pushed as far as credible, these condom campaigns formed the bulk of the advertising.

Safer Sex on Holiday

Each year, advertising has run urging young holidaymakers to take and use condoms on holiday.

Since Winter 1992/1993 there has been no large, high profile advertising campaign for HIV/AIDS. The successes of the UK's preventive efforts have been such that UK prevalence of AIDS is low, and levels of HIV infection are estimated at lower levels than those previously predicted.

Attention is now turning to other aspects of sexual health, with the structure of the HEA altering accordingly. The expectation is that mass media will continue to be used as a key sexual health education tool in the UK.

---

10. The advertising featured a range of testimonies and included gay men infected with HIV. This campaign provided the first opportunity to talk to gay men without risking the marginalisation of AIDS as a gay-men only problem.

'SASKIA'

IF THIS WOMAN HAD THE VIRUS WHICH LEADS TO AIDS.
IN A FEW YEARS SHE COULD LOOK LIKE THE PERSON OVER THE PAGE.

WORRYING ISN'T IT.

Consecutive right hand pages

'HOW FAR'

'STEVE'

"Had a drink in the hotel and I met this girl at the bar and we got on really well. She was the picture of health, very pretty. I suppose the little devil inside my head would have been saying "go on, son". So I suggested we went upstairs. We had a drink and Bob's your uncle. That's what it's like on holiday. I mean, I really wish that I'd taken some condoms with me but, it's easy to say that now."

MVO: Steve is 28, heterosexual and HIV positive.

'PAUL'

"We'd lived together for a little while and it didn't work out ... and I didn't expect to meet up with him you know. But we went for a few beers ... then one thing led to another ... and I'd known him, you see ... and it were the last thing that entered my head that he's positive. But I just didn't think it could happen to me. But it happened, you know."

MVO: Paul is 22, gay and HIV positive.

'EXPERTS I'

"We know for certain that HIV, the virus that causes AIDS, is spread by sexual intercourse from man to man, from woman ...

... to woman and from woman to man. It is also spread by sharing syringes and needles during drug abuse."

"It's possible for someone to have the virus for up to ten years without knowing it and during that time they can pass it on to others through sexual intercourse."

"It may not seem very serious now, like the greenhouse effect, but if we do not act, it could have a disastrous effect on the future of our children and grandchildren."

'MRS DAWSON'

"Of course, working here we're the first to notice the change in people's behaviour.

We're making more of these things than ever before.

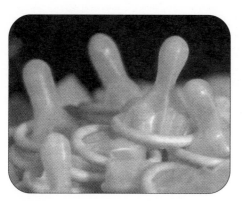

Obviously it's down to AIDS and HIV.

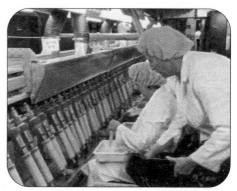

Young people can't afford to take chances these days.

Seems they've got their heads screwed on though. I've never been so busy."

EVALUATING THE EFFECTS OF THE HEA'S ADVERTISING

It is difficult to isolate the advertising's contribution.

i)   Advertising about HIV/AIDS has never taken place in a vacuum. Media coverage, school lessons, even what Madonna writes on the inside cover of 'Like A Prayer' has had its part to play. Indeed, as has been explained, part of the advertising's objectives has been to affect and stimulate these other influences.[11]

ii) The HEA's press office continually supported advertising's messages, talking to journalists, editors, programme makers and parliamentarians. As a result the HEA has been able to benefit from 'unpaid for' media.

iii) The HEA has been scrupulous in fulfilling its remit on a national basis. No region has been omitted or upweighted: the imposition of tests and controls in health education is difficult to justify on ethical grounds.

iv) There are issues around key data sources[12]. There have been three major quantitative studies commissioned by the HEA over the period in question with differing samples and questionnaires, making long term analysis problematic.

However, we will argue that advertising achieved the objectives set and so represented the catalyst for behaviour change. Without this advertising it is likely that AIDS in the UK public's perception would have 'gone away' and any appropriate attitude changes unsustained, resulting in significantly less condom usage among young, sexually active heterosexuals.

WHAT HAS BEEN ACHIEVED?

There is evidence of achievements against both sets of objectives: the maintaining of HIV/AIDS on the public agenda, and behaviour change involving condom use among the sexually active young.

Preventing HIV/AIDS Slipping Off The Public Agenda

This has represented a constant challenge for the HEA in the face of a public and press eager to believe that AIDS isn't the problem originally suggested.

---

11. Hence, for example, the launch of major campaigns around World AIDS Day (1st December), to benefit from and contribute to a yearly crescendo of 'noise' around AIDS. This makes it difficult to separate out the effect of the advertising from the 'seasonal' effect of World AIDS Day.

12. The HEA has monitored public awareness and understanding of AIDS and the response to the advertising via three commissioned quantitative studies.
    i) BMRB AIDS Strategic Monitor (December 1987 - February 1991)
    ii) ICM Waves (December 1989 - September 1991)
    iii) BMRB Communications Monitor (October 1991 onwards)

AIDS as a serious ongoing threat

The 1986/1987 DOH campaign had over-emphasised the seriousness of AIDS. It dominated public concern in November 1986.

TABLE 3: PUBLIC HEALTH CONCERNS
Diseases or infections that might seriously affect the health of people in the UK
Base: All respondents

	Feb 1986 %	Nov 1986 %	Dec 1987 %
AIDS	34	83	53
Cancer	73	65	54

Source: BMRB for COI

However, as concern began to fall away in 1987, the objective was prevent it slipping to previous lows. Since the HEA/BMP campaigns began the proportions of people rating AIDS as a "disease or infection that might seriously affect the health of people in the UK" never fell below 41%, and was consistently rated second only to Cancer.

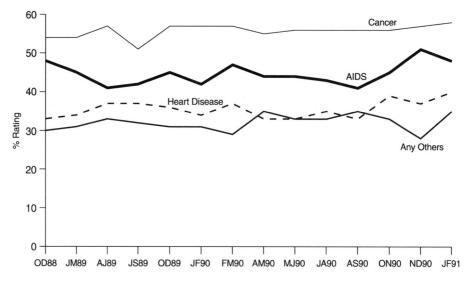

Figure 2. *Diseases or infections that might seriously damage health of people in UK*
Source: BMRB Strategic Monitor, all adults aged 13+

With the change in research methodologies at the end of 1991, the question was re-framed as "factors having a great deal of influence on long term health". Throughout 1992 and 1993 "whether people practise safer sex or not", (the AIDS-linked statement) has remained second only to "whether people smoke or not", (the Cancer-linked statement).

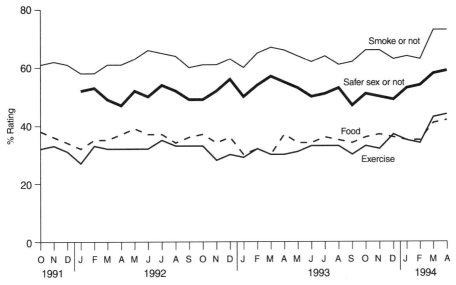

Figure 3. *Factors having a great deal of influence on long term health*
Source: BMRB Ad Monitor

AIDS had been retained as a key health concern in the public mind.

Understanding AIDS as an increasing problem relevant to heterosexuals

Keeping HIV/AIDS on the public's health agenda has involved sustaining the perception that AIDS is a growing problem among heterosexuals.

Throughout the period tracked by the Strategic Monitor, the majority of the public believed it would be "much more common" over the next few years (albeit with a dip in 1989, a reflection of the public scepticism generated in that year described earlier).

TABLE 4: 'AIDS MUCH MORE COMMON OVER NEXT FEW YEARS'
Base: All adults aged 13+ who have heard of AIDS

	1988 %	1989 %	1990 %
Agreeing	64	59	61

Source: BMRB Strategic Monitor

The Communications Monitor, introduced in November 1991, asked people's agreement with the statement "more and more people in this country are getting HIV from sexual intercourse between men and women". From November 1991 to February 1993 (the last major burst of TV advertising) between 85% to 87% of all adults (16-54) agreed.

TABLE 5: "MORE AND MORE PEOPLE IN THIS COUNTRY ARE GETTING HIV
FROM SEXUAL INTERCOURSE BETWEEN MEN AND WOMEN"
Base: All adults aged 16-54

	Nov '91 %	Nov '91-Feb '92 %	Feb '92-May '92 %	July '92-Aug '92 %	Dec '92-Feb '93 %
% Agreeing	87	86	85	85	86

Source: BMRB Communications Monitor, AIDS Module

Linking HIV with AIDS

By the end of 1988, only 24% could spontaneously name HIV as the virus that leads to AIDS. This has risen dramatically.[13]

TABLE 6: SPONTANEOUS NAMING HIV AS AIDS VIRUS

O/D'88 %	O/D'89 %	O/D'90 %	N/F'92 %	D/F'93 %	D/J'94 %
24	38	51	87	87	90

Source: 1988-1990: BMRB Strategic Monitor, all adults aged 13+
          1992-1994: BMRB Communications Monitor, all adults aged 16-54

This is a considerable achievement. Understanding HIV is an important starting point for understanding the risks posed by AIDS.

We have demonstrated that the first set of the HEA's objectives have been met. AIDS has been prevented from slipping off the public agenda. The backdrop of 'sufficient concern' around AIDS had been set as a context for appropriate behaviour change.

Condom Use Among Sexually Active Young

Recent evidence from the 'National Survey' confirms that today's 16-34 year olds use condoms to an extent their predecessors didn't.

The proportion of people using a condom the first time they have sex has risen noticeably each year amongst those first having intercourse from 1985 onwards. (See Figure 4.)

Commenting on the increase, the National Survey concludes: "This supports the view that the revival of the method in the 1980s was largely attributable to AIDS public education, suggesting considerable success in motivating public response"[14].

This survey also provides the link with behaviour change because of AIDS.

When asked "Have you changed your own sexual lifestyle in any way or made any decisions about sex because of concern about catching AIDS or HIV virus?" 19.5% of men and 14.2% of all women said 'Yes'. (See Table 7.) This rises among younger respondents[15] and among men and women with two or more heterosexual

---

13. NB: The changes of sample from all adults aged 13+ to 16-34 year olds will have exaggerated the changes: the inclusion of older respondents (55+) in earlier monitoring reducing overall levels of awareness. Direct comparison of 16-34 year olds is not possible. Nevertheless, 16-34 year olds across both samples still reveals a doubling of the percentage able to name HIV as the virus leading to AIDS.

14. National Survey, Chapter 4, p88.

15. Some allowance must be made for the 1% of the male sample (n = 118) reporting behaviour change who have had a homosexual partner, 65% of whom have changed lifestyle, 68% of which named condom use.

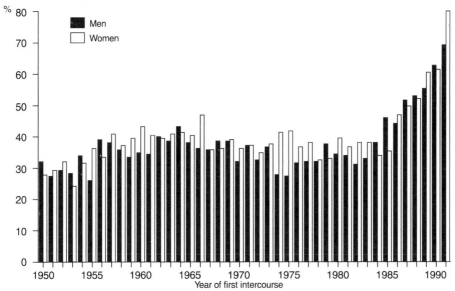

Figure 4. *How many poeple used a condom when they first had sex?*
Source: National Survey of Sexual Attitudes and Lifestyles

partners in the last five years. The majority of that change is represented by condom use.

TABLE 7: PROPORTION WHO REPORT SEXUAL LIFESTYLE CHANGE
BECAUSE OF AIDS BY AGE GROUP

	Men			Women		
	16-24 %	25-34 %	All %	16-24 %	25-34 %	All %
Any change	**36.2**	22.9	**19.5**	**29.7**	15.7	**14.2**
Using condoms	26.4	13.7	12.1	16.8	7.5	7.1
% change accounted for by condom use	75%	60%	62%	57%	48%	50%

	Men 2+ heterosexual partners (all ages) %	Women 2+ heterosexual partners (all ages) %
Any change	**38.3**	**36.8**
Using condoms	26.2	20.5
% change accounted for by condom use	68%	56%

Source: National Survey of Sexual Attitudes and Lifestyles

A tangible indicator of increased condom use is the remarkable and continued growth in the sales of condoms. Approximately 40 million more condoms were sold in 1992 than in 1986.

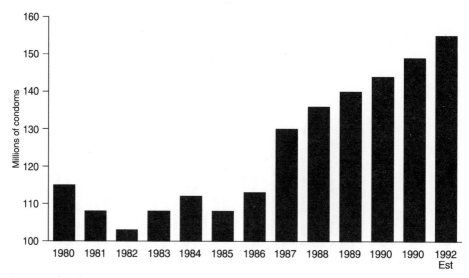

Figure 5. *Condom sales*
Source: Pre-'87: LRC
'87 Onwards: Mintel

EVIDENCE OF ADVERTISING'S ROLE

As has been said, it is difficult to isolate the contribution of advertising to these considerable achievements. Nevertheless the campaigns can be demonstrated to have had a role in the successes against both sets of objectives.

Advertising and the Public Agenda

Seeing AIDS as a serious threat

Whilst AIDS concern has never slipped down to February 1986 lows (Table 3 and Figure 2), it has nevertheless fluctuated, primarily in response to advertising or the lack of it.

The upward movements, representing a re-establishment of the importance of AIDS, coincide with periods of TV advertising and higher levels of the public's advertising awareness.[16]

The relationship exists (albeit to a lesser degree) with the reframing of the question to "Factors having a great deal of influence on long term health". (Figure 3). Noticeably "whether people practise safer sex" was in the public's view becoming less important through 1993, following lower weights of advertising and hence less advertising awareness.

---

16. An important learning made early on in BMP's work for the HEA was that even heavy weight national press did not appear to sustain AIDS on the public agenda; it had to be TV.
    The peak around Oct-Dec '89 can therefore only be attributed in part to the running of advertising on World AIDS Day. It is also likely to reflect the noise and debate created around the Kilbracken affair. The fall back to 48% following the 'Testimonies' launch can be explained by the way in which the media for the campaign was bought. The launch of the campaign was geared around re-raising the profile of AIDS. As the campaign progressed towards the Spring of '91, the media schedule focussed on 16-34 year old programming.

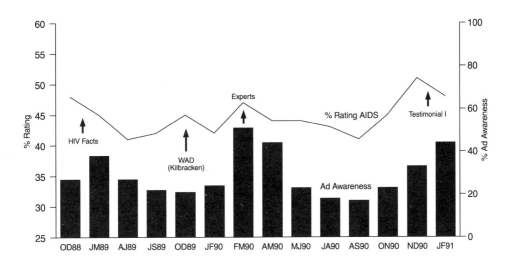

Figure 6. *Relationship between advertising and perceptions of seriousness of AIDS*
Source: BMRB Strategic Monitor, all adults aged 13+

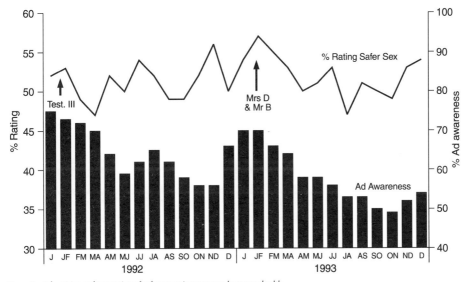

Figure 7. *Advertising and perception of safer sex as important to long term health*
Source: BMRB Advertising Monitor, 16-54 year olds

The topicality of AIDS as an issue (newly tracked by the Communications Monitor) also appears to respond to advertising and the lack of it. (See Figure 8.)

An increase is shown alongside the final 'Testimonies'. Media scheduling from then on became focussed on 16-34 year olds, and the topicality of AIDS among the general public begins to decline. Then, with no TV advertising for AIDS, the decline accelerates.

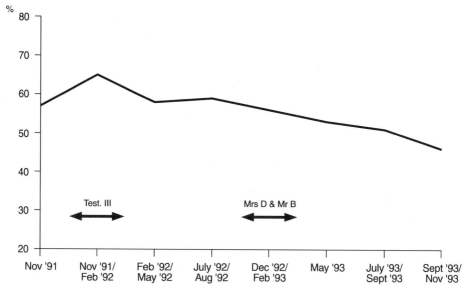

Figure 8. *"I can remember talking about AIDS recently with friends or family or people at work"*
Source: BMRB Communications Monitor, 16-54 year olds

These relationships all suggest advertising is the key (if not solus) driver of the public's perception of the importance of the disease.

As an HEA Paper has observed: "In the absence of any visible signs of AIDS around them, the press and public may be using levels of 'government' advertising on television as a proxy measure of the scale of the problem".[17]

AIDS as an increasing problem relevant to heterosexuals

The extent to which advertising contributed to this perception is demonstrated by two pieces of evidence.

a)   The proportions of people believing that AIDS would be "much more common over the next few years" threatened to fall away through the period tracked by the Strategic Monitor but were successfully reasserted by key campaigns, most notably around the 'Testimonies' campaign launch.[18] (See Figure 9.)

b)   A recent *decline* in perceptions of increasing heterosexual infection has been observed, coinciding with the recent lack of a high-profile, mass media campaign. This retrospectively supports the argument that advertising played a key role in achieving this objective. (See Figure 10.)

In summary, there are relationships in the data which suggest key campaigns were responsible for either reasserting or enhancing the desired attitudes around AIDS among the general public, preventing AIDS from slipping off the public agenda.

17. Perl S, *Reflections on using mass media for AIDS public education.* HEA AIDS programme Paper
     No. 13.

18. As 16, the media strategy explains the slight fall back on this dimension for the *general* public.

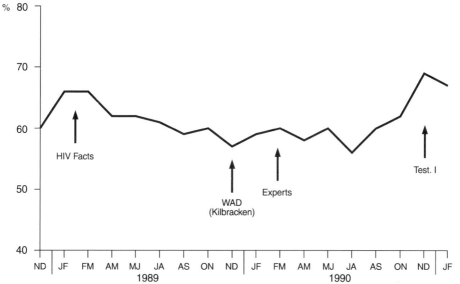

Figure 9. *Perceived commoness of AIDS over next few years: "Much more common"*
Source: BMRB Strategic Monitor

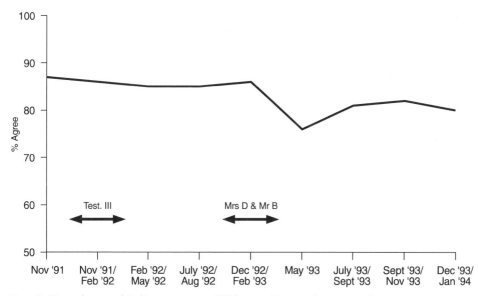

Figure 10. *"More and more people in this country are getting HIV from sexual intercourse between men and women"*
Base: *All adults aged 16-54*
Source: BMRB Communications Monitor

Linking HIV to AIDS

Advertising's role in linking HIV to AIDS can be seen by the *acceleration* of the ability to name the virus at key campaign times – most notably around the first wave of 'Testimonies'. (These all end stating the person speaking is HIV positive.)

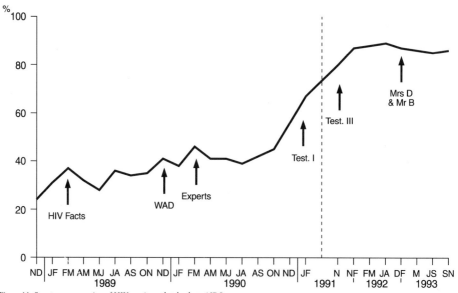

Figure 11. *Spontaneous naming of HIV as virus that leads to AIDS*
Source: BMRB Strategic Monitor, all adults aged 13+
　　　　BMRB Communications Monitor, all adults aged 16-54

Advertising has proven a valuable driver behind the linking of HIV with AIDS.

Advertising's role in encouraging condom use

If it can be shown that advertising created and sustained the conditions for behaviour change outlined by the Health Belief Model, then it is reasonable to suggest that advertising helped encourage condom use among young heterosexuals.

　　Advertising has indeed played a demonstrable part for young, sexually active heterosexuals in
i)　encouraging a personal identification with the risk of HIV;
ii)　the promotion of condoms as the means of prevention;
iii)　the reduction of a key 'barrier' to condoms: embarrassment.

Personal identification with risk

The proportion of 16-34s denying the risk (ie agreeing "I don't believe I'll ever get HIV" – Figure 12) declined from 77% in 1989 to around 56% by Nov-Dec 1991, the final round of TV advertising specifically designed to encourage a personal identification with risk.

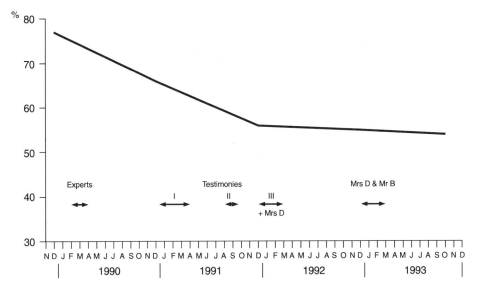

Figure 12. *"I don't believe I'll ever get HIV": Percentage of 16-34 year olds agreeing*
Source: BMRB Strategic Monitor
          BMRB Communications Monitor

The latest point at which the question was asked shows that this level has been broadly maintained. Unsurprisingly, campaigns focussing on reducing the 'barriers' (eg 'Mrs Dawson') have not increased peoples perceptions of risk in the way in which the 'risk' campaigns did (eg 'Testimonies').

Another measure of personal risk taken during the ICM Waves (pre 'Experts' to post 'Testimonies II') indicates an increasing perception of risk over the time of campaigns focussing on this objective.

TABLE 8: PERCEPTION OF RISK
"With your present lifestyle, how much risk are you at personally of catching HIV
(the AIDS virus) in the future?"
Base: 16-34 year olds, 2+ partners

% agreement	W1 Dec '89 %	W2 Apr '90 %	W3 Dec '90 %	W4 Mar '91 %	W5 Sept '91 %
Greatly at risk	3	3	4	3	4
Quite a lot at risk	9	12	14	17	17
Not very much at risk	50	50	50	50	49
Not at risk at all	33	30	25	24	23

Proof of a *direct* link between the advertising and the increase in peoples sense of personal risk is the large increases in calls to the National AIDS Helpline (NAH)[19] around these 'risk' oriented campaigns.

Figure 13 demonstrates the increase in number of calls prompted by 'Experts' and the 'Testimonies' campaigns.

The first four weeks of the 'Experts' campaign averaged 20,895 calls per week, nearly doubling the 1989 weekly average of 11,839 calls, and surpassing even the

---

19. The National AIDS Helpline is a free 24 hour telephone advice service, supported by the HEA and promoted as a referral point in all TV advertising for AIDS.

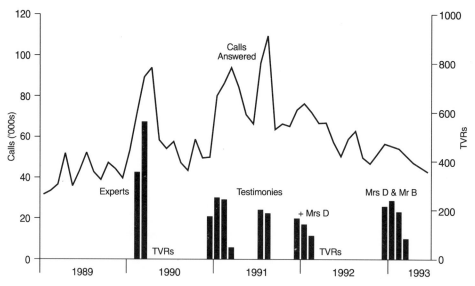

Figure 13. *Calls to national AIDS Helpline*
Source: NAHUK

busiest week of 1989 (16,455 calls). Callers were asked where they'd got the number: 60% cited advertising. 86% of callers in this period were heterosexual. The NAH observed an effect of the campaign:

> "During the course of the HEA campaign in Spring 1990 a subtle change in attitude become apparent. Many callers decided that they had been, or probably had been, at some risk. There was a high incidence of callers who had already decided to take an HIV test. The question itself has changed from 'Should I take a test?' to 'Where can I have a test?'"

> NAH 1990 Report

In 1991 the weekly average rose to 18,542 (vs 14,057 in 1990 and 11,839 in 1989). A similar proportion of callers were heterosexual. (Source: NAH[20].)

Condoms as solution

Nowadays there is an almost exclusive association of safer sex with condoms.

However, early in the epidemic's history a range of other risk reduction strategies were also talked about in press and advertising, including a reduction in the number of partners and "being careful who you slept with".

---

20. *National AIDS Helpline 1992 Report*
    1992 and the first 6 months of 1993 saw a tailing off of the calls to the Helpline. The lesser effect of the final burst of testimonies supported the view that 'risk' had been pushed as far as it could go. It is unsurprising that there is less prompting of calls from condom normalisation advertising (which 'Mrs Dawson' and 'Mr Brewster' represent). In itself this lesser reaction is confirmation of the success of 'Personal Testimonies' and 'Experts' in encouraging heterosexual audiences to identify with the risk of HIV infection.

Condoms as the primary means of protection from HIV was increasingly singlemindedly promoted by the HEA in its advertising[21], and this is recognised by the consumer, as a recent piece of qualitative research points out:

> "The condom message has now become a familiar part of the campaign in its own right. It was in fact this message that identified the ads as being from the HEA rather than the use of the HEA logo itself"

> Strategic Research Group
> *Condom Climate Part III*, January 1994

The National Survey proves the link between safer sex and condoms is very strong. (Table 9) Over 75% of men and 80% of women say "use a condom" when asked "From what you have heard or read, what does the phrase 'safer sex' mean to you?" (This was the only open-ended question asked in the survey.)

TABLE 9: MEANING OF PHRASE 'SAFER SEX' BY AGE GROUP

	16-24 %	25-34 %	All Ages %
Men			
Use a condom	75.6	79.0	75.3
Restrict no. partners	31.8	28.6	27.1
Know partner	21.5	22.8	20.4
Women			
Use a condom	80.5	84.8	81.0
Restrict no. partners	44.5	37.3	35.6
Know partner	28.4	26.1	23.2

Source: National Survey of Sexual Attitudes and Lifestyles

The HEA's ICM surveys show a similar if less pronounced picture. Importantly, "don't sleep around/have fewer partners" declined in importance from 32% to about 24%.

TABLE 10: "YOU MAY HAVE HEARD OF THE TERM 'SAFER SEX'. WHAT DO YOU UNDERSTAND THIS TO MEAN?"

	W1 Jan/Feb '90 %	W2 Apr '90 %	W3 Nov/Dec '90 %	W4 Mar '91 %	W5 Sept '91 %
Use condoms	62	60	62	61	66
Don't sleep around/have fewer partners	32	28	23	23	25
Take precautions/Use contraception	16	11	21	21	15

Source: ICM: 16-34 year olds, 2+ partners. Self-completion survey

---

21. It must be noted that this single-minded promotion of condoms is in itself the subject of debate and criticism. There are concerns that it could be seen as an encouragement to 'promiscuity' (ie it doesn't matter who or how many, as long as you use a condom). However the HEA firmly believed condom use was the form of prevention that would be both safer and acceptable to the target ("being careful who you sleep with" is unsatisfactory from a safer sex point of view as there is no way of telling by sight who is infected, and the HEA recognised that abstinence was unlikely to be accepted by a target already sexually active). The HEA was careful to ensure its advertising did not appear to condone or encourage promiscuity.

Table 10 suggests a relationship between 'condom use' being increasingly the take-out of the advertising, and understanding of condoms as safer sex.

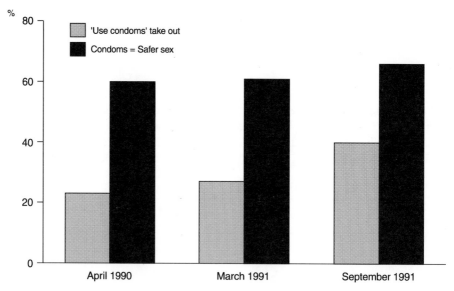

Figure 14. *"Use condoms" – Relationship between key take-out from ads* and understanding of safer sex*
Note: * *All claiming to have seen ads*
Source: ICM: 16-34 years olds, 2+ partners

A further indicator of the success of 'Testimonies' in suggesting condoms as the solution is the way in which they not only maintained but strengthened the target's intentions to use condoms with a new partner.

As can be seen in Table 11, at Wave 3, the pre-stage of the ICM's monitoring of the campaign, 67% agreed: "If I had a new partner I would definitely use a condom". This significantly increased to 72% at the post stage and was maintained at Wave 5 – confirming the role the advertising had in promoting condoms as the primary means of prevention.

TABLE 11: "If I had a new partner I would definitely use a condom"

	W1 Dec '89 %	W2 Apr '90 %	W3 Dec '90 %	W4 Mar '91 %	W5 Sept '91 %
Agreeing	68	67	67	72*	71

Note: * Statistically significant change at 95% confidence level

Source: ICM: 16-34 year olds, 2+ partners

If it is, as we believe, a result of the HEA advertising's singleminded promotion of condoms that condoms are seen as the primary means of prevention, then the advertising must have contributed to the increased use of condoms nowadays.

Reducing the 'cost' of the solution: Normalising condoms

It is not enough for people to understand that condoms are the solution. As the Health Belief Model suggests, the 'cost' of the solution needs to be acceptable. For condoms, the 'costs' are primarily social and emotional.

It was through qualitative work that these costs were usefully understood and monitored.

Evidence of the successful removal of embarrassment around condoms comes from a debrief of a large piece of qualitative research[22]:

"Attitudes evidenced in this sample demonstrated that condoms have become 'normal' both in the realm of conversation and the realm of understanding. The only evidence of unease was in communication between parents and children, and teachers and students.
   At this juncture it could be said that the establishment of knowledge and awareness proved to be a more or less completed task"

Strategic Research Group, March 1993

This report makes explicit reference to the advertising's role:

"Recall of current advertising ('Mrs Dawson' and 'Mr Brewster') was strong across all groups in the sample. Opinion was that these have succeeded in going some way towards establishing condoms as normal, everyday items in that condoms have entered everyday vocabulary and do not, in themselves, constitute embarrassment".

Strategic Research Group, March 1993

Mintel's 1992 Contraceptives report offers further evidence of successful 'condom normalisation'. They point to the changing share of condom sales by the various outlets (Table 10) as indicators that condoms are a less embarrassing and more everyday purchase, notably the large increases in the share of grocery stores.

TABLE 12: SALES OF CONDOMS, BY TYPE OF OUTLET, BY VOLUME, 1989 AND 1991

	1989 %	1991 %	% point change
Chemists & drugstores	55	49	−6
Vending machines	14	16	+2
Grocery stores	10	15	+5
NHS	11	9	−2
Service stations	3	3	−
Mail order	3	2	−1
Others	4	6	+2
	100	100	

Source: Mintel, 1992

Condoms are now a 'normal' part of everyday life – and we believe advertising has had a key part to play in making them so.

We have shown how advertising has played a vital role in the prevention of HIV transmission – by preventing AIDS from slipping of the public agenda and encouraging condom use among young heterosexuals.

However, before concluding, we will first eliminate the possibility of other factors playing this key role.

22. Strategic Research Group *Condom Climate Advertising Research* March 1993. An extensive sample comprising: 7 peer group discussion, 17-34 year olds; 2 Family group interviews; 2 'couples' depth discussions; 1 male friendship depth discussion; 3 minority ethnic group discussions; 1 'health professional' extended group and 1 'opinion formers' extended group.

WHAT ELSE MIGHT HAVE ACHIEVED THESE RESULTS?

Preventing AIDS slipping off the public agenda

One could contend that it was press coverage of AIDS, not the advertising which has kept AIDS 'top of mind'.

Press coverage of AIDS has increased over the years[23]. However, whilst advertising awareness appears to correspond with people's perceptions of the seriousness of AIDS (Figures 8 and 9), the peaks and troughs in press coverage do *not*. (See Figures 15 and 16.)

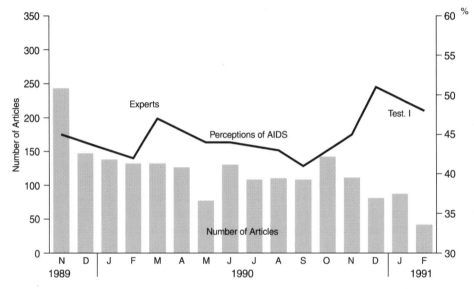

Figure 15. *Perceptions of seriousness of AIDS* vs amount of press coverage*
Note: * As "disease/infection that might seriously damage health of people in UK".
Source: BMP Press Audit/BMRB Strategic Monitor, all adults aged 13+

It would therefore seem reasonable to conclude that press coverage is a support rather than a driver of the public's awareness of AIDS.

---

23. BMP Press Audit monitored number of articles about HIV/AIDS from November 1989 to July 1993, on
    behalf of HEA. The Audit only tracked National Press coverage (dailies and Sundays), and doesn't
    comprise magazine articles and local press.

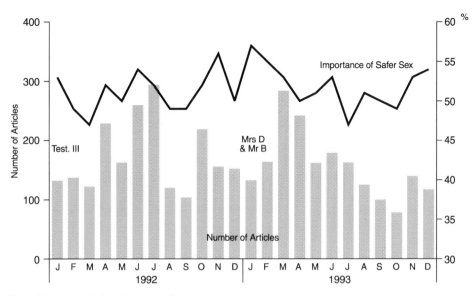

Figure 16. *Importance of safer sex* vs amount of press coverage*
Note: * As *"factor having great deal of influence on long term health of UK"*
Source: BMP Press Audit/BMRB Communications Monitor, all adults aged 16-54

Encouraging condom use

Advertising from condom manufacturers

Durex, Mates and Jiffi have advertised over the last five years. (Table 13), and two new condom launches received advertising support.

TABLE 13: CONDOM MANUFACTURER ADVERTISING SPEND

	1989 £m	1990 £m	1991 £m	1992 £m	1993 £m
Durex	0.4	0.2	0.4	*	*
Mates	0.6	0.4	0.2	*	*
Jiffi	–	–	*	*	0.2
LeCondom	–	–	0.1	–	–
Femidom	–	–	–	0.8	0.9
HEA[24]	3.6	3.7	3.8	2.1	1.7

Note: * = < £100K

Source: Register-MEAL

However, condom manufacturer spends, even in total, were small in absolute terms and minimal relative to the HEA's levels of spend. It is therefore unlikely this activity can take the credit for increased condom sales.

---

24. Register/MEAL spend differs from actual spends previously quoted:
    – likely to be about 30% under-reported because of premiums paid due to programming constraint;
    – actual spend is gross, and includes VAT and COI commission.

Education in schools

Many schools probably incorporate AIDS into their curriculum[25]. However, it is unlikely that all the changes described above can be attributed to school education, given a relatively small proportion of the 16-34 year old target would have been at school in the period in question.

Gay men accounting for the majority of condom sales

Two factors suggest this is unlikely:
i)   1.1% of men (16-59) had at least one homosexual partner in the last year. For less than 200,000 men to account alone for the extra 40 million condoms sold in 1992 vs 1986 seems unlikely[26];
ii)   Moreover non-penetrative sex has increasingly become a means of having safer sex for gay men (Table 14) much more so than for heterosexuals.

TABLE 14: REPORTED BEHAVIOUR CHANGE BECAUSE OF AIDS

	Men Homosexual Partners %	Men 2+ Heterosexual Partners %
Using a condom	44.2	26.2
Avoiding some sexual practices	40.2	5.5

Source: National Survey of Sexual Attitudes and Lifestyles

Condom sales would have continued to grow without subsequent advertising

A sizeable increase in condom sales occurred in 1987 in response to the advertised 'advent' of AIDS.

We believe that this increase would not have continued without our advertising, as demonstrated, sustained perceptions of risk of HIV/AIDS despite negative press coverage and no 'signs' of AIDS in daily life.

This suggests 'natural' condom sales trends would have been downward or static after 1987 in the absence of continued advertising.

---

25. Sex education in schools during the period covered by the paper was discretionary with no fixed curriculum. Qualitative evidence suggests many schools did not choose to cover issues relating to safer sex and condom use.
26. The National Survey found 1.1% of men aged 16-59 had a homosexual partner in the last year. Number of men in UK in 1991 aged 15-59 = 16.8m (OPCS Census figures).

COST EFFECTIVENESS

We have shown that the advertising achieved its objectives. But was it money well spent?

A strong case for the advertising spend representing a sound investment can be made wholly on the basis of the primary reason for the spend alone: AIDS prevention.

The estimated cost of supporting an individual with AIDS is about £30,000 per annum[27]. (This is a very conservative estimate of the cost, as it does not include HIV related illnesses.)

Prognosis for people with AIDS varies, but we have assumed for the purposes of this calculation, that the average is 2 years from diagnosis.

Based on this assumption, the total spent on advertising (about £15.4m) can be considered to have 'paid back' if it has contributed to the prevention of, on average, 51 cases of HIV infection a year[28].

Without a national HIV testing programme we do not know how many people are HIV positive, or the likelihood of a heterosexual encounter involving someone who is infected. Nevertheless, the National Survey suggested 26% of men and 21% of women with two or more heterosexual partners in the last five years use condoms because of AIDS. This amounts to 2.3 million people[29], (and considerably greater number of sexual occasions during which HIV could otherwise have been transmitted). Given this degree of behaviour change it is likely that the commitment to prevention programmes have been more than justified in terms of monetary cost effectiveness.

SUMMARY

The concept of financial 'pay-back' for an investment in any public health concern seems brutal. The real cost savings from investing in AIDS prevention are of course human.

We will never know what would have happened if we hadn't used advertising as the primary 'driver' of the AIDS prevention programme.

We hope to have demonstrated convincingly, however, our belief that advertising *was* a key driver, maintaining an appropriate level of public concern regarding AIDS and against this backdrop encouraging condom usage amongst young people at risk.

If this advertising had not achieved these aims, the situation we face today in the UK as a 'low AIDS prevalence' country, might have been very different.

---

27. Source: House of Commons, Committee of Public Accounts, *HIV and AIDS related health services.* London HMSO, 1992.

28. Based on the current assumption that HIV invariably leads to AIDS.

29. Calculation based on:
   OPCS: men, 15-59 in UK in 1991 = 16.8m; women, 15-59 in UK in 1991 = 17.0m
   National Survey: 34.7% men had 2+ partners in last 5 years, of which 26.4% claimed to have condoms because of AIDS; 23.5% of women had 2+ partners in last 5 years, of which 20.5% claimed to have used condoms because of AIDS.

4

Cadbury's Roses

"Thank you very Much"

INTRODUCTION

This case examines the progress of Cadbury's Roses from its repositioning in 1979 to its position at the end of 1993.

It will show how Roses grew from a (distant) second brand to become brand leader in spite of a direct and considerable competitor, Quality Street, initially more than twice its size and with a higher advertising spend.

It will demonstrate that Roses achieved this change in its fortunes by, firstly, clearly identifying a new positioning opportunity based on a key usage role which enabled the brand to create new rules for the market, and resulted in significant growth for its sector; and secondly, by communicating that positioning through motivating, compelling advertising that helped to achieve brand leadership.

It will then go on to show how consistent and single-minded support of a strong positioning has ensured that that brand leadership has been maintained by Roses in the face of continuing stiff competition from Quality Street.

BACKGROUND PRE–1979

The Market

The assortments market can be divided into three sectors – economy, mainstream and premium. At the premium end lie handmade chocolates and the more expensive Continental assortments. The mainstream sector consists of the traditional boxed chocolate assortments such as Black Magic. The economy sector features the cheapest assortments designed for more informal usage, and is dominated by a sector within this known as 'twistwrap'.

The twistwrap sector takes its name from the packaging used for individual chocolates within these particular assortments.

Like the rest of the assortments market, the twistwrap sector has always been highly seasonal, with 80%+ of sales taking place at Christmas and Easter.

The twistwrap market differs from the other assortments sectors in one other, particularly notable, way. It is, and always has been, a two-brand sector (even today, own-label accounts for less than 10% of volume).

The Brands

The two brands that dominate the twistwrap sector are Roses and Quality Street.

Quality Street was launched by Mackintosh (later bought by Rowntree) in 1936, and Cadbury's launched Roses in 1938.

Both assortments were very similar in product terms. Both consisted of a variety of different centres individually and colourfully wrapped. Their only difference lay in the proportion of chocolate to toffee within each. Roses' centres were all covered in Cadbury's chocolate. Quality Street, as befitted an assortment created by a manufacturer with a heritage of toffee-making, had a higher proportion of toffee centres, not all of which were covered in chocolate.

The two brands were also close in pricing terms. Roses was (and has been ever since) slightly more expensive than Quality Street, but the difference was marginal.

In 1969 Quality Street repositioned itself as the ideal brand for 'sharing with all the family'. Thus it overtly recognised the difference between twistwraps and formal boxed chocolate assortments. Its key consumer benefit was the variety of units, each individually wrapped and tumbled into a box/tin, making it ideal for sharing.

Roses, however, remained rooted in chocolate assortment values. Its heritage was Cadbury's chocolate, a point of difference which at once made it more desirable but also less accessible.

> "Respondents placed Quality Street in the *toffee* area... while Roses are seen to fall closer to the *chocolate box* market."
>
> Gregory/Langmaid Associates 1975

Quality Street's repositioning moved it away from Roses on to a more everyday, mass market platform and at the same time widened its appeal. This left Roses in a difficult position. It was neither one thing nor the other – more special than Quality Street, but not as special as the mainstream boxed assortments. Roses had fallen between two market sectors.

> "Roses are more of a luxury"
>
> "They are too expensive for everyday"
>
> "Roses would make me feel guilty"
>
> "Roses are more sophisticated than Quality Street"
>
> Gregory/Langmaid Associates 1975

While in reality both brands possessed remarkably similar characteristics, their personalities and appeal were quite different. In order to avoid limiting the growth potential for Roses, it was vital that a positioning with broader appeal was found.

> "There are strong reasons for avoiding any further up market pressures on Roses, which must only tend to limit its appeal in relation to the more vulgar and cheerful Quality Street. What is needed is a vehicle in which Roses can sit without any major repositioning and which will bring it closer to the front of mind of consumers."
>
> Gregory/Langmaid Associates 1975

Roses was a brand in search of a role – and this quest was reflected in its advertising

The Advertising

Since 1969 Quality Street had been advertising consistently on the 'family sharing' theme. The advertising was upbeat, energetic and fun.

> "Present time happy people… very jolly, from the younger kids to their parents, through to their grandparents. Crowded rambling, bustly houses, lots going on. The happy chocolate".
>
> Market Behaviour Ltd. 1978

> "There is an extremely favourable and high level of recall of Quality Street advertising. Quality Street advertising generally communicates suitability of sharing amongst the family and suitability for every type of person"
>
> Market Behaviour Ltd. 1979

Quality Street's consistent approach and spend allowed it to own the generic twistwrap market benefit of sharing.

Roses' advertising positioning was more blurred. The Norman Vaughan campaign of the late '70s using the line 'Roses Grow on You', was generally well liked but its message was unclear.

> "The Norman Vaughan campaign seems to have resulted in the product being associated with his perceived personality – 'jolly, bright and cheerful', 'lively and gay' and with flowers, rather than having left many definitive impressions of Roses as a product."
>
> Market Behaviour Ltd. 1978

More importantly, it did not provide Roses with a clear role with which consumers could associate it, and which could bestow upon Roses the distinct emotional brand values it needed to compete with Quality Street.

By the end of the 1970s Quality Street was clear brand leader and looked unassailable. In 1978 Quality Street was more than double the size of Roses in volume terms.

REPOSITIONING ROSES – 1979

Clearly Roses had a number of strengths. Its name, packaging and product were well liked by consumers. It had image strengths in the 'special' area. Yet these very strengths were also its limitations. Roses' specialness limited its ability to grow and to take on Quality Street. Roses lacked a clear role.

Having found that the Norman Vaughan campaign had not succeeded in significantly denting Quality Street, Cadbury looked for an alternative positioning.

It was important that Roses' existing strengths should be capitalised upon, rather than abandoned, in the search for a new positioning. Roses' 'specialness' needed to be reframed to add value within the market context.

In examining the total assortments market closely, it became clear to Cadbury that there was a gap between the mainstream and twistwrap sectors that no one had yet clearly identified, or been able to occupy.

The mainstream chocolate assortments were struggling with the problems thrown up by their 'romance' positioning. Marketing from this platform meant that usage perceptions, and therefore purchase opportunities, were distinctly narrowed.

The brands' perceived values were formal, intimate and for very 'particular' relationships.

Quality Street, meanwhile, was presenting itself successfully as an everyday, informal, value-for-money purchase for sharing with the family.

However, no one was taking up that territory that lay between the two – the territory of the *informal* gift.

When it comes to gift-giving, mainstream chocolate assortments are often the first consideration. Cadbury realised, however, that there are occasions where the gift of a 'romantic' box of chocolates would be considered inappropriate – and equally, occasions where the proffering of an assortment such as Quality Street, marketed as non-special and everyday, would also be inappropriate.

These were occasions where Roses could fit the bill perfectly – positioned as special, but informal enough to be given in a way that would embarrass neither giver nor recipient.

This was a positioning that offered the potential to exploit Roses' existing strengths in a way that was more accessible and therefore more appropriate for the consumption habits of the day.

The proposition used to brief the creative team was 'Roses are the best informal gift'. This led to the advertising that was to change Roses' fortune.

Getting the Other Elements of the Mix Right

In optimising the repositioning exercise, all elements of the Roses brand were looked at and some small changes were made. The mix of centres was revised slightly in line with consumer preference to contain fewer soft centres. The packaging, both the box and wrappers, was modernised and brightened and a new larger pack size introduced.

THE ADVERTISING – 1979-1989

The 'best informal gift' brief led to the advertising idea 'Say thank-you with Cadbury's Roses', devised by Y&R in 1979. Roses was portrayed as a small gift that could be given and received without fear of embarrassment. Importantly, it was a gift that didn't say too much.

The advertising featured vignettes of occasions when a small, non-romantic, informal gift was required.

The advertising idea researched well.

"It was generally felt that this was the first time a manufacturer had used this idea in connection with advertising a product. It came across, therefore, as an original and unique idea".

Sloane Research 1979

'SAY 'THANK YOU' WITH CADBURY'S ROSES'

THE BBH ADVERTISING – 1990-1993

By 1989 the Y&R advertising had begun to track less well than in the past. Awareness levels were average. The vignettes had become formulaic and had begun to look a little weary and old-fashioned.

> "It's getting a bit like wallpaper, that one. I don't think they say much to you, when they've had the same one on all the time."
>
> "They've had the same advert on now for at least ten years… might change some of the situations, but basically it's identical."
>
> Hallam Associates 1990

Tracking and qualitative research were taken as an early warning signal that the campaign was becoming tired. As a result of client conflict, Cadbury changed advertising agency from Y&R to BBH in 1989.

Moving the Campaign On

1989 research confirmed that Roses was strongly associated with 'Thank You'.

> "This campaign seems to have fixed the notion of a 'small thank you gift' as a Roses property."
>
> Winstanley Douglas & Partners 1989

BBH and Cadbury believed that the 'Thank You' positioning remained right for Roses. It was the brand's point of difference from Quality Street. However, BBH believed, and research confirmed, that there was an opportunity to increase the empathy consumers felt with the advertising.

> "Roses does have an advertising heritage – all about 'thank you'. This recall contributes to the sense of an established brand, a brand with nostalgia and therefore warmth. However research endorses that previous Roses advertising was not itself particularly emotional and warm… The indications are that the brand has been waiting for advertising to literally tap the warmth of Roses."
>
> Patrick Corr Research 1990

BBH's objective was to give 'Thank You' a stronger, clearer focus by imbuing the advertising with a greater depth of emotion than the Y&R 'vignette' executions had allowed.

This brief to the creatives resulted in advertising that moved the 'Thank You' campaign idea on significantly. The campaign was freed from the vignette format, thus enabling the advertising to tell one story in which consumers could become more emotionally involved. It approached the scenario of someone doing a good deed and being rewarded with Roses in a more imaginative and lateral way, which no longer depended on the scenario being true to life. This allowed for more interesting and memorable stories to be told giving the advertising greater impact.

BBH has produced three commercials in the 'Thank You' campaign. The first, and most exposed to date, was the 30-second 'Supergrans' (produced in 1990), followed by the 30-second 'Submission' and 10-second 'Steamroller' (both produced in 1993).

'Supergrans' featured two little old ladies spontaneously performing an act of kindness – the act itself being a memorable stunt which gave the commercial great impact. It went on air at Easter 1990.

'SUPERGRANS'

MEDIA SPEND – 1978-1993

Both Roses and Quality Street have had consistent media support over exactly the same seasonal periods. The difference has been that Quality Street has outspent Roses for the majority of the period we are examining.

Despite this, Roses' advertising has been demonstrably more effective, as we will go on to prove.

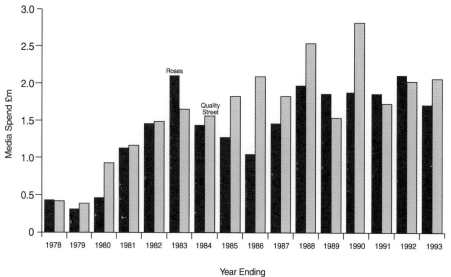

Figure 1. *Roses and Quality Street advertising spend*
Source: MEAL

THE RESULTS OF THE REPOSITIONING

Sales 1979 to 1990 – Achieving Brand Leadership

The success of the 'Thank You' campaign for Roses in volume terms began to be seen soon after it was aired in 1980. Over the next ten years Roses steadily closed the gap with Quality Street, achieving brand leadership in the late '80s.

To show this volume growth it is unfortunately necessary to look at two data sources as one continuous source does not exist. Nielsen data can be used for the period 1978-1984 whilst AGB covers the period 1983 onwards.

The figures from these two sources do not match exactly as Nielsen and AGB do not use the same market definitions. As this paper is looking at the long-term trends, this is not a problem (see Figures 2 and 3).

Not only did Roses grow its own share of the twistwrap market, its activity resulted in significant growth for its sector as a whole. From 1980 to 1993 the twistwrap sector almost doubled its share of the total assortments market (see Figure 4).

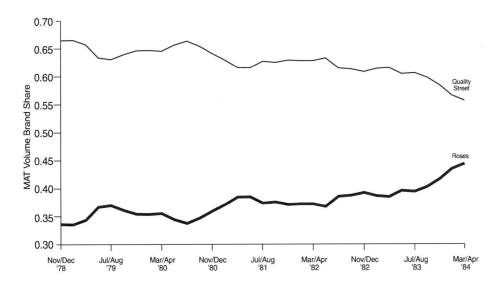

Figure 2. *Roses and Quality Street MAT volume brand share – 1978-84*
Source: Nielsen

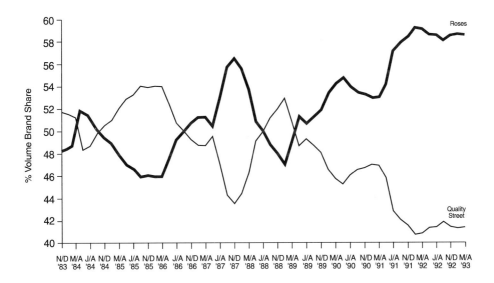

Figure 3. *Roses and Quality Street MAT volume brand share – 1983-93*
Source: AGB

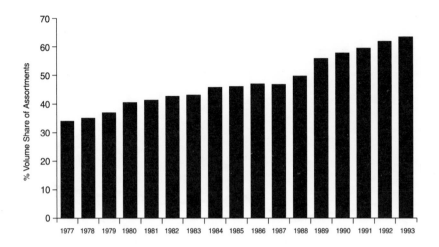

Figure 4. *The growth of the Twistwrap sector*
Source: BCCCA

It is our contention that, whilst the twistwrap sector had shown some growth, it was Roses that caused the significant growth seen in the 1980s. Weight is added to this claim by comparing the relative performances of Roses and Quality Street. Market growth alone would have maintained their relative positions ie brand shares would have been constant. Yet what we see is Roses come from a (distant) second place to take brand leadership. The explanation to this lies in the positioning and advertising of the two brands.

Sales Since 1990

Since the BBH campaign commenced in 1990 the gap between Roses and Quality Street has been steadily widening. Figure 5 highlights this latest period.

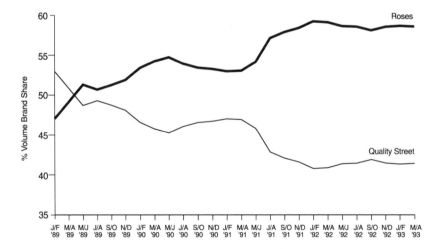

Figure 5. *Roses and Quality Street MAT volume brand share – 1989-93*
Source: AGB

Reactions to the 'Thank You' Campaign – 1979 Advertising

Consumer reaction to the new campaign was very favourable. The music ('Thank You Very Much' by The Scaffold) was likeable, catchy and memorable. The central idea of the 'thank you' gift was well received and consumers recognised that Roses had created a new and motivating role for the brand.

Roses was felt to be entirely suitable as such a 'thank you' gift and some even felt that the advertising would encourage an increase in the giving of gifts as a sign of gratitude for small favours.

> "It's a way of showing gratitude for what they've done for each other, isn't it? For any reason at all, if you want to give a box of chocs to somebody, make it Roses."

> "I think the message was, if you wanted to give a little gift, buy Roses."

> "It's just a little thank you. Appreciation"

> "Small gift, an ideal way of saying thank you".

> > Sloane Research 1979

Importantly, the 'thank you' positioning did not limit Roses' role. Consumers felt that Roses could as easily be a little gift to oneself or one's family, and therefore bought and consumed on an everyday basis.

> "Although consumers played back the fact that Roses were being advertised principally as a gift, this did not appear to limit them to thinking that Roses was appropriate only as a gift. It was more liberally interpreted as a 'little something'"

> > Sloane Research 1979

Reactions to the 'Thank You' Campaign – 1990 Advertising

The aim of the BBH campaign was to raise awareness levels and to generate more consumer empathy in order to ensure that Roses maintained its brand leadership. The following table compares the empathy levels of the Y&R vs BBH campaign

TABLE 1: EMPATHY

	TYVM Xmas 1989 (143) %	Supergrans Easter 1990 (76) %
Enjoy watching more than most ads	31	46
I like the people in it	15	19
It's an unusual ad	17	42

Source: Millward Brown

This makes 'Supergrans' the best-liked chocolate assortment advertising measured by Millward Brown.

Qualitative research confirmed the Millward Brown findings.

> "All felt the sentiment was right, from the heart."

> "A big ad for a brand of stature."

> "The focus was no longer simply the line 'Thank You' but on the emotion and intent behind the act."

> > Patrick Corr Research 1990

The clear perception of Roses' role, however, continues not to restrict usage.

"There are no indications that it [Thank You] restricts usage or emotion and indeed it has become an invaluable advertising property."

Corr Research 1992

Growth in Advertising Awareness

Advertising awareness increased with the introduction of the 'Thank You' campaign in 1980.

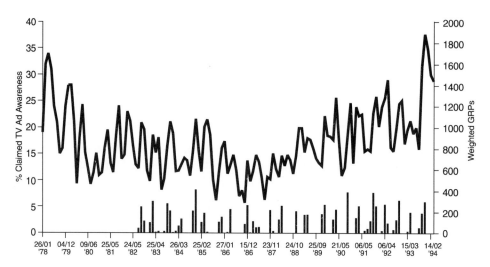

Figure 6.   *Roses TV advertising awareness vs GRPs – 1978-94*
Note: *GRP data only available from 22.11.82*
Source: Millward Brown

Indeed, an examination of Roses versus Quality Street TV advertising awareness shows that the two brands were almost parallel, *despite* the consistently lower spend for Roses shown earlier.

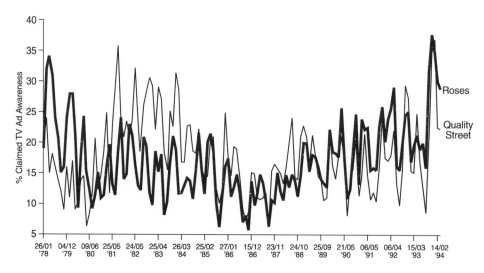

Figure 7.   *Roses vs Quality Street TV advertising awareness – 1978-94*
Source: Millward Brown

The BBH campaign has also been successful at generating awareness. The chart below focuses on Roses TV advertising awareness from 1990.

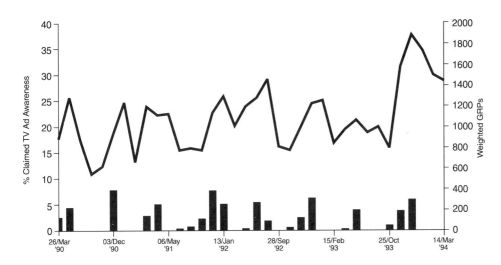

Figure 8. *Roses TV advertising awareness vs GRPs Easter 1990-94*
Source: Millward Brown

As advertising awareness grew, so did consumer preference for Roses the brand. From being clearly behind in the 1970s, Roses became the 'most preferred' brand and the one bought 'most often'.

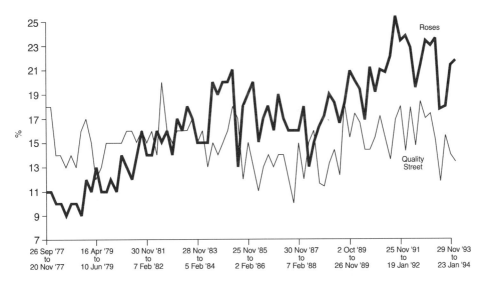

Figure 9. *Personal favourite*
Source: Millward Brown

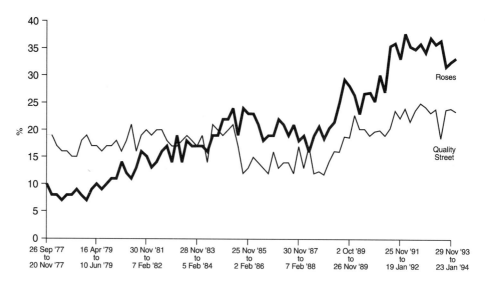

Figure 10. *Brand bought most often*
Source: Millward Brown

DISCOUNTING OTHER INFLUENCES

Clearly *all* changes made to the brand contributed in some degree to its success. It was vital that the total brand offering was optimised in order to take full advantage of the opportunity. Our contention is that advertising played a fundamental role in the brand's growth.

We have looked at, and discounted, a number of other possible influences on Roses' undeniable success.

The Product

Roses had a product strength in that it was more associated with chocolate than Quality Street. The success of the brand cannot be attributed to this, however, as this known fact about Roses was unchanged over the repositioning period.

"Roses are chocolate and Quality Street are sweets"

Gregory/Langmaid Associates 1975
(pre 'Thank You' advertising)

Advertising turned this well-understood product fact into a brand benefit.

Nor is it the case that Roses was a more acceptable eat than Quality Street. Both brands enjoyed a high level of acceptability with only 5% rejecting either brand and at least 58% having eaten both brands.

TABLE 2: EATING THE BRANDS

	Roses %	Quality Street %	
Ever eaten yourself	77	81	(ie. 58% overlap)
Eaten within last year	35	45	
Personal favourites	10	15	
Not liked	5	5	

Base: 803 Men and women, buyers of boxed assortments

Source: Millward Brown 1978

Packaging

At the time of repositioning Roses, Cadbury introduced a larger, pack size into the range – to be almost immediately copied by Quality Street. Although other new pack sizes were added over time, these were always mirrored by Quality Street (and vice versa). In fact, the similarities between Roses and Quality Street pack sizes are a direct reflection of the unusual nature of this two-brand sector, where both key competitors can easily observe and mirror any presumed competitive advantage in the presentation of each other's brand and product.

The next table illustrates the point by listing the top four by volume pack sizes available from both brands from 1983 to first quarter 1993. Few differences will be spotted. As Quality Street and Roses performed very differently over this time period, we believe performance is attributable to something other than packaging changes.

TABLE 3: PACK CHANGES OVER TIME
Top 4 Package Types by Volume Sold, (1983-1993)

	Roses	Quality Street
1983	½ lb box	½ lb box
	1 lb box	1 lb box
	3.5 lb jar	3.5 lb jar
	4.4 lb tin	5 lb tin
1985	½lb box	½ lb box
	1 lb box	1 lb box
	3.5 lb jar	3.5 lb jar
	4.4 lb tin	5 lb tin
1987	½ lb box	½ lb box
	1 lb box	1 lb box
	3.5 lb jar	3.5 lb jar
	4.4 lb tin	5 lb tin
1989	½ lb box	½ lb box
	1 lb box	1 lb box
	3.5 lb jar	3.5 lb jar
	3.9 lb box	5 lb tin
1991	½ lb box	½ lb box
	1 lb box	1 lb box
	3.5 lb jar	1.2 lb
	4.4 lb tin	5 lb tin
1993 (1st 4 mths)	½ lb box	½ lb box
	1 lb box	1 lb box
	3.5 lb jar	1.2 lb
	4.4 lb tin	3 lb tin (note 5lb tin is seasonal – likely to come in for Xmas)

Source: Cadbury

Price

Roses has always been sold at a slight price premium to Quality Street. Over time this price differential has decreased, although Roses remains more expensive. The following price differential chart illustrates this.

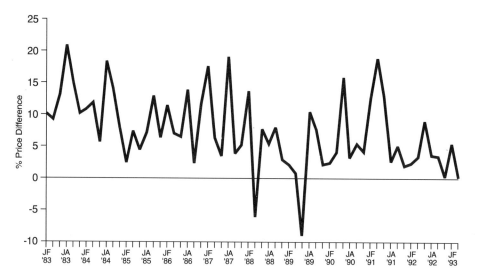

Figure 11. *Roses price differential over Quality Street*
Source: AGB

As a decreasing price differential may have influenced sales, a way of isolating its possible effect was found. The regional analysis we undertook, and which is described later, takes the regional relative price into account, enabling us to factor for price as an influence.

Distribution

Distribution data for this period was not available. However, it is reasonable for us to make a number of assumptions.

With the rise of the multiple grocers in the 1980s it is likely that the twistwrap market saw distribution gains. It is equally *unlikely* that one brand would have been stocked solus.

We have therefore assumed that where distribution gains were made, they benefited Roses and Quality Street equally. If this is the case, it does not explain Roses share gain.

Further weight is added to our argument in that in the last three years we know there have been no significant distribution gains nor losses for either brand, yet Roses share continues to grow.

THE ROSES REGIONAL MODEL

To add further weight to our argument that advertising was the main influence on growth we have undertaken some statistical analysis using regional data. At any one point in time, packaging, product, promotions etc would have been national, making weight of advertising the only regional variable.

Details of the analysis

Calculating the sales effect of the advertising presented a number of difficulties that it was necessary to overcome.

The first problem was the enormous seasonality of the market and the fact that advertising activity was always timed to coincide with the seasonal peaks. It was, however, our contention that advertising *increased* the seasonal peak.

The second problem was that weights of advertising on a national level were similar from year to year preventing us from looking at the varying effect of different weights of advertising over time. Regionally, however, weights of advertising did vary sufficiently over time.

Using AGB data we undertook a regression analysis of the regional Christmas peaks from 1983 to 1992. Unfortunately AGB data does not allow us to go back before 1983. This does, however, provide a more than adequate time period.

Christmas peaks were chosen as they represented the most robust data points. This methodology allowed us to overcome the problem of separating seasonality from advertising effect. Regionally, we found sufficient differences to estimate the relationship between advertising weight and sales volume.

It is reasonable to assume that factors influencing one region eg new packing sizes, incentives to retailers etc influenced all other regions in much the same way. We therefore approximated these other factors using a constructed variable that took account of the underlying growth not attributable to advertising.

Making the Regions Comparable

It was obviously necessary to put all of the regions on a comparable basis by looking at sales and advertising in terms of the number of *households* available in any one region.

So sales were looked at in terms of sales per household (ie regional volume divided by number of households in the region) and advertising in terms of impacts per household (ie impacts divided by the number of household in the region).

Price data was available for all regions and was taken into account in the analysis in the form of the relative prices of Roses and Quality Street.

The Model

We set ourselves a hard task in seeking to produce one regression equation that approximated the sales levels across nine regions over ten Christmas snapshots. In other words we were looking for a consistent price effect and a consistent advertising quantification both across region, and over time.

Figure 12 shows how the equation fits the various regions. Some 70% of the variation is explained by the equation. Such a fit on cross-section data like this, over an extended time period, is extremely good.

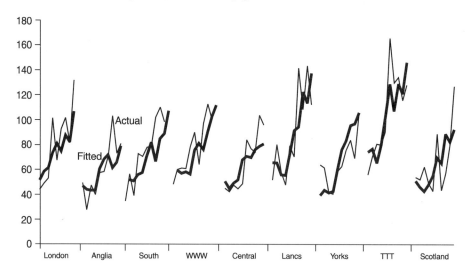

Figure 12. *Model vs actual*
Source: AGB

We therefore feel confident in using the model to calculate the advertising effect.

Quantifying the Effect

The effect of the advertising was determined by calculating the consumption effect per household of the advertising by region. This was then scaled up by the number of households in each region and each region then summed to obtain a total, national, figure.

Figure 13 shows the difference between actual sales and the models' prediction of what sales would have been without advertising.

Using the difference between actual and predicted 'no advertising' sales and scaling these down to ex-factory sales levels, it is possible calculate the volume of extra sales generated per annum. This in turn can be related to media spend. Table 4 makes this comparison.

Over the period 1983-1992, we calculate that 36,709 tonnes were generated by advertising. Over the same period £22,403,898 was spent on advertising.

To break even, Cadbury must, therefore, generate a profit of £610.31 per tonne. Although confidentiality prevents us from giving the exact level of profit, we can state that it is considerably more than that amount.

Although we have been unable to include distribution in our calculations, even if distribution gains accounted for *half* the volume generated, the advertising would still have more than paid for itself.

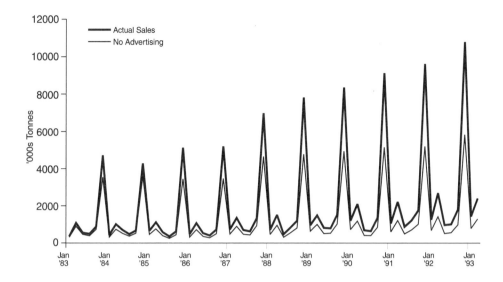

Figure 13. *Predicted sales without advertising*
Source: AGB

TABLE 4: ADDITIONAL SALES GENERATED

	Additional Tonnes Generated	MEAL Media Spend at Today's Prices £
1983	1,457	3,501,000
1984	1,257	2,284,762
1985	2,309	1,907,015
1986	2,336	1,523,188
1987	3,270	2,030,556
1988	3,982	2,592,105
1989	4,493	2,264,634
1990	5,426	2,108,989
1991	5,958	1,976,596
1992	6,221	2,215,053
Total 1983-1992	36,709	22,403,898

Source: Cadbury/AGB/MEAL

SUMMARY

The absolute benefits of a consistent long-term advertising campaign can be seen in this Roses case history. However, the additional benefit of the Roses campaign is that it has enabled Roses to own, in its 'Thank You' positioning, the biggest potential benefit of the twistwrap market. This has made it difficult for Quality Street, a very considerable competitor, to fight back effectively.

By identifying a gap in the market, the key market dynamic switched from 'family sharing' to 'informal gift'. Quality Street was left in possession of a still relevant, but more limited platform once Roses had claimed 'Thank You' for its own.

'Thank You' has the ability to encompass both 'sharing' (a thank you to myself or my family) *and* 'informal gift' (particularly relevant to the new volume coming from the mainstream).

Since 1991 Millward Brown have been recording the percentage of people who feel Roses is suitable as a thank-you gift. Respondents are able to choose from a number of brands but a large, and growing, percentage choose Roses.

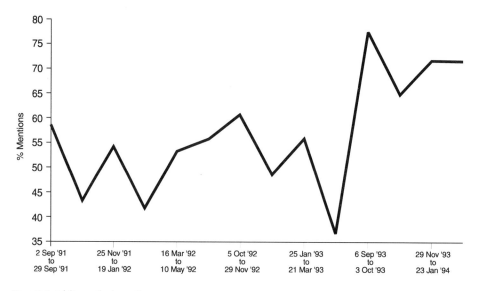

Figure 14. *Suitability as a thank you gift*
Source: Millward Brown

Unsurprisingly, Roses has not been alone in recognising the benefits of the 'Thank You' positioning. In recent years Quality Street has recognised that the market has moved on and has attempted to follow Roses into the wider, 'informal gift' sector by producing a commercial with a 'Thank You' theme, called 'Lollipop'.

Yet such is the power of Roses' hold over the 'Thank You' positioning, that much of the awareness and benefit achieved by Quality Street's Lollipop execution is attributed to Roses. In attempting to copy Roses' success, Quality Street is in actual fact contributing to it.

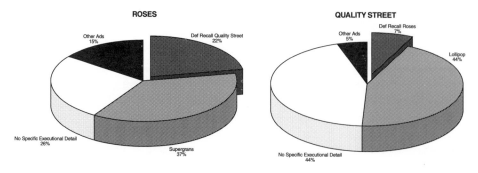

Figure 15. *Misattribution – Claimed ad recall*
Base: *Claimed recallers: Roses 692, Quality Street 455, 4/10/93-20/3/94*
Source: Millward Brown

CONCLUSIONS

— The 'Thank You' advertising campaign successfully repositioned the Roses brand, by building on Roses' heritage of being more special than Quality Street to present Roses as the perfect informal gift.

— From being (distant) second brand in the twistwrap market in 1978, Roses has grown to become brand leader, and has continued to maintain brand leadership at an ever-widening distance from Quality Street.

— The success of Roses has resulted in the growth of the twistwrap market as a whole.

— Roses now owns the 'Thank You' territory making it difficult for Quality Street to compete on the same ground, despite Quality Street's considerable best efforts.

— All this has been achieved with a media spend that has been consistently lower than Quality Street's.

— Regional statistical analysis has allowed us to factor out other variables and isolate the effect of the 'Thank You' advertising. This analysis allows us to quantify that effect and suggests that over 36,000 tonnes have been generated between 1983 and 1992. As the profitability of Roses is considerably greater than £611 per tonne, the advertising can be said to have paid for itself several times over.

— In this uniquely two-brand sector, the battle with Quality Street continues – but the advantage is Roses'.

5

Smoke Alarms
"Every home should have one"

INTRODUCTION

This case history describes an advertising campaign which has been instrumental in changing the lives of three quarters of the UK population.

Over the last seven years smoke alarm penetration has grown from 5% to 70%.

An advertising campaign on behalf of the Home Office by FCO and continued after its merger with Euro RSCG has been the dominant driving force behind this growth and in giving people the knowledge they need to maintain their alarms properly.

When all other variables have been discounted it can be seen that a campaign with an aggregate spend of under £7 million has directly resulted in the reduction of deaths and non-fatal casualties.

This paper covers 3 phases of development:

1. The creation of the market.
2. Addressing the issue of the vulnerable elderly.
3. Reinvigorating growth and reorienting the strategy to confront the unforeseen need to provide 'after sales' care in the form of maintenance information.

BACKGROUND

The fire brigades attend around 60,000 fires a year in occupied buildings, accounting for around 10,000 injuries and 700 fatalities each year. All three increased steadily throughout the 1980s.

By 1987 the Home Office was concerned that half of those killed by fires died because they were trapped by a fire that they weren't aware of. (53% of deaths occur between midnight and 10am. 67% are the result of being overcome by gas and smoke, often when the victims are asleep.)

There was evidence from other countries, where smoke alarms are often fitted by law, that they could make a contribution to reducing deaths and injury.

Smoke alarm penetration was believed to be around 5%. However, without legislative enforcement, it was, in the words of the Policy Division at the Home Office, "Doubtful that the wall of apathy could be breached".

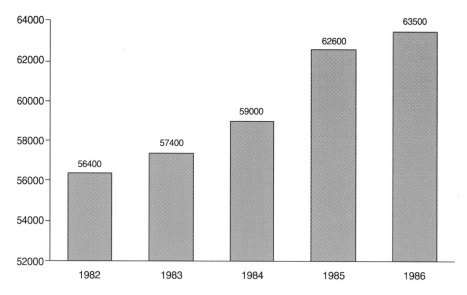

Figure 1. *National fire statistics, England & Wales: Number of fires*
Source: Home Office Statistics Division

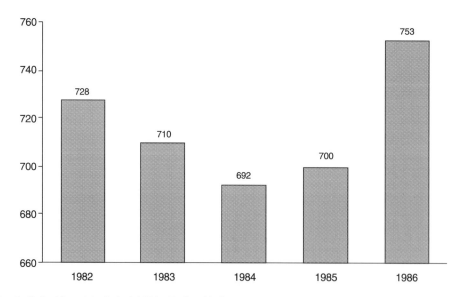

Figure 2. *National fire statistics, England & Wales: Number of deaths*
Source: Home Office Statistics Division

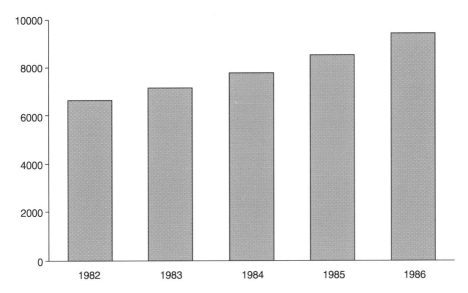

Figure 3. *National fire statistics, England & Wales: Number of injuries*
Source: Home Office Statistics Division

Nevertheless, ambitious targets were set:
  55% penetration by 1992;
  70% penetration by 1994.

ASSESSING CONSUMER ATTITUDES

Qualitative research, through Reflexions, across a wide band of ages and social classes, showed fire to be a barely considered threat, and that nearly everyone felt they would be aware of a fire in their home and able to take appropriate action quickly to stop it spreading.

Whereas parents of young children, when probed, acknowledged the danger posed to them and were able to recall anecdotal references to young children being trapped and dying in a fire, elderly respondents showed resistance to the concept of risk and had a "have a go" mentality.

Ignorance was widespread. The majority knew only of hotel-type alarm and sprinkler systems, which were felt to be prohibitively expensive for home use and would require specialist fitting.

For the few who were 'semi-aware', alarms were felt to be expensive (up to £50 each), with one needed per room.

A dozen concept statements were explored, from which emerged three emotionally charged 'building blocks' which showed how heightened feelings could overcome rational scepticism.

— Firstly, the idea of children dying in a fire was particularly emotive.
— Secondly, the idea of dying in your sleep and "just not waking up" horrified people.

— Thirdly, the speed at which smoke and fumes spread through a house was a shock to those who imagined fires smouldering, bonfire-like for hours.

From this research was devised the key message that:

"Only a smoke alarm can buy the precious minutes that can save your family from dying in a fire while they sleep."

PHASE I – CREATING THE MARKET

Creative Development

A TV commercial, 'Doll's House' was developed, showing a little girl playing with her dolls in her bedroom, which is later engulfed with smoke as she and her family sleeps.

Parents were judged to be the most receptive segment and to be likely to represent the fastest market growth opportunity.

Tested in animatic form by Reflexions, the qualitative pre-test found that the idea communicated clearly:

"You can't be relied upon to avert disaster if you're asleep, so don't take chances, get a smoke alarm."

"The communication that smoke would kill a small child in under a minute came as an unpleasant revelation and emphasise the need for an early warning system."

Area Test Market

The commercial was run on test in Tyne Tees, immediately after Christmas, when airtime is cheapest and domestic fire tragedies attract most news coverage.

The rest of the country showed a general fire prevention commercial at an equivalent weight of 400TVRs, as a control.

Since the Home Office is required to show commercial impartiality, it was the agency that held briefings with smoke alarm manufacturers and retailers, particularly the DIY multiples, to alert them to the campaign and to attempt to maximise supply and distribution. This was reinforced by Local Fire Brigade activity.

This has become the accepted practice for every year of advertising since.

A national Omnibus of 1,000 adults, by Millward Brown, showed penetration doubling and intention to purchase tripling, in the test area. The rest of the country showed little change, demonstrating a clear advertising effect.

TABLE 1: PENETRATION/INTENTION TO BUY A SMOKE ALARM

	Pre %	Post %
Claiming to own	6	11
Claim will definitely or probably buy	14	50

Source: Millward Brown

Based on this evidence, plus unprecedented demand and virtual out of stocks in the retail trade in Tyne Tees, the campaign was rolled out to London and Granada in December 1988 and nationally in December 1989.

'DOLL'S HOUSE'

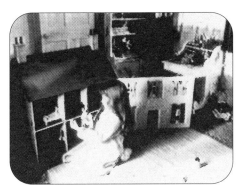

MVO: When you tuck your children in at night …

… are you putting them to bed or laying them to rest?

If inhaled, the smoke from a house fire …

SFX: *Eerie cries*

… could kill a small child in under a minute. They'll rely on you to wake them up and get them out.

What are you relying on?

SFX: *Eerie noises become more intense*

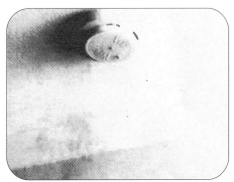

MVO: Wake up. Get a smoke alarm.

SFX: *Alarm beeping*

Measuring the National Campaign

The results were monitored in 3 ways:

1. Penetration by region, age group, social class and tenure via the twice-yearly AGB Home Audit (25,000 sample).
2. Penetration, awareness, attitudes, intention to buy and advertising via an annual study by BJM Research. (2,000 sample.)
3. Market sales, from AC Nielsen.

(NB: With different bases and timings AGB and BJM vary slightly.)

Although the Home Office campaign was not the only advertising for smoke alarms in 1988, 1989, 1990, it was the dominant publicity.

TABLE 2: SMOKE ALARM ADSPEND 1987-1990

	1987 £'000s	1988 £'000s	1989 £'000s	1990 £'000s
Home Office	328	527	707	912
Black & Decker	107	—	72	—
First Alert	—	559	396	130
Plasplugs	—	118	—	—
Polycell	—	121	—	—
THORN	—	113	—	—

Source: MEAL

TABLE 3: OWNERSHIP OF SMOKE ALARMS

	Mar '88 %	Sept '88 %	Mar '89 %	Sept '89 %	Mar '90 %
Penetration	10	15	23	26	31

Source: AGB

Against overall growth from 10% to 31%, penetration was highest and grew fastest among more upmarket households, who have easier access to the major distribution points and who, unlike council or private tenants, were less likely to view alarms as "home improvements which should be done by someone else". (See Figure 4.)

An indicator of the poignancy of 'Doll's House' was the rate of growth in households with young children being double that of those without.

TABLE 4: SMOKE ALARM PENETRATION BY PRESENCE OF CHILDREN

	1988 %	1990 %
None	8	25
Children 0-5	13	45
Children 6-15	13	42

Source: AGB

However low ownership levels among the elderly remained a concern, especially since they accounted for nearly half of all fatalities.

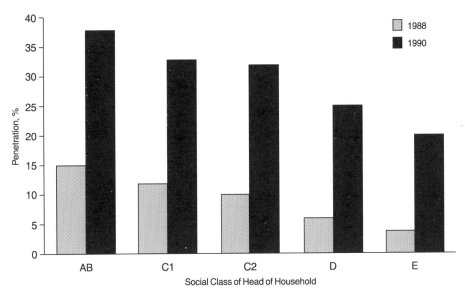

Figure 4. Smoke alarm penetration by social class: March 1988 vs March 1990
Source: AGB

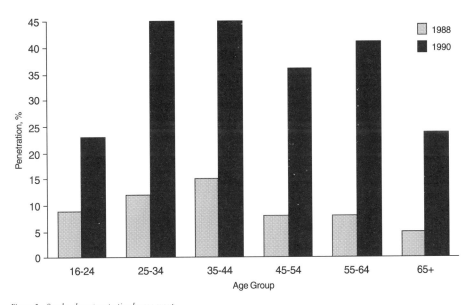

Figure 5. *Smoke alarm penetration by age group*
Source: AGB

The Advertising Contribution

The 1990 BJM Survey, showed 61% spontaneous awareness of advertising for smoke alarms, rising to 69% prompted awareness of 'Doll's House'.

Among respondents with children, advertising awareness was higher at 70% spontaneous, 79% prompted.

Prompted reactions indicated a strong educational effect and motivation to purchase:

61%: "it made me realise how quickly smoke can kill."
50%: "it made me realise how quickly fire can spread."
40%: "it made me think about the dangers of fire."
29%: "it made me think about buying an alarm."

Source: BJM; Base = all recalling advertising

Advertising recall was highest amongst those who had bought, or were considering buying, showing a contribution to both.

During the campaign period, both purchase and intention to buy among non-owners had increased significantly, with the proportion of non-owners definitely or probably intending to buy rising from 45% to 51%.

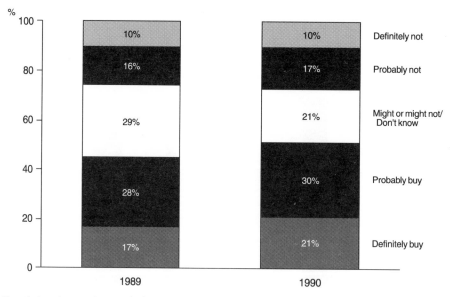

Figure 6. *Intention to purchase a smoke alarm*
Base: *Non-owners*
Source: BJM

There was a significant difference between those aware and not aware of 'Dolls House', which pointed to a strong advertising effect, with a purchase intention of 55% and 43% respectively.

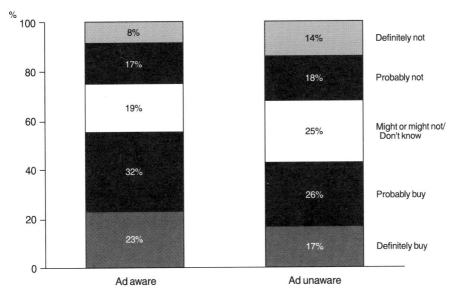

Figure 7. *Intention to purchase: ad aware vs Ad unaware*
Base: *Non-owners*
Source: BJM

PHASE II – ADDRESSING VULNERABLE GROUPS

Despite the rapid rise in penetration, ownership remained low amongst the elderly.

Penetration amongst DE 55+ was only 20% and intention to buy among non-owners was 26%, compared with 51% for all adults.

It was also clear that the limited amount of branded expenditure would be targeted in content at younger, more affluent households, and their TV buying strategy, with a strong ABC1 conversion reinforced this.

Qualitative research amongst the elderly, through Research Perspectives in June 1989, had shown that they:

— were less aware of alarms;
— over-estimated their cost;
— perceived them to be complex and difficult to install;
— felt themselves to be somehow "immune" to the threat.

Based on this the key message for this next advertising phase was expressed as:

"Smoke and fumes can kill anyone while they sleep. the elderly are particularly vulnerable. only a smoke alarm can keep watch for you."

A new execution, 'Dying', was devised to:

— directly address the elderly;
— demonstrate the speed and lethal effect of smoke at night;
— remove the misapprehension that something would wake you in a fire (BJM showed a quarter of respondents relying on their pets);
— draw attention to the affordability of a smoke alarm.

'Dying' was evaluated as an animatic in qualitative research by Andrew Irving Associates amongst elderly people and their friends and relatives.

The report spoke of the "stunned silence" that met just an animatic, and concluded that

> "Overall this approach suggests that the high impact, emotional route adopted for this campaign is both appropriate and likely to be effective in
> — persuading some to take action.
> — making others more conscious of/interested in the idea of installing an alarm."

30 and 10 second versions were aired at Christmas 1990/91 and 1991/92.

The Home Office campaign now accounted for 87% of all adspend in 1990 and 73% in 1991 and 68% in 1982.

TABLE 5: SMOKE ALARM ADSPEND 1990-1992

	1990 £'000	1991 £'000	1992 £'000
Home Office	912	898	614
First Alert	130	175	—
London Fire Brigades	—	161	294

Source: MEAL

The Results of 'Dying'

Alarm penetration continued to grow during the campaign period, and respondents aged 65+ showed the highest rate of increase, from 24% to 40%, and whilst the percentage of non-owners expressing a purchase intention grew, it was now fastest among older respondents.

TABLE 6: SMOKE ALARM PENETRATION

	1990 %	1991 %	1992 %
AGB	31	41	49
BJM	38	48	52

Source: AGB, BJM

Awareness of the TV campaign showed a cumulative uplift and again was higher amongst past purchasers and future intenders. (See Figures 10 & 11.)

Awareness of advertising detail and recall of the main message showed a startling level of clarity for a modest budget and showed that the campaign dominated awareness of fire safety.

'DYING'

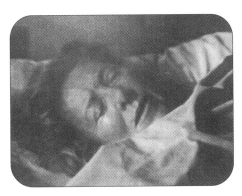

MVO: This woman's dying. She's dying because there's a fire. The smoke from the fire is already in her lungs, killing her while she sleeps.

Her last hope is her husband. But her husband's dying. The smoke from the fire is already in his lungs, killing him while he sleeps.

WAKE UP
GET A SMOKE ALARM
From £5

His last hope is Max. But Max is dying. He's dying because there's a fire.

MVO: Wake up. Get a smoke alarm.

SFX: *Alarm beeping*

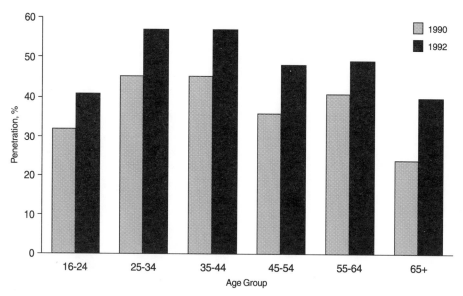

Figure 8. *Smoke alarm penetration by age group: 1990 vs 1992*
Source: AGB

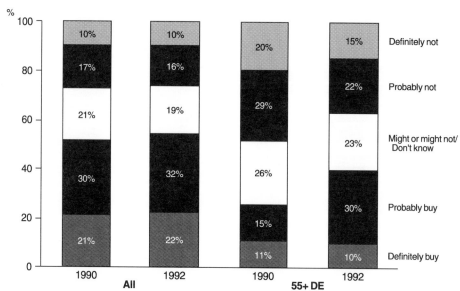

Figure 9. *Intention to purchase a smoke alarm: 55+ DE vs All, 1990 vs 1992*
Base: *Non-users*
Source: BJM

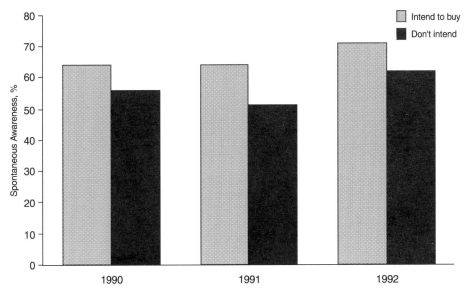

Figure 10. *Spontaneous awareness of TV campaign*

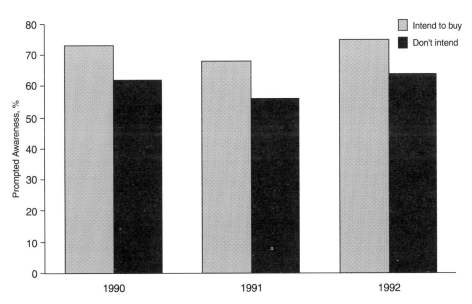

Figure 11. *Prompted awareness of TV campaign*

TABLE 7: RECALL OF THE ADVERTISING

	All Aware of Advertising (% Recalling)
Old lady in bed dying of smoke inhalation	43
Dog dying of smoke inhalation	36
Old man in chair dying of smoke inhalation	41
Main Message	
Buy alarm	54
Smoke kills	37
It made me think about buying an alarm	45

Contribution to Overall Market

Prior to the advertising campaign in 1987 the smoke alarm market had shown no discernible seasonality.

Since then, the annual profile of sales shows a distinct uplift during the advertised period, with the levels reverting to a higher plateau each year after the short term peak.

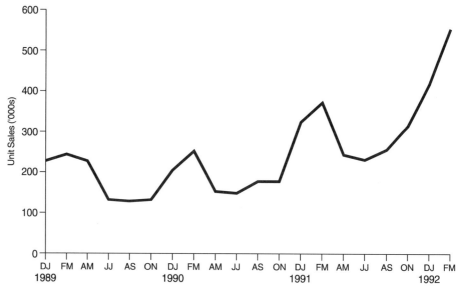

Figure 12. *Unit sales of smoke alarms*
Source: Nielsen

Cost had always been a factor in causing consumer resistance, especially in less well-off households.

In store average prices had fallen, but it was important that this was realised by those who might never look out for alarms.

The simple statement, "from around £5" was added to the end of 'Dying' and consumer price perceptions fell accordingly.

TABLE 8: AVERAGE PRICE PERCEPTIONS

	Considered £	Not Considered £
1990	11.23	15.33
1991	8.60	12.15
1992	8.54	12.45

PHASE III – ADDRESSING HARD CORE RESISTORS AND EDUCATING OWNERS

Despite the success of the campaign over 5 years, the rate of increase in penetration had slowed, with only a 4% increase overall in 1992 and 1991, but 10% among 65+.

There was also an unexpected requirement to address a completely different issue, owing to concern at the Home Office that the level of *working* alarms might be substantially lower than the installed base, due to ignorance of maintenance procedures.

Evidence for this came from the United States, a more mature market with 75% penetration in 1986, but where a survey had shown that 30% were inoperative owing to dead or missing batteries. (Source: US Fire Administration.)

In addition, between 1989 and 1992 a survey carried out over a three year period in Tameside on council installed alarms showed 10% were inoperative.

Only 1% of owners had replaced batteries after one year, as recommended on alarm instructions.

Although 70% claimed to have cleaned their alarm, only 1% had done so according to the manufacturer's instructions.

Apart from 'accidental' testing, only 38% had pressed the button on the front of the alarm to test it, and only 2% had tested the alarm with smoke.

The key maintenance procedures (changing the battery once a year, checking the battery monthly, doing a monthly smoke test and annually vacuuming the interior of the alarm) are typically outlined on-pack or in the leaflet advising on fitting.

However it was suspected that these were read cursorily at best and rarely retained and the Tameside evidence reinforced this.

Qualitative research by Bridget Galeotti in 1991 showed ignorance of maintenance procedures and strong resistance to carrying them out:

"All rejected the routine and were not prepared to take on the burden of carrying out weekly button checks, monthly smoke tests, annual vacuuming."

For some there was the feeling of betrayal:

"Manufacturers' instructions, they were sure, did not suggest anything as elaborate, and the impression created by advertising was of a relatively maintenance free item."

Respondents appeared unable to envisage a situation which would change their minds:

"Advertising to promote the recommended maintenance routine would have very little likelihood of making a serious impact on owners' current practices."

Despite the implicit possibility that a maintenance campaign might depress sales, it was decided that a smaller number of working alarms was preferable to a larger number of indifferently maintained ones.

Advertising concepts were qualitatively assessed by Reflexions in July 1992 in a study comprising 13 group discussions and 13 paired interviews.

The research concluded that despite the success of 'Dying', younger people with families still lacked the emotional motivation of thinking of their own family in the context of a fire.

It was clear that maintenance procedures required *demonstration* to imply ease, not hassle. Next, people needed to have a mechanism to remember how often they should be done.

Finally and most importantly, it was apparent that people would only be inclined to even *consider* maintenance if it was linked to the concept of protecting their family or suffering the consequences of not doing so. This was the insight that earlier research had failed to draw out.

In other words, installation and maintenance share the same emotional benefit. It was this finding that gave the realisation that the two could be addressed in a way that was positive, rather than detrimental for each.

The key thoughts generated for each strand of the campaign were:

Installation
"The consequences of not have a smoke alarm can stay with you for a lifetime."

Maintenance
"Not having a properly maintained alarm is as bad as not having one at all."

Two animatics were developed for qualitative pre-testing. One, 'Rewind', depicted a mother endlessly watching a video of her daughter, who had since been killed by a house fire, opening her Christmas presents. The second, 'Resuscitation', showed a young woman being pulled from a fire and counterpointed the desperate attempts of firemen to revive her with the simple procedures involved in checking and maintaining an alarm, with the implicit message that doing one could have prevented the other.

The approaches were tested qualitatively among owners and non-owners by Andrew Irving Associates.

The findings were:

In 'Rewind', "the case for installing a smoke alarm as put by the ad is compelling and hard to refute".

Structurally, "the disguised and late message catches the audience off guard and hits home".

The Christmas setting, coinciding with the traditional time of the advertising "added poignancy to the sense of loss and gave a strong emotional charge".

'Resuscitation' performed well in

"telling an involving story"

"credibly putting the case for maintaining smoke alarms"

"making the messages interesting and easy to understand"

However, there was evidence of deflection of the message among some owners, demoralisation at a false sense of security, particularly among women and the elderly, and reinforced resistance to buy among more sceptical non-owners.

The agency and client agreed the case for 'Resuscitation' was proven but concluded it should be run *after* 'Rewind'.

Both commercials ran in December 1992 – February 1993 and again in 1993-1994.

'REWIND'

Open on a fuzzy home video quality film of a little girl unwrapping a Christmas toy. Her mother comes into frame and kisses her. The film rewinds and plays again.

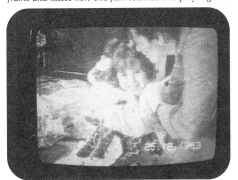

GIRL: Thank you mummy.
GIRL: Thank you mummy.

Cut to the same woman sitting in tears on the settee. She is obsessively watching the same sequence over and over again. Close up on her face brimming with tears.

GIRL: Thank you mummy.

Her husband enters the room carring two mugs. He gently takes the remote control from her.

MAN: Leave it now, lovely.

Close up of the woman on the video cuddling her daughter and looking at the camera.

The husband puts his arms arond the woman as she collapses sobbing in his arms.

FVO: The smoke and fumes from a house fire can kill a child in under a minute.

Visual of smoke alarm with smoke under it.

Spend was £807,000 in 1993 and £820,000 in the first quarter of 1994.

With an increased budget in 1994, 'Dying' was used again as well to give a breadth of targeting and message.

TABLE 9: PHASING OF ACTIVITY

	December	January	February	March
1992	'Rewind' <———293 TVRs———>		'Resuscitation' <———292 TVRs———>	
1993	'Rewind' <———195 TVRs———> 'Resuscitation' <———312 TVRs———>			'Dying' <-177 TVRs-> 'Resuscitation' <-239 TVRs->

The Results

After a slowing of penetration after the second burst of 'Dying', and fears that a hardcore was being reached, despite encouraging intention to purchase figures, penetration has continued to rise.

TABLE 10: SMOKE ALARM PENETRATION

	Sept '91 %	Mar '92 %	Sept '92 %	Mar '93 %	Sept '93 %
Owned	44	49	52	57	60
Installed	41	46	49	54	57

Source: AGB

BMRB, replacing BJM since 1992 show an acceleration of penetration with the last, increased weight burst, reaching the original target of 70% installed, with an additional 4% not yet fitted.

TABLE 11: SMOKE ALARM PENETRATION

	1991 %	1992 %	1993 %	1994 %
Owned	48	52	63	74
Installed	45	47	59	70

Source: BJM/BMRB

Despite the expectation of reaching a hard core of resistors, a majority of non-owners still express an intention to purchase.

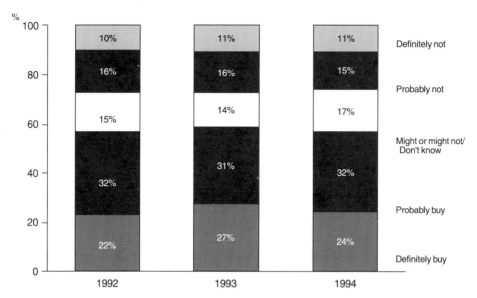

Figure 13. *Intention to purchase a smoke alarm*
Base: *All non-owners*

As in the years up to 1992, the correlation between advertising timing and sales peak continued to be striking. February/March remains the most buoyant period, accounting for nearly 25% of annual sales.

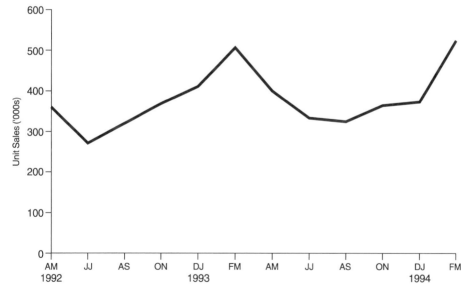

Figure 14. *Unit sales of smoke alarms*
Source: Nielsen

Spontaneous advertising awareness has remained steady, with a slight peak in 1992.

Prompted awareness for 1994 (with a greater spend and more ads to choose from), reached the highest levels measured.

TABLE 12: ADVERTISING AWARENESS

	1989 %	1990 %	1991 %	1992 %	1993 %	1994 %
Spontaneous	53	61	61	67	60	62
Prompted	62	69	66	73	63	78

Base: Total sample

Amongst non-owners claiming they were definitely or probably going to buy, spontaneous awareness was 69%, and prompted 80%, again suggesting an advertising effect.

Of spontaneous mentions of any advertising relating to smoke alarms or fire prevention, 75% are provably related to this campaign.

Maintenance

Because the maintenance issue was such an unknown, a pre-advertising check had been carried out by BMRB to gauge awareness of measures.

All have shown spontaneous and prompted increase from a low base, however four things are notable:

(i)   That the most dramatic increase has taken place for the least familiar maintenance measures.
(ii)   There remains a significant disparity between spontaneous and prompted knowledge suggesting the job is by no means complete.
(iii) The difference in awareness between owners and non-owners is small, showing that the message has been relevant to all groups.
(iv)   The cumulative effect of two bursts and a higher weight have been necessary to accelerate change. Beyond the advertising, there is no other known source of this information for the consumer.

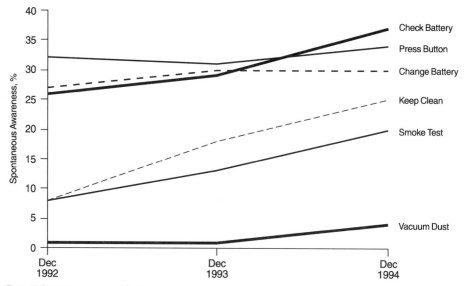

Figure 15. *Spontaneous awareness of maintenance measures: Owners*
Source: BMRB

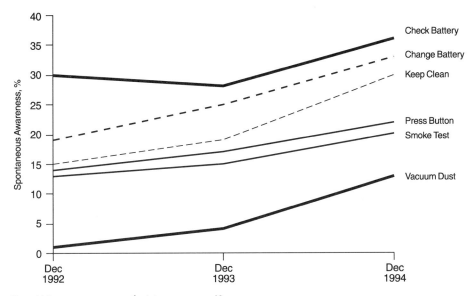

Figure 16. *Spontaneous awareness of maintenance measures: Non-owners*
Source: BMRB

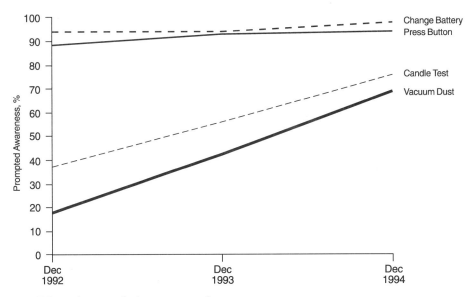

Figure 17. *Prompted awareness of maintenance measures: Owners*
Source: BMRB

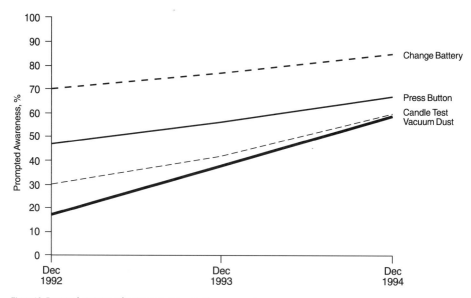

Figure 18. *Prompted awareness of maintenance measures: Non-owners*
Source: BMRB

Since qualitative development research showed a high resistance to carrying out maintenance measures, the acid test lies in the extent to which the advertising might have contributed to changes in behaviour.

Monitoring actual behaviour for measures which have to be repeated monthly or annually is clearly impossible, so we have to rely on *claimed* behaviour as a measure of how the advertising message has worked.

The table below shows the way in which practice of the basic measures has been supplemented by those which in the qualitative pre-test were greeted with incredulity.

TABLE 13: MAINTENANCE MEASURES – CLAIMED BEHAVIOUR

	Dec '92 %	Feb '93 %	April '94 %
Changed batteries in last year	72	72	75
Tested alarm in last month	55	59	58
Carried out candle test in last month	9	15	18
Vacuumed alarm in last year	12	22	36

Source: BMRB

Importantly, given the concerns raised by the qualitative concept testing, only 2% of non-owners claimed that 'Resuscitation' had put them *off* buying an alarm.

A major benefit of running three advertising executions has been the multiplicity of different messages that the consumer has received. They accomodate the broad range of motivations to purchase with a distinct link to purchase intention among non-owners.

TABLE 14: MAIN ADVERTISING MESSAGE

	Rewind %	Resuscitation %	Dying %
It made me realise how quickly smoke can kill	34	42	**50**
It made me realise everyone needs an alarm	38	39	40
It shows that the effects of fire can last a lifetime	**51**	26	22
It made me realise smoke will not wake me	17	21	**42**
It gave useful advice	26	**43**	31
It made me think about buying an alarm*	40	41	37

Base: All aware of advertising

Note: * Base = All non owners aware of advertising

Source: BMRB

Effect on Battery Sales

In the past two years, when the need for maintenance has been advertised, seasonality has been affected in the battery market. 9 volt sales have begun to show a post-Christmas peak which did not previously exist, and which is not characteristic of the total battery market.

ISOLATING THE EFFECTS

Price

Although price perceptions have fallen aided, by the final ad frame, actual minimum RSP has remained static for the past 3 years at around £3.99. However penetration growth has still been rapid.

Distribution

Since 1988, distribution in the DIY multiples which account for the majority of sales has been 100% (Nielsen). What *has* happened is that foreknowledge of the Home Office campaign has encouraged greater levels and visibility of stocks during the advertised periods.

Brigades' Efforts

Since the start of the campaign, the focus of Brigade activity (leafleting, demonstrations etc) has concentrated on alarms. Its effects, although significant are impossible to isolate. However, without the presence of the umbrella campaign, its impact would have been reduced.

PR

This has either been constant, at the time of the annual bursts, and hence dependent on them, or ad hoc, when deaths occur. However we have been unable to detect significant changes from one year to the next.

Effect on Fires

Of fires attended by brigades, the number initially discovered by smoke alarms tripled between 1988 and 1992.

The Home Office Fire Statistics for 1992 (the most recent year available) show that in homes *with* alarms, 70% of fires were discovered within 5 minutes, compared with 53% in homes without.

The death rate of 3 casualties per 1,000 fires is one third that of homes without alarms.

Research carried out by Lothian and Borders Fire Brigades have shown that if a working smoke alarm is installed, then:

— there is a third of the need to be rescued;
— there is one third the amount of direct fire damage;
— there is half the risk of a fire spreading to upper floors.

IN CONCLUSION

The last word is with those who have to risk their lives to tackle fire and too frequently are exposed to its consequences:

"The Home Office should be commended for their innovative and effective approach to their campaign."

Asst. Chief Fire Officer
London Fire & Civil Defence Authority

"We believe the effectiveness of these strategies can be demonstrated by the fact that the total numbers of persons injured in fires in our region dropped from 2,223 in 1990 to 621 in 1993."

Asst. Chief Fire Officer
West Midlands Fire Service

Section Two

New Brands or Advertisers

6

Boddingtons

"By 'eck!"

INTRODUCTION

This paper is not easy to write. Not concisely, anyway. The reason for this is the *scope* of Boddingtons' success. Attempts to isolate advertising effectiveness usually deal with the success of *one* product in *one* market. This case encompasses the success of *two* products that operate in *two* geographical areas.

The two products are Boddingtons Bitter (the pub pint) and Boddingtons Draught (the canned version). For the sake of clarity the canned product will be referred to as Canned Boddingtons.

The two areas are the North West (Granada) which represents the brand's heartland region and the remainder of the country which represents an obviously larger, relatively untapped region for Boddingtons.

Only by covering both products in both regions can we fully appreciate the brand's achievements.

We wish to show that advertising has:

— helped grow Boddingtons from a regional brand to a *nationally* available brand with regional roots;
— helped maintain, and even strengthen, Boddingtons credentials in its heartland.

We will argue that the advertising has done this by *carefully building and nurturing the brand*.

The case is divided into five parts:

1. Outlines the background behind Whitbread's acquisition of Boddingtons, the role it was to play and the resultant advertising/media strategy and executions.
2. Describes in detail the achievements of the brand since 1991 when BBH advertising began.
3. Identifies the specific contribution that advertising has made to these achievements.
4. Explains how we believe the advertising has worked.
5. Sets out the benefits of the advertising in terms of payback and secondary effects.

BACKGROUND, ADVERTISING AND MEDIA STRATEGY

Whitbread and Boddingtons

The UK beer market has within it a sector called 'standard bitter'. The products in this sector are not particularly strong in alcohol. They are predominantly used to enjoy a prolonged evening's drinking. Consequently, this is an important volume sector for brewers.

Historically, Whitbread competed in this sector with its brands, 'Whitbread Trophy' and 'Whitbread Best'.

By the late 1980s, there were indications that these brands did not enjoy the levels of appeal to consumers they had done in the past. Cask conditioned bitters (unpasteurised) were becoming increasingly popular. Trophy and Best's keg format (pasteurised) hampered their brand image.

> "Its nature was perceived to be mass produced (keg) rather than crafted (pump) and so Trophy suffered from all the growing prejudices against keg bitters".

> "...there was little enthusiasm for this perceived 'keg' brand (Whitbread Best)..."

Qualitative Research, SRG 1991

Trophy and Best were unlikely to be able to take advantage of the emerging cask sector, unlike John Smiths and Tetley which did appear as cask beers. Nor did they possess the regional heritage that national success increasingly required.

The decision was made to develop a brand of cask bitter that could better match the needs of the bitter consumer.

In November 1989 Whitbread bought the Boddingtons brewery in Manchester. Peter Jarvis, Group Chief Executive of Whitbread Plc, said of the brand at the time:

> "Boddingtons was a declining regional bitter brand that sold at pretty ordinary prices in the North West"

The clear majority of Boddingtons volume came from Granada. The rest was largely 'overspill' from the region, and not the result of 'planned' marketing.

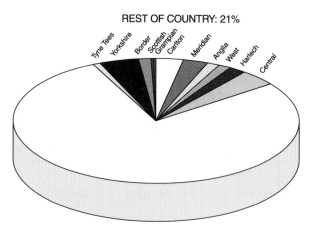

Figure 1. *Regional profile of Boddingtons – May 1991*
Source: Whitbread Marketing Information

The regionality of Boddingtons was part of its appeal for drinkers in Granada.

The brand had a Manchester birthright, a loyal local following and even a nickname, "Boddies".

Boddingtons, therefore, had the credentials for development that characterised the market's success stories and Whitbread's plans for Boddingtons were ambitious.

It wanted to *grow Boddingtons Bitter into a national brand* to rival the likes of John Smiths and Tetley. This would also present the opportunity to launch, nationally, a new canned Boddingtons product (which employed a new dispense system called 'Draughtflow'). Both of these initiatives would involve expanding the focus of the brand's marketing beyond the North West for the first time in over 200 years.

Although the opportunities were considerable, there were clear dangers with this plan.

Disenfranchising the Heartland

First, becoming a national brand ran the risk of *disenfranchising existing Boddingtons drinkers* in Granada. As we have said, the regionality of the brand is part of its appeal to these drinkers and that regionality would become diluted. Boddingtons would cease to be exclusively "our beer" for these loyal drinkers.

The problem is magnified when a national operator, such as Whitbread, is behind these changes. Bitter drinkers generally do not perceive national brewers as having the best interests of the local drinker at heart.

Qualitative research in 1990 confirmed this danger:

> "Whitbread are right buggers. They buy up these little companies and almost immediately close down the brewery. As someone on radio said recently, 'if they don't want the breweries, why do they buy them in the first place?!' I think I go along with that…"
>
> Boddingtons Drinker

> "However, as drinkers have had time to follow the events going on… a feeling appears to have developed that the soul of Boddingtons has been lost…"
>
> Qualitative Research in Manchester, Research Partners Ltd 1990

Anecdotal evidence from the marketing team in Manchester revealed that, prior to Whitbread's take-over drinkers blamed the landlord if they ever received a sub-standard pint of Boddingtons, after the take-over, drinkers were blaming Whitbread.

Local media attention fuelled these concerns.

> "Mr Boddies – They don't give a damn!"

> "Brew shock at Boddies"

> "Heaven preserve our Boddies!"

> "Boddy's £54m sell-out deal"

> "Sack the board call on Boddington's sell-out"
>
> Headlines from *Manchester Evening News*

Boddingtons could expect to be under growing competitive pressure in the North West from Tetley and John Smiths, as they continued to develop from their heartland, so preserving the credibility of the brand in Granada as it extended nationally was critical. Indeed competitive advertising spend in Granada had increased nearly 400% ahead of the national average between 1989 and 1991. (Source: Register -MEAL).

Swapping Profit for Distribution

The second danger for Boddingtons as it rolled out was to succumb to the inevitable pressure to trade on price to gain distribution.

With the five big brewers (with high fixed costs) competing for the very limited space on the bar, demand exceeds supply. In a rush for volume the temptation to discount is very high.

Boddingtons needed to preserve its value as it grew in volume in order to maximise Whitbread's profit.

So, to recap, the objectives were;

1. To grow Boddingtons Bitter outside its heartland region.
2. To preserve and protect the volume and appeal of the brand in the North West.
3. To gain distribution in a way that didn't compromise profit.
4. To launch Canned Boddingtons nationally.

Launch activity began at the start of 1991. The new canned product was launched in the March of that year. Advertising broke in July 1991.

The Marketing Strategy

Whitbread and BBH concluded that, in order to achieve these marketing objectives, the following three principles needed to govern the strategy;

—   the success of Boddingtons would depend on its strength as a brand;
—   the Boddingtons brand should always remain true to itself;
—   the growth of Boddingtons should be gradual and patient.

The tasks ahead all had one thing in common – *the brand*. By *focusing our attention on the brand* we could positively influence all those tasks.

To retain Boddingtons strong sense of heritage and integrity the brand should not be seen to have compromised after the take-over. Heartland drinkers needed to feel that their favourite pint hadn't changed. New drinkers in the rest of the country would then be presented with a truly authentic regional offering with a depth of credentials.

Gaining credentials is a process that is difficult to rush. Bitter drinkers enjoy a sense of discovery and 'ownership' of new brands. Their 'grass roots' acceptance is valuable. This had implications for targeting. Instant awareness and ubiquity, in pursuit of short-term volume, could actually be harmful.

Target Audience

The target for Boddingtons was defined as much by attitude as by behaviour. We developed a targeting hierarchy along an axis of drinking discernment:

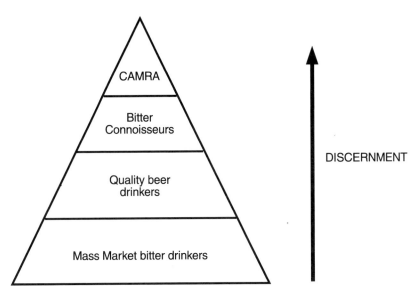

Figure 2. *Boddington's targeting hierarchy*

To build the credentials of Boddingtons outside its heartland, we initially targeted those towards the top of the triangle, to gain acceptance first amongst those most difficult to impress. Only when credentials had been established would we gradually move to the wider audience.

The Advertising Strategy

Advertising had an important role to play in developing and nurturing the brand.

To preserve the integrity of Boddingtons, the strategy was born from going back to the brand's heartland and discovering its *inherent strengths* amongst those who knew it best; the 'brand truths'.

Research revealed that Boddingtons possessed both product truths and image truths.

The *product truths* about Boddingtons are that it is creamy-looking when poured and that it settles into a clear, golden-coloured pint with a thick white head on the beer. At 3.8% ABV (alcohol by volume) Boddingtons is smooth and refreshing making it ideal for 'long-haul' drinking.

> "Boddingtons was felt to have a distinctive taste and to be particularly smooth, palatable and easy to drink".
>
> Source: Summary, Qualitative Research SRG 1991

The *image truths* about Boddingtons are essentially Mancunian in character: solid, straight-talking, irreverent, urban, contemporary.

> "It's a decent pint with no pretentions. Your 'Boddies Man' is a regular bloke with a good sense of humour"
>
> "No flies on 'Boddies'."
>
> Source: Boddingtons Drinkers, Manchester. Qualitative Research 2CV 1991

We decided to primarily focus on the product truths about Boddingtons. (This is in tune with the way bitter drinkers feel about their drink – product first, image second.)

The advertising could therefore be described as following a path of *product-led brand building*.

Of all the product truths we felt that the most important truth was that of *smoothness*.

The way we decided to execute smoothness was in line with the personality of the brand – straightforward and contemporary.

This approach broke with the conventions of bitter advertising at the time.

Advertising for bitter brands had predominantly focused on the user, rather than the product (Arkwright, Chas 'n' Dave, Tetley Bittermen etc). Indeed, previous advertising for Boddingtons in Granada had used Frankie Howerd.

The use of regional stereotyping was also prevalent. Advertising could easily have followed this convention given its Manchester roots.

The bitter brands which had avoided talking about user values were largely using brewing and ingredients stories to elevate perceptions of their product. Pictures of oats and hops abounded. Boddingtons also avoided this potentially prosaic solution.

By remaining true to the brand, we managed to steer our way past these over-familiar creative routes to a more unorthodox creative brief; one linking product appearance with product delivery.

Boddingtons Creative Brief

1. **Why are we advertising?**
   — To position Boddingtons as a quality pint without putting the brand on a pedestal.
   — To thereby confirm the brand's standing in the North West and to build its reputation outside its homeland.

2. **Who are we talking to?**
   — North Westerners for whom Boddingtons is part of the local fabric. They are very proud of the brand and will be nervous that by going national the brand is 'selling out'.
   — Premium beer drinkers who will drink from a range of quality products. They will be impressed by brands of heritage, although they won't necessarily be beer bores. They see themselves as unpretentious ordinary blokes. They have probably heard of Boddingtons but have no real knowledge of it.

3. **What must the advertising say?**
   — Boddingtons is the ultimate smooth-drinking pint.

4. **And why should the consumer believe it?**
   — Boddingtons is creamy pouring, settles out into a light clear golden colour with a tight creamy head.

5. **What tone of voice?**
   — Mancunian

— Pride in the product's quality and distinctiveness should be central, however, this should be done in an accessible, humorous and unpretentious way. Avoid the tone of the beer bore.

The Strategic Insight

It is worth pausing here to consider how different this creative brief could have been if we had decided upon an alternative strategy.

Qualitative research amongst bitter drinkers outside Granada cast some doubt on the potential of the Boddingtons product to become the focus for the brand.

"I must admit, I don't like the colour at all. Looks too wishy washy for a bitter"

Bitter drinker, London

"If you didn't know what he was drinking you'd think he was drinking lager"

Bitter drinker, Sheffield

"It annoys me when I've been given a pint and its half an inch from the top and its full of bubbles. I am paying for something and not getting it"

Bitter drinker, Devon

"The head afterwards gives you the impression it was a keg."

Bitter drinker, Sheffield

This was the pivotal moment in the development of the brand and its advertising. We believed that it was crucial to remain true to the brand, notwithstanding the research. Our perspective on managing the brand – in a careful, controlled way, preserving its integrity – left us in no doubt.

Media Strategy

In 1990, £100m was spent on advertising some 144 brands of beer. In this crowded marketplace most of the brands were following a similar media strategy, building awareness and trial as quickly as possible, and sustaining a mass presence. Television and posters dominated.

This conventional strategy contradicted Boddingtons strategy of gradual growth. Television, in particular, was felt to be too 'broadcast'.

Despite television's importance in launching beer brands – instilling trade confidence and driving distribution – it was rejected as the main medium for advertising.

In order that the media strategy contributed to the brand strategy, it had to be able to efficiently reach our more discreet target audience without over-exposure.

The requirement was for a measured approach.

The resolution of these strategic requirements was a tightly targeted press campaign. Weekend supplements (eg Guardian Review) allowed us to reach our prospects at the most appropriate time; relaxed moments eg before they went out for a lunchtime drink. Specialist titles (eg Punch, Economist) allowed us to reinforce the credibility of the brand for our discerning audience.

The advertising consistently appeared on the outside back covers of magazines. Historically, these positions had always been the province of cigarettes and book clubs.

Outside back covers were strategically right for Boddingtons as the advertising could be more visible without appearing desperate to be seen, in line with our marketing approach.

The single-minded use of this position has built a valuable media property for the brand in a very crowded market. Our sheer dominance has built this media franchise to the exclusion of other brands.

National television was added only after nearly two years in press. (The heartland region, Granada, received TV support earlier given its familiarity with the brand.) Even then, the strategy of controlled exposure meant that the TV executions were only rolled out gradually, letting different parts of the country see more of the brand. Today, Boddingtons TV advertising only appears nationally on Channel 4.

This strategy was not only unconventional in its choice of media, but in its *weight* of media activity. In 1991, Boddingtons spent £1.8m on advertising. That represented only 55% of John Smiths' spend in that year and only 60% of Stones' expenditure (source: Register-MEAL) In subsequent years Boddingtons gradually increased its spend in line with our overall approach.

TABLE 1: BODDINGTONS MEDIA SPEND

Year	Media Spend
1991	£1,836,000
1992	£2,365,000
1993	£4,497,000

Source: Register-MEAL

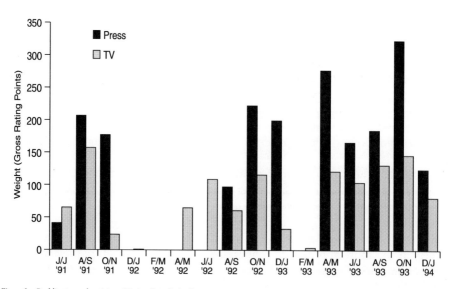

Figure 3. *Boddingtons advertising – National media laydown*
Source: Register-MEAL

The Advertising

In developing the advertising we felt that creaminess was the best evocation of smoothness. It had significant creative potential.

Other images that we explored, often expressing the negative of smoothness (eg sandpaper), we felt were not right.

All the executions in the campaign are of cream analogies. The press executes these in a simple, contemporary way. The television executions allowed us to wrap more of the Mancunian personality (image truths) around the core product thought of creaminess.

The advertising began in July 1991.

BODDINGTONS ACHIEVEMENTS SINCE 1991

Boddingtons has achieved some exceptional levels of overall growth and popularity over the past three years. Since acquisition the entire brand has grown three-fold. It it is now the UK's 4th largest bitter brand.

This success has been shared by both Boddingtons Bitter and Canned Boddingtons, though Boddingtons Bitter, accounting for 80% of total volume, is by far the more dominant offering.

Since 1991 we have been measuring the performance of Boddingtons in several ways – penetration, usage, awareness, image, and of course sales. (No competitive sales data are available for the on-trade since Whitbread is unconvinced of the reliability of the current source for this and do not buy it.)

This part of the paper will describe in detail how the two products have fared across these dimensions, sometimes indexed for confidentiality .

It is important to take into account the regional differences in this analysis (Granada vs national excluding Granada). We will look at the following in turn:

— Boddingtons Bitter nationally excluding Granada.
— Boddingtons Bitter in Granada.
— Canned Boddingtons nationally.

Boddingtons Bitter Nationally Excluding Granada

The task here was to grow volume outside Granada from a small base. The table below shows how awareness and claimed drinking have improved over the period May/June 1991 (pre-advertising) to December 1993. The figures in brackets represent a ranking vs the competition on these dimensions.

TABLE 2: AWARENESS AND CLAIMED DRINKING OF BODDINGTONS BITTER
Nationally Excluding Granada

	May/June 1991 Base = 547	Dec 1993 Base = 263
Spontaneous awareness	13 (8th)	34 (3rd)
Total awareness	77 (7th)	93 (4th)
Drunk at all (ever drunk)	11 (7th)	79 (4th)
Drunk most often	4 (8th)	14 (3rd)

Base: Bitter drinkers. Base sizes have varied over the years due to a requirement to manage research costs as the brand expanded.
Source: MRSL

SOME OF THE BODDINGTONS PRESS ADS

'FACE CREAM'

SOUND: *Music to end*   FEMALE: Soft, smooth, …

… luxurious …   … sensation of …   … pure cream.

MALE: By 'eck, you smell georgeous tonight petal.

FEMALE: Pamper yourself with Boddingtons …   … the cream of Manchester.

Boddingtons Bitter is now a famous brand. Almost everybody (93%) has heard of it. It rubs shoulders with the established big brands, John Smiths and Tetley.

Penetration of Boddingtons has increased sevenfold but perhaps more significant is the increase in claimed 'most often' drinking, an increasing degree of loyalty to the brand.

These increases in claimed drinking are reflected in the actual sales for Boddingtons Bitter.

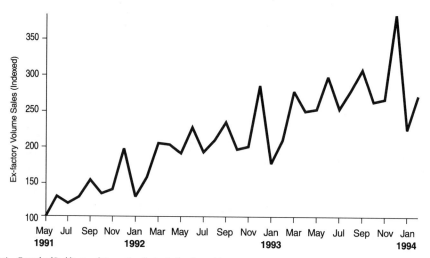

Figure 4. *Growth of Boddingtons bitter nationally (excluding Granada)*
Source: Whitbread Marketing Information

Sales are now three times as high as at the beginning of the period (though obviously from a small base).

This growth outside Granada has changed the regional profile of Boddingtons Bitter.

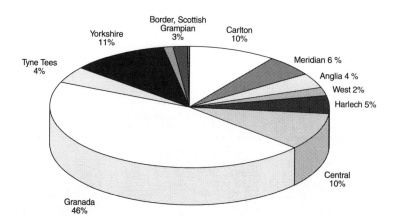

Figure 5. *Regional profile of Boddingtons sales – April 1994*
Source: Whitbread Marketing Information

Granada now accounts for less than half of all sales compared to 79% in 1991. There is now a significant presence in nearly all regions. After only three years, Boddingtons can now be fairly described as a national brand.

Boddingtons Bitter in Granada

The task in this region was one of maintenance. Already the brand leader in Granada Boddingtons needed to defend that position. Table 3 shows how awareness and claimed drinking have changed over the period.

TABLE 3: AWARENESS AND CLAIMED DRINKING OF BODDINGTONS BITTER IN GRANADA

	March 1991 Base = 174 %	Dec 1993 Base = 147 %
Spontaneous awareness	65 (1st)	72 (1st)
Total awareness	96 (1st)	100 (1st)
Drunk at all (ever tried)	57 (1st)	*69 (1st)
Drunk most often	31 (1st)	40 (1st)

Base: Bitter Drinkers
Note: * Probably interpreted as 'drink nowadays' in Granada as, of course, almost everyone will have tried it.
Source: MRSL

As one would expect, the movements are less dramatic than in the rest of the country because the brand is more familiar. Indeed, it would not have been unreasonable for the scores to have remained the same or even declined as the brand moved beyond Granada and competitive activity continued in the region. However, the brand has become more salient than before and has renewed the interest of some drinkers.

Again, the increase in 'most often' drinking suggests that, if anything, the bond between the brand and the drinker in its heartland has been strengthened.

Sales of Boddingtons Bitter in Granada have remained stable.

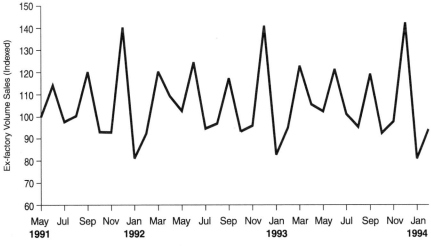

Figure 6. *Boddingtons bitter ex-factory indexed sales volume in Granada*
Source: Whitbread Marketing Information

Just as sales of a new product have nowhere to go but up, sales of a brand leader in its heartland region perhaps have nowhere to go but down! Given concerns of disenfranchising the loyal drinkers and the competitive threat from other brands we were heartened by this performance. (Indeed later in the paper we will see that, in certain accounts, Boddingtons Bitter has increased its share of the cask bitter market.)

Canned Boddingtons

This was a national new product launch in March 1991. At that time only Guinness Bitter employed a similar in-can system. By 1993 most of the big brands had entered this market with similar systems.

Table 4 shows awareness and claimed drinking.

TABLE 4: AWARENESS AND CLAIMED DRINKING OF CANNED BODDINGTONS

	June 1991 Base = 643 %	Nov 1993 Base = 301 %
Spontaneous awareness	15 (2nd)	49 (1st)
Prompted awareness	31 (5th)	61 (2nd)
Drunk nowadays	13 (3rd)	48 (1st)

Base: Bitter drinkers
Source: MRSL

Canned Boddingtons has been the most famous can of draught bitter for the last two years. (Only John Smiths heavyweight 'widget' advertising at its launch in late '93 has pushed that brand's prompted awareness ahead of Boddingtons, by 4% in the short term).

Nearly half the sample claim to drink Canned Boddingtons nowadays. This is the highest level of claimed drinking for any brand (the next nearest scores 36%).

Consumer sales of the can shows the extent of its success.

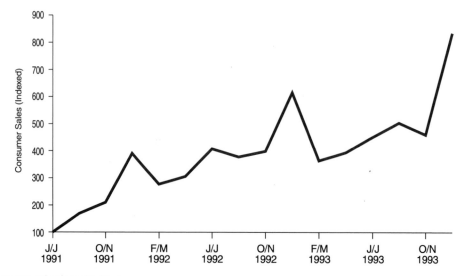

Figure 7. *Sales of canned Boddingtons*
Source: Stats MR

Canned Boddingtons is now the brand leader with a value share of 13.7%.

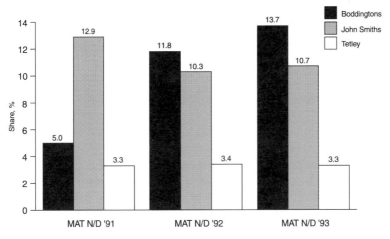

Figure 8. *Brand shares of total canned bitter*
Source: Stats MR

THE CONTRIBUTION OF ADVERTISING

Many factors have played a part in the success of Boddingtons, yet there is clear evidence that advertising was particularly important.

In presenting that evidence, the contribution of advertising to Boddingtons Bitter will again be treated separately from its contribution to sales of Canned Boddingtons.

Advertising's Contribution to Boddingtons Bitter

Increased Sales

Boddingtons Bitter is currently available in nearly 7,000 accounts. This figure has nearly doubled in three years.

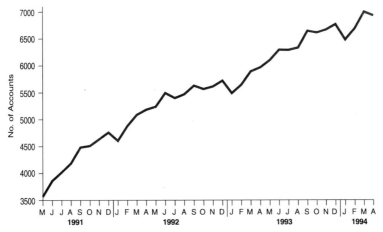

Figure 9. *Growth in distribution of Boddingtons bitter*
Source: Whitbread Marketing Information

These distribution gains have been vitally important for the growth of Boddingtons outside Granada of course.

Eliminating the effects of distribution in this market is a notoriously difficult task. Pubs aren't shops and the traditional FMCG measure of rate of sale (sales/sterling weighted distribution) needs to be viewed with some caution here. The reasons for this are;

— There is no accepted standard measure of sterling weighted distribution in this market.
— Gross distribution of bitter brands can and do fluctuate wildly month by month (a net increase of, say, 50 accounts can mask much greater losses and gains of accounts because of short-term showcasing of brands).
— Where a brand is used as a 'guest beer' (available for only a short period) in a pub its volume will never be as high as when on the bar full-time. Different qualities of distribution would need to be assigned to take this into account. No analysis of this kind exists.

We recognised, therefore, that simply dividing sales by the number of accounts that Boddingtons Bitter appears in to get a rate of sale figure could be misleading. We developed a different approach to eliminating the effects of distribution.

Boddingtons Bitter Core Account Analysis

We have used in our analysis an unchanging base of 'core accounts'. A 'core account' is defined as one which has bought Boddingtons from Whitbread every month for the past three years and sold it freely onto consumers. Distribution becomes a constant and we can then examine how sales or 'thruputs' have changed over time in these pubs. This approach also eliminates the sales uplift that a new beer gets in a pub simply because it is novel. We start our analysis at the earliest period the data allows – March 1991.

We isolated a 'core' containing 959 accounts. This represents 14% of all Boddingtons distribution. It also represents every channel of trade (Whitbread Inns, Whitbread Pub Partnership, Independents, Multiples, Retail and Leisure).

The core was split between Granada (399 accounts) and the rest of the country (560 accounts). Every region is represented.

The monthly sales of Boddingtons to these accounts was recorded along with the total sales of cask bitter from which Boddingtons' share could be calculated.

Nationally excluding Granada

Figure 9 shows how Boddingtons share of cask ale has increased in these core accounts.

As can be seen, in Figure 10, Boddington Bitter has grown its share from 51% to 66% of all the cask ales sold to these core accounts.

In Granada

The same analysis has been done in Granada (see Figure 11).

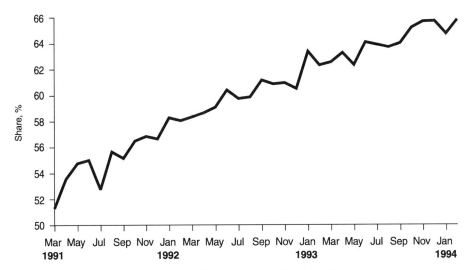

Figure 10. *Boddingtons bitter share of total core account cask bitter market nationally excluding Granada*
Source: Whitbread Marketing Information

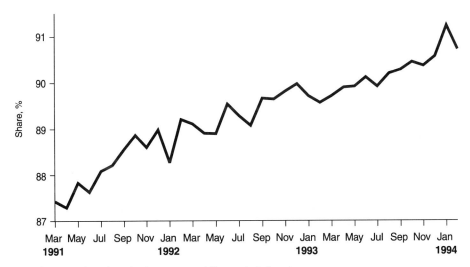

Figure 11. *Boddingtons bitter share of total core account cask bitter market in Granada*
Source: Whitbread Marketing Information

Boddingtons share has grown from 87% to 91%. This growth is happening in the core accounts where nearly all cask ale drunk is Boddingtons Bitter anyway. There is not much 'headroom' left.

Discounting Other Factors

The reasons to believe that the advertising is responsible for the growth in share that we have shown is that the growth occurred since the advertising was on air and no other factors can explain this growth. (Remember also that sales of Boddingtons were in decline when Whitbread acquired the brewery.)

We can discount the other factors which might have caused this growth.

Distribution

This is constant in our core account analysis.

Product

The product did not change.

Market

This is taken out of the equation by using market share.

Price

Not only is there no evidence of price cutting, Boddingtons has actually increased its price.

Seasonality

This is taken into consideration by using share data.

Promotions

There was some small-scale point of sale material in April 1993 and also a framed Boddingtons poster for the trade. We do not consider these activities could have affected sales to any great degree.

Advertising's Contribution to Canned Boddingtons

Canned Boddingtons was launched in March 1991. It sold at a 46% premium over ordinary canned bitters. It quickly gained distribution. As shown previously, it has grown considerably since June/July 1991.

An analysis of rate of sale shows that not all the growth came from distribution growth (see Figure 12).

To quantify the sales effect of advertising within this rate of sale growth we undertook a simple regression analysis of that rate of sale from which the volume implication could be calculated.

A common-sense approach led us to choose four key explanatory variables – price, seasonality, competitive advertising and Boddingtons advertising.

Figure 13 shows how closely our regression equation fits the actual data. The degree of fit, coupled with the battery of statistical diagnostic tests gave us confidence in the values we assigned to those variables.

We were now in a position to understand how each variable affected Boddingtons rate of sale growth. We could assign to any given variable the value 0 and see how rate of sale *would* have been affected without that variable.

Using this method we could see what rate of sale *would have been if there had been no advertising for Canned Boddingtons*. The rate of sale would then only be driven by price, seasonality and competitive advertising (see Figure 14).

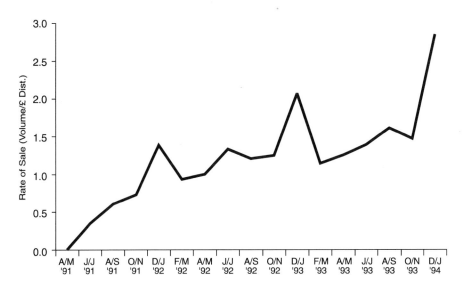

Figure 12. *Canned boddingtons rate of sale*
Source: Stats MR

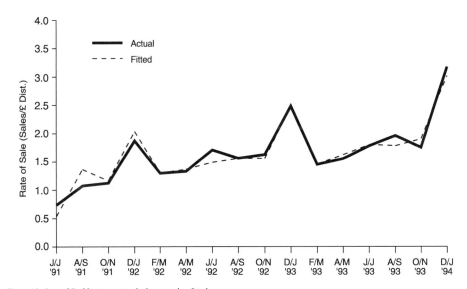

Figure 13. *Canned Boddingtons rate of sale – actual vs fitted*
Source: Stats MR

The difference between the two lines represents advertising's contribution to rate of sale (see Figure 15).

To convert this contribution into volume sales we simply need to multiply rate of sale by distribution.

As we can see, volume as a result of advertising has been increasing. In the latest period (D/J '94) advertising was responsible for increasing sales by over 8000 barrels.

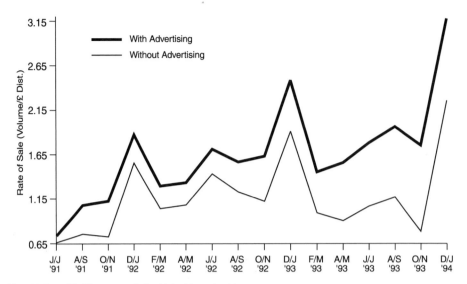

Figure 14. *Canned Boddingtons rate of sale with & without advertising*
Source: Stats MR

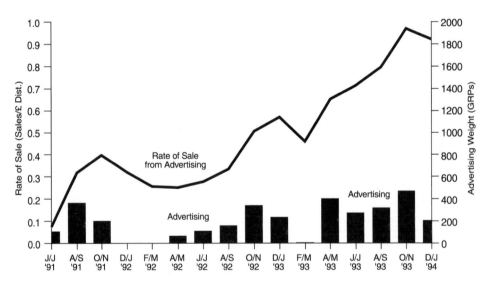

Figure 15. *Advertising's contribution to canned Boddingtons rate of sale*
Source: Stats MR, Media Register

Summing the volume contributed by the advertising for every period, we reach the total volume of Canned Boddingtons that the advertising has contributed; 62,618 barrels.

However, the effect of the advertising does not cease at this last data point. Not because we continued advertising after that period (even though we did) but because there would be residual effect from the advertising up to that period (adstock).

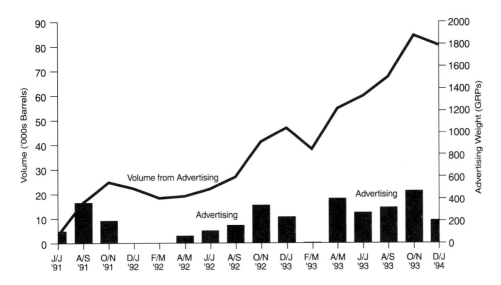

Figure 16. *Advertising's contribution to canned Boddingtons volume*
Source: Stats MR, Register-MEAL

We can measure adstock in our analysis and determine the rate of decay. This allows us to add the sales effect of that adstock to our existing sales effect.

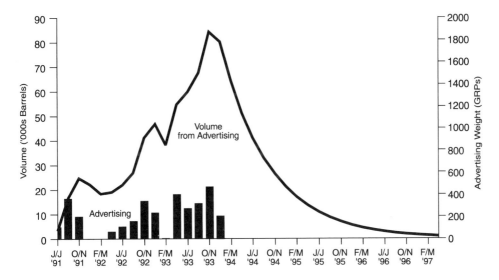

Figure 17. *Advertising's contribution to canned Boddingtons volume (including effects of adstock)*
Source: Stats MR

The area under the line, 'volume from advertising', represents the total contribution of the campaign to sales of Canned Boddingtons. This area is equal to 62,618 barrels until the last data point and 94,341 barrels including the adstock effect.

Discounting Other Factors

Our analysis has already discounted distribution, price, competitive advertising and seasonality.

We need to discount any other factors that could have affected Canned Boddingtons rate of sale.

Product

The current canned Boddingtons product uses the new 'Draughtflow' technology to create a superior product to 'ordinary' cans of bitter. However, Whitbread do still sell their previous Boddingtons product in a can, albeit in much smaller quantities. This can does not employ the Draughtflow system.

Sales of the 'old' can have been concentrated in Granada. However, since the launch of the Draughtflow can, the 'old' can has gained modest distribution outside that region.

It is effectively a parallel launch to that of the Draughtflow can except on a much smaller scale.

An analysis of the rate of sale of the old can reveals that it is also growing.

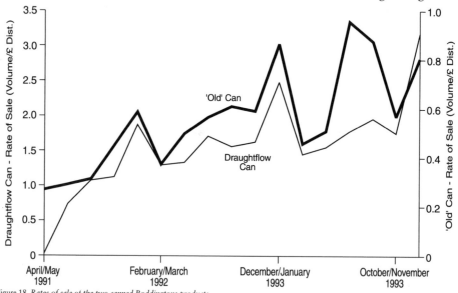

Figure 18. *Rates of sale of the two canned Boddingtons products*
Source: Stats MR

This figure shows how the rates of sale of the Boddingtons Draughtflow can and the 'old' can are both growing. Indeed, their rates of growth appear to be remarkably similar. An analysis of these rates of growth reveals that they are highly correlated (at a level of 0.79).

This suggests that there is a *common cause* for both these growth rates. That cause cannot, by definition, be the Draughtflow technology which does not exist in the old can.

We believe the common cause is the advertising.

Promotional Activity

Boddingtons Draught has been promoted below the line since launch. The majority of this activity has been money-off promotions. Sales effects from these promotions will have been taken into account within the price variable in our statistical analysis.

The remaining promotions took the form of free gifts (T-shirts, beer mats etc). Although the redemption figures for these promotions are well above average, the *scale of the redemptions* is not large enough to significantly affect the bi-monthly sales data of Boddingtons.

By way of example, in Oct/Nov 1993 there was a promotion that gave away free beer mats on 4-packs featuring photographs used in the advertising. This was deemed one of the most successful added-value promotions for the brand. In part it could be argued that this success was down to the success of the advertising. However, even if this weren't true, rate of sale for that bi-month does not clearly out-perform rate of sale for the identical periods in 1992 or 1991. This suggests that although it may have been a successful promotion its effect on rate of sale was not large enough relative to the total to make a significant difference.

Given that this promotion was the most successful for Boddingtons, the other added-value promotions would have had a smaller effect on total rate of sale.

Therefore, promotions (either added value of money-off) have either been taken into account in our analysis or have been too small to have had a significant overall effect.

The Market

The total canned bitter market has shown some modest growth, some of which will be the result of Boddingtons increasing popularity. We do not believe this will have significantly benefitted the brand, or should alter our analysis.

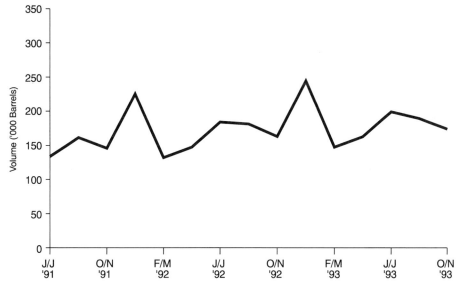

Figure 19. *Total canned bitter market*
Source: Stats MR

HOW THE ADVERTISING WORKED

One of the strengths of the campaign has been its memorability. Awareness of the advertising is testimony to that.

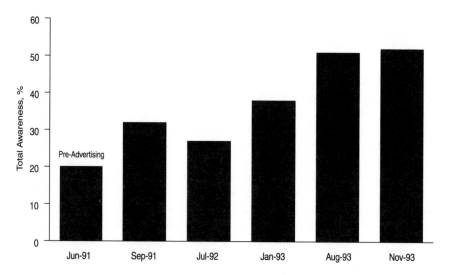

Figure 20. *Boddingtons advertising awareness – National*
Base: Bitter drinkers
Source: MRSL

Awareness is not the sole reason for advertising's ability to drive sales. We believe the most important factor has been its ability to build and fortify the brand.

We have been measuring various dimensions of the brand over time. Some of the dimensions have been tracked since before the advertising (Pre) and some have been added later (Mid 1 and Mid 2). The Post score refers to the latest period available – November 1993.

The brand has fared as follows:

TABLE 5: PERCEPTIONS OF BODDINGTONS NATIONALLY
Base: Bitter Drinkers

	% Agreeing	
	Pre Base = 643	**Post** Base = 301
A pint with a creamy head	19 (2nd)	49 (1st)
Brands liked best	6 (2nd)	18 (1st)
Has good advertising	7 (4th)	39 (2nd)
	Mid 1 (1991) Base = 503	**Post** Base = 301
A smooth pint	22 (2nd)	31 (1st)
Very good quality	30 (1st)	35 (1st)
	Mid 2 (1992) Base = 324	**Post** Base = 301
A pint with a clear golden colour	21 (2nd)	31 (1st)
A bitter from Manchester	41 (1st)	65 (1st)

Source: MRSL

The brand image of Boddingtons has improved across all the dimensions. It can now be reasonably considered the strongest brand of bitter in the country.

As can be seen, the desired positioning of the brand has been achieved. The product truths that were originally identified are now a strong part of the brand – 'creamy head', 'clear golden colour'. It is seen as a brand of high quality and a brand with 'roots' (Manchester). It has fast become the nation's favourite.

If we look at the brand in Granada, we can also examine whether we have managed to maintain our loyalty in this core region despite these national increases.

TABLE 6: PERCEPTIONS OF BODDINGTONS IN GRANADA
Base: Bitter Drinkers

	% Agreeing	
	Pre Base = 643	Post Base = 301
A pint with a creamy head	40 (1st)	68 (1st)
Brands liked best	21 (1st)	34 (1st)
Has good advertising	19 (3rd)	64 (1st)
A smooth pint	22 (1st)	51 (1st)
	Mid 1 (1991) Base = 400	Post Base = 301
Very good quality beer	47 (1st)	55 (1st)
A pint with a clear golden colour	45 (1st)	62 (1st)
A bitter from Manchester	71 (1st)	96 (1st)

Source: MRSL

Perceptions of Boddingtons have clearly improved, though one wouldn't have imagined there was much room for improvement.

It is significant that Boddingtons has a similar image in Granada compared with the rest of the country. The way drinkers feel about the brand in Granada is the way drinkers feel about it nationally.

We firmly believe that the advertising has played a significant role in building this brand. Evidence for this can be found if we compare perceptions of Boddingtons amongst those who drink the brand and have seen the advertising with those who drink the brand but haven't seen it across the core measures of 'creamy head' and 'smooth'. (It is important to use a consistent base of Boddingtons drinkers for this analysis.)

TABLE 7: ADVERTISING'S CONTRIBUTION TO THE BRAND IN GRANADA
Base: Boddingtons Drinkers in Granada

				% Agreeing
	Aware of the Advertising		Unaware of the Advertising	
	Pre*	1993	Pre*	1993
	Base = 105	Base = 236	Base = 18	Base = 61
A pint with a creamy head	42	77	50	48
	Base = 259	Base = 179	Base = 36	Base = 48
A smooth pint	34	58	39	38

* These people are aware of the previous advertising for Boddingtons featuring
   Frankie Howerd.
Source: MRSL

TABLE 8: ADVERTISING'S CONTRIBUTION TO THE BRAND NATIONALLY EXCLUDING GRANADA
Base: Boddingtons Drinkers Nationally excluding Granada

	Pre	Post, 1993	
		Aware of the Advertising	Unaware of the Advertising
A pint with a creamy head	Base = 54 35	Base = 171 68	Base = 65 35
A smooth pint	Base = 32 29	Base = 107 43	Base = 46 25

Source: MRSL

Amongst those people who have seen the advertising there is a more widespread perception that it is a pint with a creamy head and that it is smooth.

Given that the advertising was intended to communicate these core product truths, it is clear that the advertising has played a part in building the brand.

Indeed, we believe that the brand and its advertising are now inextricably linked. When people see the brand they are seeing it through the 'window' of the advertising. That window highlights the product truths about Boddingtons.

THE BENEFITS OF ADVERTISING

Second-Order Effects of Advertising

We believe that the advertising has not only had an effect on sales volume. There is significant evidence to suggest that there are layers of second-order effects beyond volume.

Price

The average price of a pint of Boddingtons has steadily risen since the advertising began in 1991. This rise has been in excess of the competition. Boddingtons was cheaper than the average in September 1991 and has gradually increased its price until in December 1993 it was nearly 12 pence a pint more expensive on a national basis (see Figure 21).

Part of this rise in price will be due to the brand moving into more expensive areas. However, this does not account for all of the increase as the price increases *within* some regions (see Figures 22 & 23).

Consumers are willing to accept these increases for Boddingtons otherwise we would not see the growth we have. Moreover, they actually see it as good value. (see Figure 24).

This perception of value cannot be the result of Boddingtons being a better product than the competition. Boddingtons does not outperform competitive products when they are tested unbranded (see Figure 25).

Indeed, as a weaker beer than the competition (3.8% ABV) one might expect that the brand would find it difficult to sustain any price premium. Strength and price normally go hand in hand in this market.

Boddingtons remains good value for consumers because of the added-value that the brand and the advertising bring.

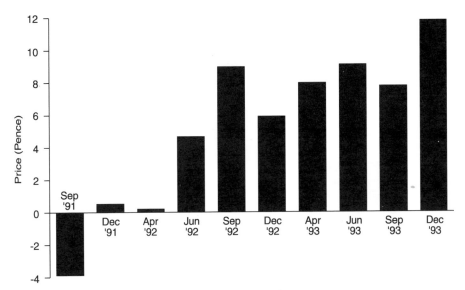

Figure 21. *Cask Boddingtons price relative to major competitors (John Smiths, Tetley, Stones)*
Source: NEMS

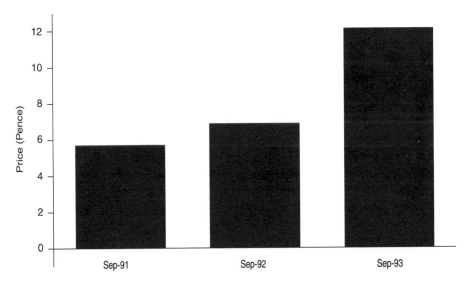

Figure 22. *Boddingtons bitter relative price – Northern Region*
Source: NEMS

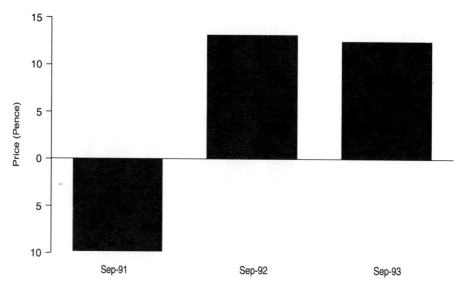

Figure 23. *Boddingtons bitter relative price – Southern Region*
Source: NEMS

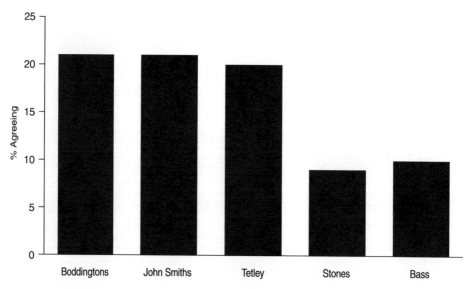

Figure 24. *'Good value for money'*
Source: MRSL November 1993

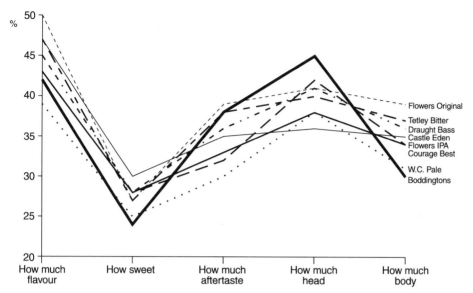

Figure 25. *Boddingtons cask product vs the competition*
Source: Martin Hamblin 1992

Distribution

The extent of a beer brand's strength can also be measured by looking at the type of distribution it has. The ability to penetrate the free trade (pubs that are not tied to a brewer) is a hard test to pass. The free-trade need only stock a brand if they can make a profit from it. Boddingtons Bitter has been very successful in this regard.

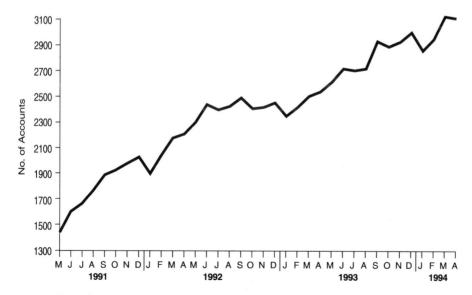

Figure 26. *Boddingtons bitter free trade distribution growth*
Source: Whitbread Marketing Information

Advertising has helped the brand gain extra distribution directly through its ability to drive volume and value, as we have shown earlier. However, the advertising also plays a role in actual trade negotiations.

Interviews with Whitbread's free trade salesmen have highlighted this role.

"The advertising has definitely smoothed the path for the brand."

Account Director, South East

"The ads have been successful in focusing our customers (free trade publicans) view on Boddingtons"

Account Director, North East

"The ads are an integral part of the package."

"They are a great pre-emptive discussion-point, at least half of the new accounts mention the ads... customers often lead in with them"

Salesman, East Midlands

Corporate/City

Whitbread has benefitted corporately from the success of Boddingtons and its advertising.

Miles Templeman, Managing Director of the Whitbread Beer company, speaks about the campaign in the following way;

"If I look within the Whitbread Beer Company there is no doubt in my mind that the advertising campaign has played a fundamental role in the success of the brand (in conjunction with the Draughtflow introduction.) It has provided us with a spearhead for our whole branded business."

"We have tried to differentiate ourselves from other brewers by our ability to build premium brands and Boddingtons has reinforced that story. Many people now believe that Whitbread are the best branded beer manufacturer."

"The City is very aware of the Boddingtons' advertising. Particularly because of the media selection. It now credits Whitbread even more with the ability to build strong brands. As a result our marketing pedigree has been notched up which is of value to the whole Plc."

"The Boddingtons advertising is perhaps the best 'corporate campaign' that Whitbread has ever had."

Peter Jarvis, Group Chief Executive, said of the advertising;

"It says as much about the professionalism of Whibread's management as the successful introduction of Pizza Hut and TGI Friday's to the UK."

Through-the-Line

The advertising has become so central to the brand that many elements of the marketing seem inseperable from it.

An example of this is how the below-the-line activity feeds off the advertising. Promotions, direct mail, point of sale no longer work in isolation from the advertising. They are a coordinated and integral part of the brand building process.

The advertising has provided a focus for all this activity. In short, the advertising property has become a part of the brand.

Publicity

The popularity of the advertising and the brand has prompted many column inches in the consumer and marketing press. Since 1991, Boddingtons has been mentioned in over 400 articles, some of which have been international.

PAYBACK

The contribution of advertising comes from both Boddingtons Bitter and Canned Boddingtons.

Advertising's Contribution to Boddingtons Bitter

If we average the first five data points that represent Boddingtons Bitter share of cask bitter in core accounts prior to the advertising, this represents a pre-measure. The extra share points occurring after this point represent advertising's contribution.

Multiplying the share gain for each period by the total size of the cask market in the core accounts for each corresponding period we reach a volume figure for advertising's contribution.

In Granada, the contribution is 2,731 barrels. For the rest of the country, the contribution is 8,640 barrels. Therefore the total contribution of advertising in core accounts is 11,361 barrels. This is equivalent to 6.1% of total Boddingtons Bitter in core accounts.

Outside core accounts, we strongly suspect that the volume uplift from advertising could be greater than in core accounts due to novelty and lack of knowledge of Boddingtons prior to the campaign. However, for the purposes of this paper, we shall assume that the uplift would be the same as in core accounts – 6.1%

6.1% of total Boddingtons Bitter sales in the country (both within and outside core accounts) over the 18 months of advertising is equal to 53,639 barrels.

Advertising's Contribution to Canned Boddingtons

Earlier it was explained how the advertising was responsible for an extra 62,618 barrels (excluding adstock) and 94,341 barrels (including adstock).

Total Contribution

Together the volume uplift of Boddingtons Bitter and Canned Boddingtons due to advertising is equal to 116,257 barrels (excluding adstock).

Cost of Advertising

Given that our choice of media for the campaign was predominantly press, we have produced a large number of executions over the period. It is also important, particularly for beer advertising, for the advertising to look good. Consequently, a significant amount of money has been spent on *production*.

It therefore seemed reasonable for us to include money spent on production in our costs.

Since July 1991 total media and production costs have come to £7.3m. (The Register-MEAL figures quoted earlier exaggerate the negotiated media spend.)

In order for the advertising to have recouped this cost given the volume uplift above, Whitbread would need to make a minimum average net profit on both products of £63 per barrel. We can confirm that Whitbread do achieve this minimum level of profit and more. Therefore, the advertising has at the very least paid for all the costs of creating and showing it.

This analysis of payback does not take into account any of the second order benefits of price and distribution that we described earlier and also omits the potential payback from adstock. We would estimate the contribution of these effects to be considerable.

CONCLUSIONS

We believe we have demonstrated the value of the Boddingtons advertising to Whitbread Beer Company. This value is not simply in terms of the advertising's ability to pay for itself in the short-term, although it has achieved that and more.

It is our conviction that the foundations for the long-term success of Boddingtons have been laid. By concentrating on building the brand with the greatest care and patience, and by avoiding the temptations of being conventional, Boddingtons has credentials that will surely endure. Perhaps even longer than Gladys Althorpe can resist buying 'er own! By 'eck!

7

Marston's Pedigree

How Victorian values strengthened a brand

INTRODUCTION

The campaign described here was developed primarily to build the Marston's Pedigree brand and, thus, grow profitable sales in the increasingly competitive cask bitter market. However, this case will not only document a revenue increase that has more than paid for the advertising, but also describe far more wide ranging effects on other aspects of Marston's business (see Figure 1). These additional benefits are important, particularly in the medium and long-term, though it is difficult to quantify their financial value.

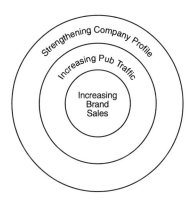

Figure 1. *The ripple effect of Marton's Pedigree advertising campaign*

It will be argued that both the effect directly on sales, and indirectly on the broader business, can be achieved only by advertising which gives stature and visibility to Marston's in a way that no other marketing support can.

Marston's is a Long Established Local Brewer

Marston's was established over 150 years ago and has operated predominantly in a small area in the East Midlands (approximately defined by the Leicester, Derby and Stoke postcodes). This area, referred to as the 'Heartland', contains 2% of the GB population, but has traditionally accounted for over 70% of Marston's Pedigree's total managed and tenanted trade volume. Marston's Pedigree is a premium, cask bitter (high gravity: 4.5% alcohol by volume) and is the brewer's largest volume

161

product. Well-known and respected in the 'Heartland', but a relatively unknown bitter elsewhere (albeit enjoying a cult status amongst the small minority of real ale fanatics), Marston's Pedigree had not been significantly advertised before: Marston's believing that word-of-mouth and point-of-sale were sufficient to maintain volumes in what were predominantly local areas of distribution.

Government Legislation was a Catalyst for Change

In the late 1980's the Government's Beer Orders were passed which attempted to loosen the tie of the big brewers and increase wider availability of different bitter brands to the consumer. For Marston's, this accelerated the process of reciprocal trading (in which one brewer takes a second brewer's brand in exchange for the second brewer taking a brand from the other) which was making Marston's Pedigree far more widely available than ever before. As the brand appeared in 'new' outlets and 'new' areas a few bitter afficiandos would relish it as a distinctive, respected bitter: however, to the majority of drinkers it would be relatively less well known, their attitudes to it might be less enthusiastic or indifferent. As a cask ale, Marston's Pedigree is 'live' and, thus, if its rate-of-sale is poor, the bitter's quality declines, consumers become even less enthusiastic about it and the publican decides to stop stocking it.

There was some qualitative evidence of this decline in Marston's Pedigree's quality from CAMRA (Campaign For Real Ale). Annually, their membership of many thousand submit appraisals on the cask bitters they drink in pubs. Throughout most of the 1980s the Good Beer Guide was unequivocal in its praise for Marston's Pedigree. However, in 1989 and the 1990s they were reporting declines in beer quality which were related to deterioration due to slow sell-through rates in pubs/areas in which Marston's Pedigree was newly appearing.

"...quality noted to be poorer in Whitbread outlets"

"A famous beer whose quality now varies enormously given its wider availability"

Good Beer Guide

At the same time, reciprocal trading meant that Pedigree was being put under pressure in Marston's own estate because the 'in-coming' products from its partners were popular, heavily supported brands. This would boost the traffic and sales in Marston's outlets, by giving their customers a wider choice of familiar brands, but it would, doubtless, lead to substitution of Pedigree for these newly arrived and popular brands.

The evidence of this pressure can be seen in the decline in Pedigree volumes in Marston's own channels of trade – particularly in tenanted and loan-tied outlets in which Marston's has a less strong control over stocking policy.

TABLE 1: VOLUMES OF PEDIGREE IN MARSTON'S ESTATE

	% Volume Change 1991 vs 1990
Marston's managed outlets	−7%
Marston's tenanted and loan-tied outlets	−25%

Source: Marston's

Investment was Needed to Maintain and Build Marston's Pedigree Volumes

Marston's Pedigree was in danger of being hit by a double whammy!

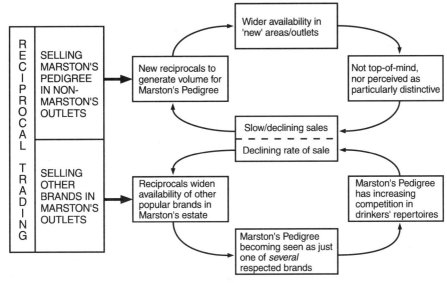

Figure 2. *The potential impact of the new trading environment on Marston's Pedigree*

In this situation, it was critical to maintain or strengthen the brand in order to retain it's place in consumers' repertoires (in its traditional areas/outlets) *and* to establish, or increase, its presence in drinkers' repertoires in its 'new' areas. In simple terms, as consumers were being faced with increasing choice, the *brand had to be more top-of-mind and seen as more distinctive and preferable.* Maintaining the status quo would simply worsen the decline.

Building a Successful Brand in the Premium Cask Bitter Sector

Premium cask bitters are generally local or regional whose recognition and reputations are established by word-of-mouth. None was widely seen as being better than any other as the market was relatively fragmented. In contrast to the far more 'developed' standard bitter or lager market, the premium cask bitter sector was characterised by a variety of 'embryonic' brands which were seen as simply just different and preferable amongst a minority who were closely involved with them.

To build a successful brand the challenge was to 'lift' Marston's Pedigree above these other brands and adopt the vacant 'high ground' for the sector as the definitive premium cask bitter. Marston's Pedigree had excellent credentials to occupy this 'high ground' and, it's reputation as a bitter amongst those who knew it was as one (of many) strong, satisfying taste but highly drinkable, as opposed to many premium gravity bitters that were seen as heavy, dark and not as drinkable.

Figure 3. *Consumer perception map of premium bitters: The opportunity for Marston's Pedigree*

THE IMPORTANCE OF ADVERTISING

There was a need for highly sensitive brand building to avoid any perceived 'sell out': reputations are earned not invented. Over the years, word-of-mouth had made Marston's Pedigree a distinctive, albeit embryonic brand. It was important to *manage* word-of-mouth to protect Marston's Pedigree's integrity and *accelerate* it to build its reputation for those less familiar with it.

In an ideal world 'public relations' might have been a candidate medium: in practice, however, it would be slow, too narrowly targeted at the beer aficionado, almost impossible to implement regionally and difficult to control over time. Direct marketing could have had a role to stimulate short-term trial/re-trial but would have been unable to build a brand long-term. Point-of-sale could act as a reminder but it is a low impact medium that the retailer, not the brewer, controls.

Advertising was the most appropriate lead communication medium to help build the brand. It could be accurately targeted in consumer and regional terms, it could add stature to the brand and, if executed sensitively, could 'nourish' Marston's Pedigree's reputation.

The Role For Advertising

The overall marketing task of maintaining and strengthening Marston's Pedigree's place on consumers' beer repertoires required advertising to make it *more prominent* and *more distinctive* in consumers' minds.

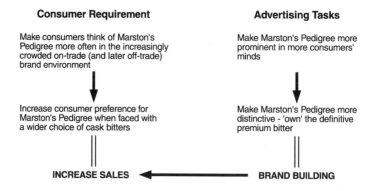

Figure 4. *The role for advertising*

Given the enormous significance to Marston's of making this first commitment to invest significantly behind Pedigree, the agency went to great lengths not only to understand the premium cask drinker and the bitter advertising environment but also to understand the culture, attitudes and ambitions of Marston's the company. Two key areas of learning arose from this research which helped drive creative development.

1. To position Marston's Pedigree on the 'high ground' as the definitive premium bitter it was essential to have 'high ground', but not high brow, advertising. Analysis of competitive bitter advertising 1989/1990 showed that most campaigns either tried to ape lager by portraying trendy lads telling jokes to each other in a bar (where the brand was almost incidental) or by dramatising the brand's regional roots to help strengthen local loyalty (relatively parochial). The advertising of Bass, the premium brand leader, adhered to the former formula. It revealed that there was a great opportunity to develop distinctive advertising that gave reverence to the brand (in tune with the discriminating bitter drinkers' interests) but in an approachable, entertaining way without being overly serious.

2. This competitive analysis identified that no brand campaigns were appropriating core generic values of quality cask ales. The opportunity to own such values was important for Marston's Pedigree: it reflected the long-term aspirations of Marston's for Pedigree to be perceived of the definitive premium cask ale and was in line with the warm perceptions of its drinkers. Furthermore, the agency were convinced that if Marston's Pedigree was the first to brand these values to itself it would make it more difficult for other campaigns to be as effective against consumers.

The Creative Brief

Role for Advertising
To position Marston's Pedigree as the definitive premium cask bitter.

Target Audience
Men, aged 25-45, who prefer cask bitters and have a wide repertoire of brands. They take an interest in what they are drinking, but are not connoisseurs or real ale buffs, neither are they 'session drinking lads'.

Proposition
Marston's Pedigree is a quality, traditionally brewed bitter.

Support
Marston's is unique in still using Burton Unions – a traditional brewing process. Marston's origins were in the mid 19th century, an important period for British brewing.

The Creative Work

Like much good advertising, the creative idea arose directly from the brand and the company. The creative idea was a 'celebration of the greatness of the Victorian era': this was initially dramatised via its famous people, famous inventions and discoveries. The 'highlight' of this era was John Marston, his brewery using Burton Unions and his pursuit of quality beer – the most acclaimed of which nowadays is Marston's Pedigree. In research, consumers had talked about great bitters having genuine history and tradition and were often wary of brands which had been launched or re-badged to jump on the real ale bandwagon. Thus, the campaign took the 'high ground' of quality traditional bitters, was tonally in keeping with the company's culture and would motivate a preference for Marston's Pedigree both emotionally (Victorian-period feel) and rationally (traditional Burton Unions).

Media Selection and Targeting

Television was the best lead advertising medium. It was proven to add stature to brands yet it could be used sensitively to avoid a 'blockbuster' campaign that would suggest Marston's Pedigree was 'selling out'. Television has good regional flexibility to match Marston's Pedigree's current, and future, availability and could be targeted precisely to reach our audience of the more discriminating bitter drinkers. In this respect the agency used qualitative research to understand the type of programmes that the target audience *preferred* to watch and would, doubtless, be more attentive to during the commercial breaks. This was matched with quantitative research which monitored actual viewing levels.

A Media Planning Conundrum – Reaching the BBC Viewer on ITV/C4!

Many of the target audience's preferred programmes are BBC1/BBC2 current affairs, documentaries, dramas and comedies. Innovative analysis was conducted to identify the viewing profiles of these BBC programmes and find the closest match in an ITV/C4 programme. Additionally, media experience was used to qualitatively pair ITV programmes with similar BBC programmes. This fresh media thinking provided a very accurately targeted media schedule that reached the target audience by quality programme selection rather than simply planning to reach fixed targets of weekly and/or demographic ratings. In effect, it gave Marston's a far more cost effective way of reaching its target audience than conventional media planning techniques.

The Media Plan

Rigorous analysis of brand volumes by postcode areas was conducted to priorise TV area selection. Overlaid on this was an analysis of the exact revenue and profit contribution of each barrel sold. These margins varied according to whether the barrel was sold via Marston's own estate or not, and if not, which other brewer's estate it was sold through. It was immediately clear that Central was the most important area (accounting for approximately 62% revenue) but within this it was possible to accurately priorise the East, West and South sub areas which could be

'TEAM PORTRAIT'

MVO: Remember when Britannia ruled the waves …
My! What a team we had then! Boots Wellington …
Chopper Dickens … Dangerous Darwin … Nobbler
Nightingale … Bomber Brunel …

John Marston …

JUDGE: Who?

CHOIR: Good old John Marston, a great Victorian
bloke.

He brought us Marston's the finest ale from casks of
oak brewed the Burton Union way up until the present
day…

… and Pedigree's his finest brew in all the land!

CROWD: Hurrah!

MVO: Thank heavens some things are what they used
to be.

bought separately at different weights as they had separate transmitters. The TV media schedule is outlined below.

Figure 5. *Marston's Pedigree brand TV plan (incl. approximate ABC1 men ratings)*

EVALUATING THE EFFECT OF THE MARSTON'S PEDIGREE CAMPAIGN

The effectiveness of the advertising can be evaluated in 3 principal ways: increasing prominence, volumes and profits for the *brand*, indications of increasing pub traffic for Marston's the *retailer* and strengthening the profile of Marston's as a *publicly quoted company*.

Advertising Effect on the Brand Marston's Pedigree

Campaign Cuts Through Competitive 'Clutter'

The impact of the advertising has been strong and immediate: this has been demonstrated by Millward Brown advertising research amongst cask bitter drinkers which has consisted of a series of 'dips' before and after each burst. After only two bursts, spontaneous awareness of Marston's Pedigree advertising was already higher than that of any other brand recorded over the six 'dips'. This was achieved with TV rating levels that meant it was only the fourth most advertised brand in the 18 months from September 1992, and in competition with brands that had consistently advertised for many years previously.

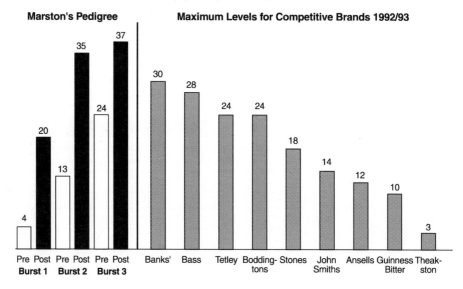

Figure 6. *Marston's Pedigree spontaneous advertising awareness compared with the competition*
Source: Millward Brown

The high level of residual awareness of the advertising, when not on air, is indicative of the 'extra value' that the company derives from the advertising extending its benefit for a considerable period beyond any individual burst.

Marston's Pedigree Becomes More Prominent In Bitter Drinkers' Minds

As more brands become available it is imperative to strengthen the prominence of Marston's Pedigree in consumer's minds. The extent to which Marston's can merchandise Pedigree in pubs is limited (controlled largely by the publican) so advertising is important. Spontaneous awareness of established cask brands tend to change only gradually so this measure is tracked less often. However, in both the Heartland and Non-Heartland areas of Central, spontaneous awareness of Marston's Pedigree has increased significantly, both in absolute terms and relative to a competitive set of premium bitter brands.

TABLE 2: SPONTANEOUS AWARENESS OF MARSTON'S PEDIGREE
In context of competitive premium brands

	Pre-Burst 1 %	Pre-Burst 2 %
Heartland		
Spontaneous awareness of Marston's Pedigree	48	59
Share of mentions of total premium bitters	40	44
Non-Heartland		
Spontaneous awareness of Marston's Pedigree	20	30
Share of mentions of total premium bitters	29	40

Source: Millward Brown

An Increasingly Favourable Consumer Image

The target audience has varied cask bitter repertoires. Reciprocal trading means that Marston's Pedigree has the *opportunity* to appear in more repertoires – however, it will only do so if consumers' attitudes to the brand are favourable. Several key brand perception measures are tracked. These image attributes were derived from qualitative research in which consumers used them to describe the premium brands that they respected and would prefer to drink if given the opportunity. Without exception, Marston's Pedigree's association with these attributes has strengthened both in absolute terms and relative to representative group of competitive premium brands. There has been limited PR which might have helped contribute to this improving perception – but it is judged that it is closely related to the improved prominence of the brand due to advertising (see Figure 7).

Marston's Pedigree as a Higher Quality Bitter

One of the most relevant barometers of consumer preference for a bitter has been found to be a brand's rating on a linear scale from being described as 'the best bitter' or 'one of the best bitters' through to being called 'average' or 'poor'. The more highly rated a brand the greater the likelihood the consumer will purchase

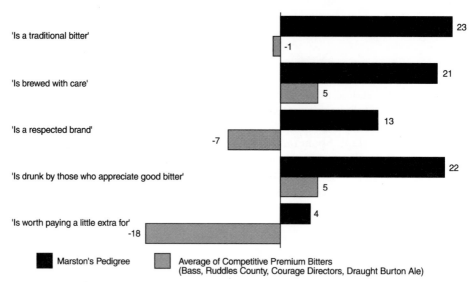

Figure 7. *Percentage change in Marston's Pedigree's and other premium bitters' image ratings, August 1992-November 1993*
Source: Millward Brown

that brand when offered the choice. This rating reflects the quality of the bitter itself as well as its perception.

Marston's Pedigree's rating in the top 2 (of 7) options (ie 'the best' or 'one of the best') in Non-Heartland has increased consistently since the advertising commenced whilst its main volume competitor (Bass) has remained constant. During this period there has been no changes to its recipe, nor in the methods of keeping and dispensing in pubs, so the improvement in perception must be related to the favourable impressions generated by the advertising.

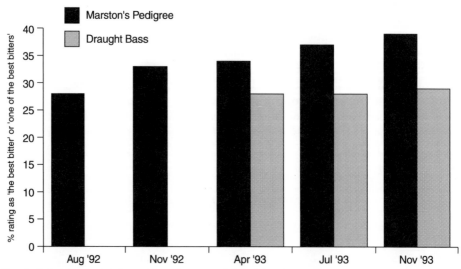

Figure 8. *Ratings of Marston's Pedigree and Bass as bitters in non-heartland (Central)*

In the Heartland, Marston's Pedigree has had an unassailable lead on this rating scale – 60%+ rate it as 'the best' or 'one of the best'. This score has remained consistent while that of Bass has fallen slightly.

Greater Inclusion In Bitter Drinkers' Repertoires

Marston's does not subscribe to on-trade consumer panel data so it is difficult to measure actual levels of repertoire inclusion. As a guide, however, the advertising research elicits brands drunk nowadays.

Over the first full year of the campaign Marston's Pedigree ranks as the top brand (alongside Boddingtons) in terms of the proportional increase in the number of consumers who claim that they drink that brand regularly nowadays (see Table 3). It is interesting to note, moreover, that if the brands are placed into three groups reflecting the changes in claimed regular drinking, the top group contains the highest proportion of advertised brands and the bottom group the lowest. This adds weight to the inference that advertising is positively correlated with consumer consumption and that Marston's Pedigree is among the most top performers in this respect.

TABLE 3: PROPORTIONAL CHANGE IN LEVEL OF CLAIMED REGULAR CONSUMPTION OF BITTERS
August 1992-July 1993

	% Change in Claimed consumption	Proportion of Brands advertised
'HIGHER THAN AVERAGE CHANGE'	Boddingtons (+12%) Marston's Pedigree (+12%) Courage Directors (+11%) John Smiths (+11%) Marston's Bitter (Burton Best Bitter) (+9%) Worthington Best (+6%) Tetley Bitter (+5%)	71%
'ABOUT AVERAGE CHANGE'	Draught Bass (–2%) Banks's Bitter (–5%) Theakston XB (–7%) Ansells (–10%) Flowers Original (–10%) Ruddles County (–13%)	50%
'LOWER THAN AVERAGE CHANGE'	Draught Burton Ale (–15%) Greene King IPA (–20%) Abbot (–22%) Stones Best (–23%) Ruddles Best (–23%) Everards Tiger (–27%) Davenports (–27%) Wadworth 6X (–29%) Websters (–29%) Courage Best (–30%)	20%

An important 'halo' effect of Marston's Pedigree advertising is the improved standing of their standard strength cask bitter (Marston's Bitter). During the period of the research there has been little direct investment specifically behind this brand that would account for this.

Sales Increase

It is clear that there has been an immediate, and building, sales increase for Marston's Pedigree related to the advertising. This section will document the extent of this increase and, subsequently, dispose of other significant explanations.

Marston's principal source of volume and market share data is the Beer Market Survey (BMS). In the year prior to advertising Marston's Pedigree's monthly sales in Central had been showing a gradual, largely consistent decline. After the advertising started, volumes showed large and consistent increases compared with the equivalent non-advertised months. These *short-term* gains have surprised Marston's as the expectation was for a *medium-term* response (imagining the brand to be relatively mature). However, these increases add weight to the argument that the on-trade bitter market is more open to consumer demand forces than it was prior to government legislation, so advertising can play an even more valuable role.

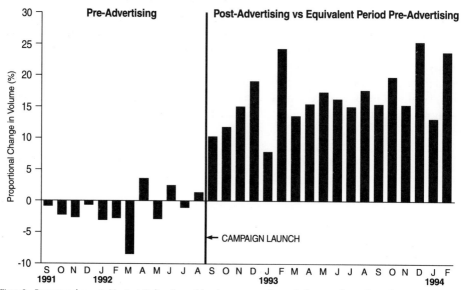

Figure 9.   *Percentage changes in Marston's Pedigree's monthly volumes compared to equivalent non-advertised period (Central)*
Note: *All changes expressed as percentages for reasons of confidentiality.*
Source: Beer Market Survey

These increases are far in excess of those shown by the recovery of cask bitter sales generally. Figure 10 demonstrates that Marston's Pedigree has achieved *large and sustained increase in its volume brand share* (premium cask bitter market) after the declines of the previous year.

Marston's firmly believe that these volume increases are not due to reciprocal trading making Marston's Pedigree available more widely in Central, because reciprocal traders prefer to distribute it *outside* Central to give their pubs a point of difference. (If reciprocal partners made Marston's Pedigree available only in their pubs in Central their outlets would lack a competitive advantage as it is widely available in Central via Marston's own outlets.) Distribution of Pedigree within Marston's own trading estate in Central has remained generally static over the last two years (see Table 4). Again, this is evidence of real growth in volumes due to increased consumer demand.

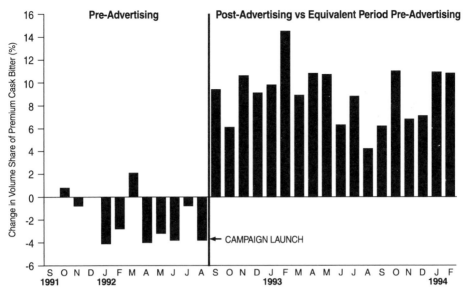

Figure 10. *Percentage changes in Marston's Pedigree's monthly volume share of premium cask bitter market in Central area compared to equivalent non-advertised period*

Note: *Percentage increase in brand share, eg change from 20% share to 22% share is +10%*

Source: Beer Market Survey

TABLE 4: AVERAGE NUMBER OF MARSTON'S ACCOUNTS TAKING DRAUGHT PEDIGREE IN CENTRAL

	Pre-Advertising Apr '92-Aug '92	Post-Advertising		
		Sep '92-Feb '93	Mar '93-Aug '93	Sep '93-Dec '93
Managed outlets	96	104	102	110
Tenanted outlets	335	331	329	332
Free outlets	358	357	351	355
Total	789	792	782	797

Source: Marston's

Conversely, in the period since the Marston's Pedigree campaign began, reciprocal trading has resulted in high penetration levels of other brewers cask ales, stouts and 'quality' lagers in Marston's own estate in Central (see Table 5). This has given Marston's customers a far wider choice of well known (and well supported) brands. For Marston's Pedigree to have achieved volume increases, while the availability of competitive brands was widening in its estate, is further evidence of increased consumer desire and demand for the brand, fuelled by the campaign.

TABLE 5: THE INCREASING PRESENCE OF RECOGNISED COMPETITIVE BEER BRANDS
IN MARSTON'S ESTATE IN CENTRAL
Numbers of accounts stocking reciprocal brands

	July 1992	October 1992	Change
Murphys }			
Heineken }	Relatively constant availability in Marston's outlets		
Stella Artois }			
John Smiths	—	275	+275
McEwans Export	2	54	+52
Ansells Mild	—	376	+376
Banks's Mild	196	336	+140
Beamish Stout	—	181	+181
Becks (draught)	2	109	+107
Castlemaine	33	60	+27
Fosters	—	300	+300
Kronenbourg	—	60	+60
McEwans Lager	2	166	+164
Tennents Extra	—	246	+246

Source: Marston's

Revenues Up

It is possible to evaluate incremental revenue and profit resulting from these volume increases. Calculations have been made using actual volumes, revenues per barrel and profit per barrel. However, the data is presented here in indices for confidentiality. In this evaluation two assumptions have been made.

1. Without advertising, Marston's Pedigree volumes would have continued the decline shown in the year prior to September 1992 for the *next 12 months*. For 18 months after that a static benchmark is assumed reflecting trends in cask ales but, probably, underestimating the impact of reciprocal trading on Marston's Pedigree sales in Marston's own estate.

2. BMS provides sales volume up to February 1994. If Marston's Pedigree received no more advertising there would be a considerable 'carry over' effect from the campaign which would yield further incremental volumes. To be conservative, incremental revenue projections in this respect have been made only for a further 12 months (at half the previous period's increment).

TABLE 6: INDEXED COMPARISON OF INCREMENTAL REVENUE FROM MARSTON'S PEDIGREE AND
COST OF ADVERTISING (MEDIA AND PRODUCTION)

	Advertising Cost	Revenue From Incremental Sales
Period		
Sept '92-Feb '93 (actual)	100	322
Mar '93-Aug '93 (actual)	111	264
Sept '93-Feb '94 (actual)	127	308
Mar '94-Feb '95 (projected)	—	196
Total Sept '92-Feb '95 (incl. projection)	100	355

Note: Airtime costs paid by Marston's are significantly different from those quoted in published sources due to regional test discounts, media negotiations, etc.

Thus, it is estimated that *for every £100 Marston's spent on advertising they would receive £355 in extra revenue.*

In understanding the *real* financial gain for Marston's Pedigree it is important to estimate the net incremental profit achieved (after production, transport and overhead costs have been accounted for). Using a comparable analysis to that above, *for every £100 spent on advertising Marston's would receive £164 in additional profit.*

TABLE 7: INDEXED COMPARISON OF INCREMENTAL PROFIT FROM MARSTON'S PEDIGREE AND COST OF ADVERTISING (MEDIA AND PRODUCTION)

	Advertising Cost	Profit From Incremental Sales
Period		
Sept '92-Feb '93 (actual)	100	149
Mar '93-Aug '93 (actual)	111	122
Sept '93-Feb '94 (actual)	127	142
Mar '94-Feb '95 (projected)	—	90
Total Sept '92-Feb '95 (incl. projection)	**100**	**164**

So using only the relatively narrow measure of short-term profit increase, we can demonstrate that the advertising was highly cost effective. However, the full effect of the campaign is much broader helping Marston's in other ways.

Advertising's Effect on Marston's as a Retailer

The campaign is strongly branded Marston's and evokes very positive feelings about Marston's as a traditional company. It was envisaged that the advertising could have a halo effect on Marston's outlets and generate additional consumer interest in visiting them. The company does not collect pub traffic data so we must turn to the Millward Brown research to help evaluate the 'popularity' of Marston's pubs.

This source provides two pieces of evidence to demonstrate that Marston's pubs have grown in appeal and popularity. Just as with brand image, qualitative research had indicated a number of attributes which the target audience associated with 'good' pubs and which would influence their outlet choice. Figure 11 shows that perception of Marston's outlets has improved relative to the average for a set of competitive brewery branded pubs: a general decline for competitive brewery branded pubs reflects the impact of the recession in the on-trade.

Secondly, the proportion claiming to visit Marston's pubs regularly has risen significantly (+25% in the 16 months since the campaign began.) At the same time the average proportion claiming to visit competitive brewery pubs has fallen (see Table 8). If the claimed increase for Marston's was reflected across the adult beer drinking population in Central this would equate to an additional 200,000 regular customers over the campaign period. Clearly, these additional customers would generate considerable revenue for Marston's retailing division over time (unfortunately no data are available to quantify this revenue increase). Since the number of Marston's pubs in Central has remained relatively unchanged and no significant refurbishment programme has occurred, this increase in the popularity

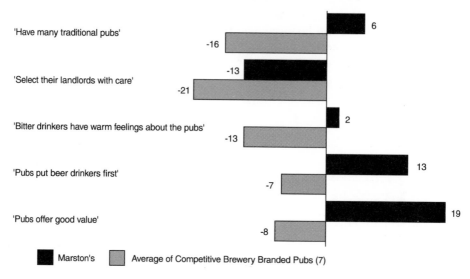

'Have many traditional pubs' 6 -16

'Select their landlords with care' -13 -21

'Bitter drinkers have warm feelings about the pubs' 2 -13

'Pubs put beer drinkers first' 13 -7

'Pubs offer good value' 19 -8

■ Marston's   ▨ Average of Competitive Brewery Branded Pubs (7)

Figure 11. *Percentage change in Marston's and other brewers' pub image ratings, August 1992-July 1993*
Source: Millward Brown

of Marston's outlets can be attributed to the effect of the campaign on improving consumer perceptions.

TABLE 8: PROPORTIONS VISTING BREWERY BRANDED OUTLETS REGULARLY

	August 1992	November 1993	% Change
Marston's outlets	28%	35%	+25%
Total mentions for other brewery owned outlets	167	159	−5%

Source: Millward Brown

Advertising Effect on Marston's as a Publicly Quoted Company

In the past Marston's has been owned by a mix of employee, private, institutional and corporate shareholders. The largest has been Whitbread which has owned a 35% stake. To comply with the Government Beer Orders, Whitbread had to sell a large proportion of its holding by 1993. It was placed very successfully with institutional investors, as their analysts – and the financial community in general – have confidence in Marston's future. The company had shown a 25% increase in profits, despite tough trading conditions. In this respect, the *Financial Times*, a good barometer of City opinion, praised the company's sales performance and cited *recent advertising and promotional activity as being an important factor.*

CONCLUSIONS

The advertising has been very effective as it is highly involving and entertaining communication that creates and stimulates genuine enthusiasm for the brand. It makes Marston's Pedigree more important in consumers' lives by proudly embodying Great British, and great beer, traditions.

Since the Marston's Pedigree campaign started there is clear evidence that Marston's has benefited in several ways and a regional roll out plan has been implemented. As a *brand* Marston's Pedigree has become more prominent and increased volume significantly while retaining and improving its respect amongst bitter drinkers. As a *retailer* Marston's pubs appear to have experienced increased traffic well beyond that which could be expected due to the usual refurbishment and acquisition programme. As a *publicly quoted company*, Marston's last financial year was its most profitable ever and the informed view was that the company's advertising investment was a significant factor.

Just as importantly, the 'Victorian' campaign has provided a clear focus for the salesforce and employees to talk about Marston's Pedigree with renewed enthusiasm. It is highly visible and celebratory advertising which has acted as a source of much pride and confidence for those who work for Marston's.

8
Nissan Micra

INTRODUCTION

Major car companies are not noted for their willingness to risk something new, untried, and radically different. So Nissan took a brave step when they approved the design of the new Micra. It was a radically different approach to small car design; it has repaid Nissan's bravery through an extraordinary level of success.

The advertising that helped to launch the new Nissan Micra matched the car. It was a radical departure from previous car advertising. And it required an extraordinarily brave marketing management to buy this campaign for a new company's first major launch – the launch of a car replacing their top selling model. This bravery was also repaid, as we shall demonstrate.

It's not only in design and advertising that the client was brave. **In the midst of a major recession, and at a time when competitive prices were falling, Nissan chose to introduce a premium-priced car to replace one that sold mainly because of its low price.** This from a brand whose main image associations were to do with price-led value.

MARKETING BACKGROUND

Nissan used to occupy the 'price-led value' end of the UK car market. Through the '70s and most of the '80s this was a highly successful strategy, which played to the strengths of most of the products imported by Nissan from Japan. Nissan produced very practical, durable, well-equipped, easy-to-drive and well-made cars very efficiently. Most UK and European mass-market competition was unreliable, shoddily and inefficiently made, poorly equipped and more demanding (though more rewarding) to drive. So it didn't really matter that Nissan's cars weren't designed with European roads, driving conditions and behaviour, or æsthetics in mind.

This was aided by a distributor who piled them high and sold them cheap, making much of his money via financing the car sales. He could sell as many cars as he was allowed to import and was doing very nicely, thank you, and didn't feel the need to make the marketing investment that would be required to sell further up-market.

With European competitors making inroads into if not matching Nissan's product strengths, and a consumer who was becoming more demanding as standards generally rose, Nissan did feel the need. To develop new cars that would enable Nissan to compete successfully on product rather than price, with major design input from and production in Europe. To make the marketing investment required. And ultimately, since the distributor did not concur, to set up an owned distributorship: Nissan Motor (GB) Limited (NMGB) opened its doors on 1 January 1992. Its first major new product launch was the new Nissan Micra.

MARKETING OBJECTIVES

While NMGB has no objection to selling lots of cars, increasing volume over the previous Micra was not a key objective. Nissan's ambitions are to compete across a balanced range of products, not to become overly reliant on a single model in the way that Volkswagen is with Golf. The previous Micra already represented 40% of Nissan's volume.

More important was how Nissan competed. The previous Micra cost, on average, 20% less than the average of its competitors. The most important, and difficult, task for the new Micra was to compete successfully on its own merits, at parity, or even premium, prices.

Nothing would have been possible without the excellence of the product itself, well worth a premium. But the product benefits of the new car, and the pricing, meant that we had to sacrifice some existing customers and attract a new type of consumer to Nissan. People who weren't totally price-led. People who demanded more from a car than just getting from A to B. People who previously wouldn't have been seen dead in a Nissan.

CAMPAIGN DEVELOPMENT

We were impressed by the car. Nissan suffers from a firmly held (if nowadays mistaken) consumer perception of producing what are most charitably described as functional, worthy and good value, but hardly exciting small cars. This one oozed personality, distinctiveness and driver appeal. It would also have that price premium over the outgoing model. We would have to overturn expectations of a new Nissan model. **Which suggested that whatever we wished to claim for the new model would have to be firmly backed up by rational support or demonstration.** Especially as the new model would carry the same name as the old, to avoid further alienating existing customers.

Technical briefing provided a raft of product advantages. As did simple observation: the Micra is roomy enough to seat four overweight advertising executives in comfort.

Mr Hosaka, the Principal Project Director for Micra, explained in inimitable Japanese style his inspiration for the Micra concept. He had noticed that people tended to avoid petting his neighbours' Japanese Tosa dogs, presumably because they wanted to keep their hands, whereas they loved making a fuss of his little terrier. He wanted to design a car that evoked a parallel response: lively and friendly, rather than sharp and aggressive.

The consumer clinic results indicated that he succeeded, though there was a degree of polarisation. Some people found it hard to come to terms with the new Micra's radically different styling, but more found it highly attractive: friendly, characterful and lively.

So, armed with fistfuls of product detail, clinic results and Mr Hosaka's wisdom, we set out to develop the communications strategy.

We were very mindful that **it is at the launch of a new car when you have the greatest opportunity to shape perceptions that will last throughout the model's lifespan**. So while we knew that we would need advertising that communicated the rational product advantages, we needed something bigger. We needed something that would encapsulate and dramatise the whole of the car: its emotional as well as its rational appeal.

We developed a number of propositions, supported by product facts and photographs of the car, to be explored in qualitative research.

It was in developing the stimulus material for this that we encountered a problem. The rounded styling that contributes so much to the car's character and appeal also makes it, according to the art director, "a bugger to photograph". Photographs are flat. We were worried that the photography available to us at the time wouldn't provide enough of an indication of the personality contributed by the car's styling. And that consequently there would be a real danger that research respondents wouldn't look at our propositions in the right context, and we could be given a mis-steer.

So, in an attempt to provide a better feel for the styling, we included in the research a graphic derived from some of the original concept drawings for the car, and from a symbol used in some Japanese promotional material. That graphic was eventually developed into this:

Incorporating the graphic worked in two ways. Firstly, it helped us develop a powerful, distinctive and relevant rational proposition which complemented the looks of the car.

Cars in Micra's class are regarded as city cars. And they're seen to be pretty good at the job: nipping in and out of the traffic, parking in tight spaces, and suchlike. Respondents expected that any new 'supermini' would be a good city car.

So we looked at what small cars are traditionally not so good at: longer distance, motorway travel. Which, even if you're not going to do very often, you want your car to be able to do. For longer distance higher speed travel, small cars were generally seen to be too noisy, too cramped and uncomfortable, not safe enough, and (apart from GTi's) underpowered. But not the Micra. With rational supports such as safety features, large interior space, and in particular 16-valve engines across the range, we could develop a proposition that credibly presented the new Micra as a much more complete car than any of its rivals: **the new Micra – the city car that's equally at home on the motorway**.

But rational argument is not enough. Particularly in this sector of the market, character is vital. And something much more powerful than the rational proposition emerged from the research. The 'shape' that we put in to give a better impression of the car's styling and personality turned out to have the potential to become an extraordinarily powerful and attractive icon. It also engendered a highly accurate expectation of what the car itself was like – a more accurate (and immensely more attractive) impression than the photographs gave. Responses to the symbol almost mirrored the positive responses to the car itself in the consumer clinic.

The rational proposition and the shape, together with its associated personality values of being friendly, approachable, characterful and lively, were incorporated into the creative brief – not just for advertising, but for through-the line communications at national and dealer level.

The concepts that emerged – press, poster and TV – were examined and refined in three stages of creative development research, during which we were also able to add a further support: the Micra was voted European Car of the Year by an international panel of motoring journalists.

One of the reasons for such exhaustive research is that client, and to some extent we at TBWA, were understandably nervous about launching such an important new car with advertising that starred a cartoon rather than the car itself.

But whenever we compared the shape approach with more conventional concepts we found that it gave a more positive, more intrusive, more attractive and above all more accurate impression of the car and its abilities.

It was only in pre-testing that a further strength emerged for the shape-based campaign: because the shape itself communicated instantly, we could visually communicate important product detail such as turning circle or catalytic converters much more simply, clearly and effectively than conventional advertising could. As should always be the case (but rarely is in car advertising), the creative treatment enhanced rather than obscured product communication.

MEDIA CONSIDERATIONS

This is a difficult market in which to be noticed, in which to gain advertising awareness. Without constant heavy expenditure, it is an impossible market in which to maintain it. **The average consumer sees two car commercials every day.** Over the eight weeks of our campaign, the average new car buyer would have seen one of our commercials **once a week**, twice in the week of the launch. Our tracking respondents mention an average of 2 brands for unprompted advertising awareness, 4 when prompted by a brand list. So we can expect (and indeed we see) that awareness for any individual brand falls off rapidly once advertising ceases.

This has important implications for how the advertising – creative as well as media – must work:

1. It must be able to cut through an intense amount of competitive clutter to be able to register at all.
2. Every opportunity should be taken to extend the impact of the campaign.
3. When front-of-mind awareness of the campaign fades, as it surely will, it's the residual effect on awareness of and attitudes towards the car and marque themselves that counts towards long term success.

Media planning was dominated by two criteria: making the most of what by car market standards (see below for comparison) was a limited budget; not just placing but contributing to the creative content to enhance the media effect.

The graphic impact of the shape-based advertising suggested that it would work disproportionately well in print. It was the media planner's suggestion that its simplicity also meant that it would be highly prominent even in small spaces.

270 small space 'teaser' insertions, using nearly 40 different executions tailored to editorial ("Size does matter" was the headline for the women's page) were placed in the national press in the week leading up to launch. According to feedback from the newspapers themselves, we dominated Fleet Street for a week at a total cost of £300,000.

The small space campaign combined for a week with a simple 'Shape' poster and a 10 second teaser commercial, before the launch proper, which combined the main display media with extensive below-the-line continuation of the shape theme – extending the campaign in time and to point of sale.

The budget summary, with the Vauxhall Corsa's subsequent launch included for comparison, was as follows (all figures are Register-MEAL and cover the respective launch periods, assuming a two month launch):

TABLE 1: BUDGET SUMMARY: MICRA AND CORSA

	Micra	Corsa
TV £'000s	1,726	4,165
TV share of (automotive) voice	6.2%	12.9%
Press £'000s	1,992	2,195
Press share of voice	5.7%	4.7%
Poster £'000s	612	1,193
Poster share of voice	24.1%	26.6%
Total £'000s	4,330	7,553
Total share of voice	6.6%	9%

Source: Register-MEAL

"FIENDISHLY DIFFICULT"

Looking at past papers regarding car advertising, it has become customary[1] to point out the special circumstances of the car market which make it "fiendishly difficult"[2] to isolate the effect of advertising, particularly launch advertising.

The key point is that car purchase is a complex and protracted (3-4 year purchase cycle) process, with many stages coming between advertising and a sale. And with a launch, we are limited to identifying short-term effects.

Without wishing to labour this point, it is important to acknowledge it, before we consider the effectiveness analysis.

---

1   See in particular Macdonald and Buck, 'The Volkswagen Golf 1984-1990', and Chandy and Thursby-Pelham, 'Renault Clio: Adding Value during a Recession', both in *Advertising Works 7*, for a fuller exposition.

2   *IPA Guide for Entrants 1994.*

SHAPE BASED 'TEASER' ADS

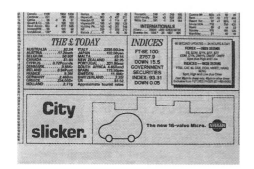

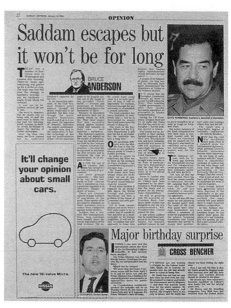

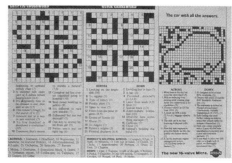

'COMBO'

SOUND: *Music to end*

MALE: The new Nissan Micra has a completely new 16-valve engine …

… giving it amazingly low fuel consumption.

It also has a nine point four metre turning circle …

… twin catalytic converters …

… and has been voted 'Car of The Year 1993'.

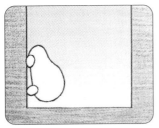

The new Nissan Micra …

… lives in the city, loves the open road.

The new 16-valve Micra.

NISSAN

Lives in the city, loves the open road.

VOLUME AND MARKET SHARE

Gavin Macdonald and Antony Buck illustrated[3] through many examples that as a general case "following launch, one would predict a couple of years of increasing share followed by gradual share decline up to the point of launch of the new car's replacement". Accepting this, it makes it difficult to make any case for advertising effectiveness based simply on short term volume increase over the preceding model. Indeed, this pattern of sales is built into the manufacturer's volume predictions and targets.

We do not wish to make a case for advertising effectiveness based simply on achievement of target volumes, though it is of course vital that the car has indeed achieved them.

TABLE 2: MICRA REGISTRATIONS AND SEGMENT SHARE

	1991	1992	1993/94[4]
Micra registrations	32,571	31,002	40,108
Segment share	8.1%	7.8%	8.5%

The new Micra sold 29% more than its predecessor (which as we see from comparing '92 with '91 sold well even in its final year) in a segment which itself grew by 18%. It exceeded Nissan's initial volume target for the first full year by 40%, and its revised target (taking account of market growth) by 11%.

The Micra would seem to be on course for share growth as predicted by Macdonald and Buck. Segment share in the latest month available at the time of writing – April 1994 – was up to 10.9%.

MODEL PRICING

The key demonstration of the new Micra's success is not that it exceeded sales targets, but that it did so at a price 20% higher than that of its predecessor, in a market where prices were falling.

Segment Prices

Figure 1 shows the price/volume relationship in the B Segment of the car market for 1992 and the twelve months to March 1994[5]. For any price the point directly above on the curve shows the percentage of segment volume below that price.

Between the two periods prices didn't change a lot. In each year around a third of volume comprised cars priced at under £7,000. The slope of the line in '93/94 is steeper than in '92, indicating fewer low-priced cars (10% below £6,300 compared with 20% in '92) but also fewer high-priced ones (13% above £9,000 compared with 23% in '92).

---

3 Op. Cit.

4 This is the 12 months to March 1994. We have excluded the launch quarter of the car a) because of confusion between old and new Micras and b) we are more concerned with longer term effects.

5 Quarter 1 1993 was excluded because both old and new Micra were on sale in this period and it is difficult to distinguish between them from SMMT data.

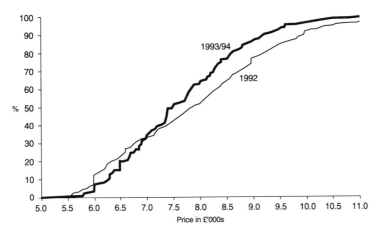

Figure 1. *Car market B Segment cumulative price/volume, 1992 vs 1993 Q2-1994 Q1*
Source: SMMT/NMGB

Model Prices

Looking at the Micra price/volume relationship in 1992 (see Figures 2 and 3), we see how the previous Micra competed at the bottom end of the price spectrum. Two thirds of Micra volume sold for below £6,500, compared with under 25% for the segment; less than 10% of Micra volume sold for more than the segment median price of £8,000. In 1993/4, however, the new Micra successfully competed across the spectrum, with an identical median price of £7,500. Indeed, it is relatively weak at the bottom end of the spectrum: 10% of its volume was below £6,750, compared with 20% for the segment.

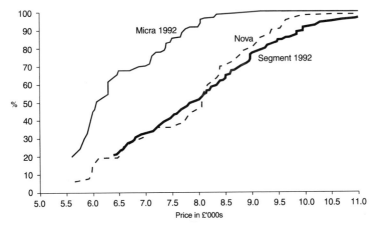

Figure 2. *Micra, Nova and B Segment cumulative price/volume, 1992*
Source: SMMT/NMGB

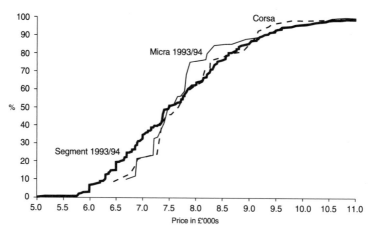

Figure 3. *Micra, Corsa and B segment cumulative price/volume, 1993 Q2-1994 Q1*
Source: SMMT/NMGB

Comparing old and new Micra, (see Figure 4) we see that two thirds of the previous Micra's sales were below the starting price of the new Micra.

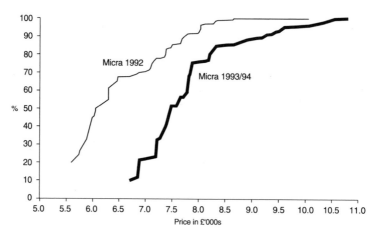

Figure 4. *Micra cumulative price/volume, 1992 vs 1993 Q2-1994Q1*
Source: SMMT/NMGB

When we consider average prices, we see the following:

TABLE 3: AVERAGE PRICES: B SEGMENT, MICRA AND NOVA/CORSA

	B Segment	Micra	Nova ('92)/ Corsa ('93/94)
1992	£7,927	£6,465	£7,799
12 Months to Mar '94	£7,666	£7,758	£7,845
% change	–3%	+20%	+1%

The magnitude of the new Micra's achievement becomes evident. The previous Micra sold largely on price to the price-sensitive: the average Micra cost 19% less than the average B Segment car. The new Micra has exceeded its volume and share targets competing at a parity price.

TRACKING STUDY FINDINGS

The main indications that directly implicate the advertising in the success of Micra come from Nissan's tracking study, conducted by Harris. At the time this comprised 75 interviews per week amongst new car owners and fleet 'user-choosers' across the B (Micra/Fiesta), C (Sunny/Escort) and D (Primera/Cavalier) segments of the car market. The main reporting period was eight weeks, giving an overall sample of 600 per wave, 6 waves a year, and a four week break over Christmas. Recruitment screening and analysis weighting ensured that the findings were representative of those market segments, both demographically and by brand shares.

Advertising Awareness

Figure 5 shows that unprompted awareness of Nissan advertising grew from what seemed to be a base level of 8% to 12% in response to some end of year promotional advertising. The launch of Micra saw awareness rise to 19% across the heavy spending month of launch, and then maintain itself at around 12% (through heavy competitive activity including the launch of Corsa) before, ironically enough, dropping back to the base level following some promotional television activity for Nissan's Primera. It should be remembered that our 'share of automotive voice' as measured by Register-MEAL was only 6.6% through the launch period.

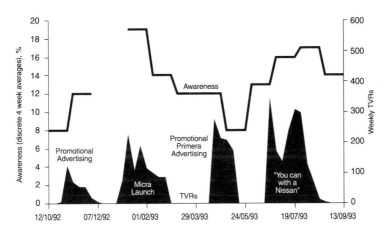

Figure 5. *Nissan unprompted advertising awareness*
Source: NMGB/Harris

Reactions to the Advertising

Beyond the qualitative development research mentioned earlier, the only specific quantitative feedback we have regarding the content of the advertising relates to the launch commercial. A regular feature of Nissan's tracking study is the exposure of a set of (unbranded) stills from commercials, followed by a standardised set of awareness, branding and attitude questions. We now have a bank of eighteen Nissan and competitive commercials that have been tested in this way, which can form the basis for comparison. Before giving the results, we should acknowledge that there are a number of caveats that should be borne in mind when considering this data, notably:

— An additional variable is included in terms of how well a set of stills can represent each commercial, which can of course have a strong effect on level of recognition.
— A standardised list inevitably ignores the fact that different commercials have different objectives that are not necessarily well represented by the questions.

The average score for recognition of stills is 38%, yielding an average sample size of 230 'aware' respondents replying to the branding and attitude questions. The score for the Micra was 36%, but as this was spread across two waves of the tracking study, the sample size for the subsequent questions was 430.

Figure 6 shows branding and attitude responses to the Micra launch commercial compared with the 'norm' from the other seventeen commercials tested to date. A number of the findings are worthy of note.

— Correct marque and model identification is substantially better than the norm. It really does seem that the shape device, thanks no doubt to print advertising as well as the commercial, has become very closely identified with the Nissan Micra.
— The simplicity and straightforward communication noted in the qualitative research is reflected in a high agreement level for "it is informative" and a low score for "I didn't understand it".
— We would have been alarmed if there hadn't been a high score on "different from most car commercials"
— Even though qualitative research indicated that the graphic shape gave all the right cues as to the styling character of the car, it was a relief to see a commercial that concentrated on that shape scored well on "makes the car seem attractive".

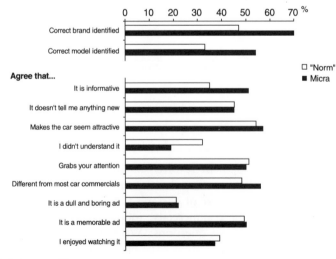

Figure 6. *Attitudes to car commercials*
Base: *Those aware from stills*
Source: Harris/NMGB

Developing interest in considering the car

One particular question in the attitude bank deserves more detailed consideration. It is "makes me more interested in... (manufacturer)... cars". As a more purchase-related question, we have analysed the answers to this only within the relevant segment of the sample for each model/ad. So the sample sizes are smaller – 143 for the Micra, around 75 as an average of the 17 competitive commercials – but still enough for the difference between Micra and the average, see Figure 7, to be statistically significant[6]. The Micra launch commercial was the best scoring commercial, and significantly better than average, in terms of agreement with the statement "Makes me more interested in Nissan cars".

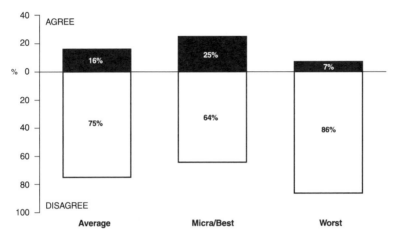

Figure 7. *"Makes me more interested in... cars"*
Base: *Those aware from stills*
Source: NMGB/Harris

CUSTOMER FEEDBACK

Nissan, as is common practice in the motor industry, routinely check on customer satisfaction following purchase. This Customer Satisfaction Index (CSI) survey allows us to examine, on a large sample base, differences between buyers of the old and the new Micra.

Reasons for Choosing a New Car

Table 4 shows, from a check-list, reasons given by buyers of the old and new Micra for their choice. The large sample sizes involved make all of the scores (save 'luggage capacity') significantly different at the 95% level, but we have highlighted the major changes.

It is notable that buyers of the old Micra were much more concerned in particular with price-related issues. Buyers of the new Micra were much more concerned with styling, safety, spaciousness and aspects of performance, all of which are not only real benefits of the car itself, but are also features that were strongly highlighted in our campaign. **The biggest single difference between owners of the two cars was the higher importance placed upon advertising and road tests in magazines as a reason for choice by buyers of the new Micra.** It is unfortunate that

---

6 Chi-Square test, 99% confidence.

we cannot separate the individual effects of the road tests and the advertising. We must acknowledge that most of the published road tests have been very positive, with the car being rated towards the top, and often at the top, of its class. We also note that may of the road tests have made use of and reference to our Shape advertising, again helping to extend its effect.

TABLE 4: REASONS FOR CHOOSING NEW CAR

	New Micra %	Micra '92 %
Fuel consumption/economy	65.4	63.7
Dealer location	22.7	24.0
Reputation of make	60.2	58.7
Exterior styling/design	**30.0**	17.7
Price/deal/trade-in	36.6	**51.8**
Previous experience of Nissan	49.6	**57.8**
Advertising/road tests	**26.8**	5.6
Safety/safety features	**25.4**	6.6
Luggage capacity	5.9	5.4
Sportiness	4.4	3.4
Amount/level of equipment	22.4	19.6
Interior roominess/comfort	**42.6**	29.6
Availability/delivery time	18.6	**23.6**
Reliability/durability	56.3	59.2
Performance/roadholding/handling	**35.8**	26.7
Exterior size	16.4	12.9
Dealer reputation	15.2	17.2
Resale value	13.8	15.4
Servicing/parts costs	11.8	10.0
Recommendation	16.5	**20.6**
Warranty	41.0	39.7
Other	6.2	1.8
Not stated	0.9	0.6
Unweighted sample total	18,421	10,953

Source: NMBG Customer Satisfaction Index

Previous Car and Other Cars Considered

Other indications of Micra's success in attracting a new and more demanding consumer were evident in the CSI. The balance of sales moved from loyalty to conquest (previous Micra 47% conquest, new Micra 55% conquest), and the other cars considered formed a much richer mix, see Table 5. The major differences, not just the statistically significant ones, are again highlighted.

Whereas the old Micra was more likely to compete successfully against the ageing Ford Fiesta and Fiat Uno, and the 'bargain basement' Hyundai, Lada, Proton and Seat, buyers of the new Micra were more likely to have considered and rejected the more upmarket sexy French models, and the new Vauxhall Corsa.

TABLE 5: OTHER CARS CONSIDERED

	New Micra %	Micra '92 %
Considered others	61	56
Citroën	20.4	16.9
Daihatsu	3.9	2.8
Fiat	12.2	13.7
Ford	41.6	54.6
Honda	8.3	6.3
Hyundai	3.4	5.1
Kia	4.0	4.0
Lada	0.9	2.3
Mazda	5.7	5.9
Mitsubishi	2.8	2.6
Peugeot	40.0	36.0
Proton	5.1	9.3
Renault	30.2	21.7
Rover	27.7	28.1
Seat	3.5	5.1
Skoda	0.9	1.6
Subaru	2.2	1.3
Suzuki	3.7	2.7
Toyota	10.2	9.6
Vauxhall	51.5	35.7
VW	14.9	15.6
Volvo	2.8	2.8
Unweighted sample total	11,103	6,134

Source: NMGB Customer Satisfaction Index

CONCLUSIONS

There is no doubt about three things:

1. The launch of the new Micra has been very successful. It exceeded its volume targets, and it has done so by competing on its merits rather than on price, defying all past and ingrained attitudes and imagery.
2. The main contributor to this is the car itself: an excellent and highly competitive product.
3. The advertising campaign has been very successful in the eyes of the advertising industry. To date, it has won over 60 creative awards, plus awards for media and account planning.

We believe that – within the constraints of a market where isolating advertising effectiveness is acknowledged to be "fiendishly difficult" – we have demonstrated that the advertising has also been a significant contributor to the success of the launch.

9

The Launch of CICA

How advertising helped Clarks gain entry into the premium trainer market

INTRODUCTION

Most effectiveness case histories seek to demonstrate how advertising resulted in large sales increases for a product. This case shows how advertising can contribute in a different way. Clarks used advertising to replace their own label trainer product with a branded equivalent and overall trainer sales did indeed rise. However, the primary role for advertising was to justify a significant price premium for the new branded product, which in turn led to an increase in revenue. We believe this case goes some way to proving that using advertising to simply sell more of a product is not always the only (or even the best) way to increase profit.

Advertising is often said to 'add value' to a product. Since in this case there was (initially) no difference between the own label and branded product other than advertising, it also provides an unusually 'pure' example of how it added value in a literal and measurable way.

BACKGROUND

The Growth of the Trainer Market in the Late Eighties

The shoe market is not known for its radical innovation, yet in the late 1980s it experienced a fundamental restructuring with the rise of the trainer as everyday footwear.

Trainers originally gained popularity from the jogging and aerobics booms. However sales only grew dramatically when they began to be used for everyday wear (because of their comfort and fashion value).

The results of this trend were remarkable. Over the 5 year period before 1992 (when our story begins) sales rose by 24% (see Figure 1). Not only did consumers buy more trainers, they were also prepared to pay more for them as the brands became more prestigious. So that over the same period the value of the market increased by an astonishing 125%.

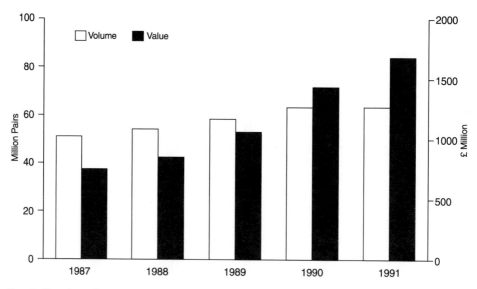

Figure 1. *The trainer market*
Source: TMS

The Impact of the Trainer Boom on Clarks

Around 55% of Clarks shoes are sold for casual use. As trainers were increasingly being substituted for casual footwear, the core of the Clarks business was being eroded (see Figure 2).

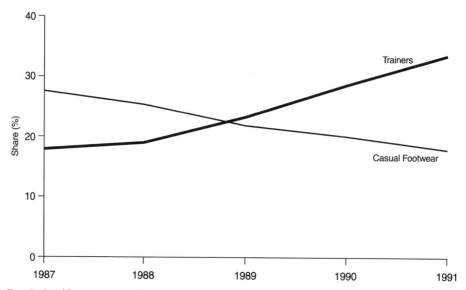

Figure 2. *Casual footwear vs trainers value share of total footwear market*
Source: TMS

Clarks had an own label trainer business which, however, suffered from two problems:

— The product competed on price at the budget end of the market so earning low profits.
— In 1990 sales began to drop as consumers increasingly moved towards premium trainers.

Gaining Entry to the Premium Market

Clarks wanted to enter the premium sector but there were two obstacles to doing this, both of which concerned the Clarks brand name:

— Clarks is a well loved brand which however has been traditionally associated with infants' shoes and comfortable 'practical' shoes for older people. Neither of these associations provided the young, sporty, slightly glamorous image a trainer brand required.
— Premium branded trainers are sold mostly through sports shops or the sports sections of department stores. Clarks would find it difficult to get this distribution because its trainers bore the name of a rival retailer.

Ironically, the strength of the Clarks brand worked against the company in this market!

CICA: A New Brand

Early in 1991, as the sales decline became increasingly evident, it was decided that the Clarks own label trainer was not a suitable vehicle with which to enter the premium market. A new trainer brand would have to be launched.

The Clarks marketing manager devised the name CICA while on a train journey toying with the initials CIC. These had been patented back in the nineteenth century by the original Clarks company, C&J Clarks along with their own initials CJC, in order to prevent another manufacturer taking them and causing confusion.

Although the initial range included models for adults, children and infants it was decided to bias the range towards children since Clarks had a distribution strength with this group which would be buying school shoes in their shops.

Roughly half of sales would come from Clarks' own outlets and half from independent Clarks stockists – a distribution pattern similar to that of own label.

In the summer of 1991 the first CICA trainers came off the existing Clarks production line. Because of the urgency of the task there was no time for lengthy new product development, so for CICA's first year these new trainers were not significantly different to the existing own label product in terms of styling, product quality or specification. Indeed several of the key models were actually the same product simply re-badged with a CICA logo.

In September 1991 they were launched to the Clarks retailers and stockists and were introduced into stores in October.

Difficulties Facing CICA

There were some difficulties which made the tasks of successfully launching and sustaining the new brand seem almost impossible:

— Trainers are a very publicly consumed product. Their 'badge' value is probably the single biggest reason people are prepared to pay more for premium brands (even if they will not always openly admit it!). As a new trainer, CICA had no heritage and therefore no real 'cred'.

— In the premium sector, which CICA was entering, the competitors were to be the sports equipment giants: Nike, Reebok, Adidas, Puma and Hi-Tec. These brands had been around for along time and have an almost magical attraction for consumers, standing alongside Levis or Sony in their appeal for widely different types of people. This appeal depended largely on the sports credentials which CICA lacked.

— This market was one with historically very high historic advertising spend (see Figure 3). In the year preceding CICA's launch total spend for the market was £13.9m. (Nike alone spent £3.8m.) It had been gaining by 31%pa and looked likely to continue to do so.

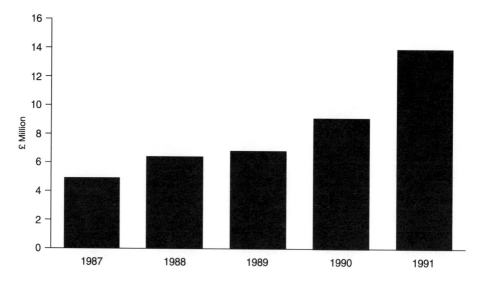

Figure 3. *Sports shoe advertising spend*
Source: Media Register/MEAL

It was clear that to 'catch up' with these brands CICA would have to be advertised. The advertising budget was considered an 'entry fee' to the premium sector. Yet the amount available (£490,000) was dwarfed by the rest of the market. In its first year CICA had a 5% share of spend.

— Most of the major competitors had endorsement by top athletes or sports stars. Since part of the 'symbolic' appeal of trainers was their association with (and implied promise of) sporting success, this was very important. Consumers are unsure how to judge the quality of trainers and the assurance that "if it's good enough for him it's good enough for me" gives some guarantee that they are worth paying extra for. Unfortunately, in its first year CICA was not going to get any such professional endorsement.

— CICA had no special feature with which it could differentiate its shoes, (such as the Nike Air sole or the Reebok Pump.) These features had a significance out of all proportion to their function – they implied a professionalism and technical know-how which radiated over the whole brand and added greatly to its credibility.

— CICA would initially only be sold through Clarks shoe shops. This meant that it was excluded from the majority of sports shoe purchase occasions. Moreover, because they were shoe shops, Clarks outlets lacked perceived sporting expertise.

MARKETING OBJECTIVES

In the face of these difficulties the following marketing objectives seemed very difficult indeed:

1. *Price Premium*
   The principle objective was to increase the profitability of the Clarks trainer business by selling CICA at a premium over the own label equivalent (of over 15%), without any significant change in product specification.

2. *Volume Sales*
   Overall volume sales of Clarks trainers had to be at least maintained at their 1990 level despite of this increase.
   (This would be done both by encouraging some existing Clarks buyers to trade up, and by taking share from the 'second-tier' (ie cheaper) models of the premium brands.)

3. *Value Share*
   To reverse the decline in value share that Clarks trainers had suffered since 1988.

DEVELOPING AN ADVERTISING STRATEGY

Targeting

Our targeting task was not straightforward. Although the launch range was biased towards children, making CICA a kid's brand was not an option since Clarks wanted to extend it to adults in later years. The obvious strategy would be to target the 'centre of gravity' in this market: the 16-24 age group (which both children and adults looked towards for guidance about which were the 'right' brands). However getting them to visit 'uncool' Clarks shops would be very difficult. In any case they were devoted to the major brands which, in turn, concentrated most of their advertising spend on them.

Qualitative research revealed a way in which we could overcome our disadvantages. It showed that, surprisingly, attitudes towards trainers amongst adults (over 25) and children (under 12) were actually quite similar. Teenagers, it seemed, were the odd ones out. Adults and children were quite pragmatic and wanted only a reasonable level of brand reassurance. This finding raised the possibility of addressing both groups with the same sort of advertising.

The Purchase Process

Children have very clear lists of trainers they find either acceptable ('alright') or unacceptable ('sad'). Crucially, this mental list is drawn up *before* shopping, usually in conjunction with their peers. When the children went shopping they would only be inclined to consider shoes on this list, and then would choose between them in store on the basis of colour, style and fit. Their choice would then be subject to parental approval.

There was one all-important criterion for inclusion on this list – the perceived fame of the brand. Children above all wanted their brand choice to be endorsed by their friends. For this to happen, their friends had to have heard of the name. Unfortunately no one had ever heard of CICA.

There emerged from this finding a very clear role for advertising – to get CICA on list of acceptable brands before they went shopping by making it famous.

Creative Strategy

There was nothing inherently different about the product which we could build an advertising story around. However, in research we stumbled over an interesting product attribute: people seemed unsure how to pronounce the name. At first this appeared to be a handicap in a brand which needed to become well known. However we realised that making a game out of the name was an excellent way of focusing attention on it, and one which was ideally suited to the playground!

Taking a Fresh Approach to Make Our Small Budget Work Harder

Looking at other trainer advertising, there seemed to be a remarkable uniformity of style. It was nearly all 'sweaty', male and aggressive and took itself very seriously. We felt that humour might be a more appropriate way to talk to children and would certainly make the CICA advertising stand out. Puncturing the pretensions of the big trainer brands a little would also appeal to our chosen adults. By taking this alternative route we could turn the size and might of our competitors against them.

Creative Brief

Target Audience
Primary: Boys and girls under 12.
Secondary: Adults over 25 (principally their parents).

What Exactly Do We Want to Do as a Result of the Advertising?
– Trade up from Clarks own label sports shoes and pay a premium for CICA.
– Choose CICA in preference to the 'second tier' models of other premium trainers.

Proposition
The trainers with the name no one knows how to pronounce.

Guidelines
– Humour will appeal to children and mark CICA as being different.
– By implying names are not important we can implicitly ridicule the other
  premium brands.
– The ads should make clear that CICA is available from Clarks stores.

The Launch Campaign 1992

'Mispronunciations', the launch campaign, comprised 4 ads (10-40 seconds). They featured various people trying unsuccessfully to work out how to pronounce 'CICA'. Set in California in order to confer a 'ready made' trainer heritage, the ads also reflected the relaxed, fun-loving spirit of the place. This style was echoed in the use of bright primary colours and the bouncy Harlem Globetrotters' theme, 'Sweet Georgia Brown'. The light-hearted tone defied trainer advertising conventions.

The Second Campaign 1993

After the first year's burst it was felt that the name had been established. A second campaign was needed which would concentrate more on the new shoes which were to be introduced in the summer of 1993 and bestow some sporting credentials on the brand.

The new campaign, 'Closer Look', retained the same tone, visual style and music, but this time the action was seen through the lens of a cameraman who was trying unsuccessfully to get a close-up shot of the shoes.

The campaign had 3 ads (40, 20 and 10 seconds). The Olympic hurdler Kriss Akabussi featured in two of them who, with his giggly, irreverent style, seemed to personify CICA's new 'sunny' positioning.

MEDIA

The seasonality of children's trainers sales (see Figure 4) dictated that we concentrate the small budget in April, in both 1992 and 1993. £490,000 was spent in the first year and £470,000 in the second, on national campaigns.

We deliberately biased our children's TV schedule towards Saturday morning programmes for two reasons. This was an effective way of reaching our secondary audience of parents in a relaxed frame of mind as they played with their children and watched them enjoying the advertising. Secondly, the 'wacky' anarchic humour of programmes like 'What's Up Doc' was a complementary environment for the style of humour used in the CICA ads.

Table 1 illustrates how concentrating our spend away from our competitors gave CICA high share of voice amongst its target for a lower share of spend.

'MISPRONUNCIATIONS I'

Hey Cliff, what's that on your foot?
That darned puppy …

No, the shoe.
Ah, tha's a CICA.
Shouldn't that be pronounced
'Shesha'?

I think it's a 'Cheeca' man.

CICA, the C is an S, the I is an E.
What's the other C?
That's a C.
Right …

Hey man, it's one of those names
that's spelt wrong like haemoglobin.

C–I–C–A, C–I–C–A …?

I don't care if it's pronounced …
Jeff, I love 'em

MVO: CICA, Sika, whatever. I'm
afraid we spent more time on the
shoe than the name.

Hey, give me a closer look at that.

'CLOSER LOOK'

I'm here to get a closer look at
CICA's new sports shoes.

(Camera looks around for players)

Guys where are you going?
Down here?

Alright, in for the logo, here we go ...

*(Camera is kicked accidentally and
falls on the floor)*

Ugh!
Afternoon ladies.

*(Camera bobs up and down to avoid
balls coming over net)*

Excuse me ... perhaps ... Could you ...
would you ...

OK Mr Bigshot.
Oh! *(Is hit with skipping rope)*
Ah ... nice shoes!

Alright and we're off.

(Falls down manhole)

This is a good shot!

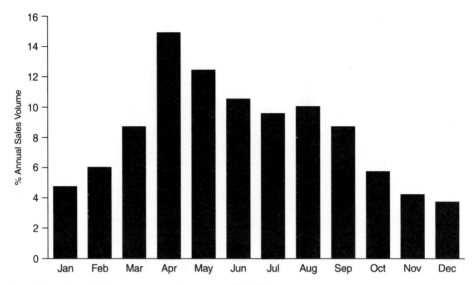

Figure 4. *Seasonality of children's trainers sales – Average pattern, 1988-1994*
Source: Clarks

TABLE 1: SHARE OF SPEND VS SHARE OF VOICE AMONGST CHILDREN

	1992		1993	
	Share of Spend %	SoV (Children's TVRs) %	Share of Spend %	SoV (Children's TVRs) %
Nike	50	34	35	19
Reebok	21	20	17	15
Puma	8	23	11	22
Pony	–	–	10	8
CICA	5	16	6	22
Adidas	–	–	5	9

Source: Media Register/BARB

WHAT WAS ACHIEVED?

Objective 1: The Price Premium

CICA was successfully launched at a premium over own label of 18.3%. This premium was maintained in both 1992 and 1993.

The real extent of this achievement can only properly be seen when put in the context of what happened in the rest of the market. In 1992-93 children's trainer prices dropped sharply as the recession bit into clothing and footwear and children's disposable income was diverted into computer games.

TABLE 2: AVERAGE PRICES OF CHILDREN'S TRAINERS

	Y/E 1991 £	Y/E 1993 £	% Change
Clarks /CICA	19.32	25.99	+34.5
Nike	27.85	29.14	+4.6
Adidas	21.94	22.85	+4.1
Pony	17.04	16.73	−1.8
Parrick	18.70	17.83	−4.7
Reebok	30.42	27.98	−8.0
Matchstick	13.36	12.14	−9.1
Hi-Tec	19.73	17.54	−11.1
Nicks	11.05	9.58	−13.3
LA Gear	28.80	22.29	−22.6
Pirelli	16.99	12.74	−25.0
Arrow	19.92	14.60	−26.7
Gola	14.14	10.31	−27.1
Puma	19.57	14.16	−27.6
Dunlop	11.14	7.80	−29.9
K Shoes	13.95	8.98	−35.6

Note: Average prices paid (includes discounts). Based on a home audit.

Source: TMS specially commissioned price analysis

Table 2 shows that out of the 16 brands audited, only 2 were able to increase their price, while Clarks went from selling own label trainers at £19.32 to CICA at £25.99. All the other brands saw their prices drop, usually through discounting.

It is interesting to note that the brands which invested significantly in advertising over 1992-93 were Nike, Reebok, Puma, Pony, Adidas and CICA. With the exception of Puma, these were the same brands that either increased their price or suffered relatively small drops.

Objective 2: Volume Sales

Despite this large price increase, overall sales of Clarks trainers were not only maintained but increased following the CICA launch (see Figure 5).

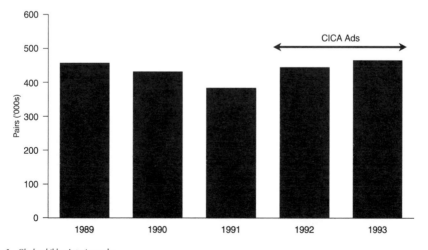

Figure 5. *Clarks children's trainer sales*
Note: *We have excluded adults' sales from our analysis because adults were not a primary advertising target. Infants' sales (below 4 years) have also been excluded because the mother makes the purchase decision. These will be dealt with later.*
Source: Clarks

Objective 3: Value Share

The combined effect of volume and price increases led to a marked rise in value sales (see Figure 6)

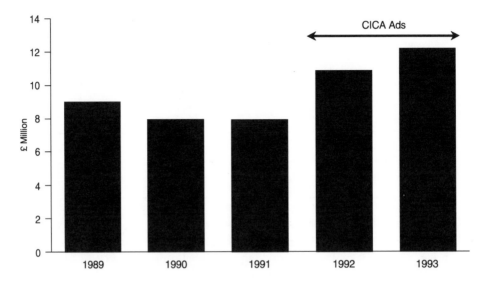

Figure 6. *Clarks children's trainers sales value*
Note: *Excludes infants.*
Source: Clarks

Clarks' value share was restored within 2 years (see Figure 7).

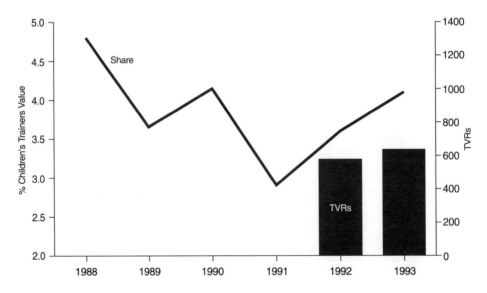

Figure 7. *Clarks' share vs ads*
Sources: TMS, BARB

Moreover, within 2 years, CICA had almost entirely replaced sales of own label (see Figure 8).

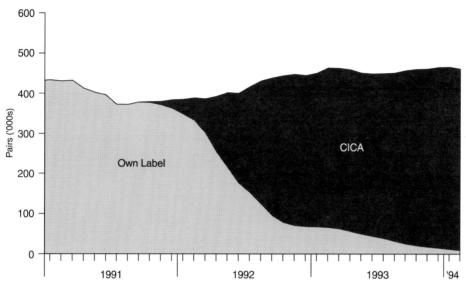

Figure 8. *Children's trainers sales – MAT volume*
Note: *Excludes infants.*
Source: Clarks

HOW THE ADVERTISING WORKED

Brand Awareness

It was our belief that fame was the most important factor in the credibility of a premium trainer brand for children. For this reason, brand awareness was always going to be the crucial measure of whether or not the advertising had worked in the desired way (see Table 3).

TABLE 3: BRAND AWARENESS OF CICA AMONGST CHILDREN

	Pre '92 Advertising %	Post '92 Advertising %	Pre '93 Advertising %	Post '93 Advertising %
Spontaneous	4	19	10	17
Prompted	24	68	54	66

Source: Carrick James

In fact CICA's prompted awareness rose dramatically so that two thirds of children were aware of the brand. It even exceeded Fila in both years (51%/52%), which was a much more established name.

Advertising Awareness

A majority of children recall seeing the first burst. Indeed recall was greater than that of Puma's advertising for the new 'Disc' shoe (at 29%), which was on air at around the same time with a higher share of children's TVRs (see Table 4).

TABLE 4: ADVERTISING AWARENESS OF CICA AMONGST CHILDREN

	Pre '92 Advertising %	Post '92 Advertising %	Pre '93 Advertising %	Post '93 Advertising %
Spontaneous	3	22	4	15
Prompted	8	54	21	40

Note: Lower awareness in '93 probably caused by lower SoV while on air.

Source: Carrick James

The Effect of Advertising on the Desirability of the Brand

Table 5 shows pronounced increases in CICA's desirability amongst children at the expense of other brands after advertising.

TABLE 5: CICA PREFERENCE RATING
"Which of these 5 makes would you most like to have?"
(Average of a 5 Point Scale)

	Pre '92 Advertising	Post '92 Advertising	% Change	Pre '93 Advertising	Post '93 Advertising	% Change
Reebok	3.97	4.03	+6	4.05	4.04	−1
Nike	3.85	3.60	−25	4.00	3.91	−9
Adidas	2.99	2.69	−30	2.81	2.66	−15
Hi-Tec	2.87	2.61	−26	2.60	2.37	−23
CICA	1.45	2.19	+51	1.70	2.10	+24

Source: Carrick James

Preference for CICA was also higher amongst those children who recalled seeing the advertising (see Table 6).

TABLE 6: CICA PREFERENCE RATING
"Which of these 5 makes would you most like to have?"
(Average of a 5 Point Scale)

	Pre '92 Advertising	Post '92 Advertising	% Change	Pre '93 Advertising	Post '93 Advertising	% Change
All children	1.45	2.19	+51	1.70	2.10	+24
Recall CICA advertising	–	2.58	–	2.10	2.61	+51

Source: Carrick James

Of course, it is always impossible to prove the causality of such effects, but the fact that preference dropped when CICA was off air (and that the pre and post checks were taken immediately before and after bursts) makes it reasonable to infer that they were caused by advertising.

Further evidence is provided by a syndicated survey amongst children called Youthtruth (see Table 7).

TABLE 7: MAKES OF CLOTHING LIKED NOW
(% Endorsing Each Brand)

	Pre '93 Advertising	Post '93 Advertising
Trainer Brands		
Reebok	56	54
Nike	41	47
Hi-Tec	32	38
Fila	25	9
CICA	17	27
Clothing Brands		
Levis	33	26
Wrangler	18	13

Note: 'Post' fieldwork conducted immediately after CICA advertising.

Base: Primary school children

Source: The Research Business

The advertising appears to have moved CICA into the popularity league of Adidas and Hi-Tec and elevated it above such revered brands as Fila, Wrangler and Levis.

A similar effect was observable in qualitative research. Before advertising, children were generally unimpressed by the CICA product. After advertising, one miraculously heard quotes like the following:

"They're pretty good... you wouldn't get laughed at with those on."

Boy 10, London

Nothing had changed but the advertising.

Appeal and Communication

After both campaigns, qualitative research confirmed that humour had indeed been an excellent way to gain the involvement and attention of children. The following quotes are typical:

"It's really good, I love this advert"

Boy 6, Birmingham

"It's a very happy advert"

Girl 8, Manchester

"They're really colourful... and funny too."

Boy 12, Birmingham

In the Clarks tracking study amongst adults, 50% of mothers who could remember seeing the ads themselves said they believed their children also liked them.

Moreover, the children seemed also to have noticed the different approach this advertising had taken:

"It's not taking itself too seriously"

Boy 12, Birmingham

"They're taking the mickey out of the American ones, saying they're such good shoes you don't need to worry about the name."

Boy 10, London

"They're a lot calmer"

Girl 9, Manchester

Perhaps most importantly, the game of mispronouncing the name had, as we had predicted, been taken up in the playground:

"No one knows how to say it right... none of my friends can tell"

Girl 8, Manchester

The follow up campaign was received with similar enthusiasm, particularly the ads featuring Kriss Akabussi.

WAS THE ADVERTISING RESPONSIBLE FOR THE SUCCESS?

There are two direct pieces of evidence which suggest that the marketing success was a result of advertising:

1. The Timing of Volume Uplifts

We know from experience with previous Clarks children's shoes that any new launch could expect to see an initial rise in sales.

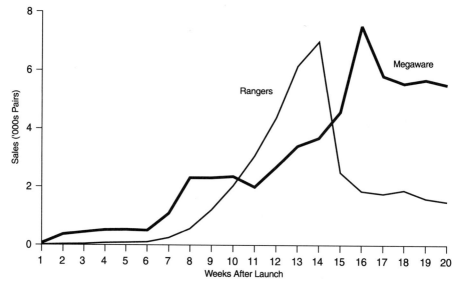

Figure 9. *Other product launches*
Source: Clarks

Figure 9, which shows examples of two recent launches (neither of which was advertised at this point), illustrates that typically sales rise after launch. This is due to novelty value and (mainly) enthusiasm on the part of the sales staff. However, these effects work through after 14-16, weeks whereupon sales peak. A plateau or decline usually follows.

This is exactly the pattern CICA showed after its launch (see Figure 10).

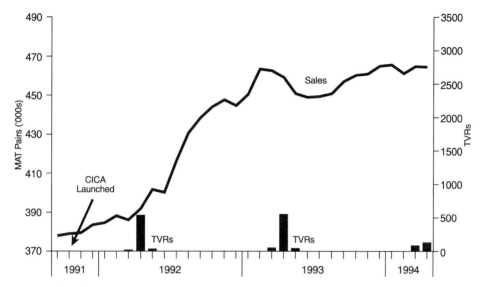

Figure 10. *Clarks children's trainers – MAT sales vs advertising*
Note: *Excludes infants. MATs used to remove seasonal effects.*
Sources: Clarks, BARB

Sales rose modestly until March 1992 (the month before the advertising) when they started to fall slightly. However in April the first advertising campaign caused overall sales to rise rapidly again and to continue doing so. (There are long intervals between purchases of trainers, and so the total effect of the advertising is delayed and can be seen to be spread across the rest of the year.)

In the beginning of 1993 sales started to decline slightly as brand awareness (which seems to decay rapidly in children) diminished. It took a second burst of advertising in April 1993 to restore sales levels. On this occasion, the response to advertising was slower because of higher base levels and a deterioration in trading conditions.

The primary objective of the advertising was not to gain incremental sales (although these were obviously very welcome). However the timing of the uplifts strongly suggests that the trading-up process (which was the main aim) was being driven by the advertising.

2. Regional Analysis

CICA's share of voice amongst children varied because there was a regional spread to competitive spend. Correlating regional share of voice against percentage uplifts in volume sales allows us to see that, broadly, the greater CICA's share of voice the greater its sales growth (see Figure 11).

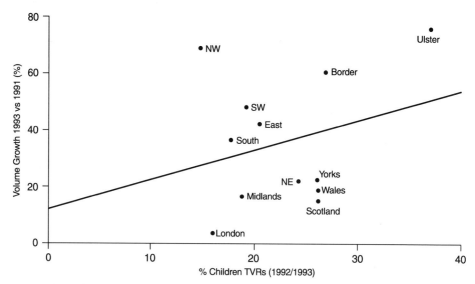

Figure 11. *Sales growth vs share of voice – First two years*
Note: *Children's trainers excl. infants*
Source: Clarks, BARB

ELIMINATING OTHER POSSIBLE CAUSES OF SUCCESS

Would Mothers Have Bought CICA Anyway as Clarks Own Label Became Unavailable?

No. Own label was only phased out as CICA sold through. For about 9 months both types of shoe were available in shops, yet CICA was preferred. Indeed, much own label stock had to be discounted to be sold. Furthermore, anecdotal evidence from sales supervisors suggests that the preference came from children, as planned. There are stories of disputes in the shops caused by children insisting on CICA shoes which seemed to parents to be remarkably similar to own label.

Would Simply Having a Name Other Than Clarks on the Shoes Have Had the Same Effect?

No. We know that a brand name does not mean anything in this market until it is widely known. It was only after advertising that CICA gained significant brand awareness.

Better known brands than CICA (eg Puma, Gola, LA Gear) found their name no guarantee of price stability.

Would Raising the Price of the New Product Have Raised its Perceived Value and so Become Self Justifying?

It is possible that some consumers might rationalise purchase in this way. But it is more probable that in a market where prices were dropping, without advertising or a product change, a price increase would result in considerable volume loss.

Did Product Specification Change?

Central to this case is the fact that in CICA's first year there was no real difference between it and own label. In the second year several models with higher specification were introduced but these accounted for less than 10% of total volume.

Did Distribution Change?

Precise figures are unfortunately unavailable. However CICA has had consistent 100% distribution in Clarks outlets since launch (accounting for half of volume). In independent stockists distribution has not 'widened'. It did 'deepen' in 1993 as retailers were persuaded to take more expensive models following the success of 1992. However, if the initial success is attributable to advertising, then so must this extra stocking. Sales force feedback confirms that advertising was an important tool for them.

EVALUATING THE CONTRIBUTION OF ADVERTISING

Advertising was viewed as a long term investment to establish a presence in the premium sector. It was not expected to pay back immediately. Yet, although the immediate effect of the incremental sales was in some ways the least important, we hope to demonstrate that with these alone, the advertising more than paid for itself within 2 years.

If CICA had not been advertised, it seems likely it would have followed the pattern of other recent Clarks launches (eg Megaware and Rangers as previously discussed). We have seen that typically sales peak after 14-16 weeks and are followed by a decline. CICA followed this pattern until it was advertised, whereupon sales started rising again.

It seems reasonable to assume then that without advertising sales would have reached a plateau or declined further. If we (optimistically) assume a plateau, we can see that all the sales above this level (illustrated in Figure 12) would be incremental and produced by the advertising.

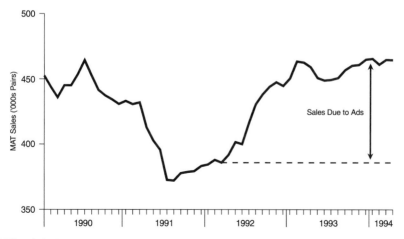

Figure 12. *Effect of advertising*
Source: Clarks

Table 8 shows that the incremental sales totalled 142,000 extra pairs over the advertised period. These generated £3.9m in revenue. Clarks receives profits from two sources on this: wholesale margin on all the shoes and a retail margin on those sold through its own shops. It can thus be seen that the total profit generated on the incremental sales was £1.3m.

This is in return for an advertising expenditure of £960,000.

TABLE 8: SHORT TERM PROFITABILITY OF CICA

	Extra Volume	Extra Revenue	Wholesale Margin Per Shoe	Avg. Retail Margin Per Shoe	Total Extra Profit Due to Advertising
	Pairs	£m	£	£	£
1992	58,730	1.42	2.50	5.43	466,000
1993	79,006	2.06	3.31	5.87	725,000
1994*	14,878	0.39	3.60	5.86	141,000
Total	142,613	3.87			1,332,273

Note: * January and February 1994

Source: Clarks

This scenario however we believe represents the absolute *minimum* effect of advertising because:

1. **It Ignores the More Important Long Term Effect**
   Most importantly, Clarks have established a profitable and enduring brand.

2. **It Assumes Sales Would Have Reached a Plateau**
   In fact we believe they would probably have declined. Some evidence of this is found in Figure 13 which shows that up until CICA's launch, sales closely followed the pattern of Clark's shoe sales.

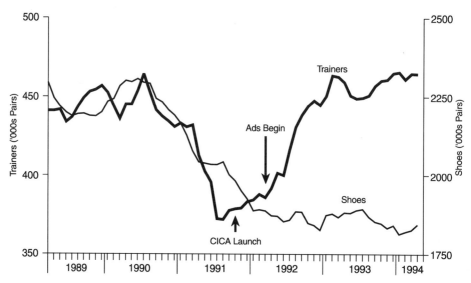

Figure 13. *Clarks trainers vs shoes – MAT sales, children*
Note: *Excludes infants.*
MATs used to remove seasonal effects.
Source: Clarks

There is no reason to suppose that after the initial 4 month growth CICA would not have continued to follow shoes into slow decline.

3. **It Assumes that the Price Premium Would Have Been Maintained**
In fact we believe this is most unlikely. Most other brands were forced to drop their price. K Shoes (perhaps the audited brand most similar in personality to Clarks) suffered the most severe price drop (of 35.6%). There is no reason to suppose that Clarks would have been an exception to this trend.

4. **It Ignores the Effect on Adults and Infants**
95,000 pairs of infants' CICA were sold over 1992 and 1993. CICA's success in 1992 encouraged Clarks to launch a small range of adults' CICA in 1993 which sold 50,500 pairs. It is impossible to evaluate the extent to which advertising influenced parents to buy CICA for themselves or for infants, either directly or through their children's preference (although some indication of its impact is given in Table 9). However, any advertising generated sales would increase the return on the investment in advertising.

TABLE 9: AWARENESS OF CICA ADVERTISING AMONGST PARENTS OF CHILDREN AGED 0-15

	Post '92 Advertising (July) %	Pre '93 Advertising (March) %	Post '93 Advertising (May) %
Men	21	17	24
Women	20	10	24

Notes: A pre '93 measure is not available.
There is also considerable qualitative evidence that parents noticed and enjoyed the advertising.

Source: TABS Tracking Study

5. **It Ignores Secondary Effects**
Clarks now sell a small amount of CICA merchandise which is expected to grow with time.
Clarks also believe CICA has enhanced the credibility of their shops with children. Some evidence of this is suggested by sales of character shoes (eg Sonic the Hedgehog) which have improved since the CICA advertising.

SUMMARY

The main points are as follows:

1. Existing own label trainers sold at low profit at the budget end of the market and were in decline.
2. CICA was launched with a product no different to own label.
3. The advertising strategy concentrated on the unpronouncibility of the name as a means of getting it known, and found a different approach in the use of humour.
4. CICA successfully maintained a price premium of 18.3%.
5. It not only maintained but increased overall trainer sales.
6. Clarks' value share was restored.
7. Increases in brand awareness and CICA's desirability appear to have been caused by advertising.
8. The timing of volume increases and regionality data suggest more directly that advertising was responsible for the success.
9. Advertising was more than paid for by incremental sales which we believe to be its minimum effect.

CONCLUSION

We believe that the main achievement was to reverse the fortunes of the Clarks trainer business and give it a position in the high profit premium market sector. The full effects of this have yet to be seen. CICA is now in an excellent position to introduce high specification, innovative products which will win it new customers and greater distribution. Advertising played a crucial part in launching this brand and gaining it this position.

10

The Launch of Halls Soothers
"It started with a kiss"

INTRODUCTION

The development of Halls Soothers was designed to expand Warner Lambert's medicated confectionery portfolio by creating a brand which combined mainstream indulgent confectionery values with the throat and nose therapy for which Halls was famous with Mentho-lyptus.

This new mildly mentholated confection was hard boiled on the outside with a fruity liquid centre. The brand name Halls Soothers signalled cold symptom relief whilst the brand's packaging owed more to impulse confectionery.

Advertising was required to communicate these dual benefits of therapy and indulgence stimulating usership which extended beyond the normal winter season for medicated confectionery and without cannibalising the existing Halls Mentho-lyptus franchise.

During its launch season the brand rose to a profitable 12% share of the medicated market. This increased further in its second year, and in both years the brand sustained its volume beyond the natural seasonality of the market. This paper will demonstrate the pivotal role of the advertising to this success.

MARKET BACKGROUND

There is a blocked nose and sore throat season. This generally runs from October through to March and accounts for 60-65% of sales. Sales are clearly boosted by the viruses and bugs which take hold over the winter months. Traditionally the market has responded to the classic need for medicated confectionery at this time of year and has advertised over this period to promote the therapeutic value of the brands on offer.

The brands in this market place, Halls Mentho-lyptus, Tunes, Lockets, Strepsils, Fisherman's Friends, Victory V, Hacks and Macs, were the same brands that were available twenty years ago and consumer loyalties were entrenched. The launch of Lockets twenty years ago was the last new product innovation and whilst it provided a new product proposition (a liquid centre and dual action claim) it did not expand the role of medicated confectionery.

The market splits into high efficacy and low efficacy brands. Medicated confectionery relieves sore throats or blocked noses. Brands differ in their levels of therapy according to their positioning and their strength of flavour. This tends to be directly related to menthol content. Some of the brands are so low in menthol that the flavour is much milder. Generally brands that are thought to be very effective are not expected to offer a wide range of flavours, or indeed, confectionery flavours. They are suitable for a severe cold as opposed to a mild one, and are therefore consumed less frequently. Those which have a more confectionery taste are often used more frequently and are seen to be less effective.

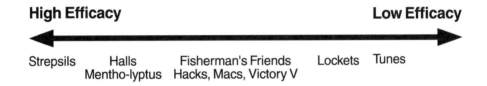

High Efficacy ← → **Low Efficacy**

Strepsils   Halls   Fisherman's Friends   Lockets   Tunes
            Mentho-lyptus   Hacks, Macs, Victory V

The Opportunity

The idea that medicine has to be unpleasant to work is diminishing. Very few people today would be willing to persevere with cod liver oil for their health. Across many OTC categories we see examples of therapeutic products which have been made more palatable – fruit flavoured Tums and Rennies, Remegel, Lemon Alka Seltzer, Chewable Vitamins all in an effort to make medication easier to take. Furthermore here we're talking about medicated confectionery. Confectionery is a more emotional purchase, it's something which should be enjoyed whilst delivering the more rational/practical benefits. No other brand in the market place had recognised the importance of indulgence.

Penetration of medicated confectionery is, according to TGI, 54% of the total population. This leaves many consumers who would prefer to soothe a sore throat by sucking a mint or some other confectionery than by using any of the medicated products on offer. A more enjoyable concept would attract some of these people to the market as well as steal share from competitors.

Brand Development

The idea for a brand which was therapeutic but could also be enjoyed was carried through to all aspects of brand development.

The product combined menthol and real fruit juice. The name combined Hall's heritage and a descriptive evocative name – Halls Soothers. The packaging used fruit to emphasise taste values – very important as the name 'Halls' can have negative taste perceptions. However, the advertising was crucial. We knew that trial was essential and that this brand had to stand out and change people's attitudes to what is an uninvolving category.

THE ROLE OF ADVERTISING

1. To create awareness of the new brand

2. To redefine medicated confectionery to include indulgence, and to position Halls Soothers at the heart of that.

3. To create trial of what we knew to be a good product.

THE CREATIVE STRATEGY

The creative strategy was to demonstrate how Halls Soothers could work against a sore throat in a way which was enjoyable and indulgent.

The target was to be young females who, at present, can only be tempted by fruit flavoured Tunes as the mildest form of medicated confectionery. This target was not only ripe for conversion but was a completely separate franchise from Halls Mentho-lyptus. Whilst the personality was to be overtly feminine and modern, the required tone of voice was 'fresh and fruity'.

MEDIA PLANNING

Why Television?

Television was essential in order to generate high interest in what is a short medicated season.

Historically, the medicated confectionery market has concentrated advertising into television due to the medium's ability to generate high levels of cover and frequency not only with impact but with the full creative story (problem/solution). Television was essential to build awareness quickly.

The plan had to meet several strategic requirements.

1. *Careful Targeting*
   We were setting out creatively to keep the two brands separate and we had to replicate this as far as possible in the media plan. Halls Mentho-lyptus was to target its older users and was given an all adult focus. Halls Soothers was targeted younger with a female 15-34 focus.

2. *Seasonality*
   A November start date was extremely desirable for the launch of Halls Soothers – with a limited budget we had to get Halls Soothers heard early on in the season with minimum competition for share of voice.

3. *Timing*
   The two campaigns had to be carefully planned to cover the sales season for as long as possible whilst avoiding a high degree of overlap which would cannibalise awareness, confuse consumers and reduce efficiency of budgets.

Creating Impact in a Low Interest Category

Advertising in the medicated confectionery arena is not particularly impactful, in fact it is a low interest category. Amongst groups of users few ads come to mind, some may remember Tunes "help you breathe more easily" but that is where it stops. As launch advertising we aimed to be impactful but what was to create this stand out had to be integral to the product proposition, had to be part of a campaignable idea. We knew that much of our competitors' success could be attributed to consistent strategy and long term support.

The Creative Idea

The creative idea was developed with an understanding of how our young female target relate to confectionery and how they deal with the symptoms of a sore throat. When they have a sore throat they like to feel pampered and comforted. They look to confectionery at this time for self indulgence, something which will pleasantly soothe and take their minds off how bad they are feeling. For some the association with Halls Mentho-lyptus may have given cues of too strong a flavour and too harsh an effect, so we had to be clear in portraying the emotional values of the brand.

The idea of "kissing it better" researched well and as an analogy it clearly demonstrated the soothing and pampering nature of the product. The kiss execution provided stand out and a clear link with the product benefits.

Reactions to the execution were very good particularly amongst our core female target. It caught their imagination and they became very involved in the fantasy, (substituting fantasy characters) and were motivated into recognising Halls Soothers as a remedy/sweet they could identify with in preference to more serious alternatives. It was clearly understood that Halls Soothers are new and different and that the real fruit liquid centre would taste good as well as soothe – a combination of the best facets of Tunes and Lockets.

The Launch

Halls Soothers Blackcurrant and Cherry flavours were launched to the trade in September. The commercial broke in November and ran nationally for five weeks with rapid cover build to create maximum awareness before the biggest period of medicated confectionery sales in December and January.

'KISS'

FEMALE: Having a sore throat …

… used to be a real pain in the neck …

… but now I have it kissed better …

… with these fruity Halls Soothers.

Just allow one to dissolve slowly …

… in your mouth.

Mmm. First, the smooth eucalyptus gets to work …

… before the gentle kiss of the real fruit liquid centre.

Have your sore throat kissed better with Halls Soothers.

I can't wait to try the cherry flavour.

TABLE 1: MEDIA SCHEDULE FOR THE LAUNCH

Week commencing Monday	November					December				Actual Total TVRs
	2	9	16	23	30	7	14	21	28	
Television: ITV/CH4/SAT **Length:** 30" **Target Audience:** 16-34s										
London										424
Central										580
Granada										617
Yorkshire										541
Tyne Tees										561
STV										489
Grampian										510
HTV										613
TVS										460
Anglia										506
TSW										545
Ulster										522
Border										604
Sky/UK Gold										37
Total										563

RESULTS

The launch was a great success.

Volume Share

Whilst both Tunes and Lockets share declined, the Halls brands grew. Halls Soothers achieved a share of 12% at the height of advertising, more than double the objectives. And it didn't take a point from Halls Mentho-lyptus whose share increased by 2% from 20.4 to 22.3%.

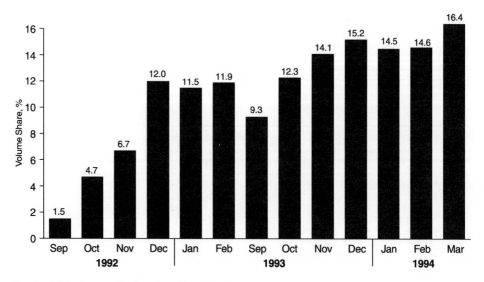

Figure 1. *Halls Soothers monthly volume share of the total market*
Source: Nielsen

Rate of Sale

Halls Soothers rate of sale increased dramatically from 12.0 at launch to 53.1 in December 1992 (at the height of Halls Soothers' TV advertising).

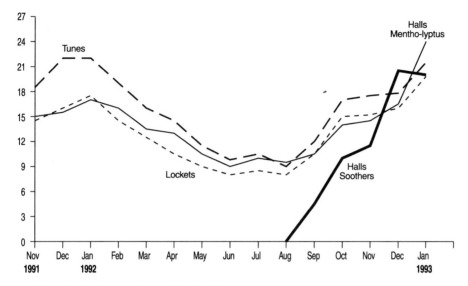

Figure 2. *Medicated confectionery – Cash rates of sales – GB: Grocers and CTNs.*
Source: Nielsen

Distribution

Distribution grew well, largely due to the trade's appreciation of the unique positioning of the brand and the power of its advertising. The following are a series of quotes from Mintel's 1993 Retail Intelligence Report on Personal Care and Healthcare Goods retailing which endorse the trade's attitude to medicated confectionery and Halls Soothers in particular.

"We were all taken aback by the launch of Soothers, demand exceeded supply and there were a lot of out of stock situations"

Buyer, Wholesaler

"Soothers are doing well, they're on the telly"

Buyer, Grocery multiple

"Halls Soothers have done very well. It's a fairly static market, and you're looking at relatively low retail values so we wouldn't normally pay much attention to it"

Director, Chemist multiple

Halls Soothers achieved 52% distribution well above all expectations and in most cases both flavours were stocked with nominal delists of Halls Mentho-lyptus flavours.

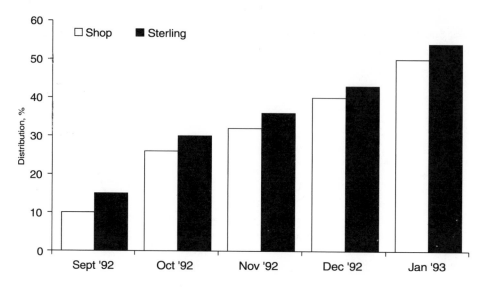

Figure 3. *Distribution of Halls Soothers*

Extending the Season

Halls Soothers extended the medicated season. Sales of Halls Soothers remained high in March and April when the market was following the seasonal pattern.

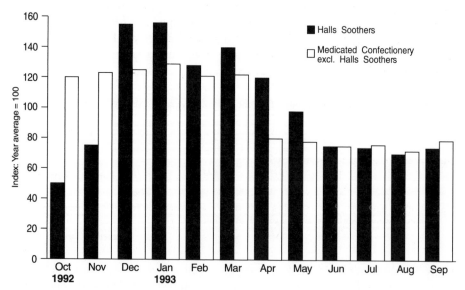

Figure 4. *Sales volume, index versus year average*

ISOLATING THE EFFECT OF ADVERTISING

The launch was clearly a success. Sales exceeded Warner Lambert's expectations without cannibalising Halls Mentho-lyptus in any way. However all elements of the marketing mix were strong. What part of the success can we ascribe to the advertising?

The Pattern of Halls Soothers' – Sales Year 1

i) Sales of Halls Soothers took off in December 1992. Sales shot up at the peak of advertising and began to fall back in February a month after the advertising had finished.

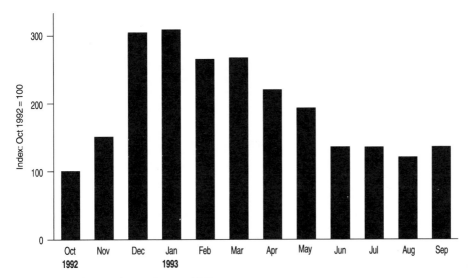

Figure 5. *Halls Soothers unit sales – GB: Grocers and CTNs*
Source: Nielsen

ii) The market only increased marginally in December and this increase is likely to be due to seasonality. But Halls Soothers' growth was far higher than the market. Halls Soothers' volume sales grew by 101% from November to December and 103% from November to January. The corresponding figures for the market excluding Halls Soothers were 5% and 12% (see Figure 6). This growth rate was much more than Halls Soothers experienced before the advertising broke. Growth between October and November was only 50%.

iii) Other activities remained constant.

Pricing

Pricing was the same throughout the launch and could have worked against us as we were operating at a premium of 2 pence to Lockets and at least 5 pence above any other medicated sweet. If anything, pricing would have had a negative influence on rate of sale.

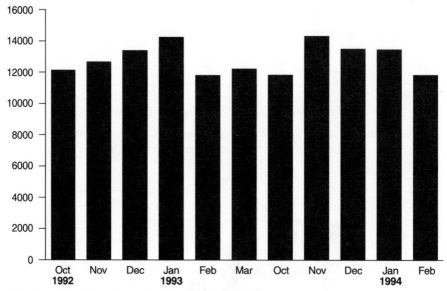

Figure 6. *Market volume sales excluding Halls Soothers – GB: Grocers and CTNs*
Source: *Nielsen*

Sampling

Throughout the launch sample packs were available – this was the only promotion during the season. A box of 48 packs of 2 sweets costing 5 pence with 5 pence coupons on pack to be redeemed against a packet of Halls Soothers were supplied to about 20% of independent grocers and about 50% of independent CTNs. This promotion was not carried by any of the multiples. These packs were popular and lasted in store for an average of 72 hours and we are sure that they must have had a positive influence on trial. However, sampling was a constant throughout the launch and cannot account for the high increases in rate of sale during the advertised period. There is also no evidence to suggest that independent CTNs and grocers performed better over the advertised period than the multiples as one might expect if the sampling had real impact (see Figure 7).

Competitive Activity

Unusually, Lockets and Tunes did not advertise in the first quarter of the '92/93 season. Strepsils was the only competitor to advertise before Christmas. Lockets heavyweight campaign began in the first week of January and continued until the end of March. Tunes came on air very late in the day for four weeks from the last week of February to the third week in March. The shares of voice over the 1992/93 medicated season are shown in Table 2.

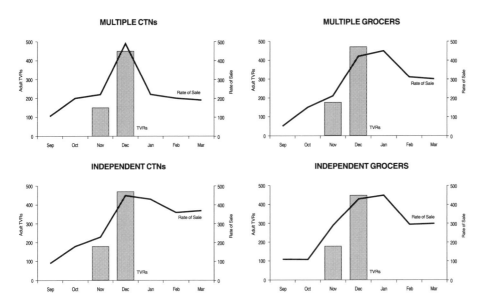

Figure 7. *Halls Soothers rate of sale by outlet type*
Source: Nielsen/AGB React

TABLE 2: MEDICATED CONFECTIONERY: SHARE OF VOICE
1992/93

	%
Halls Soothers	20.7
Halls Mentho-lyptus	27.1
Strepsils	24.2
Lockets	25.1
Tunes	2.9
Fisherman's Friends	—

Note: Adult TVRs weighted by expenditure

Source: AGB

The fact that the Halls Soothers launch was unopposed in the first two weeks of advertising undoubtedly helped Soothers to cut through with its advertising message but cannot detract from the success of the message. As we will demonstrate we have also seen high increases in rate of sale this season with much increased competitive activity – particularly the new advertising campaign from Tunes. During our main December burst shares of voice were 42.4% Halls Soothers, 32.4% Tunes.

The Health of the Nation

If there had been a particularly bad flu epidemic over the advertising period then this may have caused an uplift in sales. Unfortunately we don't have week by week data but we do know that there were no massive epidemics over the advertised period. If this had been the case we would also have seen a huge uplift in the market which we know was only 12% up as opposed to 105% as in the case of Halls Soothers.

Distribution

As we have already seen distribution built steadily over the launch period but not significantly enough between November and December to account for the huge increases in sales.

Packaging

This remained constant throughout the launch.

Product

This remained constant throughout the launch.

The Pattern of Halls Soothers Sales – Year 2

Brand Share Increased Again in October 1993 and Every Time the Ad Was on Air

There were three bursts of advertising in the '93/94 season – 18th-31st October, 29th November - 25th December and 21st February - 27th March.

The brand went from strength to strength. Share continued to grow. Halls Soothers now accounts for 16.8% of the market despite a much lower share of voice than achieved last year. Again it has shown itself to be advertising responsive.

Growth began earlier than usual as we had the advantage of 2 weeks of advertising in October and continued with our second burst in December. Value share reached 15.5% in December and fell back to 14.7% in January when we were off air. This share was then continued into February highlighting its increasing status as an established brand. Responsiveness to advertising is extremely well demonstrated in March when we come back for our final burst of the year. Against market seasonality, value share peaked at 16.8%.

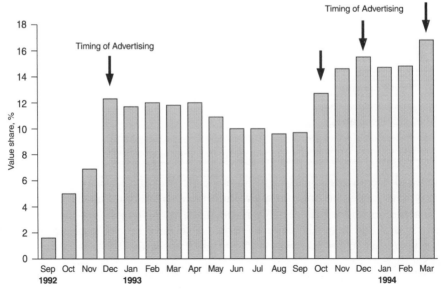

Figure 8. *Halls Soothers value share*

Sales of Halls Soothers Continued to Grow in Year Two

Every month of the 1993/94 winter season exceeded 1992/93 figures, building on that successful launch. Sales peaked in December with the height of the advertising.

What this means is that within two years Halls Soothers has established itself as a major brand in the medicated confectionery market.

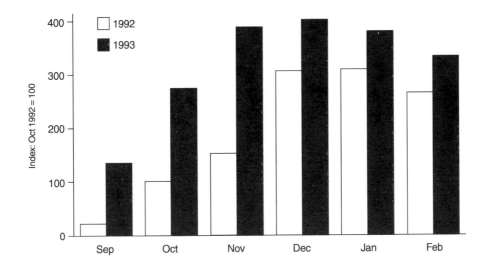

Figure 9.   *Halls Soothers value sales – GB: Grocers and CTNs*
Source: *Nielsen*

There were no other variables which could account for such high sales increases every time we advertised:

Seasonality

Volume sales for the market declined in December whilst Halls Soothers grew (see launch results). Volume share figures indicate that Halls Soothers' share of the market grew every time it was on air.

Sampling

Again there was some sampling throughout the season but at a much reduced level compared with launch and could not account for the sales peaks.

Pricing

This was constant throughout year 2.

Competitive activity

This was heavy in 1993/94, Tunes came back with a very heavyweight campaign and our share of voice was markedly lower, particularly at the peak of our campaign in December.

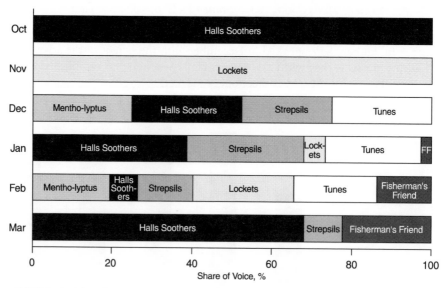

Figure 10. *Halls Soothers' share of voice, 1993/94 season*

Product

The product is of excellent quality and at time of launch was a completely new offering – prior to this a fruit flavoured liquid centre did not exist. However, this year we have seen the launch of Blackcurrant Lockets as a direct competitor to Halls Soothers. Despite the fact that its distribution is high and the Lockets brand has a strong identity it has not had the same success (see Figure 11). The brand values of Lockets have not been strong enough to affect Halls Soothers. The advertising has created something which goes beyond the product offering.

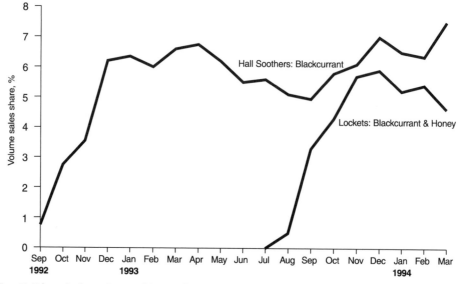

Figure 11. *Volume sales shares – Grocers and CTNs: Halls Soothers and Blackcurrant Lockets*

HOW DID THE ADVERTISING WORK?

The advertising broke through and established a new product offering.

The Halls Soothers commercial created rapid and high awareness in a way which consumers found extremely involving.

TABLE 3: ADVERTISING AND BRAND AWARENESS

	Year 1		Year 2	
	Pre %	Post %	Pre %	Post %
Advertising Awareness				
Spontaneous	0	14	4	18
Total	0	51	25	50
Brand Awareness				
Spontaneous	2	17	9	19
Total	36	73	58	77

Note: The dates for the tracking were:
Year 1: Pre Oct 23-31 1992, Post Dec 21-Jan 5 1993.
Year 2: Pre Sep 27- Oct 9 1993, Post Dec 13-19 1993.

Source: HPI Tracking

From the rational message played back by consumers having seen the ad it is clear that they have understood the product benefits – taste and soothing qualities are strongly recalled. 15% claimed the ad made them want to buy the product – double the score achieved by any competitor.

Where Halls Soothers really emerges as being different is on enjoyment as expressed in a more approachable personality.

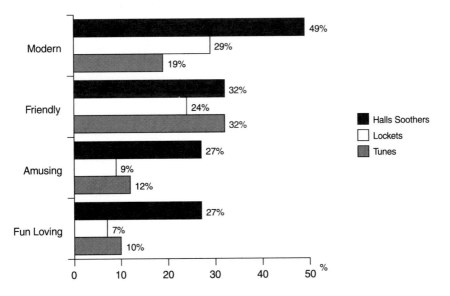

Figure 12. *Perceptions of brands*
Note: *Perceptions of brands among all respondents aware of brand (Tunes 426, Lockets 418, Halls Soothers 312). These measures were taken post the first launch burst of advertising. There was no pre-advertising measure.*
Source: HPI Tracking

This distinctive image has been maintained in year 2.

Importantly, the advertising generated more involvement than we have seen previously in the marketplace. Our tracking uses the 'Framework' approach so we were able to understand how the ad was working. Whereas most ads in the category work purely on persuasion – the more strongly a piece of information is communicated, the more consideration of the brand will be increased, our ad was working on involvement.

We were able to measure how strongly consumers identify with what is in the advertising, how they relate to it and how strongly it captures their imagination. Respondents were asked, how strongly they get caught up with the advertising, how interesting and entertaining they find it and whether they enjoy seeing it.

Our involvement scores have always been higher than those of the competition:

—   19% of consumers felt they were quite or very strongly caught up in the advertising for Halls Soothers – Tunes scored 6%, Lockets 5%.

—   19% of consumers found the advertising interesting and entertaining – Tunes scored 14%, Lockets 4%.

—   22% of consumers enjoyed seeing the advertising – Tunes scored 16%, Lockets 4%.

Post that first burst of advertising only three months after launch, 73% of medicated users claimed to have heard of Halls Soothers and 32% had tried them. They were buying lots of them. Most had purchased two or more packs and a healthy eight out of ten said they would buy them again.

Halls Soothers has continued its impressive growth on all attitudes relating to taste, containing real fruit, having a variety of flavours, a liquid centre and being up to date.

Consequently more people are claiming to have tried and bought Halls Soothers. After the launch 44% of consumers were claiming to need no symptoms to purchase. Obviously the advertising communicates great taste and enjoyability as opposed to pure therapy.

THE BOTTOM LINE

The purpose of the launch was to profitably expand Halls' business. This was done comfortably.

In its first year Halls Soothers exceeded sales expectations by 500% and the brand generated almost four times as much profit by year two as the company had expected.

All of this was achieved without any loss of Halls Mentho-lyptus' sales. Indeed Halls Mentho-lyptus saw a 6% growth in sales value in 1993 vs 1992.

The launch has paid for itself already, and Halls has an expanded business base in medicated confectionery which augurs well for future profits.

CONCLUSIONS

Halls Soothers not only met but far exceeded its first year sales targets. This was achieved in a market place which had been virtually static for many years. It had also achieved this without any adverse affect on Halls Mentho-lyptus, in fact the opposite, it seemed to have breathed new life into the Halls brand.

The advertising campaign had proved to be impactful, involving, well branded and extremely successful in communicating the desired strategy.

Specifically, the advertising had ensured a clear positioning for Halls Soothers in the marketplace and one which was very motivating for the consumer. It brought some excitement to a category which has never previously created a stir. We believe we have harnessed an emotional benefit which goes beyond the functional characteristics of the product with an advertising idea that has many years to run.

Section Three

New Campaigns for Previously Advertised Brands

11

Peperami

The Consequences of Unleashing a Beast

INTRODUCTION

This story demonstrates how the insight into peoples' intimate relationship with 8"
of meat led to one of the most exciting, provocative and undoubtedly successful
food campaigns ever to be produced.

BACKGROUND

Peperami arrived in this country by mistake back in 1982.

Mattessons, the importer, was expecting a 40' container load of pâté from
Germany but instead were lumbered with 5 tonnes of salami sticks on the Dover
quayside. Unwilling to apportion blame, they off loaded the surrogate pâté with
their van delivery system and the Brand has never had to look back since.

Well only once. On 4th December 1987 a warning appeared on the *News at
Ten* not to eat Peperami for fear of catching Salmonella. The brand was
immediately de-listed and returned 12 months later in a pasteurised form and
protected by a 'sheath'. Within 8 months, sales had regained the rate of sale
enjoyed before the scare.

This miraculous recovery can be partly accredited to the advertising at the time.
When Peperami reappeared on the shelves, it was accompanied by new advertising.
Advertising which cleverly confronted the apparent contradiction between meat
and snacks by turning the meat aspect into a competitive edge, delivering a more
assertive taste over other snacks such as crisps. Sales grew year on year consistently
thereafter by approximately 15% in volume up until the end of 1991.

Although the campaign was still alive and kicking in 1992, penetration of
Peperami had plateaued and volume growth likewise had slowed (see Figure 1).

There was little doubt the relaunch ads had achieved their objective of
establishing awareness and knowledge of Peperami. In fact, by 1992, 90% of the
Millward Brown sample knew it was a snack made of meat compared with only
38% back in 1987. However, with trial generation at an all time low, the
executions were obviously no longer provoking a relevant and motivating reaction.

The business objective defined, therefore, was to regain the rate of trial
experienced in earlier years whilst increasing the frequency of purchase among core
users.

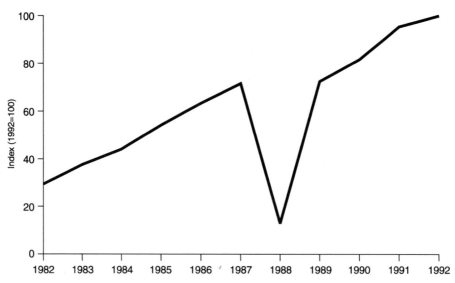

Figure 1. *Perperami volume development, 1982-1992*
Source: Van den Bergh Foods

PUTTING PEPERAMI UNDER THE MICROSCOPE

We were in no position to decide whether the successful but tired campaign merely needed refreshing or whether a new approach was needed to achieve this business objective.

What we did know, however, was that this was no ordinary, conventional product. The way it arrived in this country, the way it recovered its sales after a national health alert and the way *Anglers' Weekly* would enthusiastically endorse Peperami to its readers as an effective fishing bait merely suggested there was more to this product than we really knew about!

Our first step, therefore, was to conduct a semiotic analysis of the Brand: a psychological interrogation of the product which would hopefully unearth the root cause behind this mystical behaviour. These couch sessions revealed Peperami suffered from (or enjoyed) a truly schizophrenic personality. It appears the brand has a unique ability to straddle both meat values (power, masculinity, real food) and snack values (fun, unisexual, improper food) simultaneously. Because these two *paradigms* (meats and snacks) are so diametrically opposed, Peperami is literally pulled in opposite directions and, as a result, is left hanging there, suspended in a confused state of flux – in a world of its own with its own rules and its own agenda.

All the additional product features, the phallic shape, the condom inner-wrap, the tactile, bright green, deceptive packaging and the explosive taste act as material evidence for this frenetic, wild confrontation between meat values and snack values, thus ensuring Peperami's schizophrenia remains well and truly incurable.

So, the brand's extra terrestrial origins were confirmed. But without confronting the consumer to bring some earthy realism to this madness, we would be no closer to finding out how to develop new advertising.

THE CONFESSIONS OF A PEPERAMI EATER

In March 1992 we conducted a piece of qualitative research to attempt to understand the consumer relationship with the brand and its advertising. We discovered something no one had anticipated.

By conducting *confessional* depth interviews and friendship groups with Peperami users, it materialised they had an almost fanatical relationship with the brand which, over time, had become far more powerful than its advertising.

This 'bond' consumers shared was evident in how they ate it, where they ate it and how they talked about it. Whether they be 7 year old little girls in playgrounds or 20 year old lager louts in the 'local', there was this common, almost ritualistic appreciation for the brand and its personality.

> "It's great for when you come back pissed from the pub, yank open the fridge, pull out a Peperami and rip it open – you don't need any manners for it."

> Male, 20

> "Peperami is my wicked willie!"

> Female, 13
> Source: The Research Practice

It appeared Peperami had this eerie ability to bring out the child in everyone – their regressive streak – but in a humorous way.

Children and young adults alike would affectionately refer to the Brand as being bizarre, mischievous, anarchic, impulsive, rebellious and manic in personality.

The only ones who were less inclined to be so expressive were their mums who were buying the product for the family at the supermarket. They were simply happy to endorse the consumption of something more nutritional than chocolate. It was almost as if young consumers were intentionally keeping their special, somewhat crude relationship with Peperami to themselves.

It was clear the existing advertising did little to contribute to this relationship. It was perceived to be far too 'well-behaved', conventional and clinical for a brand which is eaten in a regressive mode, with a bottle of cheap wine and a dirty video or with a fag behind the bike sheds.

It was also clear that, thanks to the semiotic work we did earlier, this bizarre but incredibly intimate relationship had evolved from the product itself and its schizophrenic identity crisis rather than from some weird youth phenomenon that had nothing to do with the product.

These consumer confessions not only highlighted why the existing advertising was no longer inspiring usage but also how the new communication strategy could be developed. If non-users already knew of Peperami and its meat content (as Millward Brown would suggest) and still were not being tempted, we could use this controversial, manic personality to reinvigorate interest in the brand. After all, because this brand personality is so deeply rooted in the product's rational make-up, using it would have the effect of dramatising Peperami's meatiness in a much more relevant and provocative way.

57 WAYS OF SKINNING A PEPERAMI

Using the personality of the brand to excite and provoke trial was all very well but with such a personality disorder the creative challenge was as much dangerous as it was exciting.

Not only could this anarchy and rebellion turn into a destructive, vicious, uncontrollable force but how do you find a creative expression for it which appeals equally to 7 year olds and 20 year olds without alienating Mums by letting them into their offspring's secret world?

And because of the varying interpretations of Peperami's multi-faceted personality, according to consumers, the character portrayal could take the form of Arnold Schwarzeneger, Nigel Kennedy, Fred Flintstone, Roy Chubby Brown, Alf Garnett, James Belushi, Vinny Jones or Iago!

So, to ensure we exhausted all possible creative expressions, four working propositions were written from a matrix which reflects the parameters of Peperami's personality. All four rely on the mischievous personality of the brand to communicate the product's meatiness but tonally in very different ways.

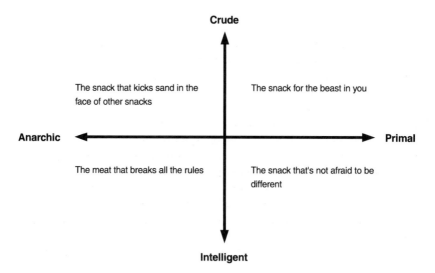

Figure 2. *The Peperami personality matrix*

Adcepts were produced to these four propositions – 57 in all. They are literally advertising concepts or perhaps better defined as 'scamp creative expressions', in this case of Peperami's personality. They have the benefit, in research, of being treated as rough ideas rather than 'real' ads by consumers and by their very nature are much more efficient in exhausting the strategic opportunities. Handled like a deck of cards, they became the focal point of a qualitative project. Kids, young men and mums alike would use them as an essential crutch to help express and clarify their feelings towards the brand and its persona.

Out of this research we learned exactly how to *manage* this personality.

For example, adcepts with crude and base connotations, although true to the brand, not only alientated mums but distanced young users by making an aspect of the brand public which they would rather keep to themselves.

Similarly, sheer agression, although a by-product of the brand, failed to represent the shrewd, deceptive side of Peperami's mentality.

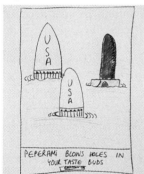  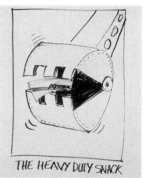

However, three adcepts in particular hit the mark spot on.

  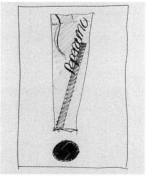

All three cleverly depicted the deceptive nature of the product, as if the brand is getting some sort of kick from deceiving, surprising and even shocking the consumer without being overtly aggressive.

"It's mischievously going out of its way to shock. You can't cage the taste."

Male, 17

"It's untamed. You don't know how it will behave."

Male, 18
Source: RDS Research

References to 'beast' and 'wild' in these adcepts were suggestive of an untamed, uncontrollable animal constrained by the confines of its packaging: an image which not only reflected Peperami's manic personality but also its blatant spicy, carnivorous product nature. The exclamation mark, on the other hand, boldly epitomised the ballsy confidence of Peperami and its mischievous desire to shock.

Suspense, surprise and deception – all the essential ingredients to provoke the necessary intrigue and trial among potential users.

CALCULATED MADNESS

The creative brief became the distillation of all the accumulated learning: the semiotic analysis, the confessional research and the reactions to the adcepts. Learning which was clearly reflected in the one idea which the creative team presented 4 weeks later.

The creative idea centred on an animated Peperami character. A *creature* with an attitude whose antics embodied all the brand's manic personality traits identified by consumers, wrapped up with an arresting, controversial and disarmingly honest endline "It's a bit of an animal"!

The risqué nature of the creative idea demanded we sensitively validated the campaign both in qualitative research in concept form and quantitative pre-testing with finished film. The initial concept research confirmed the richness and appeal of the idea.

> "The product and personality mirror each other in the advertising and are inextricably linked. By dramatising the provocative, deceptive side of Peperami, the campaign successfully nurtures the unique relationship with the Peperami consumer whilst creating the necessary intrigue and curiosity among non-users. Both young adults and young children alike feel the campaign was written for them personally and no one else, whilst mums turn a blind eye knowing their children will love it!"
>
> Source: Crucible Research

Likewise, the Millward Brown pre-test research endorsed the campaign on every measure from branding to impact, from comprehension to appeal and from product communication to likelihood to try. At this point of time, however, the validity of its predictions, were yet to be proven.

THE MEDIA STRATEGY AND PLAN

All the accumulated learning which fuelled the development of the advertising, equally played its part in driving the media strategy.

With the smallest budget in the snack market our ambitions were to make the biggest noise. We wanted Peperami to be on everyone's lips, in pubs, at school, at home, everywhere. Because we knew we could not out-shout *Suede, Sega* and *Jurassic Park* we relied on the very tactics Peperami himself would deploy: surprise, deception and suspense...

1. Spend 75% of the budget in the first two weeks to generate the initial hype, attain a satisfactory level of exposure of the six executions and reinforce the manic energy of the creative idea.
2. Then withdraw swiftly from television altogether to initiate a *whispering campaign on the ground*. The free 'word-of-mouth' advertising we all dream about.
3. Finally, return two weeks later with a very light 'drip' strategy, teasing and reminding the audience that what hit them in the initial burst was not simply a figment of their imagination. Continue this 'drip' for as long as the money would last (10 weeks).
4. Opt for a single TV buying audience of 16-24 year old males, taking into account the aspirational nature of younger children. But in addition, intentionally avoid the obvious youth programmes. The effect of our Peperami ads in a *Coronation Street* break (and even *Songs of Praise*) would do far more justice to the brand's mischievous personality than a spot say in *The Word*. By blackballing terminally trendy programmes we could distance ourselves from overtly youthful advertisers, never wanting to appear alongside Tango, Sega and Pepsi Max.

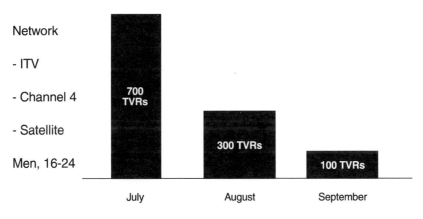

Figure 3. *Peperami media schedule 1993*

STILLS FROM "IT'S A BIT OF AN ANIMAL" ADS

'Bag'

'Hot'

'Arms'

THE PEPERAMI 'BIG BANG'

The outcome of the initial advertising concept qualitative research not only fuelled the excitement and confidence to progress to production, but also initiated a whole flurry of activity back at Van den Bergh Foods. The strength of the advertising paved the way for the successful negotiation of new listings in the key multiples and more importantly the acceptance of *dual* sitings in *all* multiples (in the chiller cabinet *and* on the Deli Counter top) – a first in the history of the grocery trade!

It was not the fact that Peperami was spending £800,000 on TV, which impressed the Trade – afterall it was a smaller budget than 1992 – but the very nature of the immediately impactful advertising idea which they gleaned from, by now, rather tatty ex-research storyboards. *They* were the ones who demanded the dual siting, not Van den Berghs: ironic, considering the million's of pounds confectionery manufacturers spend in trying to get a second listing!

For best effect, it was agreed these distribution and siting gains would start on the very day of the TV launch. In collaboration with a below-the-line Agency, a display box using the advertising idea was produced to take full advantage of the new Deli Counter top position.

The date was set for 3rd July – the day quickly became nicknamed *the Big Bang*.

THE GROSS EFFECT OF THE 'BIG BANG'

The 'Big Bang' existed *because* of the advertising. According to Van den Berghs, there is no doubt, neither distribution gains nor dual sitings would have been secured without a campaign of this creative standard. We will prove the total incremental sales by the 'Big Bang' consist of both *direct* and *indirect* advertising effects. We will only use, however, the *direct* advertising effects to demonstrate the Campaign's effectiveness.

Sales

In July, Nielsen recorded tonnage sales of Peperami were up by 54.5% on June and up 75% year on year – four times greater than any previously recorded monthly sales increase. In August, this record was promptly broken when sales were up 65% on June's figures.

But the sales effect of the 'Big Bang' was not just limited to the advertised period.

The launch of the advertising on 3rd July conveniently allows us to use the first six months of 1993 as an index to set against what happened in the following six months. From 1st January to 2nd July there was no support whatsoever for Peperami. As a result, monthly sales were constant with only a +/- 5% deviation. This consistency in sales is indicative of Peperami's normal year-round performance. There is no seasonality in Peperami sales whatsoever. We can naturally take these first six months, therefore, as a realistic base level for comparison. The effect of the advertising in July and August was dramatic against this index with 49% and 59% increases respectively, but its effectiveness was still significantly visible even in December with sales up by 22% on the first six months of the year.

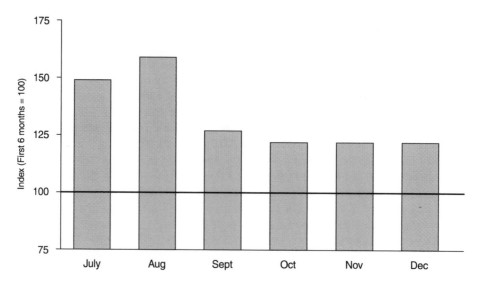

Figure 4. *Peperami volume sales: July-December 1993*
Source: Nielsen

In fact, the average running rate for the second half of the year was 21.2 tonnes/month higher than that for the first half. A 35% increase in the average monthly running rate. (Source: Nielsen)

Splitting the year up by quarters, rather than halves, quarter 3 saw a 42% increase in sales over quarter 2 whilst there was still a 23% uptake in sales in the fourth quarter over the second.

Van den Bergh Foods' own delivery figures confirm this dramatic sales uplift.

TABLE 1: PEPERAMI DELIVERIES

	Average Monthly Tonnage	% Change on Q2
Quarter 2	80.0	–
Quarter 3	121.4	+51.8
Quarter 4	96.3	+20.4

Source: Van den Bergh Foods

Peperami's market share also climbed to an all time high of 90.2% in July – a 4% share gain from Own Label. Peperami managed to defend this gain throughout the latter half of 1993.

In value terms, Peperami sales grew by 60% in 1993. Since sales were constant in the first half of the year, virtually all this growth can be attributed to the last six months.

Trial

Since the core advertising objective was that of provoking trial of Peperami, we must attempt to assess the extent to which this dramatic sales increase effected actual trial of the brand rather than merely frequency of purchase among existing users.

Based on 11 years of experience, the entry point for triallists of Peperami has been the single stick, whereas existing, loyal users are more predisposed to the multipacks (5 sticks). By splitting out sales of single sticks and multipacks over the July-December period we can tentatively demonstrate the levels of trial verses increased frequency of purchase.

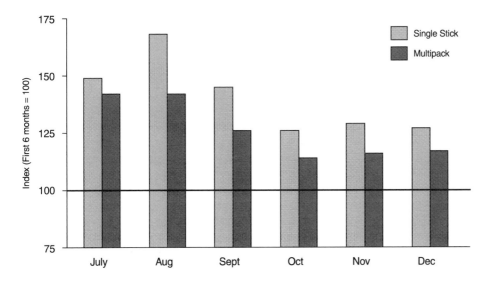

Figure 5. *Peperami single stick and multipack sales: July-December 1993*
Source: Nielsen

It is reassuring to see increased sales of single sticks holding up against the better value multipacks, suggesting new users have joined the Peperami *club*. However, although a strong relationship may exist between variant sales and 'user-type', we cannot conclusively prove the extent of the trial generation based on this correlation alone.

For more concrete evidence, an NOP Omnibus study was conducted in January 1993 and repeated 15 months later to gauge any shifts in penetration of Peperami (see Figure 6).

A total of 4,058 adults (all 15+ years) were interviewed across the two waves. By April 1994, the proportion of the population having ever tried Peperami had grown by 40% – in just 15 months. For a brand which took 11 years to achieve a 25% penetration, this is a dramatic shift.

Although we have no data on frequency of purchase and repeat purchase, this certainly proves trial contributed significantly to the sales uplift.

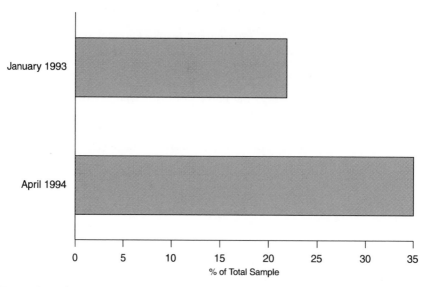

Figure 6. *Ever tried Peperami: January 1993 vs April 1994*
Base: *4,058 Adults, 15+*
Source: NOP Omnibus 1993-1994

CALCULATING THE NET ADVERTISING EFFECT

The gross effect of the 'Big Bang' was a 35% increase in the monthly running rate and a 40% increase in penetration.

   To calculate the net effect of the advertising we must subtract the sales effects from the two other elements of the 'Big Bang' (and any other influental variables), regardless of how critical the advertising was in securing such elements.

Distribution Gains

The following table details the distribution gains which were secured before the campaign but which only became active at the time of the TV launch.

TABLE 2: PEPERAMI DISTRIBUTION GAINS 1993

Store	Product Variant	Sterling Distribution Change %
Gateway	Hot 5 Pack	40-100
Safeway	Hot Single	77-100
	Hot 5 Pack	15-60
Tesco	Hot 5 Pack	0-50
Asda	Hot 5 Pack	42-100
Sainsbury	Single	0-90
	Hot Single	75-100
	Hot 5 Pack	75-100

Source: Van den Bergh Foods

It is important to point out here that these distribution gains are merely for variants of Peperami. Because the brand is already listed in all of these outlets in the form of other variants, actual number of outlets stocking Peperami remains unchanged.

The other significant factor to take into account is the degree to which multipacks cannibalise single stick sales. The introduction of a multipack into a store which lists a single stick on average cannibalises 50% of single stick sales. (Source: Van den Berghs.)

These two factors help explain why the increase in rate of sale for Peperami almost exactly mirrors the total sales increase. The average monthly ROS for the last half of 1993 was 34.4% up on that for the first six months.

Compare this to the 35% average increase in total sales and it is clear the growth has been demand-led rather than distribution led.

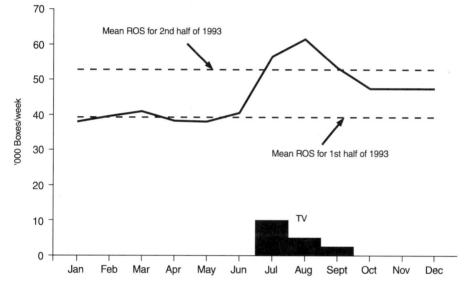

Figure 7. *Peperami rate of sale 1993: Total GB Grocery*
Source: Nielsen

Van den Berghs own data confirms this. Their delivery figures can be accessed by individual store and individual variant/pack format. We can, therefore, subtract the gross effect these new distribution gains have had on total monthly Peperami sales by totalling the last 6 months of data for 1993.

TABLE 3: VOLUME CONTRIBUTION OF NEW DISTRIBUTION GAINS
July–December 1993

Store	Additional Tonnes/Month from New Listings
Gateway	0.10
Safeway	0.15
Tesco	0.12
Asda	0.10
Sainsbury	0.50
Total tonnes/month	**0.97**

Source: Van den Bergh Foods

The total contribution to sales from these new distribution gains alone was on average 0.97 tonnes/month (40,000 sticks) between July and December 1993 – only 4.5% of the additional sales achieved.

Their contribution to trial generation must be even more negligible, since the extreme nature of Peperami Hot (which takes up most of the distribution gains) limits appeal to existing Peperami users.

Dual Sitings

Although Peperami has had ad hoc sitings on the deli counter in the past, it has never managed to secure an extra siting in *every* major multiple at the same time. Since these first appeared in the week of the new advertising they will undoubtedly have contributed significantly to the effectiveness of the advertising both in terms of sales and trial. Most of these deli-top stands were still in operation at the end of 1993.

Arguably, these deli-top stands with designs which fed directly off the campaign idea, were literally an extension of the advertising in-store. One could argue the case further that eliminating the very sales channel, designed and set up specifically to help convert the interest generated from the advertising, will unfairly downplay the advertising's effectiveness.

Regardless, we still want to isolate the second siting from the sales in order to prove the raw advertising effect. Unfortunately, neither Nielsen data nor Van den Bergh delivery data split out sales from the deli-top. And since *every* store listed the second siting we are not able to establish a control against which the effect of the extra siting can be compared. In order to negotiate permanent dual sitings, Van den Bergh's undertook a trade survey to quantify the contribution from these deli-top stands. Each retailer was asked to supply sales figures from the two sitings, which were then collated and analysed at Van den Bergh.

TABLE 4: FREQUENCY OF DELI-TOP BOX REPLACEMENT
July-December 1993

Boxes per Week	% of Stores
0-1	55
1-2	25
2-3	10
3-4	5
4-5	5

Source: Van den Bergh Trade Survey

The results of the survey show that, on average, the deli-top stands were refilled once a week during the 6 month period. In total, 4.2 tonnes of Peperami sales a month went through the deli-top stands.

Subtracting both this amount and the 0.97 tonnes generated by the distribution gains from the gross sales uplift of 21.2 tonnes, leaves a net effect of 16.03 incremental tonnes a month. For the 6 month period from July to December 1993 this running rate is 26.6% higher than that for the first half of the year.

Seasonality

We have already touched on the seasonality aspect of Peperami. Peperami sales over the 11 years in UK have shown no seasonal trends whatsoever. The greatest variance in monthly sales in the previous 4 years has been +/– 10% (source: Nielsen). Such nominal shifts can be attributed to past advertising, promotions, distribution gains and stock levels, but never has there been a climatic or seasonal relationship observed.

Variant Launches

There were no variant launches in 1993. The main Peperami variant launched was *Peperami Hot* in July 1992. Initial sales were spectacular yet subdued slightly by some cannibalisation of Peperami Original. By the time the new advertising appeared 12 months later, trial and frequency had stabilised. Although one of the commercials in this new campaign featured this new variant, thus increasing sales, its share of total Peperami sales has remained constant throughout the last half of 1993, at just under 20%.

Because of the extreme taste of Peperami Hot, we expect the sales uplift to have come from existing Peperami consumers rather than from non-users. Hence, penetration of 'ever tried' Peperami will not have been significantly effected by Peperami Hot.

Peperami-in-a-Roll was also launched in September 1992. However, it was not featured in the advertising and, as a result, sales and trial since July 1993 have remained sluggish.

Pricing

Peperami's RRP, accepted by all grocery retailers remained unchanged in 1993. The price was increased at the end of 1992 from 39p to 45p, making it two thirds more expensive than a *Mars Bar* and even more difficult for trial generation. Own label salami sticks also maintained their prices during 1993.

Promotions

The brand ran neither promotions during the advertised period nor in the subsequent months. The nearest promotion was in March 1993 for Peperami Hot in limited stores.

Competitive Influences

Peperami's only significant direct competition is from Tesco and Sainsbury salami sticks who jointly account for approximately 8% of the meat snacks market (source: Nielsen). Retailing at a price 10% below Peperami, these two competitors have never supported their salami snacks in any way which could have influenced either theirs or Peperami's performance.

At the end of 1993, both retailers delisted their own brands. We can only conclude the effectiveness of Peperami advertising had a part to play!

Other Possible Influences

In the lead up to or during the campaign period there was no relevant consumer PR positive or negative on any subject which could have impacted on sales. Any PR generated by the advertising itself was limited to business and industry press.

As for the product, since the pasteurisation back in 1988 the make-up of Peperami has remained unchanged. The packaging is still the same as it was when the product arrived in the UK in 1982.

Summary of the Advertising Effect on Sales

We earlier highlighted the Nielsen figures for Peperami, which confirmed a 35% monthly increase in volume sales for the last six months of 1993 compared to the first six months.

We have now calculated that 23% of these incremental sales can be attributed to what some may call *non-advertising factors* (which we would prefer to call *indirect* advertising factors). Discounting the fact that the advertising idea literally negotiated those crucial dual sitings and distribution gains (which have since become permanent fixtures), we can conclude the *raw*, net effect of the advertising campaign is a 26.6% volume uplift in average monthly sales during July to December.

If you were to continue to exclude those *indirect* advertising factors you would see this uplift peaking during the campaign in July and August, when net *advertising-related* sales were up 38% and 45% respectively over the first 6 months. The effectiveness of the advertising was still clearly visible later in the year contributing 17% of extra sales in December.

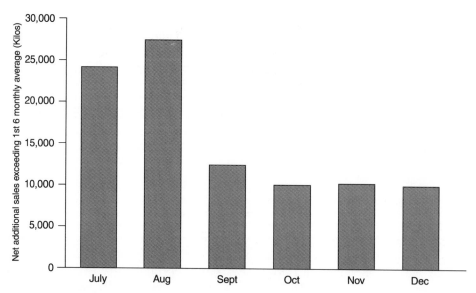

Figure 8.   *Net advertising-related sales of Peperami: July-December 1993*
Note: *Less effect of distribution an siting gains*
Source: Nielsen, Van den Bergh Foods

In total tonnage terms for the second half of 1993, this equates to an incremental gain of 96.2 tonnes (or 4 million sticks) – equivalent to an extra 1½ months worth of total Peperami sales calculated at the running rate before the campaign.

Although profit details and payback periods cannot be disclosed here, based on these net advertising effects alone, the return on investment for the campaign was phenomenal.

> "Although we had tough targets to meet, to experience such an advertising payback from a campaign for an 11 year old product is just unheard of."
>
> Simon Turner, Marketing Director, Van den Bergh Foods

As a result, business objectives for 1994 were dramatically reviewed (upwards naturally), whilst the marketing budget for the following year was doubled.

CONFIRMING THE CORRELATION BETWEEN ADVERTISING AND SALES/TRIAL

So far we have demonstrated by a process of subtraction and elimination the *raw* advertising effect on Peperami sales.

Quantitative consumer research was commissioned to gauge the degree of direct correlation between Peperami advertising and people's propensity to purchase.

A pre and post Millward Brown survey was conducted amongst the two target groups, children aged 7-14 and young men aged 16-24. A group of mothers of children aged 0-18 was also incorporated into the sample to monitor potential degree of alienation, if any. The pre-survey was conducted in mid-June, the post late September 1993.

We will demonstrate how the high levels of advertising awareness, recall, appeal and communication have directly effected Peperami's popularity, people's interest in and expectations of the product and finally their likelihood to try the brand.

Advertising Awareness

When Peperami appeared in *Marketing's* Adwatch survey in week 2 of the campaign, at number eleven, behind ten campaigns with significantly heavier advertising spends, we naturally anticipated good awareness levels amongst our core targets.

However, this did little to prepare us for the news that the advertising achieved the second highest *advertising awareness index (AI)* ever recorded in this country by Millward Brown – who have been monitoring directly or indirectly most campaigns aired in the last 18 years! (See Figure 9.)

The ad awareness index acts as a measure of *branded visibility*. The average awareness index from a random sample of 300 of the most recent campaigns tracked by Millward Brown is 4. Peperami's estimated awareness index among 16-24 year old males was 40, which would suggest for every 100 TVRs spent behind this advertising, the brand's ad awareness level would be increased by 40 percent! Ridiculous it may be but no one would question the unique ability this advertising had of immediately grabbing peoples attention – even the notoriously difficult 16-24 year old male consumers. Among 7-14 year old children the

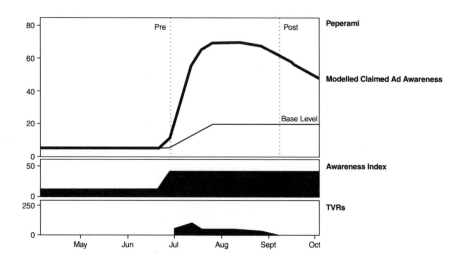

Figure 9. *Claimed TV advertising awareness: Men 16-24*
Source: Millward Brown

Peperami ad awareness index was a record-breaking 26 and for mums, who were never intended to notice the advertising, an AI of 15 was measured!

For prompted advertising awareness, Peperami was placed in a list of competitive brands – most of which were receiving above-the-line support within the first six months of 1993. After the campaign, Peperami visibly outscored all of them.

TABLE 5: PROMPTED AD AWARENESS: SNACK BRANDS
16-24 Year Old Men

Pre	%	Post	%
Mars	47	**Peperami**	67
Walkers	42	Walkers	41
McCoys	38	Mars	37
Penguin	32	McCoys	30
Kit Kat	31	Penguin	28
Baby Bel	16	Baby Bel	28
Peperami	**11**	KP Nuts	27
KP Nuts	9	Kit Kat	22
Branigans	7	Branigans	11

Base: Pre: 511;   Post: 418

Source: Millward Brown, 1993

TABLE 6: PROMPTED AD AWARENESS: SNACK BRANDS
7-14 Year Old Children

Pre	%	Post	%
Milky Way	52	**Peperami**	62
Walkers	47	Monster Munch	48
Mars	38	Walkers	44
Monster Munch	36	Baby Bel	38
Quavers	30	Mars	25
Baby Bel	29	Milky Way	24
Kit Kat	27	Penguin	24
Penguin	25	Quavers	23
Hula Hoops	16	Kit Kat	19
Peperami	12	Hula Hoops	12

Base: Pre: 225;   Post: 412

Source: Millward Brown, 1993

The media ambition of *making the largest noise with the smallest budget* had certainly been achieved. What is also certain, is that not just *any* advertising could have achieved this awareness, but only advertising of Peperami's quality with the originality, attitude and sheer intrusiveness to penetrate the hardest of consumers.

Advertising Recall

A testimony to this is the strength of the advertising recall: 87% of young men ad aware correctly recalled one or more of the executions and 75% of children ad aware played back detailed sequences from the ads. Kids in particular had an outstanding ability to quote verbatim from the Peperami character.

"He's watching a film and it's in a salami shop and a man takes a Peperami off a rack and starts slicing it up. The Peperami turns around and says "I like a good horror film" and starts laughing."

Male, 14 years
Source: Millward Brown, 1993

Even recall of the endline "it's a bit of an animal" was high considering the newness and media weight of this campaign, with 1 in 3 of those children and young men who claim they remember the advertising, playing back the line word for word.

Advertising Appeal

Overall reactions to the campaign were almost universally positive. It appeared the advertising had generated high levels of empathy amongst all samples. 81% of kids ad aware rated the advertising as good or very good whilst 84% of young men recalling the ads mentioned elements they like. As for mums, dislikes were kept to a manageable level below 25% – a level of negative comment not dissimilar to mainstream popular campaigns like *I Can't Believe It's Not Butter* or *Domestos*. We were relieved to discover alienation of mums was never to be an issue.

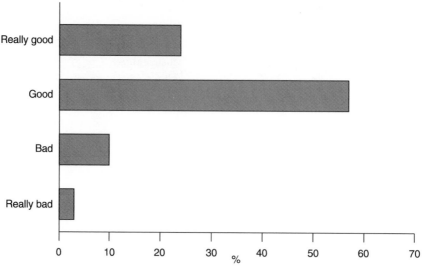

Figure 10. *Total opinion of Peperami ads: Children*
Base: *Definite recallers: 255*
Source: Millward Brown, 1993

Advertising Communication

Considering the campaign communication rested entirely in the hands of the wild Peperami personality, rational take-out from the advertising was very good. 1 in 2 mums and young men spontaneously translated the personality into a relevant, rational product benefit eg, spicy, hot, nice to eat, tasty or genuinely different, whilst 78% of children agreed the advertising clearly conveyed the spiciness of the product.

But what effect has all this advertising awareness, recall, appeal and communication had on people's perceptions of the brand and more importanly their propensity to purchase Peperami?

Brand Popularity

The campaign clearly demonstrated its ability to raise the perceived popularity of the brand across its two diverse user groups. From a list of competitive brands, both children and young men were twice as likely to mention Peperami in the post stage as a brand popular amongst people of their age.

This helps explain the 150 or so letters Van den Bergh received in 1993 from children and even mothers of younger children requesting VHS copies of the campaign.

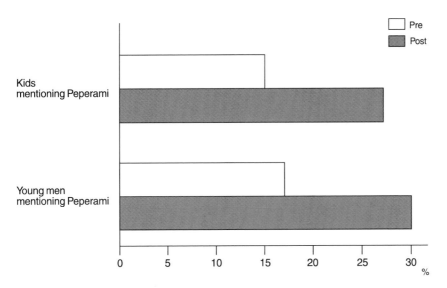

Figure 11. *Popularity of Peperami: Q. "Which of the following brands do you think are popular amongst people of your own age?"*
(List of 10 snack brands)
Source: Millward Brown, 1993

Brand Interest

The advertising has generated very high levels of increased brand interest amongst both current users and non-users – and across both men and mums.

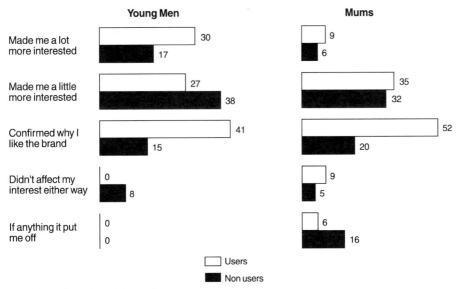

Figure 12. *Total effect on interest in Peperami*
Base: *Definite recallers. Young men: 281; mums: 220.*
Source: Millward Brown, 1993

Brand Expectations

This heightened interest is sourced in their greater expectations of the product which have improved significantly across all relevant attributes.

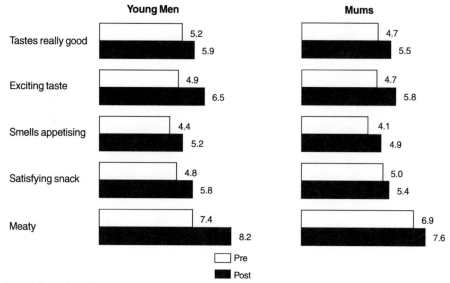

Figure 13. *Expectations of Peperami*
Base:　　　*Total sample. Young men: 418; mums: 424.*
Source: Millward Brown, 1993

Likelihood to Try

Because of the conceptual subtleties of measuring *levels of interest* in a brand among children we did not attempt to monitor this criterion. However, we did succeed in measuring their *desire to eat* Peperami.

Children were asked how much they would like to eat various snack brands, including Peperami. There was a marked improvement in their desire to eat Peperami after the campaign. In fact, boys in particular were 28% more likely to want to eat Peperami post the advertising, with their mean score out of 10 going from 3.88 to 4.96. The mean score for all kids increased by 21%.

This greater desire to eat Peperami was also shared among young men, whose mean score for *likelihood to buy for oneself* rose from 2.97 to 3.65 after the campaign launch: a 23% increase during the campaign period. Amongst those who definitely recall the advertising, the increase in mean score rises to 38%. Although this may not be causal, since it may include a greater proportion of users, at least it does not contradict the overall finding across the total sample group. (See Figure 14.)

For mums, acting as purchasers rather than core consumers of Peperami, their responsiveness to the advertising is even greater than that among young men. Their mean score for *likelihood to purchase* increases by 26%, whilst those aware of the advertising are 40% more likely to buy Peperami for their children (again, not causal but certainly not contradictory either). (See Figure 15.)

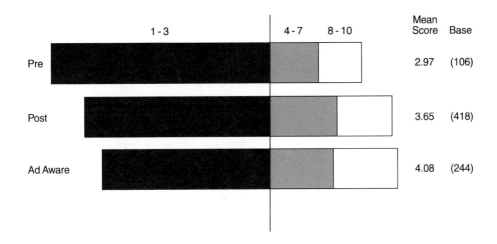

Figure 14. *Likelihood to buy Peperami for oneself: Young men*
Source: Millward Brown, 1993

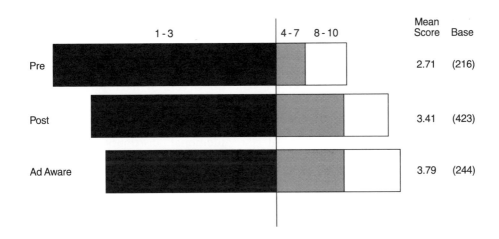

Figure 15. *Likelihood to buy Peperami for child: Mums*
Source: Millward Brown, 1993

Considering the very way in which the product itself polarises people of all ages, these shifts are even more significant.

From these results, it is clear the advertising successfully generated real interest in the actual purchasing of Peperami not just across its core user groups of young men and kids but also among the core purchasers of Peperami in the supermarket, mums.

Reassuringly, the biggest shifts in increased *likelihood to purchase* have come from non-users of the brand with rises of 25% among kids, 28% among young men and 34% among mums.

Converting to 'Actual' Trial

To what extent these potential users actually bought Peperami as a result of their 'claims' to purchase is difficult to quantify.

However, it is these particular findings which best demonstrate the relationship between the advertising and its contribution to generating trial of Peperami.

The shifts in *likelihood to purchase* among potential users, ranging from 25% to 34%, measured between June and September 1993, are not poles apart from the shifts in actual *ever tried* figures recorded by NOP, of 40% between January 1993 and April 1994. In the heart of that 15 months there was a dramatic shift in non-users propensity to buy – a shift more likely caused by the advertising than anything else. It is conceivable the dual sitings as a *vehicle* contributed to generating trial – and we hope they did, since that was what they were designed to do – but it is less conceivable they were capable of provoking the attitudinal change necessary to prompt non-users to trial. *Only* advertising, communicating the product's meatiness in a provocative and appealing way, thereby raising peoples expectations in the product, could have realistically driven this increased *desire* to try.

We can safely conclude, therefore, that the Peperami advertising was critical to generating trial of the brand and not just increasing frequency of usage among existing users.

SUMMARY – THE CONSEQUENCES OF UNLEASHING A BEAST

A Beast was identified within the make-up of Peperami. The unleashing of it, in the form of the advertising, completely reinvigorated the brand.

With *and* without the help of the additional distribution gains and unprecedented dual sitings it helped to realise, the campaign generated spectacular value and volume growth for Peperami both during and after the airing and an explosion of its customer base by 40%.

Not content with that and breaking all payback records in Van den Bergh's account books, the advertising continued to perform unabated well into the following year before the second burst picked up the fight.

The impact of this business success is clearly visible in 1994: a doubling of the brand's marketing budget, new films to complement the existing batch, increased NPD activity, acceptance in new Trade Outlet types (pubs and garage forecourts) and not surprisingly, an upward review of business targets – all the manifestations of a satisfied and more confident client.

Unilever in the States has since tested the films, and on the back of the results will be launching the brand over there! At least a dozen other countries are seriously considering usage of the campaign in their markets.

There is no doubt, that none of this would have been achievable had it not been for advertising with such originality, appeal and sheer intrusiveness.

Only such advertising, borne out of an exhaustive interrogation of the product and the consumer relationship, had the capacity to quite literally *enter people's lives* in the way we have demonstrated.

12

The Wonderbra

*How thinking big ensured the survival
of the fittest*

INTRODUCTION

This is the story of "Bra Wars", a phrase coined by the press to sum up the recent high profile battle for the Great British Cleavage.

There are two main protagonists – the Playtex Wonderbra and its arch rival the Gossard Ultrabra. And whilst "Bra Wars" is still raging, we will show two things:

1. How advertising on a very limited scale for the Playtex Wonderbra sparked a public debate of unprecedented proportions, proving that you don't need to be new to be newsworthy.
2. How at a time of serious threat and competition, advertising for the Playtex Wonderbra not only protected volume and distribution but also achieved substantial incremental sales.

But before discussing the rationale behind the Wonderbra advertising, and what it has so far achieved, it is important to understand the history behind the War itself.

BRA WARS – A BRIEF HISTORY

1964

Canadelle, a leading Canadian lingerie manufacturer designed and patented a revolutionary new push-up plunge bra, the Wonderbra. It was so called because, through intricate engineering and 44 vital components, it created a fabulous cleavage where nature had neglected to do so.

1968

Canadelle gave the UK licence for the Wonderbra to Courtaulds Textiles, who manufactured and distributed the bra through their subsidiary, Gossard.

1991

After 23 years, the Gossard Wonderbra had sold a steady but uninspiring 11 million units in the UK (on average 50 million bras are sold a year in this country. Source: trade estimates). The main reasons for this were:

— The fact that it was seen as a functional 'niche' product (a problem solving bra).
— The bra itself, and the shape it created, had fallen out of fashion by the 1980s and was seen as out-of-date and unattractive by most women. (Source: TBWA qualitative.)
— Advertising support for the Gossard Wonderbra had been negligible over that period.

1992

The situation changed dramatically, with the 28 year old Wonderbra set to become the 'essential' fashion accessory through an unforeseen chain of events:

— The fashionable image of women changed from the lean, hungry look to one of voluptuous womanly curves, and clothes were now being designed with bosoms very much in mind:

"A quick flip through *Vogue* will leave you in no doubt that visible cleavages are back in fashion"
Today

— The Wonderbra was quickly rediscovered by the less well endowed fashion cognoscenti as an inexpensive and less painful alternative to cosmetic surgery, and Wonderbras were once again being worn with pride:

"The way to be in on the breast front is to stick them out in a Wonderbra."
Sunday Times

— By the end of 1992, Gossard was producing an unprecedented 20,000 units a week for the UK and export markets.

"Wonderbra is being worn, nay flaunted everywhere"
Vogue

1993

In 1993, over 900,000 Gossard Wonderbras were sold in the UK, and the Sara Lee Corporation, who by now owned Canadelle, retrieved the Wonderbra licence from Gossard and Courtaulds Textiles.

The licence was then given to Playtex, another leading lingerie manufacturer, whom Sara Lee had bought at the end of 1992.

As of January 1st 1994 the Gossard Wonderbra would cease to be, and the Playtex Wonderbra would exist in its place.

Gossard responded by developing the virtually identical Gossard Ultrabra, which would also come into existence on January 1st.

THE PROBLEMS FACING THE WONDERBRA IN 1994

At the beginning of 1994, the Playtex Wonderbra was potentially the loser, with the Gossard Ultrabra poised to win before the battle had even begun:

1. British women tended to buy bras not brands. This was due to:
    — their traditionally functional/practical attitude to underwear, ie it serves a purpose (Source: TBWA qualitative);
    — the dominance of own label. 65% of bras bought in the UK are own-label, and only 35% are brand names. Marks & Spencer alone accounts for an estimated 40% of sales (Source: trade estimates);
    — historically, there is a very low advertising:sales ratio as lingerie brands only had minimal advertising support (see Figure 1), so women were given no reason to buy brands rather than own label.

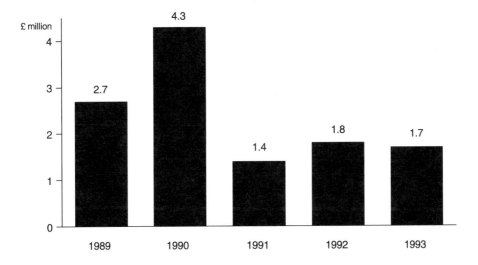

Figure 1. *Women's lingerie advertising expenditure*
Source: MEAL

    — furthermore, the average price of a bra in the UK was only £6.84 compared to the European average of £7.99 and the French average of £9.59 (Source: trade estimates). The Wonderbra was over twice as expensive, retailing at £14.99;
    — although UK women were changing their attitude to bras and were beginning to see underwear as fashionable outerwear, it was a very slow process with the vast majority of women being very unresponsive to brands.

2. However, thanks largely to its recent success with the Wonderbra, Gossard had become a very high profile brand amongst women, with a very strong fashionable image (Source: TBWA qualitative).

3. Playtex on the other hand, whilst being a major player, had no history or credibility at the fashionable end of the UK lingerie market, as its heritage and strength was in the more functional, practical sector. Playtex was regarded by

women as the *"no nonsense"* brand which made good quality *"serviceable"* garments for the more mature woman, ie *"bras my mother wore"*. (Source: TBWA qualitative.)

4. Whilst there was considerable interest in the Wonderbra licence changeover amongst the media and the trade, the Gossard Ultrabra was seen as the real, more exciting story as it was to all intents a new product, whereas the Playtex Wonderbra was largely the same as it had always been:

> "The Cup Final – Ultrabra [performance] beats Wonderbra."
>
> *The Sun*

5. This was despite the fact that both products were virtually identical in their design and performance, which was a problem in itself:

> "Customers may have problems working out the difference between the two products".
>
> *The Observer*

6. This product similarity added to the potential confusion surrounding the change in ownership of the Wonderbra. The Wonderbra was known amongst women and the industry as the Gossard Wonderbra, but whilst the Wonderbra still existed, Gossard – with their high profile sexy image – were now making the Ultrabra.

Summary

At the time of its relaunch, Wonderbra was in great danger of being seen as 'old hat' with the new Ultrabra set to steal the show, the attention and the sales. Not only did Gossard have the more sexy image, it also had the essential support of the trade and the media.

With the media, the Gossard Ultrabra was new and exciting and therefore newsworthy. With the trade, Gossard was a major fashion brand which deserved a high-profile in-store presence and was found in the sexier outlets.

Furthermore, there was the additional threat of confusion. Women, retailers and journalists were used to the Gossard Wonderbra. Now the Wonderbra was to be made by Playtex and Gossard would have the Ultrabra, and the products were virtually identical.

Given this situation it seemed optimistic to hope that the Wonderbra could maintain sales at its previous, highly successful level. In fact, such was the threat of the competitive product launch, there was real concern that the Wonderbra's share of the push-up bra market could drop from virtually 100% to as little as 50%.

And whilst the complete marketing mix would prove invaluable to the successful relaunch of the Wonderbra under the Playtex banner, there was one element which could make that vital difference.

THE IMPORTANCE OF ADVERTISING

In a highly competitive and potentially confusing market, advertising held the key to the success of the Wonderbra:

— Advertising would be the strongest way to immediately differentiate the Wonderbra from the competition.
— Advertising would consequently help alleviate the expected confusion resulting from the licence changeover and competitive product launch.
— Advertising was needed to reinforce the Wonderbra's status and credibility as *the* original cleavage enhancing bra.
— Advertising was also needed to show that not only did the Wonderbra create an amazing cleavage, but that it was still extremely fashionable and extremely desirable.

However, more specifically, there was one immediate and fundamental objective for the Wonderbra campaign, against which it would be judged, and that was the **generation of publicity** and the **domination of the media** by the advertising itself.

The relevance and importance of this is clear:

1. The media had virtually single-handedly rediscovered and revitalised the Wonderbra's flagging fortunes, aided by only minimal advertising support (see Figure 2), in 1992/1993 so it's power and effect on the behaviour of women was proven.
2. The Wonderbra's advertising budget was still severely limited – a total of £330,000 to a spend from February through to June – and therefore needed to be made to look much bigger and prove more effective with the help of publicity.

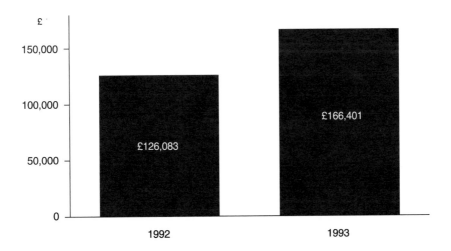

Figure 2. *Wonderbra advertising expenditure*
Source: MEAL

Summary – Advertising Objective

Ultimately, the objective was to at least maintain sales of the Wonderbra with the aid of advertising and the extensive publicity it would generate.

This meant that whilst the Wonderbra needed a high profile and newsworthy advertising vehicle, it was essential that it was not an irrelevant 'shock value' campaign that was rejected by women and banned by the authorities the moment it hit the streets.

The creative work, therefore, needed to strike the right balance between its appeal to the media and its appeal to women:

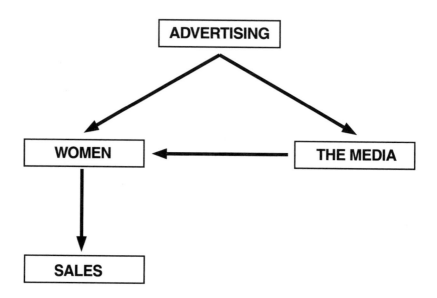

FINDING THE RIGHT BALANCE FOR THE CREATIVE WORK

In order to strike the right balance, and produce the most influential creative work, information was primarily gleaned from two sources, and the learning from this was used for the thinking behind and the development of the Wonderbra advertising:

a) Extensive qualitative consumer research which highlighted what women thought about the Wonderbra and lingerie generally, fashion, advertising, men, sexism and feminism. This was supported by extensive one-to-one interviews with women to test the advertising itself.

b) In-depth analysis of the previous media coverage of the Gossard Wonderbra in order to identify the reasons behind its potency.

What follows is a summary of this learning and its relevance to the creative work subsequently developed.

Who was the 'Wonderbra Woman'?

Talking to the right woman in the right way was essential. The most important finding was her self-confidence and the fact that she was unashamed and unafraid of her sexuality.

She was a powerful, image-conscious woman, in control of her life and angered by advertising which did not reflect that. She enjoyed *"looking good"* and was a great believer in *"if you've got it, flaunt it"*. She could just as easily be an 18 year old raver as a 40 year old mother-of-two; age was unimportant.

She was a liberated 'post feminist' who liked to demonstrate, and even exploit, her sexuality, and was certainly no shrinking violet.

What was the Wonderbra's Appeal?

The message that women were given by the fashion and mainstream press in 1992/1993 was the message that worked, and the future success of the Wonderbra meant building on that message.

Unlike ordinary bras, women were not interested in whether or not the Wonderbra was pretty, good quality or comfortable to wear. They were only interested in the unique physical and emotional benefits that it offered:

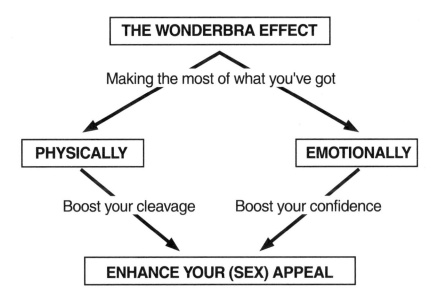

The secret of the Wonderbra was that rather than simply wearing it *"for myself"*, women also wanted the Wonderbra for the effect it would have on other people (men and women) and the subsequent ego-boost that it would give them.

Demonstrating the Wonderbra Effect

Clearly, demonstrating the Wonderbra Effect would be the best way to motivate the Wonderbra Woman. It was, after all, the media message that women had originally responded to. But, as outlined earlier, it was how this was done in advertising that would be important.

In-depth interviews were conducted amongst women aged 16-30 (Source: TBWA/Elucidation) to assess which of 13 potential Wonderbra advertisements worked best, and why. All but 3 were very well received:

1. The advertising was up-front, bold and direct, in keeping with women's view of the Wonderbra itself, and would stand out from the crowd and grab women's attention:

    "Brilliant, great. You couldn't get more to the point."

    Respondent, 16-25 Manchester.

    "It would be talked about. People would say, "have you seen this?""

    Respondent, 25-30 London

2. If sex appeal and feeling good was what the Wonderbra offered, a "*risqué, naughty*" advertising approach was appropriate, as it reflected Wonderbra Woman's **own** view of her sexuality:

    "It's a bra that makes you feel sexy, so why not promote that fact."

    Respondent, 25-30 London

3. Just as Wonderbra Woman liked to "*have a laugh*" and enjoy herself, humour was used to amuse her and reflect the light-hearted, feel-good factor of the Wonderbra. The humour itself was seen as "*for women*" and not "*aimed at women*":

    "Women are laughing at men for a change."

    Respondent, 25-30 London

4. Whilst the advertising was bold and risqué, the fact that no men actually featured in the photography meant that women did not find the advertisement offensive or sexist:

    "I wouldn't want to see a bloke. She'd only be wearing it for him then."

    Respondent, 16-24 London

5. Similarly, the confidence and self-assurance of the model was key as it showed her to be in-control of the situation, not demeaned by it:

    "She looks great and she knows it. But she isn't a tart."

    Respondent, 25-30 London

The three concepts that were less well received were rejected on the grounds of vulgarity and of going too far; ie "*too crude, male orientated and unsubtle*" or "*demeaning to women*".

The Advertisments

In essence, out of 10 possibles, three concepts which best reflected the Wonderbra and the Wonderbra Effect, and were deemed to have the greatest impact were previewed in their finished form to nearly 4,000 female lingerie sales assistants across the length and breadth of the country. And whilst this cannot be considered as conclusive research the overwhelming support for the advertising, the clapping and laughter, confirmed the potential of the campaign.

Summary

The key to the past and future success of the Wonderbra lay in sex and sexuality, and women clearly found this attractive, as long as it was not offensive or demeaning. Humour was used as a way of reducing this risk.

Extensive research showed that the 'One and Only' Wonderbra advertising campaign was seen as clever, enjoyable, appealing, motivating and relevant. And as well as appealing to women, no one could disagree with the fact that 'sex sells newspapers', and that journalists would respond very positively to a bold, raunchy advertising campaign for the Wonderbra.

However, where the advertisements were finally placed would ensure their impact and the generation of publicity.

WHERE SHOULD THE ADVERTISEMENTS APPEAR?

In terms of media choice, there were 3 key issues which needed to be considered:

1. How could maximum publicity and exposure be generated with a limited budget?
2. What was the best environment to talk to women about the Wonderbra? After all, we wanted them to buy the bra.
3. What was the least expected place to see a Wonderbra advertisement? This was essential if the campaign was to attract the media's attention and imagination.

Television, despite its undoubted impact, was unaffordable with the budget. The eventual media choice reflected the dual objective of talking to women and to the press.

Women's Magazines

This would be the back-bone of the campaign, providing an on-going one-to-one dialogue with women. Environmentally, fashion and young women's titles were perfect as they were used by women to choose what to buy and what to wear (see Figure 3).

Format:	Colour double page spreads
Budget:	£200,000
Timing:	March-June issues

'THE ONE AND ONLY' ADVERTISEMENTS

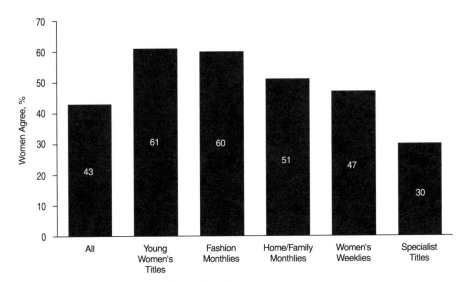

Figure 3. *"Magazines are an excellent source of ideas on buying clothes"*

Outdoor

Posters would give the Wonderbra immediate and massive impact and awareness, being a highly visible medium. Women would be able to link what they saw on the high street with what they saw in their magazines. Most important, however, was the element of surprise that the Wonderbra advertisements would have as posters, because outdoor is not a typical lingerie medium. And it was the use of posters that would provide the key to the media and publicity interest.

Format: 48-sheet posters
Budget: £130,000
Timing: 2 weeks in February
Schedule: National coverage of major connurbations with 830 sites

JUDGING THE ADVERTISING'S EFFECTIVENESS

The objectives of the campaign have already been discussed:

1. *Short Term*
   To substantially increase the power and reach of the advertising through the generation of editorial coverage.

2. *Medium Term*
   Whilst the long-term objective is to win the "Bra Wars" the objective behind this initial phase of advertising was to try and ensure that Wonderbra sales figures were maintained at their previous, pre-licence changeover levels.

It is against these two requirements that the success of the advertising should be judged, and not how the Wonderbra performed against the Gossard Ultrabra as estimates of the competitive situation vary enormously and are therefore unreliable.

Media Coverage – The Results

Subjectively, few advertising campaigns have received as much exposure and generated as much interest as that for the Wonderbra. Hardly a day went by without some debate, discussion, comment or feature.

In an effort to assess the coverage, all relevant newspaper, magazine, television and radio coverage from the end of January 1994 to the end of April 1994 has been logged. Amazingly, coverage is still on-going, but one has to draw the line somewhere.

By relevant coverage, a strict definition was used to only include features or comments on the advertisements themselves or the previously unknown model, Eva Herzigova, used in the advertising – she was, after all, a crucial part of the campaign.

The subsequent, and numerous, comments and discussions of the Wonderbra itself have not been included. But clearly none of this would have happened without the advertising and the interest it caused.

A summary of the coverage is given in Table 1:

TABLE 1: WONDERBRA ADVERTISING MEDIA COVERAGE SUMMARY
(end January 1994 – end April 1994)

Medium	Number of Features	Airtime/ Column Inches	Estimated[1] Cost £	Estimated[2] Value £
Television	18	167 mins	3,152,200	12,608,800
Radio	5	40 mins	87,600	350,400
Magazines	52	5,353 c.ins	177,172	708,688
National	95	8,998 c.ins	873,787	3,495,148
Local press	216	16,881 c.ins	150,079	600,316
TOTAL	386	207 mins/ 31,232 c.ins	4,440,838	17,763,352

1. Estimated rate card cost of buying the airtime or space for advertising

2. Institute of Public Relations estimation of the value of the editorial. The general rule is that the value of editorial is four times that of advertising in respect of its effect and influence. The estimated costs have therefore been multiplied by four.

Source: Eurospace/Jackie Cooper PR

If an advertiser wanted to buy the Wonderbra coverage as advertising space it would have cost an estimated £4,440,838 at ratecard.

If an advertiser wanted to replicate the value and potency of the Wonderbra coverage it would cost an astounding **£17,763,352**, according to Institute of Public Relations guidelines.

It has become clear that the posters led the way in the generation of coverage. And two weeks of poster advertising generated 386 features including 3 hours of airtime, which increased the £130,000 poster spend by an astronomical 13,664%.

EXAMPLES OF THE PRESS COVERAGE

Even including the £200,000 womens' magazine spend as well, the budget would have increased by 5,383%.

The media covered every possible aspect of the advertising from "have you seen the ads", to "are they dangerous for male drivers, are they sexy or sexist, who's the model and why was she chosen, who were the people behind the product and campaign, what the advertising tells us about women today' and 'what about Wonderpants for men?'

"Congratulations to Wonderbra on their eye-catching ads."

The Guardian, 17/2/94

"Heads have turned, eyes have swivelled. They're the sexiest billboards in town."

Sunday Express, 6/3/94

"The Wonderbra ads are all humour and health… they're swell."

Today, 19/3/94

"Wonder ad"

Daily Express, 4/3/94

"The current Wonderbra posters are hard to miss."

Financial Times, 10/3/94

"The [Wonderbra] advertisements are not offensive."

Daily Telegraph, 16/3/94

Such was the level of UK media interest the model, Eva Herzigova, has become an international 'star' and the advertising has been featured in the American, French, German, Italian, Spanish and Portuguese media, including CNN and the US Entertainment Tonite show.

Sales – Background

Advertising and the resulting publicity's effect on sales has been no less dramatic. To put the relaunch results into their proper context, the following points need to be specified:

— The Playtex Wonderbra was identical to the original Canadelle design.
— Apart from the addition of a front-fastening version, extra sizes and co-ordinating briefs, the Playtex Wonderbra range was unchanged from the previous Gossard Wonderbra range.
— Playtex distribution was on a par with Gossard's.
— The Playtex Wonderbra cost the same as the Gossard Ultrabra – £14.99 – and there had been no increase since 1993. However, this price was substantially higher than the UK average bra price of £6.84.

The only element of the mix that did in fact change was the advertising, along with the in-store displays and packaging which were a direct translation of the campaign.

But, before outlining the results it is important to note that the clothing industry as a whole is very difficult to monitor, and Playtex do not subscribe to the only retail audit, TMS. Monitoring is not helped by the fragmented distribution, covering everything from department stores, retail/grocery chains, to independents, mail order and market stalls. With this in mind, trade estimates are the only available means of measuring the results.

Sales – The Results

The relaunch objective was to maintain Wonderbra sales at their previous, and very high, levels. And the results themselves have exceeded all expectations.

The fact that on average 41% more Wonderbras are bought a week in 1994 than in 1993, and 118% more than in 1992 (see Figure 4) testifies to the effectiveness of the advertising and the resultant publicity.

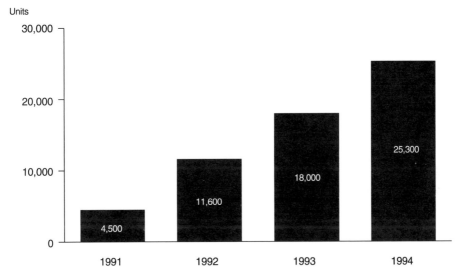

Figure 4. *Wonderbra average weekly sales*
Note: *These figures are retail only and exclude mail order*
Source: Playtex

In conclusion then, limited advertising for the Wonderbra, and the publicity surrounding it, has achieved the following:

a) Protected sales up to 9,000 units a week, assuming 50% of the 1993 figures. This is worth £134,910 a week, based on £14.99 per bra.
b) Achieved incremental sales of 7,300 units a week, worth an additional £109,427 each week.

And this success in the UK has had a substantial and unexpected additional benefit:

— Playtex has made 500 major distribution gains for the Wonderbra as a result of its successful relaunch, including Top Shop, Dorothy Perkins, Hennes, Asda and Tesco, and negotiations with other retailers are underway.
— The Wonderbra has subsequently been launched to enormous publicity and excitement in the USA, France, Germany and South Africa with the same advertising campaign, translated where necessary.
— At least three other European Wonderbra launches are planned before the end of 1994.

CONCLUSION

The first few months of the Playtex Wonderbra relaunch were absolutely critical. The advertising needed to ensure the support of the media, of women and of retailers if the Wonderbra was to survive "Bra Wars".

Far from surviving, this paper has demonstrated that by thinking big and being brave, advertising has helped create a phenomenon of tantalising proportions:

1. The media became bra crazy, with everyone from the Sunday Sport, Ruby Wax, David Frost and The Financial Times discussing, debating and enjoying the Wonderbra advertising at an estimated value of nearly £18,000,000. The advertising was still in the news three months later, despite the traditionally short life span of 'fashions'.
2. Far from rejecting the Wonderbra in favour of *"newer, more exciting models"* women have embraced the 30 year old Wonderbra with a renewed fervour. Not only have 9,000 units a week been protected, over 7,000 more Wonderbras are bought a week now than in 1993 when the bra had supposedly reached the height its of success. The total value of these sales is £224,337 a week.
3. The trade, like the media and women, cannot get enough of the Wonderbra. Not only is it now available in 500 additional and invaluable outlets in the UK as a direct result of this success, the Wonderbra has subsequently been launched in the USA, France, Germany and South Africa with additional launches planned. The trade are very firmly behind the Playtex Wonderbra:

"I'm getting the most incredible feedback from retailers. The push-up bra market has exploded yet again, with the Wonderbra pushing sales to even greater heights. My customers are telling me that the cash tills just keep on ringing."

Ken Campbell, Sales Director of Playtex

At the time of writing, it is too early to tell who has won the "Bra Wars", however after the first battle, the Wonderbra is poised for victory.

13

Cadbury's Boost

"Why Work and Rest when you can Play?"

INTRODUCTION

This case demonstrates how a change in strategy helped Cadbury's Boost to compete more effectively against a dominant brand leader.

We will show how our strategy achieved this by avoiding a head-to-head battle with the Mars Bar and, instead, focusing on an area of its relative weakness.

That weakness was 'youth appeal'. Mars had a relative lack of it as a brand, and Boost had a relative strength in this area; a result of both its more recent launch and some innate brand characteristics such as its name.

We will therefore show that advertising helped Boost carve out an 'energy for youth' positioning that enabled the brand not only to build penetration and frequency (and of course, as a result, sales) but also to build a real relationship with the notoriously fickle, but important, 16-24 year old target.

We will also show how, in so doing, the advertising still managed to avoid alienating other target groups, and, in fact, even increased sales among the rest of the population.

THE MARKET BACKGROUND

The chocolate market splits into various different market sectors (see Figure 1).

Boost operates in the largest sector – the countline sector. (This accounts for 28% of all chocolate sales, worth £865.2 million) and can be further broken down into sub-sectors, determined by the different types of 'eat' the various products deliver (see Figure 2).

CADBURY'S HISTORY IN THE GUTFILL SECTOR

For many years Cadbury had been in pursuit of a brand that could compete with the heavier, more filling bars in the market. The industry describes this sector as 'Gutfill'. The company was represented in all other sectors of the market. However, the size and maturity of the existing brands, notably Mars Bar and Snickers, had made the cost of entry high.

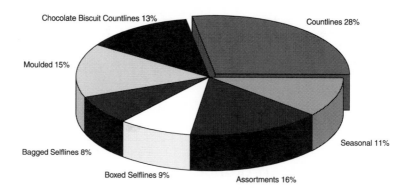

Figure 1. *The chocolate market 1993*
Note: *Seasonal = Eggs, novelties and selection boxes*
Source: BCCCA/AGB/Cadbury Estimates

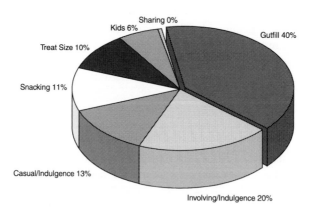

Figure 2. *The Countline market 1994*
Source: AGB (12 months ending 10th April 1994)

Over the years, Cadbury had launched brands to compete with Mars bar (the two most notable being Aztec in the '60s/'70s and Double Decker in the early '80s). Both brands were developed to compete in the 'Gutfill' sector with Mars. At launch they generated high levels of trial, but this wasn't sustained.

THE LAUNCH OF BOOST

Boost was Cadbury's first attempt on the 'Gutfill' market since Double Decker. It was launched in 1985 initially in just one variant – Coconut.

Although the product was different to a Mars Bar the advertising positioned it as a substantial, filling bar. This was another 'head on' attack against Mars Bar.

The brand's launch was unspectacular. The volume sales of the Coconut product were disappointing. Cadbury's added two variants – Biscuit and Peanut in 1989 and relaunched the brand. This increased volume significantly but even this turned out to be relatively short-term.

The brand was exhibiting the all too familiar signs of decline that Cadbury's had seen with Aztec and Double Decker.

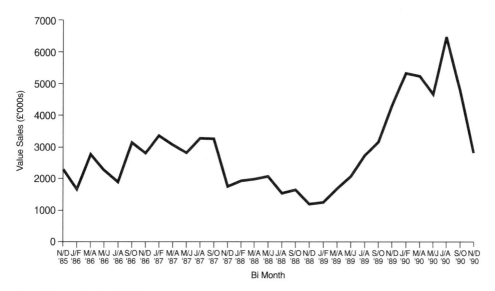

Figure 3. *Boost value sales, 1985-90*
Source: AGB Personal Purchases Index

In 1990, BBH was appointed to develop a new advertising strategy for the brand. This started with a thorough strategic review.

BOOST'S LAUNCH STRATEGY (1986-1990)

The launch strategy for Boost had been built on the product's substantialness. Boost really filled you up. This strategy had several advantages: it was clear, unambiguous and easy to communicate. It also fulfilled a real consumer need – a bar for when you're really hungry.

The advertising was targeted at all adults, with a slight bias towards the strongest part of the market – 16-34 year old males. Advertising's role had been mainly to generate high levels of brand awareness. Cadbury's had supported the brand strongly, as evidenced by the levels of support detailed below.

However, the strategy had some fundamental flaws. It was not a particularly differentiating positioning and more importantly, the brand had no credentials to

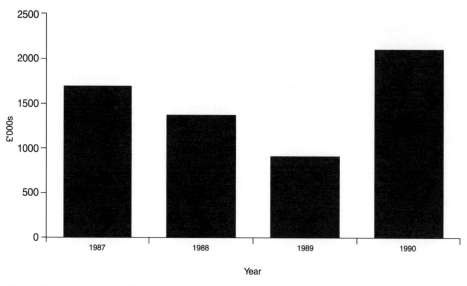

Figure 4. *Boost advertising spend, 1986-90*
Source: Register-MEAL

really own the territory with this promise alone. Mars or even Snickers were
considered to be more appropriate 'filling' brands. In addition, Mars had heritage
on its side. It was launched in 1932, making it the oldest 'Gutfill' bar in the UK
with a considerable advertising spend and heritage.

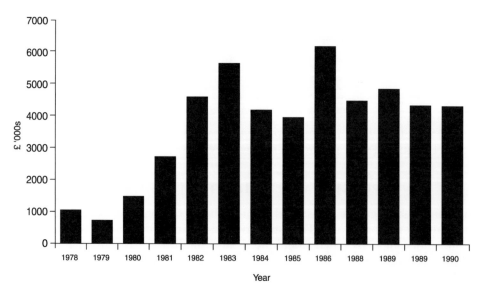

Figure 5. *Mars advertising spend, 1978-1990*
Source: Register-MEAL

DEVELOPING A NEW STRATEGY FOR BOOST (1990)

Cadbury's and BBH went back to basics. We thoroughly analysed the product, its ingredients, its packaging, its historic advertising and its existing consumer franchise. We needed to harness every potential strength.

We needed to find a way of competing efficiently and effectively. The strategic answer, we felt, was to chip away at the edges of the Mars brand by focusing our efforts on an area of relative weakness.

A quote on Guerrilla Warfare from Klaus von Clausewitz, a military expert, admirably reflects the strategic approach that we adopted:

> "Militia and armed civilians cannot and should not be employed against the main force of the enemy, or even against sizeable units. They should not try to crack the core, but only nibble along the surface and on the edges. They should rise in provinces lying to the side of the main theatre of war, which the invader does not enter in force, in order to draw these areas entirely from his grasp. The storm clouds, forming on his flanks, should also follow to the rear of his advance."

In this context, analysis of our consumer profile versus Mars was revealing:

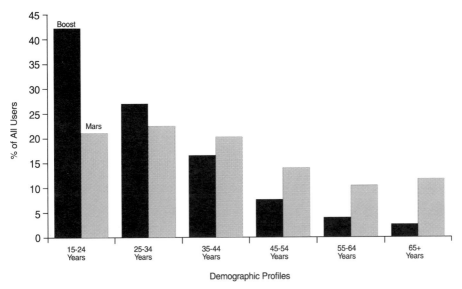

Figure 6. *1990 Consumer profile of All Users: Boost vs Mars*
Source: TGI, 1990

Mars was the universal 'filling' bar – a megabrand. Unsurprisingly, it had a flat consumer profile. It was strong across all age groups. Its advertising approach was also all-embracing summed up by the famous line: "A Mars a day helps you work rest and play".

In comparison, Boost's profile was skewed towards the 16-24 age group.

Our analysis of Boost's inherent strength in the 16-24 target audience was supported by Cadbury's own AGB data (see Figure 7).

Analysis of Millward Brown tracking data added more interesting evidence. Mars' advertising for Mars Bar, using an all-embracing approach, had particularly low levels of enjoyment amongst 16-24s (see Figure 8).

We believed that Mars' all-encompassing strategic approach could offer us a 'breaching point' of relative weakness if we were extremely focused and targeted.

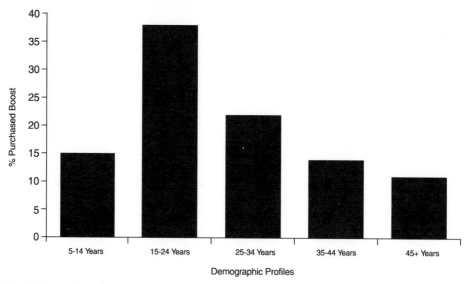

Figure 7. *Demographic profiles of Boost purchasers, 1990*
Source: AGB (52 weeks ending April 1990)

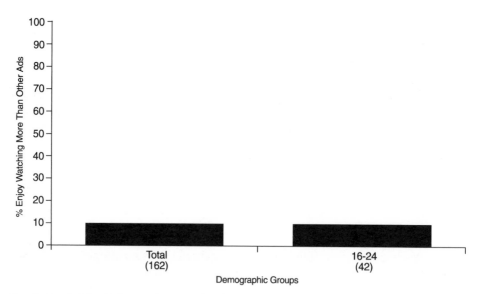

Figure 8. *Mars detailed recall: "Enjoy watching it more than other ads", 1990*
Base: *Main sample*
Source: Millward Brown (30/12/90-30/6/91)

We decided to target the brand much more precisely at our strongest target audience – the under 25s.

REFINING THE STRATEGY

We were obviously interested in isolating why Boost had developed such a strong following amongst youth. Was it the historic advertising?

Our tracking data suggested not. Boost advertising had relatively low levels of enjoyability. It was no more enjoyed by 16-24s than Mars advertising, which we knew was not particularly enjoyed by youth.

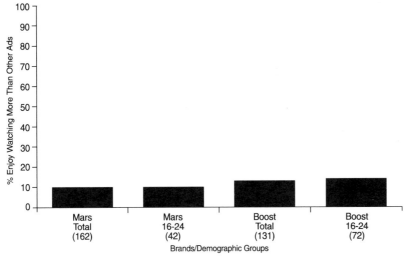

Figure 9. *Boost vs Mars detailed recall: "Enjoy watching it more than other ads", 1990-91*
Base: *Main sample*
Source: Millward Brown (31/12/90-30/6/91)

Analysis of the two most recent Cadbury product launches suggested a reason for Boost's strength amongst youth. The products analysed seemed to generate high levels of trial amongst 16-24s. It seemed that they were the most likely group to try something new.

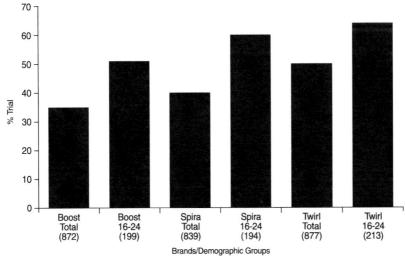

Figure 10. *Trial of Cadbury brands 6 months after launch*
Base: *Main sample*
Source: Millward Brown

We therefore needed to cultivate this launch profile, or in this case relaunch, into an ongoing relationship. The strategic challenge was to develop a personality for the brand that would help us to develop a tighter bond with our target audience.

The opportunity was to approach the market in a different way – moving away from usage (a brand that fills you up) to concentrate on users (our youth target audience).

The strategic emphasis on youth obviously affected the way in which we developed advertising. We conducted research to establish the proposition that would be most motivating to our 16-24 target audience.

The Relevance of Energy to Youth

The research was revealing. 'Gutfill' bars, like Mars or Boost, were used as a 'filler'. The end benefit was in their ability to keep you going.

Mars had reflected all the potential benefits of this ability to fill in their advertising ("work, rest and play"). Research told us however, that our audience weren't interested in an all-encompassing approach, summed up below by a young male consumer in our research:

"Why work and rest when you can play."

Source: BBH Qualitative Research

We believed that Boost could exploit Mars' generic market positioning with a more specific, active energy proposition.

Research indicated that our target audience were active and had a real need for an energy bar. Boost had the basic product ingredients to support an energy proposition – it really filled you up. The brand's name (Boost) gave it the right to own an energy claim. We believed therefore, that we could focus single-mindedly on an 'energy for youth' proposition.

Our strategic thinking led to the following creative brief.

The Boost Creative Brief

1. *Why are we advertising?*
   To make Boost a megabrand in the youth market.

2. *Who are we talking to?*
   Single, young and free males, 16-24 years old. They are confident and streetwise, leading active and exciting lives.

3. *What must the advertising say?*
   BOOST GIVES YOU ENERGY.

   And why should the consumer believe it?
   Its ingredients/its name.

4. *What tone of voice?*
    Confident
    Streetwise
    Dynamic

5. *What practical considerations?*
    ITVA
    Must conform to Cadbury mandatories:
    Deliciousness of product must be communicated.
    Product should be referred to as "Cadbury Boost" wherever possible.

SUMMARY

In summary, our strategy was:

1. To avoid taking Mars on in a head-to-head battle.
2. To chip away at the edges of the Mars brand by focusing our efforts on an area of its relative weakness, and, coincidentally, our relative strength.
3. To exploit our strength in the 16-24 age group by developing a real and longer-lasting relationship.
4. To focus on the real end benefit of the 'Gutfill' market for this specific target audience – energy.

DEVELOPING A CREATIVE MEDIA STRATEGY

Media had a critical part to play in enhancing our repositioning and helping us to make Boost feel like a young person's brand. We believed that our communication could be reinforced by using media that was owned by youth.

The mass market nature of Cadbury products in part dictated media strategy. *All* the Cadbury brands were advertised on television exclusively, as shown in Table 1.

The standard quantitative media planning sources we used were helpful but did not give us an understanding of our target audience's full, in-depth relationship with the media. We decided to commission some qualitative research to look exclusively at media consumption amongst our primary audience (16-24 year old males). The findings were helpful.

Obviously, television was seen as 'family' entertainment. It wasn't a medium that our target audience felt was exclusively for them.

"I get in and my mum is watching 'Home and Away', so I join her."

16 year old male

"There's a difference between what I watch as 'wallpaper' and what I really watch and enjoy."

17 year old male
Source: BBH Media Qualitative Research

However, young people's viewing tended to centre around a few 'cult' programmes. The research allowed us to build a qualitative picture of the sort of programmes with which our target audience had a quality relationship.

TABLE 1: CADBURY ADVERTISING EXPENDITURE 1990

Brand:	MAT £'000s	TV %	Radio %	Press %
Cadbury Buttons	305	100	–	–
Cadbury Caramel	1,034	100	–	–
Cadbury Creme Eggs	1,306	100	–	–
Cadbury Boost	2,113	100	–	–
Cadbury Crunchie	2,342	100	–	–
Cadbury Dairy Milk	2,417	100	–	–
Cadbury Double Decker	1,606	100	–	–
Cadbury Easter Eggs	100	100	–	–
Cadbury Flake	1,960	100	–	–
Cadbury Fruit & Nut	1,092	100	–	–
Cadbury Inspirations	1,139	100	–	–
Cadbury Milk Tray	1,955	100	–	–
Cadbury Mini Eggs	372	100	–	–
Cadbury Roses	1,877	100	–	–
Cadbury Spira	1,248	100	–	–
Cadbury Twirl	1,960	100	–	–
Cadbury Wholenut	1,301	100	–	–
Cadbury Wispa	1,774	100	–	–
Cadbury White Buttons	281	100	–	–

Source: Register-MEAL

TV, we believed, was essential at the initial stages of the brand's repositioning in order to help maintain the stature of the brand. However, our TV strategy used the medium in a highly selective way, with the advertising appearing only in specific youth orientated programmes.

On the other hand, our target audience listened to a lot of radio and were able to name particular stations, shows and DJs that they specifically tuned in to. Radio was a medium that they felt they owned exclusively.

"I listen all day in the workshop at work"

21 year old male

"I listen in the morning, at lunch times with my friends and in the evening doing my homework."

16 year old male
Source: BBH Media Qualitative Research

Radio, we believed, would work in a different way to television. It would give us a longevity of presence and a high level of frequency, giving us the opportunity to rotate several creative treatments, whilst maintaining freshness and interest.

Cadbury's decided to test radio in London before committing to national roll out. The test was successful and, over a three year period, the balance between TV and radio has changed (radio assuming a more important role).

The recommended media strategy, therefore, used selectively bought TV and radio. We believed that the two media working together would enable us to develop both a presence and a real personality for the brand. This would result not only in making us feel like a big brand to young people but also, and more importantly, to develop a real relationship with them.

THE CREATIVE WORK

We needed an advertising idea that communicated our energy positioning in a way that was motivating to our target audience. Overt energy claims were not possible due to the advertising regulations surrounding food and drink.

The creative team developed an advertising idea for television and radio which can be summed up as: Boost helps you solve bizarre energy problems. This idea used two rising 'cult' youth comedians, Vic Reeves and Bob Mortimer as the creative vehicle. TV and radio executed this idea in slightly different ways.

Creative development research endorsed our recommendation of Vic and Bob as advertising vehicles.

> "The use of Vic Reeves and Bob Mortimer as the main characters can be endorsed. Certainly Vic Reeves does have very strong appeal to the primary target audience for this advertising. In this context, it is important to note that the research suggests that the scripts do appeal to consumers in their own right, even those who are not Vic fans."
>
> Source: Corr Research Consultancy

Television

The television execution pastiched the cowboy and indian film genre. Vic Reeves' unusual energy problem was the threat of Red Indians attacking his stagecoach. Boost inspired Vic's solution (which was to put the horses inside the coach and pull the stagecoach with his trusty friend Bob).

Radio

The radio advertising spoofed a radio 'problem phone-in' show. Different listeners (in the guise of Bob) phoned Vic with their unusual energy problems.

THE EFFECT OF ADVERTISING

The advertising would need to fulfill four objectives to show that the change in strategy was truly successful. They were:

1. To grow the brand's sales overall.
2. To achieve greater growth amongst the 16-24 year old age group than from the rest of the demographic groups.
3. To strengthen and build the relationship within the 16-24 target audience.
4. To avoid alienation of other audiences.

1. THE GROWTH IN BOOST SALES OVERALL

The Growth in Volume Sales

Figure 11 shows Biscuit Boost volume (index of kilogrammes sold) up to April 1994. The Coconut and Peanut variants were withdrawn from the market in August 1993 as Cadbury's rationalised the brand into its biggest selling variant – Biscuit. For the purposes of this analysis we have concentrated on Biscuit Boost

'STAGECOACH'

RADIO COMMERCIAL

'MARGARET DERN'
(60 seconds long)

SFX	*Radio show jingle.*
Vic Reeves	We're at that time of the day when I like to offer a little boost to you, the public out there.
	First on the line today, we have Margaret Dern from Yorkshire, which is near Lancashire. Margaret, what's your problem?
Bob Mortimer (as Margaret)	Hello Vic. Well, I'm an unmarried mother, and to make ends meet, I've accepted a contract to build a small housing estate. But I'm rather concerned as to whether or not I can complete the 14 detached houses by the deadline, next Tuesday.
	Normally, I have no trouble with challenges like these, as last year, I successfully baked cakes for a local fête. Can you help me?
Vic	You baked them?
Margaret	Yes.
Vic	Not boiled?
Margaret	No.
Vic	Well, Margaret, although I'd really like to help, there's absolutely nothing I can do for you. But a Cadbury's Boost – it's slightly rippled with a flat underside – could help you build a space station out of delicious acorns and lemon squash.
Margaret	Oh, you've been no help at all, Vic. I wish I'd never rung you...

sales only as they represent the bulk of sales and are the only consistent base over the period of analysis.

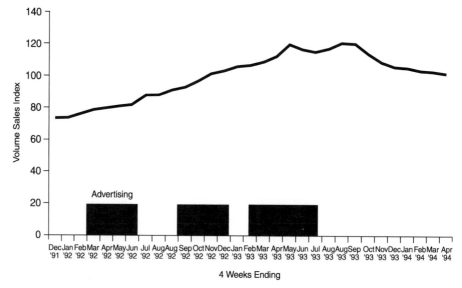

Figure 11. *Boost volume sales, 1991-1994*
Source: AGB Impulse

(The chart shows a fall-off in sales since June 1993, this coincides with a lack of Boost advertising activity for budgetary reasons.)

The Growth in Value Sales

Boost has also shown growth in total value sales (for reasons of confidentiality we have expressed these as indexed growth).

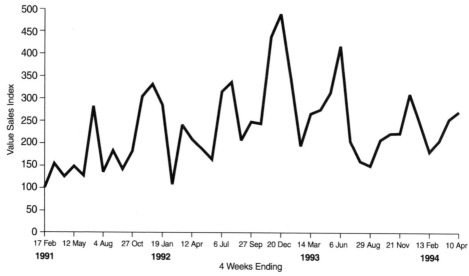

Figure 12. *Indexed Boost value sales, 1991-1994*
Source: AGB Impulse

The Growth in Boost Brand Share

Over the advertised period there has been an increase in Boost's overall value share in the 'Gutfill' market.

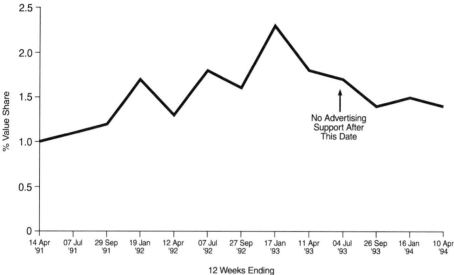

Figure 13. *Boost value share, 1991-94*
Source: AGB Impulse

ISOLATING THE EFFECT OF ADVERTISING AND DISCOUNTING OTHER FACTORS

To make an estimate of the effect of the TV and radio advertising we undertook a regression analysis to quantify, where possible, the key influences on the brand. This enabled us to factor out those influences that have contributed to the brand's growth and therefore enabled us to calculate the advertising effect in isolation.

The factors that could possibly affect the brand are discussed below. Some of these factors are included in the model. Those excluded from the model have no material effect on the brand.

Underlying Market Growth/Macro Economic Factors

Any contribution of underlying market growth had been automatically discounted by the way in which the model was constructed. The model works on the ratio of Boost sales to Mars sales and market growth would be affecting each equally.

Distribution

There have been a number of changes in the distribution of the brand. Some trade sectors have shown growth. Overall, however, the impact on total distribution has been small and consequently has not been a major influence on the brand's growth and has not been included in the model.

Boost Price and Competitive Price

The underlying price of the brand is an important influence on volume. Promotions, in the form of short-term price changes, have a large effect. By taking these factors into account in the model we have effectively discounted their influence when quantifying the effect of the advertising.

Promotions

As noted above, price promotions are accounted for in the model.

However, we have found no evidence in the data to suggest that they have distorted our quantification of the advertising effect.

Cannibalisation

In August 1993 Cadbury's withdrew the Coconut and Peanut variants of Boost.

This led us to question whether the volume of Coconut and Peanut might have switched into the Biscuit variant, even though we recognised that this switching would only affect the last 3 periods of our model.

To check out this hypothesis we went back to our model. If there had been cannibalisation one would have expected to see a decay in the sales curve that was somehow different from previous periods. On examination of the model we found that this was not the case. The decay in the sales curve after the withdrawal of the variants had *exactly* the same characteristics as previously modelled decay periods. This leads us to believe that Biscuit Boost sales have not been affected by the addition of sales from the other variants.

Mars Advertising

It might have been expected that Mars advertising effects should have been highlighted by the regression analysis. However, no robust or meaningful quantification could be determined despite a wide-ranging analysis of its potential influences.

There are several possible explanations for this: (i) Given the sampling error of the data Mars short-term advertising effects would have needed to be large to be identifiable. (ii) Given the size of the brand it is perhaps not too surprising that its advertising does not produce massive short-term blips.

There are a number of technical reasons why failure to identify exactly the effect of Mars advertising on Boost volume will not bias the quantifications of the Boost advertising.

THE BOOST ADVERTISING MODEL

The regression equation accounts for about 80% of the variation in the Boost/Mars sales/volume ratio. As can be seen from the chart below the model fits the actual movements in the brand well.

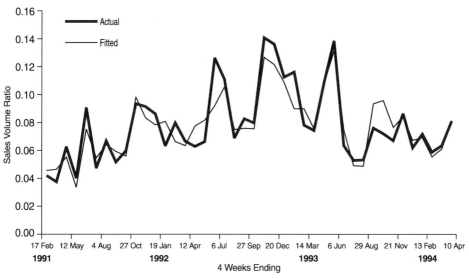

Figure 14. *Boost-Mars sales volume ratio actual and fitted, 1990-94*
Source: AGB Personal Purchases Index

The Boost Advertising Effects

Radio and TV advertising were in most instances simultaneous. It was therefore difficult to totally separate the two influences. Our best estimate is that rating for rating TV is approximately five times more powerful. This was not unexpected.

The charts below were calculated by simulating the volume effects of:

— TV advertising only
— Radio advertising only
— No advertising.

The TV Advertising Effect

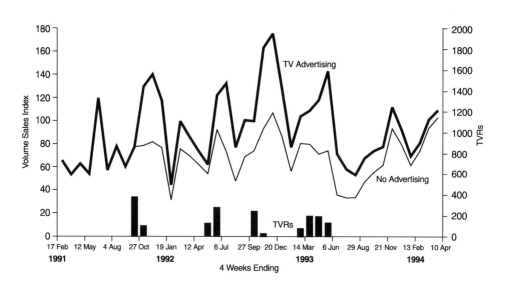

Figure 15. *Boost sales volume: Advertising effect simulations – TV and no advertising, 1990-94*
Source: AGB Personal Purchases Index

Over the three year period of the Vic and Bob campaign the television advertising contributed 50,000,000 bars.

The Radio Advertising Effect

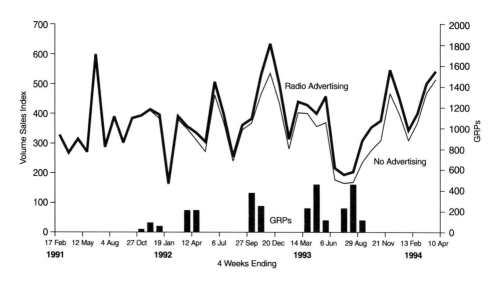

Figure 16. *Boost sales volume: Advertising effect simulations – Radio and no advertising 1990-94*
Source: AGB Personal Purchases Index

Over the three year period of the Vic and Bob campaign the radio advertising contributed 13,000,000 bars.

No Advertising

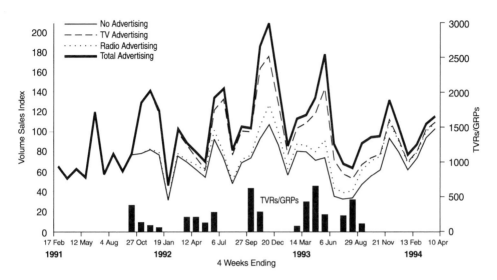

Figure 17. *Boost sales volume: Advertising effect simulations – Total, TV, radio and no advertising 1990-94*
Source: AGB Personal Purchases Index

The total advertising effect over three years is 70,000,000 bars. There is a quantifiable element of synergy between the two media. This is the difference between the total advertising effect and the sum of the radio and TV components.

ADVERTISING PAYBACK

The Vic and Bob advertising has uplifted Boost sales by 55% (over the three year period of the advertising).

The advertising more than pays for itself over the period that it has run.

However, we also believe that the advertising has started to build the sort of enduring relationship with our target audience that will continue to payback in the long-term.

2. GROWTH IN THE 16-24 AGE GROUP

The largest proportion of growth has come from our focused target audience – 16-24s (see Figure 18).

(Due to the change in AGB panels we only have demographic data available until April 1993.)

This has resulted in real change in the demographic profile for the Boost brand over the period of Vic and Bob advertising (see Figure 19).

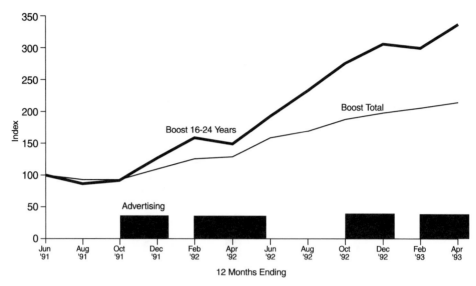

Figure 18. *Indexed Boost value sales by demographic groups, 1991-93*
Source: AGB Personal Purchases Index

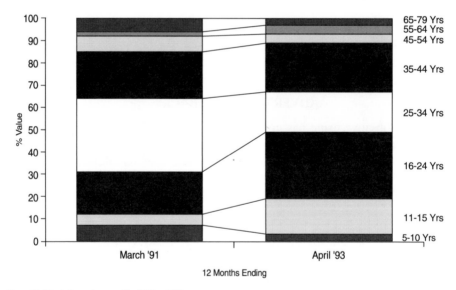

Figure 19. *Biscuit Boost demographics: 1991 vs 1993*
Base: *Purchases (value)*
Source: AGB Personal Purchases Index

STRENGTHENING THE RELATIONSHIP WITH 16-24s

The strength of our relationship with 16-24s can be examined in two areas:

— Changes in behaviour
— Changes in attitude towards the brand.

Changing 16-24s Behaviour

The growth in the 16-24 age group has come partly from increasing the penetration of Boost users. This is shown below as the growth in 16-24 users who claim to 'eat nowadays'.

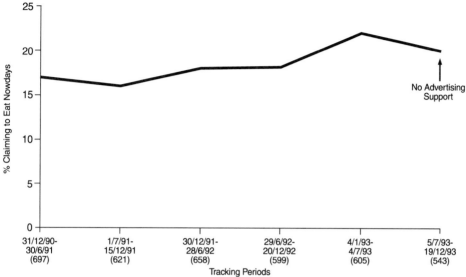

Figure 20. *Boost 16-24 penetration 1990-93: Claiming to "eat nowadays"*
Base: Main sample
Source: Millward Brown

More importantly, we have increased the frequency of purchase of Boost amongst our key group. This is shown below in the growth in 16-24 heavy eaters (defined as: claimed to "have eaten once a fortnight or more").

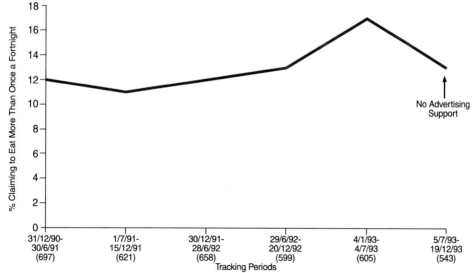

Figure 21. *Boost 16-24 frequency of purchase, 1990-93: "Heavy Eaters"*
Base: Main sample
Source: Millward Brown

16-24 growth has come from both increasing penetration *and* frequency. The frequency, we believe, has come from strengthening the relationship with our 16-24 year old target audience.

Changing 16-24s Attitudes Towards The Brand

Changing the attitudes of 16-24 year olds towards the brand is an extremely difficult task.

We have therefore broken down the changes in attitude into these areas:

— communicating the right product message;
— communicating the right image for the brand;
— communicating the brand's proposition in the most motivating way;
— communicating the brand's suitability for our target audience.

Communicating The Right Product Message

The advertising has helped to communicate the right product messages, as the charts below demonstrate.

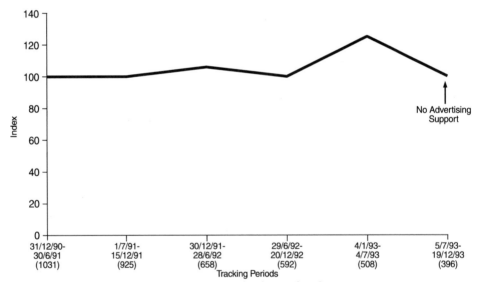

Figure 22. *Boost brand image amongst 16-24s, 1990-93: "Have a good combination of ingredients"*
Base: *Main Sample*
Source: Millward Brown

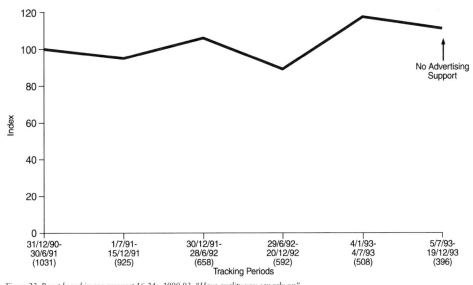

Figure 23. *Boost brand image amongst 16-24s, 1990-93: "Have quality you can rely on"*
Base: Main sample
Source: Millward Brown

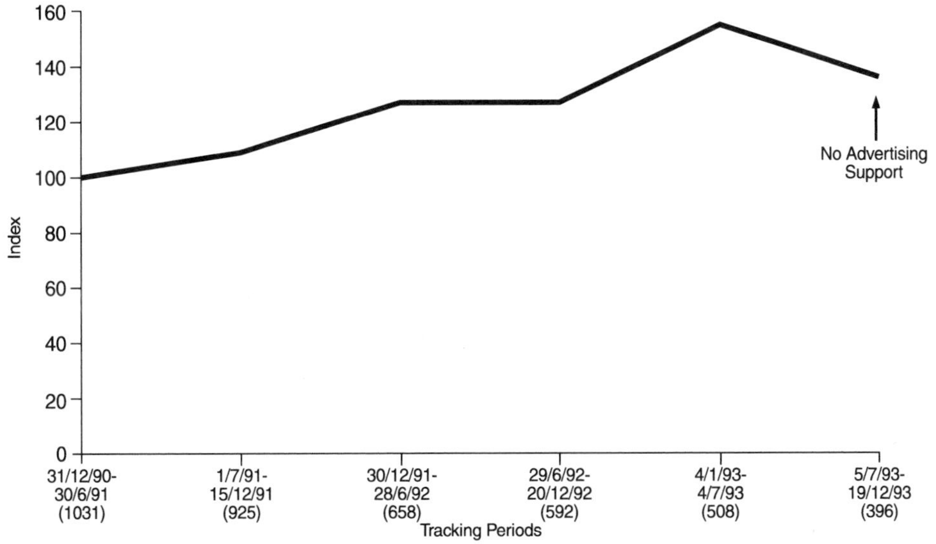

Figure 24. *Boost brand image amongst 16-24s, 1990-93: "Are more interesting to eat than others"*
Base: Main sample
Source: Millward Brown

Communicating The Right Image For The Brand

The advertising has also helped to strengthen the brand's image.

The personality of the advertising is reflected in the change in 16-24s attitude toward the product as a brand that is 'fun to eat'.

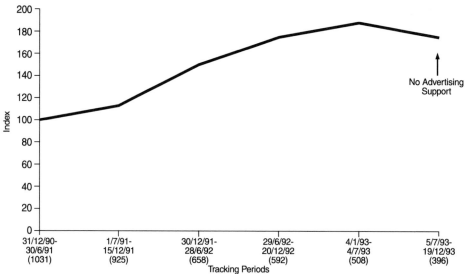

Figure 25. *Boost brand image amongst 16-24s, 1990-93: "Are fun to eat"*
Base: *Main sample*
Source: Millward Brown

Communicating The Brand's Proposition In The Most Motivating Way

The Vic and Bob advertising has proven to be an extremely enjoyable and unusual campaign for our target audience.

The advertising's distinctive style is reflected in the change in our target audience's attitudes towards the advertising on the measure 'an unusual ad' (see Figure 26).

The enjoyable nature of the campaign is reflected in the change in 16-24 attitude towards the advertising. We have demonstrated this by showing attitudes to Boost advertising before and after the Vic and Bob advertising (see Figure 27).

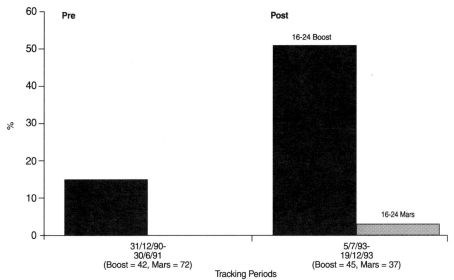

Figure 26. *16-24 Year old attitudes to Boost and Mars advertising "an unusual ad": Pre and Post Vic & Bob*
Base: *Main sample*
Source: Millward Brown

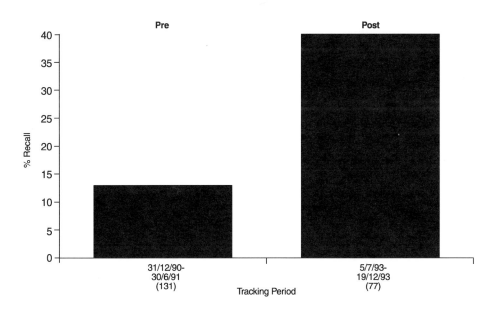

Figure 27. *Attitudes to Boost advertising "Enjoy watching it more than other ads": Pre and post Vic & Bob*
Base: *Main sample*
Source: Millward Brown

It was also more enjoyable than Mars advertising amongst 16-24s.

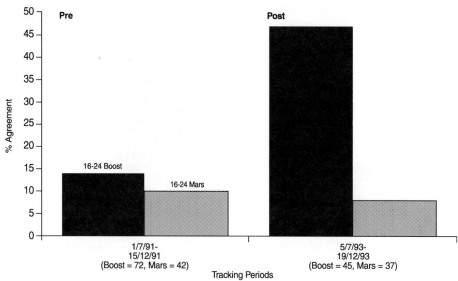

Figure 28. *16-24 Year old attitudes to Boost & Mars – "Enjoy watching it more than most ads": Pre and post Vic & Bob*
Base: *Main sample*
Source: Millward Brown

Communicating The Brand's Suitability For Our Target Audience

The most important dimension, on which to assess our relationship with youth is the proportion of 16-24s endorsing the statement "are more appropriate for teenagers". This is an important barometer and shows impressive growth. This is particularly significant given the extremely fickle nature of the audience. Overt targeting can be rejected if the execution is not executed perfectly.

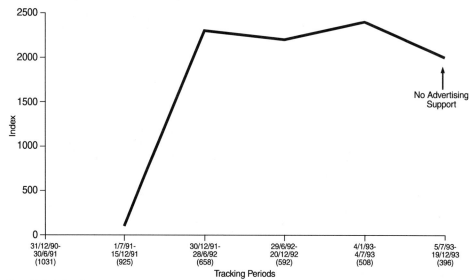

Figure 29. *Boost brand image amongst 16-24s, 1990-93: "Are more appropriate to teenagers"*
Base: *Main sample*
Source: Millward Brown

Vic Reeves & Bob Mortimer's Contribution

A lot of the personality of the advertising comes from the association with Vic and Bob. The association was immediate, as demonstrated by the detailed recall levels for Vic and Bob after the first burst of advertising and has grown over the campaign period.

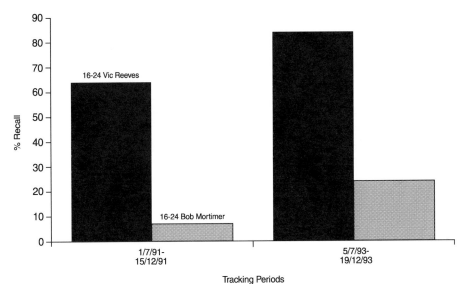

Figure 30. *Boost detailed recall amongst 16-24s: "Vic Reeves & Bob Mortimer", 1991-93*
Base: *Main sample*
Source: Millward Brown

Vic and Bob's personality and style of humour is stamped on the advertising with the rather unusual endline developed for the advertising: "Boost – It's slightly rippled with a flat underside". Detailed recall shows its growth in familiarity (see Figure 31).

It is clear that Vic and Bob's association with the brand has spilled over into the public domain. Their association with the brand is evident from press articles.

BOOST'S POSITIVE RESPONSE AMONGST OTHER AUDIENCES

Our strategy was focused on 16-24s but at the same time we did not want to alienate other audiences.

In advertising terms, we have not alienated other audiences. Our advertising itself is enjoyed by the other age groups, not just 16-24s. This is evidenced below by the positive changes in attitudes towards the Stagecoach advertising. The sample sizes are not particularly robust but they give an indication of the general trend. It is interesting to note that the 25-34 year old audience, the closest age group to our 16-24 year old audience, also shows very similar attitudes toward the advertising.

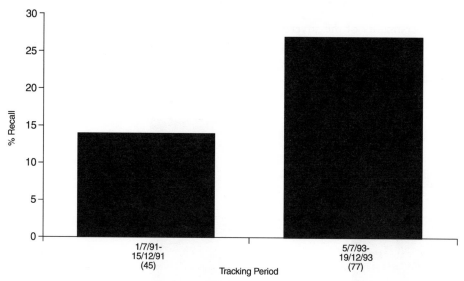

Figure 31. *Boost detailed recall amongst 16-24s: "It's slightly rippled with a flat underside", 1991-93*
Base: *Main sample*
Source: Millward Brown

TABLE 2: STAGECOACH – "ENJOY WATCHING IT MORE THAN OTHER ADS", 1991-93

	1/7/91- 15/12/91	30/12/91- 28/6/92	29/6/92- 20/12/92	4/1/93- 4/7/93	5/7/93- 15/12/93
Total	(45)	(71)	(91)	(120)	(77)
	38	42	56	37	40
16-24	(28)	(38)	(39)	(62)	(45)
	39	47	59	44	47
25-34	(9)	(16)	(25)	(33)	(21)
	22	38	44	36	43
35-44	(7)	(10)	(20)	(13)	(8)
	57	30	60	15	–
45+	(1)	(7)	(7)	(12)	(3)
	–	43	71	25	33

<————————— 'Stagecoach' —————————>

Base: Main sample

Source: Millward Brown

AGB sales data show us that growth has been achieved across all age groups. (Due to a change in AGB panel we only have demographic data available until April 1993.) The audiences closest to our 16-24 year old age group show very similar pattern in sales terms to the advertising as we found in our tracking data. In sales terms we have not alienated other audiences.

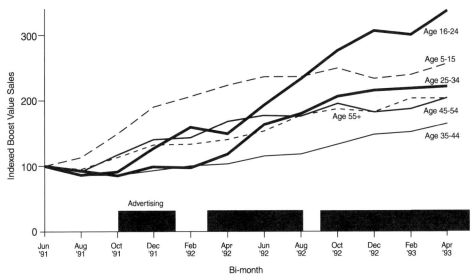

Figure 32. *Indexed Boost value sales by demographic group, 1991-93*
Source: AGB Personal Purchases Index

CONCLUSIONS

We have demonstrated how advertising helped Cadbury's Boost to compete more effectively against the dominant brand leader.

Our approach was to look at the market in a different way – moving away from usage to concentrate on users. This allowed us to avoid a head-to-head battle with Mars. We chipped away at the edges of that brand by focusing our efforts on an area of relative weakness for Mars – 16-24 year olds.

All elements of our strategy combined to produce a focused youth strategy.

The advertising that was created was in tune with our target audience and was enhanced by positioning the brand in a media environment that was highly relevant to youth. The radio in particular, has been awarded some of the industry's highest accolades, eg a D&AD Silver and the Independent Radio Advertising Award's Grand Prix for the Best Radio Campaign of 1992.

Boost has developed an enduring relationship with the 16-24 year old audience, has paid for itself in the short-term and has laid the foundations for the future growth of the brand.

14

The Edinburgh Club
Turning fatties into fitties

WHAT THIS ADVERTISING CAMPAIGN ACHIEVED

In 1990, the year prior to The Leith Agency's appointment, The Edinburgh Club was struggling to recruit new members, with only 212 new members in that year. In contrast during 1993, 911 new members joined the club – a 330% increase. During this period, the company's turnover rose by 113% and profits rose by 174%. In addition, the club commanded a single membership premium of 23% over the average cost of comparable health and fitness clubs in the Edinburgh area. This was all achieved amidst the ravages of an economic recession in what is effectively a luxury goods sector.

SETTING THE SCENE

The Edinburgh Club is a private members health and fitness club in Edinburgh's city centre. It is well established, having opened in 1965.

In 1991 The Edinburgh Club realised its advertising wasn't working. Despite a relatively high investment in advertising (during 1990 nearly 3% of turnover), membership was static. The Club had advertised virtually 52 weeks of the year, but the advertising spaces were small and the content was highly promotional. This paper will demonstrate how a change of strategy resulted in highly effective advertising.

In 1991 the world was going fitness-mad (see Figure 1), but this potential market growth was being mirrored by an explosion in the number of facilities available to users. The result was an intensely competitive, but still very immature, supply network coupled with a faddish demand.

All health clubs were chasing the 14% of the population already in the market for a health club. That is those who already participated in some form of exercise. (Source: General Household Survey 1987.)

The phenomenon of 'the gym' had grown through the '70s and '80s. It began as 'pumping iron', and evolved into aerobics (Jane Fonda, Cher, etc.). Consequently, the non-user's image of these clubs was that they were bursting at the seams with the kind of people who could easily be extras in Baywatch, and who would be competing with each other in front of full length mirrors to present the best bodies.

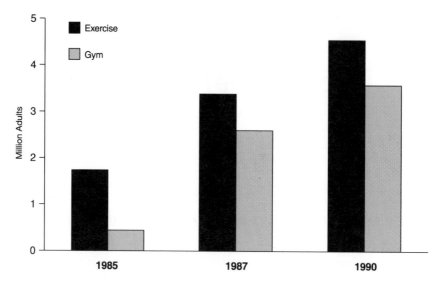

Figure 1. *Estimated number of adults in the UK who attend a private health club once a week or more (1985-1990).*
Source: TGI

The health and fitness market's confidence was high. As the data in Figure 1 suggests, it was a boom time for this industry, and Figure 2 indicated a rosy future.

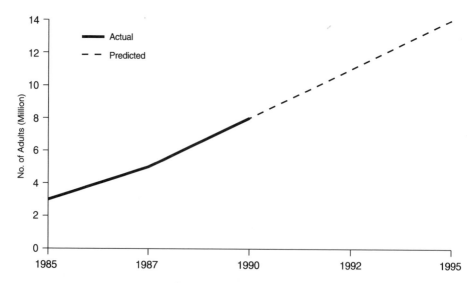

Figure 2. *Use of private health clubs 1985-1995 (as predicted in June 1991)*
Source: MINTEL

Sales of leotards – a good indicator of how fitness orientated the nation was becoming – were growing. The dip in 1990 and 1991 is probably explained by the effects of recession.

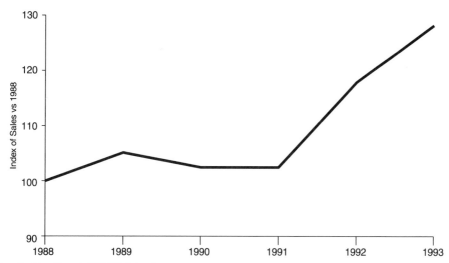

Figure 3. *Sales of leotards 1988-1993 (indexed)*
Source: TGI

The Recession

Although the future looked rosy and clearly there was a desire by people to partake in fitness and join fitness clubs, the depth, the length and the depressing effects of the by now well documented economic recession were not predicted in 1991. Nobody knew that luxuries were about to become just that to most people, and that an expensive annual subscription would be one of the first things to go.

Figure 4 shows the impact of the recession on out-of-home leisure spend. Against the boom time of 1989, we can see a 9% fall in out-of-home leisure spend compared with a 2% gain in in-home spend.

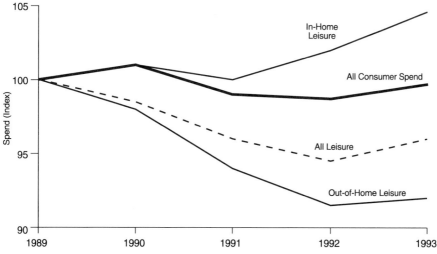

Figure 4. *The impact of recession on leisure spend indexed against 1989*
Source: MINTEL

Given that membership of a health club could cost up to £500 a year, it was a luxury that had to go by the board for many.

Looking at the rise in in-home leisure in Figure 4 it is obvious that 'staying in' became a much more common pursuit. This is backed by data in Figure 5 which shows that consumer spending on health and fitness clubs fell in real terms in 1991, 1992 and 1993.

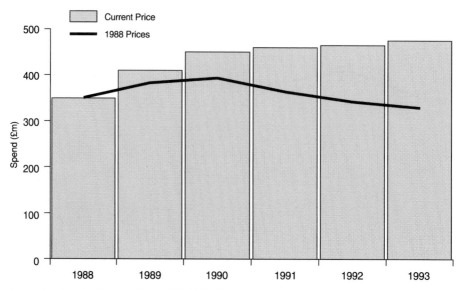

Figure 5. *Spend on private health and fitness facilities (1988-1993)*
Source: MINTEL

So the optimism in 1991 was misplaced and the recession was to become a major inhibitor to growth. Consequently the results of this advertising were achieved under extreme pressure and should be judged with this market background in mind.

THE BRIEF

The advertising brief was specific and aggressive. Increase the membership of our premium priced facility (as if the recession wasn't happening).

THE ADVERTISING STRATEGY

This paper sets out to demonstrate how lateral thinking had a significant business impact on The Edinburgh Club.

We decided not only to target the 86% of the population who were not using a health club but to identify behavioural characteristics within this group and go for the people with the greatest potential. To do this we had to establish *why* they were not using a club.

Was it because they felt that getting fit was a waste of time and not for them? Or were they inhibited by price or emotional barriers?

As we have already seen it couldn't be that the desire to be fit wasn't for them. After all, in 1991, six of the top 100 selling videos were home exercise videos. In fact, by 1994, this market sector was so popular that it had its own top seller's chart. But the fact that it was video sales for *home* consumption was the key to our understanding of the target market.

It seemed to us that the fear factor of being 'looked down on' in a health club by the beautiful people was the biggest turn-off. Price was an inhibitor (and the recession didn't help) therefore the fact that The Edinburgh Club commanded a price premium throughout the campaign makes these results all the more remarkable.

To reach the 86% of people who would no more pull on a pink Lycra leotard than refuse that extra helping of custard with their apple pie, required a new look at how to position the club. Our strategy invented a place where ordinary people could get fit without feeling inadequate. A place for fat people who wanted to become fit people in an embarrassment free zone.

TARGET AUDIENCES

Table 1 shows the profile of health club users in 1991. It suggests that the highest potential lay among young upmarket men. Logic dictated that these should be the people to whom we appealed. However, these were the people who were already using health clubs. We were after non-users.

So we disregarded received wisdom and aimed at an older, more downmarket, female-biased target audience. Not the sort you would expect to find in a health club at all. But precisely the people who were 'going for the burn' with Jane Fonda (on the video recorder).

We identified another key group. Although they followed the same demographics as the home workout brigade, they were the opposite in terms of behaviour. We classified them as 'guilty couch potatoes'.

They may once have been fit, trim and active, but in the last few years circumstance had conspired to rid exercise from their lives – children, work pressure, ageing. They wanted to get fit but wouldn't be seen dead in a health club.

In late 1992, there was a switch in emphasis towards recruiting off-peak (daytime) members so we introduced senior citizens to our target audience. They too fell into the atypical health club user profile, as Table 1 clearly demonstrates.

TABLE 1: DEMOGRAPHIC BREAKDOWN OF USAGE OF PRIVATE HEALTH AND FITNESS CLUBS
March 1991 (Base: 1,085 Adults)

	I am a member/thinking about becoming a member %
All	9
Men	**11**
Women	8
15-19	**15**
20-24	**10**
25-34	**17**
35-44	10
45-54	8
55-64	7
65+	2
AB	**16**
C1	11
C2	8
D	7
E	2
London/TVS	10
Anglia/Central	9
Harlech/TSW	11
Yorkshire/Tyne Tees	10
Granada	6
Scotland	7
Working	13
Not Working	7
Retired	3
Married	11
Not Married	8
Children	12
No Children	8

Source: MINTEL

THE CREATIVE SOLUTION

The risk of our strategy was that we might position the club as a place for freaks. So humour was both the key to creating empathy with our target audience and the way to avoid them thinking the club was too 'serious' for them. Our advertising built on the fact that although being overweight is seen by many as an imperfection, a lot of overweight people refer to their extra inches in a self-deprecating way.

These people could not be attracted through 'serious' fitness messages because they were not looking to become superhuman athletes, they were only looking to get a little bit fitter in a non-threatening environment.

The desired response from the advertising was:

"I could be comfortable there. They don't seem to be too serious so I could do something about my fitness, or fatness, without looking like a prat."

For three years now the most unlikely models have made their advertising debuts.

'PUDDING CLUB'

'UPLIFTING'

'OTHER FITNESS CLUBS'

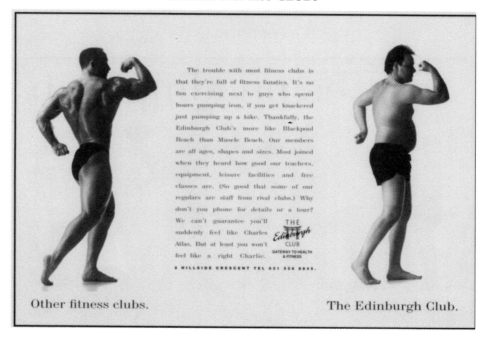

The trouble with most fitness clubs is that they're full of fitness fanatics. It's no fun exercising next to guys who spend hours pumping iron, if you get knackered just pumping up a bike. Thankfully, the Edinburgh Club's more like Blackpool Beach than Muscle Beach. Our members are all ages, shapes and sizes. Most joined when they heard how good our teachers, equipment, leisure facilities and free classes are. (So good that some of our regulars are staff from rival clubs.) Why don't you phone for details or a tour? We can't guarantee you'll suddenly feel like Charles Atlas. But at least you won't feel like a right Charlie.

THE Edinburgh CLUB
GATEWAY TO HEALTH & FITNESS

2 HILLSIDE CRESCENT TEL 031 556 8845.

Other fitness clubs.   The Edinburgh Club.

THE MEDIA STRATEGY

Local press was the obvious choice. But which title to use boiled down to the best deal we could get on appropriate spaces.

Availability of guaranteed spaces on the TV page of the *Edinburgh Herald & Post* was the deciding factor in its favour. The TV page is the most read page in this paper and was the prime place to talk to our target audience of guilty couch potatoes. *The Scotsman*, *Scotland on Sunday* and *Edinburgh Evening News* were also used occasionally when good spaces could be purchased. We even had a brief flurry of advertising on bus backs (a good place to reach guilty car seat potatoes) using an adaption of one of the press ads.

TABLE 2: MEDIA PLAN

Execution	1991	1992	1993	1994
Chocolate	✖ ✖ ✖ ✖ ✖ ✖	● ● ● ● ◆ ✖ ★ ★ ★ ★ ★	✖	
Other Fitness Clubs		✖ ✖ ✖		
Uplifting			✖ ▲ ▲	
Pudding Club			✖ ✖ ✖	✖
Sag Banner			☆ ☆ ☆ ☆ ☆	☆ ☆ ☆ ☆ ☆
Off-Peak 1 & 2		✖ ✖ ✖	✖ ✖ ✖ ✖ ✖ ✖	✖

Key: ✖ = Edinburgh Herald & Post   ★ = Bus backs   ☆ = Hanging banner outside club
      ● = The Scotsman ▲ = Edinburgh Evening News ◆ = SOS Magazine

HOW RESEARCH BACKS UP THE STRATEGY

We carried out a three part research exercise among the membership:

1.   Two group interviews of club members.
2.   Sixteen depth interviews of club members.
3.   Questionnaire survey of members (80 people, or 8% of members filled in the questionnaire).

The research was intended to establish, albeit retrospectively, whether our previously unresearched strategy was based on correct assumptions and to find out whether the advertisements were having the desired effect.

What follows is a representative selection of comments gleaned from the depth research. The comments are universally positive because it really is quite difficult to find club members who do not like the advertising:

> "The people here don't intimidate you. They are not the headband crowd and not everyone is a size 10."

> "Mr Normal, overweight, person is welcome at The Edinburgh Club – I think the ads portray the club as it is now."

> "The ads made The Edinburgh Club somewhat homely which is a good feeling. It facilitates working mothers, older, middle aged people. They are funny."

> "The ads would appeal to people because some people are turned off by young, perfect, beautiful bodies."

> "The people are just like me, not exactly glamorous: some are overweight and trying to lose weight. The 'Baywatch' figures aren't very visible."

> "The ads are comical. They don't make it sound serious."

> "This one is quite good. It shows ordinary people of different sizes so you know you won't be working out with size 8/10 model figures on each side."

> "They make the club seem very approachable and friendly and would make me more willing to come in and ask about facilities."

> "My husband would not feel he was obese in the sense that he looks like at least 90% of the people here."

> "It says the club is not draped in wall-to-wall Arnold Schwartzeneggers."

THE RESULTS

The best way to judge the effectiveness of the campaign is to measure the number of new members recruited over the course of the campaign (see Figure 6). Between 1990/91 and 1993/94 there was a 330% rise in new members, from 212 to 911.

Figure 7 compares turnover with media spend. As we can see, advertising spend is constant yet turnover increases by 113%. We will go on to prove in this paper that the change in advertising strategy was the only variable that could have had this effect.

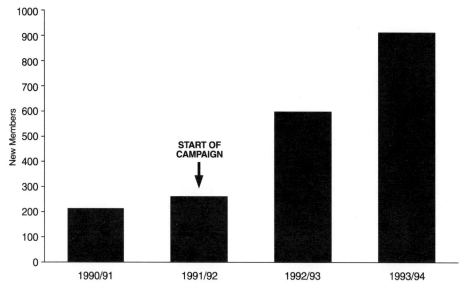

Figure 6. *New members of The Edinburgh Club 1990-1994*
Source: MINTEL, Edinburgh Club Survey

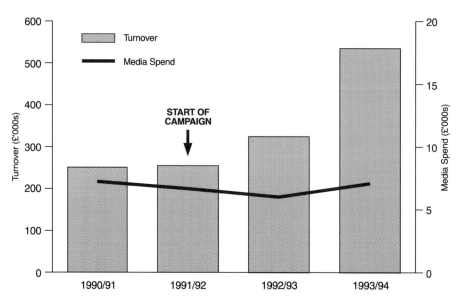

Figure 7. *Turnover and advertising spend of The Edinburgh Club 1990-1994 (Year ending April)*
Source: The Edinburgh Club Accounts

A SHIFT IN EMPHASIS

By November 1992 the club was becoming very busy during peak times; early morning and after office hours. In order to maintain a steady flow of new members the emphasis of the advertising began to shift towards off-peak customers – particularly senior citizens. Off-peak custom would lead to a more balanced use of the club across the day. This drive fitted perfectly with the positioning of the club for older, less fit people.

So, in October 1992, the off-peak rate was advertised in small ads in tandem with the main campaign.

Figure 8 shows the breakdown of new members 1990-1994 by full price, off-peak and others.

Full price members include single, double and life members who enjoy unlimited use of the facilities. Off-peak members have a 45% discount on full price but are restricted to using the club during weekdays, outside 'rush hours'. 'Others' include two groups – corporate members and judo members.

We can see that although off-peak growth, from a small base, has been dramatic since advertising began (+1,130% since 1991) the critical, high value, full members book has also grown rapidly (+169%) over the same period.

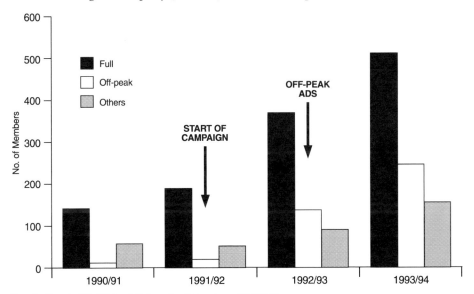

Figure 8. *Growth of The Edinburgh Club membership by category (1990-1994)*
Source: The Edinburgh Club Database

So it seems that the advertising has worked, but to prove it needs further evidence.

HOW CAN WE PROVE IT WAS ADVERTISING THAT HAD THE EFFECT?

In the membership survey people were asked why they had joined the club. We also tried to establish members' attitudes towards the advertising campaign and how they had heard of the club. We began by comparing their reasons for joining with published national figures:

TABLE 3: REASONS FOR JOINING A HEALTH CLUB

	BMRB Findings	The Edinburgh Club Members
To get fit	32%	44%
To lose weight	21%	28%

Source: BMRB/The Edinburgh Club Survey

From this table we can see that The Edinburgh Club members are more likely to join to get fit or lose weight than the national average. In addition, we know from national figures that joining for pleasure is the number one reason for joining a health club, yet this reason does not feature highly among The Edinburgh Club members.

When members were asked how they would describe their weight before joining, these findings were further vindicated.

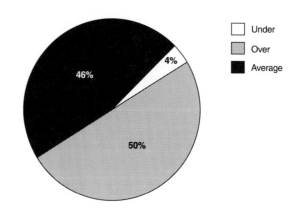

Figure 9.   *The Edinburgh Club members' perceptions of their weight prior to joining The Edinburgh Club*
Source: The Leith Agency Survey

Half of the club's new members considered themselves to be overweight. We think this is an important point given the targeting of 'fatties'. Had we asked this question in 1990 (and we didn't), we would contend that given the club's target market of beautiful people at that time, the result would have been less skewed towards people who considered themselves overweight.

Likewise, when we investigated fitness levels, the following trends emerged (Figure 10).

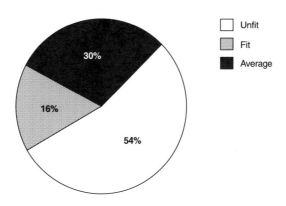

Figure 10. *The Edinburgh Club members' perceptions of their own fitness level prior to joining The Edinburgh Club*
Source: The Leith Agency Survey

Over 50% of the membership considered themselves 'unfit' on joining the club. Again, this indicates that we were attracting the sort of people featured in the advertising.

When asked how they had first heard of the club, a large number said it was through friends who were already members. This is what you would expect given that a health club is a very personal place to go, and for overweight people, the sort of place to go to with a friend for a bit of moral support.

It is indicitative of the campaign's effectiveness that advertising is as important as the recommendations of friends as a reason to join. This supports our case for the key role of advertising in the recruitment of new members (Figure 11).

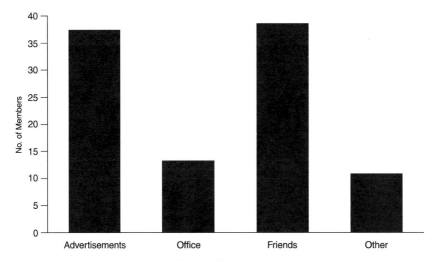

Figure 11. *Where The Edinburgh Club members originally heard of the club*
Source: The Leith Agency Survey

Table 4 shows members' responses when asked why they had first joined The Edinburgh Club.

One would assume that facilities and classes would be the main reasons for joining. Location was also important and this backed up our choice of advertising in local press.

However, the frequency of mentions for the 'non-intimidating members' (38%), and 'atmosphere' (29%) suggested that it was not functional reasons alone that were attracting new members. Emotional reasons too were important in the decision.

TABLE 4: MEMBERS' REASONS FOR JOINING THE EDINBURGH CLUB

Reasons for joining	%
Facilities	60
Classes	54
Location	43
Non-intimidating members	38
Special offer	30
Atmosphere	29
Cost	19
Café	18
Corporate scheme	11
Staff	4

Source: The Leith Agency Survey

Probably the most important aspect of the questionnaire in the context of this paper is attitudes towards the advertising itself. The results are shown in Table 5.

TABLE 5: ATTITUDES TO THE EDINBURGH CLUB ADS BY MEMBERS

	Agree %	Neither Agree nor Disagree %	Disagree %
They reflect the style of the club well	83	16	1
They make the club seem like a good place to come to	81	18	1
I like them	81	18	1
They make it seem like a place for normal people	89	6	5
There are too many overweight people in them	19	30	51
They are for people like me	45	42	13
They are not patronising	78	17	5

Source: The Edinburgh Club Members' Survey

There is an overwhelming empathy towards the advertising. People like the ads and appear to defend them against negative comments such as "there are too many overweight people in them". The warmth of feeling for the ads was also demonstrated in the qualitative research, from which the earlier quotes were selected.

So there is a great deal of evidence to show that the advertising had a positive effect. Nevertheless, other factors may have come into play. The next section considers these possible factors.

Competition

Despite the recession the number of health and leisure centres in Edinburgh has risen from 6 to 27 since 1988 (see Figure 12).

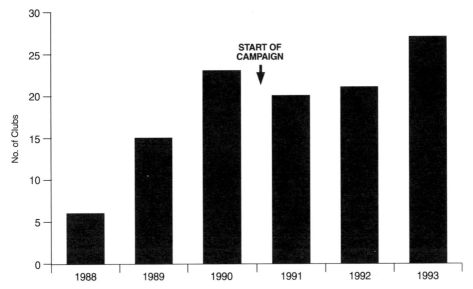

Figure 12. *Health clubs and leisure centres in Edinburgh (1988-1993)*
Source: Edinburgh Yellow Pages

The chart shows quite clearly an effect of the recession in 1991. Immediately there was a fall in the number of clubs in Edinburgh. For a short time this may have relieved some of the competitive pressure which the club was experiencing. However, the number rose in 1992 and to a record level in 1993.

So, despite consumers having more choice of clubs, recruitment of new members rose throughout the campaign.

Pricing

We conducted a telephone survey of every health club in Edinburgh to establish the cost of a single membership – including the first year's joining fee. Some clubs have no extra charge for initial membership. The Edinburgh Club has, and so we thought it was appropriate to establish the full cost of the first year's membership, as this would be the way in which new members would make a price comparison.

Of the 27 clubs in Edinburgh, eight are district council owned and offer subsidised prices, however we decided to exclude them from our calculations of relative price. These would, however, be prime competition during the recession. Indeed, the Meadowbank Sports Centre which is only one mile from the Club and has more facilities than any other centre in Scotland, charges only £15 for membership. Seven are priced on a 'pay as you go' basis and so could not be compared. Three refused to help us with our survey. The remaining nine clubs therefore represent a direct comparison. The results are graphed in Figure 13.

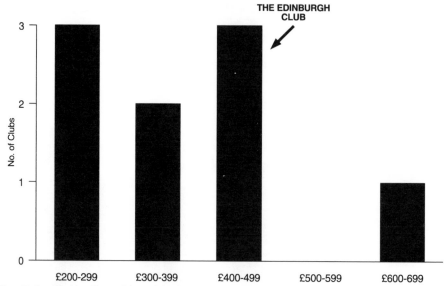

Figure 13. *Cost of health and leisure clubs in Edinburgh (1993)*
Source: The Leith Agency Telephone Survey

The average price in Edinburgh for a first year single membership is £390. The cost of The Edinburgh Club is £480 – a price premium to the market of 23%. In fact only one club is more expensive. Furthermore, in our members' survey, 25% of those questioned thought The Edinburgh Club was expensive at the time of joining the club.

It is unlikely therefore that pricing has ever been a positive factor in increasing membership of The Edinburgh Club and the campaign has almost certainly allowed The Edinburgh Club to maintain a price premium across the period.

Sales Promotions

Special offers to entice new members are a common marketing ploy in this sector. At any time several private clubs are offering new membership deals. Indeed of the nine clubs surveyed, five were running special offers at that time.

The Edinburgh Club has only ever adopted one tactic; the waiving of its £60 joining fee. This could be a factor in choosing a club.

However, waiving of joining fees is essentially a constant factor in the equation. Nearly every club does it on a regular basis. This devalues the customer's view of the real price, so that reductions are taken with a pinch of salt. Consequently, the effectiveness of the tactic is reduced.

Whatever the effect of price reductions, it seems highly unlikely that this approach could account for the sort of sustained growth we have seen in membership, especially as the tactic was also being used *before* our advertising began.

In any case, even with a £60 discount, The Edinburgh Club is still more costly than the market average. And if price was the key determinant, then the fact that

The Edinburgh Club is more expensive after the discount would surely limit the effect of the tactic.

Significantly, none of the advertising has *ever* featured a price reduction on full membership. We have run advertisements for the off-peak rate, and as we have demonstrated these have been successful, but the headline peak rate has remained sacrosanct.

The Product

The club has carried out regular upgrading of facilities since 1991. However, these have not resulted in tangible added value. Alton Towers might increase usage by adding extra rides. It would be unlikely to quadruple its visitors by repainting the roller coaster.

In The Edinburgh Club's case, no new attractions have been added. Indeed the squash courts were closed in 1993 – arguably reducing the clubs' competiveness.

It is interesting to compare the facilities across the ten clubs which provided usable answers to our telephone survey (see Table 6).

Facilities are broadly comparable between clubs. The single facility which most increases appeal is a swimming pool. In a BMRB survey in 1991, swimming was quoted as the No. 1 reason for visiting a health/fitness club. Yet The Edinburgh Club does not have one. In our club survey 68% of respondents said they would like a swimming pool to be added. It is especially important for the more sedentary members of The Edinburgh Club who may be reluctant to 'go for the burn' from day one.

TABLE 6: PRIVATE HEALTH AND LEISURE CLUB FACILITIES IN EDINBURGH CLUBS

	Tennis/ Squash	Sauna/ Steam	Cardio-vascular	Sunbeds	Aerobics	Swimming Pool	Snooker	Café
The Carlton Club	✓	✓	✓	✓	✓	✓	✓	✓
Fettes Village	✓	✓	✓	✓	✓	✓	✓	✓
Balmoral Hotel		✓	✓	✓	✓	✓		✓
Royal Terrace Health Club	✓	✓	✓	✓		✓		✓
Sheraton Hotel		✓	✓	✓		✓		✓
The Edinburgh Club		✓	✓	✓	✓			✓
Claremont Health Club		✓	✓	✓	✓			✓
Flying Scot Club	✓	✓	✓	✓	✓			
Body Talk		✓			✓			✓
Morrissons		✓					✓	✓

Source: Leith Agency Telephone Survey

Given the lack of a pool, the lack of new attractions since 1991, and the generally comparable facilities between the competition we can conclude that the club's facilities have not gained it a competitive advantage during the campaign period.

WHAT EFFECT HAS THE ADVERTISING HAD ON THE BUSINESS?

There has been a healthy impact, as a result of the advertising, on the club's bottom line. We have already noted a 113% increase in turnover. However, turnover could be a misleading measure. Instead we should consider profit. The Club moved from a loss of £3,500 in 1990/91 to a profit of £60,000 in 1993 (the latest financial data available).

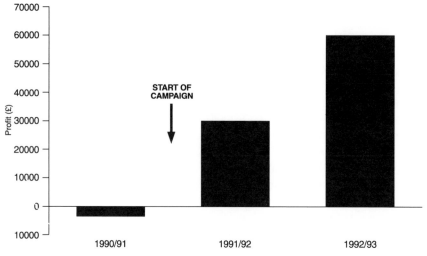

Figure 14. *The Edinburgh Club profits*
Source: Edinburgh Club Accounts

We believe a large contributory factor to this performance has been the ability to maintain a significant price premium whilst accelerating the acquisition of new members.

It is not surprising, given the constant advertising spend, that the advertising to sales ratios have dropped since 1990 (see Figure 15).

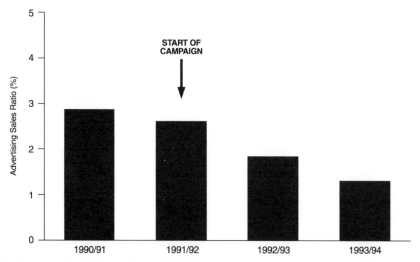

Figure 15. *Advertising to sales ratio for The Edinburgh Club (1990-1993)*
Source: The Edinburgh Club Accounts

CONCLUSIONS

We have demonstrated the value of imaginative strategic and creative thinking to a very brave advertiser.

The Edinburgh Club has operated in a highly competitive market, in a luxury sector, during a recession.

It hasn't fundamentally improved its product and its promotional activities have been limited to tactical price reductions. Even with these, it operates at a price premium to the market. No other promotions, PR or direct mail have been employed.

At the same time it has increased membership by 330%, turnover by 113% and profit by 174%.

It is the only health club in the area to run brand building advertising (as opposed to price offer and tactical advertising).

Until 1991, The Edinburgh Club ran that type of campaign too, but made a strategic move to give itself a brand personality beyond the commodity feel of the market as a whole. This was the only variable factor in the equation which changed in The Edinburgh Club's favour in the period.

We would argue that it is braver for a small concern to adopt a radical strategy than for a big brand. After all, the sole proprietor was placing his livelihood on the line. If the advertising had failed, and the recession had bitten as hard into his business as data shows it did with other out-of-home leisure operations, he might no longer have been in business.

15

The Co-operative Bank
"Profit with Principles"

INTRODUCTION

This case demonstrates the genuine contribution The Co-operative Bank's 'ethical' advertising strategy and campaign, launched in May 1992, made to the Banks' results in 1992 and 1993.

An examination of the effect of the other variables that might have affected the Bank's success lead us to conclude that the identification of a distinctive advertising message and the careful media targeting of that message was a major contributor.

The Co-operative Bank's case study is unusual in that it shows how a small player in an established and heavily advertised market-place can carve a distinct niche for itself, and introduce a new dynamic into the decision making process, on a comparatively small advertising budget.

We hope that this provides inspiration to all the marketeers who are currently struggling to find a tangible point of difference for their brand, and confounds all the cynics who said at the launch of the Bank's campaign in 1992 "money and morals don't mix". They were wrong. Read on and you will see; you can have profit with principles.

BACKGROUND

The Co-operative Bank traces its origins back to 1872. From then, when it was the bank for the Co-operative Wholesale and Retail Societies, it has evolved to become one of the eight UK Clearing Banks with a network of over a hundred branches nationwide. However, in the market for personal banking The Co-operative Bank is one of the smaller players with approximately 2% share.

The personal banking market is dominated by the National Westminster Bank and Barclays Bank, both of whom have around 20% market share, followed by Lloyds, Midland and the Trustee Savings Banks, each with 12% to 15% share (source: FRS).

These larger banks have the advantage of customer convenience, and exposure to their 'brand' name via their extensive branch networks which infiltrate every British high street.

The personal banking sector is an extremely important source of funds to the banks. By increasing their personal sector deposits, their reliance on wholesale money is decreased and they can broaden their lending margins. Furthermore, personal customers are a prime target for cross-sales of savings, loans, credit cards, insurance and pensions products. This paper concentrates on current accounts as these are the core entry product.

De-regulation in the 1980s brought some radical changes in the personal banking sector as the current account market was opened up to competition from other financial organisations, most particularly the building societies. The ensuing battle for market share resulted in a rapid increase in marketing activities in a bid to retain/gain customers and their combined advertising expenditure escalated into the hundreds of millions.

In comparison to these larger organisations The Co-operative Bank's total annual advertising investment of less than a million pounds appeared insignificant and the Bank's annual share of advertising voice registered below 1%.

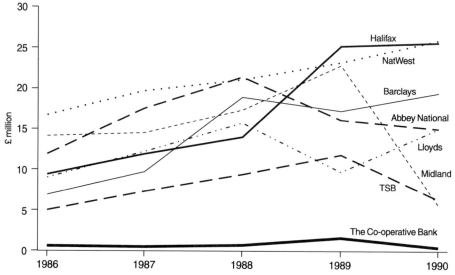

Figure 1. *Advertising expenditure by the major banks and building societies vs The Co-operative Bank, 1986-1990*
Source: MEAL

THE CO-OPERATIVE BANK'S PROBLEM

By 1990 it was readily apparent that The Co-operative Bank had problems in the personal banking sector. These lay in three related areas:

Declining Market Share

During the early part of the '80s The Co-operative Bank had experienced steady growth in the personal banking sector as a result of its many product innovations, eg free in-credit banking, interest bearing cheque accounts and extended opening hours. However, during the second half of the decade the Bank's market share fell from 2.7% in 1986 to 2.1% by 1991 in a growing market (source: FRS). And personal current account losses began to outweigh gains.

Increasingly Downmarket Customer Base

Furthermore, whilst the Bank's personal current account profile in 1990 was, if anything, slightly upmarket, 41% of customers were ABC1, there was evidence that this profile was beginning to be diluted as a growing proportion of their new accounts were being recruited from the C2DE social groups. The ramification of this was that the growth in current account deposits was slowing and the potential for profitable cross-sales was diminished.

Lack of Identity

Finally, research conducted by The Co-operative Bank in the late '80s indicated that it lacked a clear image of its own despite the advertising expenditure behind its innovative products. Furthermore, spontaneous awareness of the Bank had fallen steadily from 12% to 7% between 1983 and 1988 which was indicative of the sheer weight of financial advertising in the interim period.

THE ADVERTISING BRIEF

The Bank recognised that raising awareness and developing an image were fundamental to its future success and it looked to advertising to achieve these. As a consequence of raising awareness and developing an image the Bank sought to:

i)   Build customer loyalty and so stem the net outflow of personal current account customers.
ii) Expand the personal customer base, targeting ABC1s, and so improve current account balances and the potential for cross-sales.

Whilst the main thrust of the advertising campaign was aimed at the personal sector by raising the Bank's profile so the Bank sought to benefit in the corporate sector also.

The size of the Bank and its profitability meant that the marketing and advertising budget available was modest by comparison to the other financial organisations. Therefore, the effectiveness of the Bank's expenditure through creativity, impact and focus were recognised to be crucial.

TOWARDS AN ADVERTISING STRATEGY

The Bank could not continue with what was essentially a product-led strategy. Its product innovations in the early '80s had been quickly adopted by the other major banks and its competitive edge swiftly eroded. Furthermore, a brand positioning that relied on innovation was difficult to sustain in the long term.

However, mainstream positionings that positioned The Co-operative Bank directly alongside the 'Big Four' banks were also out of the question since the size of the Bank limited its credibility and it lacked the promotional budget that such a positioning would require anyway. Hence, we decided that a niche positioning was required that had sufficient status to increase The Co-operative Bank's business and meet its objectives but was not so large that the larger banks and building societies would seek to emulate it.

Rather than devise a new positioning and then try to weld it onto the Bank, BDDH took the Bank itself as the start point and attempted to find a unique competitive differentiator from within the organisation. We looked at three main areas. These were:

— How was The Co-operative Bank different from the other banks?
— Who had it attracted to date?
— How was it perceived by customers and outsiders?

How was it different?

We found that there were four aspects of The Co-operative Bank that differentiated it from the competition:

— Firstly, its ownership structure: it was owned by the Co-operative Wholesale Society which meant that it was not controlled by the same City interests as the other banks.
— Secondly, through its historic ties with the Co-operative Movement it had developed areas of specific banking expertise, eg for Local Authorities & Community Action Groups.
— Thirdly, it had developed products that reflected these areas of expertise, such as affinity cards for the Labour & Liberal Democrat parties and the RSPB.
— Finally, it differed in the way it sourced and distributed its funds. Due to its customer bias its deposits came from bodies such as Local Authorities and Trade Unions and its lending was to Workers Co-operatives, individuals and small businesses. Its heritage meant that its lending policy had always been governed by an unwritten ethical code, hence, it had never lent money to any of the larger environmentally or politically unsound organisations.

Who had it attracted?

Our analysis revealed that these distinctive aspects of the Bank were reflected in its customer base; a high percentage of customers were employees of organisations that had a community focus, and particularly those from the caring professions, eg teachers, nurses and health workers.

How was it perceived?

The distinctive aspects of The Co-operative Bank did mean that it had rather a different image from the other banks.

Qualitative research conducted by BDDH amongst the general public indicated that The Co-operative Bank currently fell between two stools. It did not carry the credibility of the larger banks nor engender the regional patriotism of the other smaller banks. The brand map below illustrates this point.

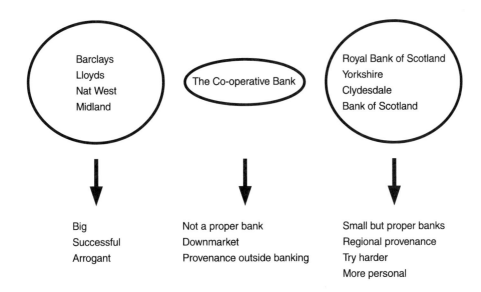

Figure 2. *Brand map*
Source: BDDH Qualitative Research, 1990

These findings were borne out by quantitative research which showed that amongst the broader general public The Co-operative Bank was perceived to be rather old fashioned, working class with left wing tendencies and was "not really a proper bank". (See Table 1.) Hence, amongst the general public there was a significant lack of identification with The Co-operative Bank and the values that it represented.

TABLE 1: THE CO-OPERATIVE BANK'S IMAGE VERSUS BARCLAYS BANK

	The Co-operative Bank %	Barclays %
Rather old fashioned	25	8
Not really a proper bank	17	3
Particularly left wing	11	3
Working class	29	12

Base: All Adults

Source: AIM Tracking Study, 1990

We found that this perception of The Co-operative Bank was not shared by its customers. They valued the Bank's heritage and one in ten claimed to have joined The Co-operative Bank because of its ethical values. However, on further exploration it was apparent that each customer had their own interpretation of the Bank's ethics based on expectations: the Bank had never actually told them what its ethics were.

In summary, we found that The Co-operative Bank was clearly a different type of bank and it had a very distinctive and personal appeal to its customers, based on its ethical heritage and provenance. However, the Bank's appeal was not apparent to the wider public at that time.

Hence, the task for BDDH was to transform the factors that set The Co-operative Bank aside from the other banks into a relevant and motivating proposition that would appeal beyond the Bank's current customer base.

THE OPPORTUNITY

From the outset, it has been established that The Co-operative Bank was never going to appeal to everyone. What was required was the identification of a profitable niche in the market. An analysis of the market trends, conducted by BDDH in 1991, indicated that a significant niche opportunity did exist that had not yet been developed by competing banks.

Our analysis indicated a growing public awareness of the wider social and environmental implications of commercial behaviour. Consumers were carrying their personal values and ethics into their purchasing behaviour; evidenced by the growth in ozone friendly, cruelty free and environmentally friendly products. We found that 40% of consumers were prepared to pay a premium for ethical products and 8% would pay as much as a 20% premium (source: 'Planning For Social Change', Henley Centre, 1990).

Furthermore, we found that there was some evidence that this new consumer behaviour was already filtering through to the financial market, indicated by the uptake of ethical unit trusts and affinity cards.

In addition the upmarket profile of these 'ethical' consumers was directly in line with the Bank's desired new customer profile.

THE POSITIONING

Thus BDDH believed that a real opportunity existed for The Co-operative Bank to target these 'ethical' consumers with a positioning that came straight out of the Bank's core values and aspirations. It was proposed that The Co-operative Bank should take the moral high ground and position itself as the "Ethical Bank".

THE CONSUMER PROPOSITION

Whilst many of the Bank's activities supported this positioning, BDDH had to identify those activities that were most relevant to the customer in order to arrive at a motivating consumer proposition. The proposition we finally arrived at was:

"The Co-operative Bank is committed to the responsible sourcing and distribution of funds."

The rationale for this proposition was that the sourcing and distribution of money was fundamental to every customer's relationship with the Bank, and so it was an aspect of the Bank's ethics that *directly* affected them.

SUPPORT FOR THE NEW POSITIONING AND PROPOSITION

This new positioning as the 'Ethical Bank' was first presented to the Bank's own customer base. In total 30,000 customers were interviewed and a very high level of support was indicated, with 84% approving the new positioning. What was particularly pleasing was that this approval was strongest amongst the Bank's more upmarket customers, which was exactly the profile of new customers that the Bank particularly wanted to attract.

Qualitative research conducted amongst non customers indicated strong potential for the positioning outside the Bank's customer base also. The consumer proposition based on "responsible sourcing and distribution of funds" served to raise an issue that they had never previously considered, but now it had been presented it was felt to be extremely pertinent.

Both pieces of research also helped clarify which organisations the consumer felt most strongly that the Bank should not be involved with. These were: organisations that used animals to test cosmetics, businesses that polluted the environment, businesses involved in the arms trade and companies that did business with oppressive regimes.

The Bank used this consumer feedback to construct a written ethical policy that stated who it would and would not do business with and it undertook a thorough audit of its corporate customer base to ensure that it lived up to its stated ethics. This resulted in the Bank actually rejecting some corporate customers who did not fit with its policy.

THE ROLE FOR ADVERTISING

Advertising's contribution was to establish the Bank's new positioning and reinforce it over time. In terms of the Bank's prime target of new customers, the advertising needed to:

a) raise their awareness of the Bank;
b) establish an emotionally based rationale for the bank that challenged them to consider it.

Given the high level of consumer apathy exhibited towards changing one's bank account a challenging approach was vital. The majority of the British public remain with the same bank all their life. (Source: FRS.)

An important secondary audience for the advertising was the Bank's existing customer base. Whilst there were other more direct means of reaching this audience (ie direct mail), advertising could provide a public declaration of the Bank's ethics and an emotional discriminator for it, hence providing customers with a justification for their banking relationship.

The Bank's staff were an equally important secondary audience for the advertising. Advertising could show them the Bank's commitment to the new ethical positioning and inspire and motivate them. As the 'public face' of the Bank it was of fundamental importance that the new positioning gained their full support.

Whilst there were other elements in the promotional mix, advertising served to inspire and lead them, setting their tone and style. Advertising was essentially the catalyst that ignited these other activities, and it was the umbrella that united them.

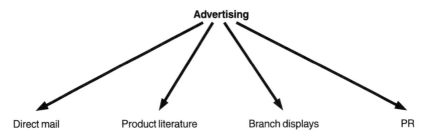

Figure 3. *Advertising's role*

THE CREATIVE SOLUTION

The creative challenge was to express the idea of "responsible sourcing and distribution of funds" in a way that the consumer could easily understand but would also find provocative and motivating. The creative work also had to remain tonally in keeping with the Bank's values of honesty and integrity and not fall into the potential pitfall of appearing sensationalist, and so undermine the credibility of the Bank's message, or, at the other extreme, to appear "worthier than thou". Further the whole notion of advertising was slightly at odds with the Bank's ethical stance and so it was important that the creative work did not appear typically commercial.

The creative solution was disarmingly simple; to use a story-line, along the lines of the well known children's tale of "This is the house that Jack built...", to tell the story of the actions and consequences in the sourcing and distribution of funds.

Four storylines were produced each focusing on a different issue; the environment, human rights, animal testing and armaments. Each story told of a very normal family undertaking an everyday purchasing activity that required money from their bank but in each case there was an ironic twist. It was revealed that their bank had loaned money to another organisation whose business was in some way detrimentally linked to what the family were purchasing.

Black and white drawings and photographs were used in order to reinforce the simplicity and the integrity of the message and to contrast with the other banks' and building societies' rather spectacular, full colour, "all singing and dancing" advertising epics. The executions were designed to run on TV and in press in a very similar format.

'THE HILLS'

The CO-OPERATIVE BANK

Why bank with one that isn't?

This is the daughter

The Hills sent to law school

*Using savings they kept
in their bank*

*Which their bank
had invested*

Abroad in a country

*That denies
most of its people*

Legal rights.

It happens.

But not at the Co-operative Bank.

Our customers know there are some things we will never invest in.

Such as companies with oppressive regimes.

Our policy is to invest only in things we believe to be as sound ethically as they are financially.

Of course, we still provide all the normal services you'd expect from a clearing bank with assets of £3 billion, 6,000 'Link' cash machines and a full telephone banking service.

The difference is that along with financial peace of mind our customers receive one other important benefit.

More peace of mind.

FOR AN INFORMATION PACK ABOUT WHAT WE DO AND DON'T DO WITH OUR CUSTOMERS' MONEY, CALL **0800 100 555**, OR WRITE TO THE CO-OPERATIVE BANK P.L.C., DEPARTMENT EW, FREEPOST 4335, BRISTOL BS1 3YX.

'THE WILKINSONS'

The CO-OPERATIVE BANK
Why bank with one that isn't?

These are the trees

The Wilkinsons planted

With interest accrued on their savings

Which their bank had lent

To a chemical giant

That ceaselessly spews

Toxic waste.

It happens.

But not at the Co-operative Bank.

Our customers know there are some things we will never invest in.

Such as companies whose activities are needlessly harmful to the environment.

Our policy is to invest only in companies we believe to be as sound ethically as they are financially.

Of course, we still provide all the normal services you'd expect from a clearing bank with assets of £3 billion, 6,000 'Link' cash machines and a full telephone banking service.

The difference is that along with financial peace of mind our customers receive one other important benefit. More peace of mind.

FOR AN INFORMATION PACK ABOUT WHAT WE DO AND DON'T DO WITH OUR CUSTOMERS' MONEY, CALL **0800 100 555** OR WRITE TO THE CO-OPERATIVE BANK P.L.C. DEPARTMENT EW, FREEPOST 4235, BRISTOL BS1 3YX.

MEDIA STRATEGY

Given the Bank's limited budget a very focused media strategy was required. We defined the target audience in the first year of the campaign as follows:

— Aged 25-50 years.
— ABC1 social grades.
— Current account holders with a rival bank (switchers).
— Caring professions.
— Socially concerned.

Our rationale for this targeting was :

— 25-50 year old, ABC1s represented the highest value customers socio-demographically.
— 'Switchers' were selected rather than the 'first time' bankers due to the 'switchers' comparative affluence and the fact that the competition was greater in the 'first time' market.
— The caring professions, eg teachers, nurses, were felt more likely to have a natural affinity with the Bank, as was already reflected in the Bank's customer base.
— Finally, we believed that the greatest opportunity lay amongst those who shared the Bank's values of social responsibility.

The media selection in 1992 was driven by two criteria;

1. the requirement to support every branch in the launch year (ie national, excluding Scotland);
2. the budget of £750,000.

National press was selected as the main medium (60% of budget) in order to provide advertising support for every branch. A tightly focused schedule was put together comprising core titles that were in tune politically and socially with the target audience; ie The Guardian, The Independent, the Independent on Sunday and The Observer, with the Times, Financial Times and Mail on Sunday included to increase cover. In addition occupational magazines that provided unique cover of key caring professions were used. The press schedule ran May to September and provided 69% cover of ABC1s.

The remaining 40% of the budget was spent on a three region TV test in Granada, Yorkshire and Tyne Tees. These three regions were selected as they represented the Bank's heartland and so presented the most ready new customer potential. They also provided good customer and staff cover (approximately 30% of the Bank's customers and branches are in these regions). TV airtime was bought by specific programmes selected for their editorial suitability, eg Dispatches, World in Action etc., in order to reach the target audience to best effect.

The TV campaign ran 1st May-12th June, 1992 and achieved approximately 500 ABC1 adult TVRs across the three stations.

In 1993 we shifted the media strategy in favour of TV on the basis of the success of the 1992 TV campaign in enhancing awareness and attitudes. London was added to the 3 core TV regions, given the attitudinal appropriateness of this region as defined by TGI 'ethical' lifestyle statements and also the ABC1 bias of the region.

The TV campaign ran 15th February to 26th April and it achieved approximately 420 ABC1 TVRs.

Cinema was also included to the media mix in 1993. Two opportunities were taken advantage of:

1. Trailing Malcolm X – we selected this film as it was particularly appropriate to the "we do not invest in oppressive regimes" execution.
2. An 'art screen' package – we believed that the Bank's target audience were more likely to be viewers of niche art films rather than mainstream blockbusters.

The cinema activity ran between 1st February and 4th April.

There was also a consistent presence in key occupational/special interest magazines from February through to October.

TABLE 2: MEDIA SCHEDULE

Medium	Jan	Feb	Mar	Apr	May	Jun	Jul	Aug	Sep	Oct	Nov	Dec	Budget
1992													
TV				1/5 <——> 12/6									£287,237
				Granada:		445 ABC1 TVRs							
				Tyne Tees:		578 ABC1 TVRs							
				Yorkshire:		542 ABC1 TVRs							
National Press				1/5 <————————————> 31/9									£334,664
						69% cover ABC1s							
Specialist Press				1/5 <————————————> 31/9									£128,825
													£750,726
1993													
TV		15/2 <——> 26/4											£881,809
		Granada:	407 ABC1 TVRs										
		Tyne Tees:	460 ABC1 TVRs										
		Yorkshire:	435 ABC1 TVRs										
		London:	421 ABC1 TVRs										
Specialist Press		1/2 <————————————> 31/9											£58,000
Cinema		1/2 <——> 4/4											£115,028
		2.1 million admissions											
													£1,054,837

THE RESULTS

As mentioned earlier, the end objectives of the advertising were to:
— build customer loyalty and so stem the net outflow of customers;
— expand the customer base, targeting ABC1s, and so improve balances and cross-sales potential;
— expand the corporate customer base also.

In 1992 personal current account closures (instigated by the customer not the Bank) were reduced by 21% from 1991's level, and in 1993 they were reduced a further 10% year on year. In terms of new account generation, openings were held at 1991's level in 1992 but rose by 6% in 1993. Hence, the net outflow of personal current account customers was brought under control and converted into a net increase. (See Figure 4.)

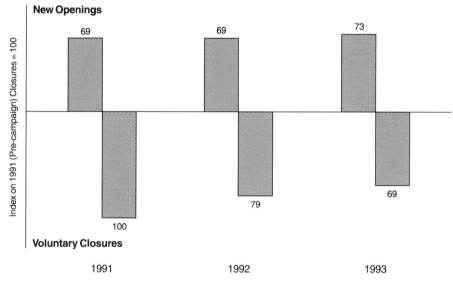

Figure 4. *Personal current account gains/loss analysis*
Source: The Co-operative Bank

Whilst market share did not actually increase over this period the steady decline in share from 2.7% in 1986 to 2.1% in 1991 was halted. (See Figure 5.)

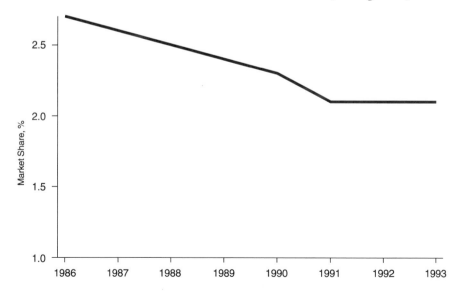

Figure 5. *Market share of personal current accounts*
Source: FRS

In addition a greater proportion of ABC1 current account customers were attracted to the Bank in 1993, compared to 1991, indicated by the Bank's new current account customer surveys conducted in both years. (See Table 3.)

TABLE 3: NEW CURRENT ACCOUNT CUSTOMER PROFILE

	1991 %	1993 %
ABC1	40	50
C2DE	60	50
Base:	300	300

Source: B & MR, 1991 & 1993

This increase in more upmarket customers would appear to have had a positive effect upon average current account balances. The Bank's average balance increased throughout 1992 & 1993, outstripping inflation in both years, (see below) resulting in a 9% increase in the Bank's personal current account deposits.

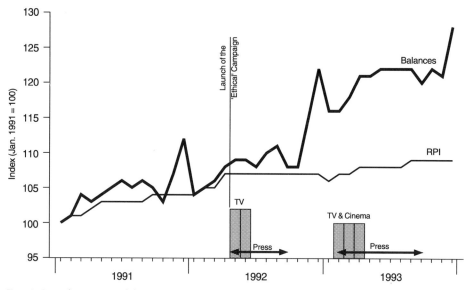

Figure 6. *Personal current account balances*
Source: The Co-operative Bank, CSO

Further, the potential for cross-sales with savings products increased (95% of the Bank's savings product sales are cross-sales) and the Bank's personal savings deposits rose by 49% (May '92 to December '93).

In addition, whilst in media terms the campaign was essentially targeted at personal current account holders, there was naturally a cross over with the business audience and the Bank experienced a significant increase in its corporate accounts – current account balances rose by 116% and deposits rose by 161%. In particular new business was generated in areas that had an affinity with the advertising campaign's ethical message, ie Education, Charities, and Health Services. (See Table 4.)

TABLE 4: GROWTH IN BALANCES IN KEY BUSINESS SECTORS, MAY 1992-DECEMBER 1993

Sector	Growth
Education	+£125 million
Health	+£20 million
Charities	+£10 million

Source: The Co-operative Bank

ISOLATING ADVERTISING'S EFFECT

We don't intend to claim that advertising alone was responsible for this upturn in the Bank's fortunes, however we do believe that it performed a vital role and enhanced the other marketing activities undertaken by the Bank. There are a number of other variables that may have potentially contributed but we do not believe that there is any evidence to support the case that any of these played a major role.

Price

The first factor requiring examination is price, both in terms of the interest rate on the Bank's current account product and in terms of bank charges on it. No advantageous changes were made to price over the period May 1992 to December 1993.

Product

The second factor that might have contributed to the Bank's recovery is the current account product itself, however that seems unlikely as it did not change in any way during 1992 or 1993.

Distribution

Clearly an increase in distribution would have helped to boost the Bank's performance, however in reality the opposite was true and 200 of The Co-operative Bank 'Handybank' outlets were closed. Which, given that 15% of The Co-operative Bank's customers use 'Handybanks' as their main point of contact might have been expected to have had a negative effect upon customer loyalty. Further, none of the Bank's branches were significantly refurbished during 1992 and 1993 and there were no relocations.

The Other Banks' and Building Societies' Advertising Expenditure

The other banks and building societies continued to spend large amounts on advertising during 1992 and 1993, so whilst The Co-operative Bank's advertising expenditure did rise from 1991's level its share of voice remained below 1% in 1992 and 1993. (See Table 5.)

TABLE 5: MEDIA EXPENDITURE BY THE BANKS AND BUILDING SOCIETIES

	1991 £ million	1992 £ million	1993 £ million
Banks	77.2	72.7	76.5
Building Societies	105.7	114.9	100.7
Total	**182.9**	**187.6**	**177.2**
The Co-operative Bank's share of voice	0.03%	0.07%	0.07%

Source: Register-MEAL

The Market

In contrast to The Co-operative Bank's increase in new personal current accounts opened in 1992 and 1993, there was actually a decline in the total market for new current accounts as illustrated below. Hence, The Co-operative Bank bucked the market trend over this period. (See Figure 7.)

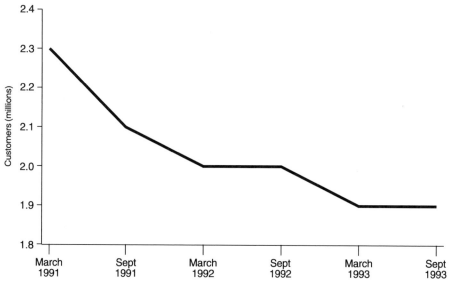

Figure 7.   *New current account market*
Source: FRS

The Co-operative Movement

One possible source of more new customers could have been through the Co-operative Movement rather than via the advertising however, the percentage of new customers through the Movement actually fell from 35% in 1991 to 15% in 1993. (Source: New Customer Surveys, B & MR.)

Other Promotional Activities

The Bank's direct mail and branch displays and literature, will doubtless have had an effect upon the Bank's current customers, however we would argue that these activities could not have instilled the sense of customer pride which was exhibited in the qualitative customer research on their own. This revealed that the public declaration of the Bank's ethics was an important factor providing stature and credibility. Furthermore, the advertising dictated the message, tone and style of these items, hence they were really an extension of the advertising campaign.

There was no direct mail to non-customers and we do not believe that the branch materials will have brought new customers into the branches given the limited branch network and the typically poor nature of the Bank's window displays.

The launch of the Bank's ethical positioning did gain a reasonable amount of media publicity in May 1992, however since then publicity has been sporadic. So, whilst PR will have facilitated we do not believe it has played a major role in account recruitment.

Finally, during 1992 and 1993 the Bank did run some product advertising for their VISA credit card, however this was purely direct response and was specifically for the credit card.

EVIDENCE TO SUPPORT THE ROLE OF ADVERTISING

Evidence to support the vital role performed by the advertising is documented below:

Evidence that the Advertising Affected Existing Customers

Both qualitative and quantitative research was conducted amongst the Bank's existing personal customers after the first burst of advertising in 1992.

The qualitative research revealed a high level of support for the Bank's advertising, in particular the TV, and there was evidence that the advertising campaign had had a significant effect upon them instilling loyalty and pride.

Typical comments about the advertising were:

"It makes me feel I'm banking in the right place."

"It makes me feel proud every time I see it."

Source: KGB Research, 1992

The quantitative research served to indicate the genuine importance that existing customers attached to the Bank's ethical positioning; there was almost unanimous support for it and over half said that they were *more* likely to do business with the Bank as a result.

TABLE 6: EXISTING CUSTOMER'S ATTITUDES TOWARDS THE CO-OPERATIVE BANK'S ETHICAL POSITIONING

	Agree %
I think an ethical policy is a very good stance to take	94
I'd do more business with The Co-operative Bank because of its ethical policy	53

Base: 377 customers

Source: B & MR, 1992

Whilst there were clearly other means than advertising by which the Bank's existing customers learned of the ethical positioning, advertising was identified as the *main* source of awareness of the Bank's ethical positioning by 11% of customers, above press articles and leaflets in branch.

TABLE 7: MAIN SOURCE OF AWARENESS OF ETHICAL POSITIONING

	%
Branch displays	25
Bank sent a letter	19
Advertising	11
Leaflets in branch	7
Press articles	5
Not aware	40

Base: 377 customers

Source: B & MR, 1992

It should be noted that this research took place in 1992, after the first burst of the ethical campaign. It is likely that advertising's role in raising awareness will have increased, by virtue of increased exposure to it, in 1993.

Evidence that the Advertising Affected New Customers

A survey was conducted amongst newly recruited personal current account customers to the Bank after the second burst of TV activity in July 1993.

This revealed that 44% of the new customers had opened an account with the Bank because of its ethical positioning and 22% cited ethics as their *main* reason for opening an account. Amongst the core target audience of 'switchers' 38% claimed the Bank's ethics was their *main* reason for opening an account.

TABLE 8: REASONS FOR OPENING CURRENT ACCOUNT

	Any %	Main %
Ethical policy	44	22
Convenience	33	15
Recommendation	30	11
Bank charges	18	7
Via employer	39	22
Other	48	22

Base: 150 customers

Source: B & MR, 1993

This clearly indicates the potency of the Bank's ethical positioning. The Bank has succeeded in putting ethics into the decision making criteria, and for these new customers it was placed above the more obvious reasons for account opening such as convenience and recommendation.

This research also indicated that 34% of all new personal current account customers were aware of the Bank's ethical advertising campaign and specifically 45% of those who claimed ethics were the main reason for opening their account attributed their awareness to advertising.

TABLE 9: AWARENESS OF THE BANK'S ETHICAL ADVERTISING CAMPAIGN

	Total %	Ethics Main Reason %
Yes	34	45
No/Don't know	66	55

Base: 150 customers

Source: B & MR, 1993

A second piece of support for the advertising's role in gaining new customers is provided by a research survey conducted amongst cinema-goers who had just seen a film within which The Co-operative Bank's commercial featured. 73% recalled The Co-operative Bank's commercial on prompting, illustrating its stand-out, and 22% claimed that they were more likely to consider switching to The Co-operative Bank as a result of having seen the commercial. This is significantly above the level of consideration that the Bank would get by right, given its 2% share.

TABLE 10: LIKELIHOOD TO CONSIDER SWITCHING TO THE CO-OPERATIVE BANK

	%
More likely	22
Less likely	7
No change	63
Don't know	8

Base: 170

Source: Gallup, 1993

ANECDOTAL EVIDENCE

A final piece of evidence that supports the role of advertising is provided by the Bank's own staff. Eight workshops (each 4 hours long) were conducted around the country in 1993, after the Spring TV burst had ended.

All the staff agreed that whereas in 1991 they were slightly embarrassed to say that they worked for The Co-operative Bank now, thanks to the ethical policy, they said it with pride. They also claimed that customers spontaneously talked about the Bank's ethical policy and its advertising.

HOW DID THE ADVERTISING WORK?

The role set for advertising was to:

— raise awareness of the Bank;
— establish a rationale for the Bank that provoked its consideration.

Examining each of these in turn:

Brand Awareness

The Bank subscribe to NOP's continuous brand and advertising awareness monitoring survey which is conducted amongst a robust sample of 2000 adults. This revealed that prior to the new ethical campaign, launched in May 1992, spontaneous awareness of The Co-operative Bank had fallen to 6% nationally and prompted awareness to 66%.

After the TV burst in May-June 1992 spontaneous awareness of the Bank rose from 6% to 10% in the three TV advertising regions and prompted awareness rose from 71% to 81%.

In 1993, again, an increase in brand awareness coincided with the TV activity in February-April. Spontaneous awareness of The Co-operative Bank increased from 6% to 12% in the four regions that TV was used and prompted awareness reached 81% post-campaign. (See Figures 8 and 9.)

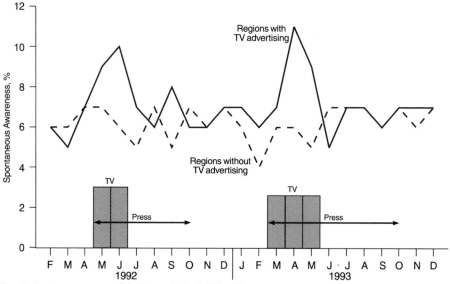

Figure 8. *Spontaneous awareness of The Co-operative Bank, 1992-1993*
Source: NOP

Increases in awareness outside the TV advertising regions were less marked on a broad basis. However, amongst the readers of the national press titles on the 1992 media schedule increases in awareness, particularly on the spontaneous measure, were apparent.

TABLE 11: SPONTANEOUS AWARENESS OF THE CO-OPERATIVE BANK AMONGST READERS OF THE CORE PRESS TITLES

	Pre (January) %	Mid (May) %	Post (November) %
Guardian	9	22	20
Independent	10	23	25
Independent on Sunday	5	28	32
Observer	14	24	20

Source: NOP, 1992

Furthermore, the overall increases in awareness, particularly spontaneous, were most evident amongst ABC1s. (See Figure 10.)

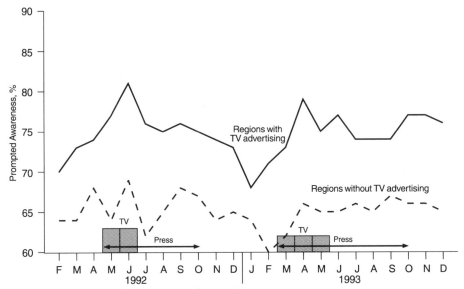

Figure 9. *Prompted awareness of The Co-operative Bank 1992-1993*
Source: NOP

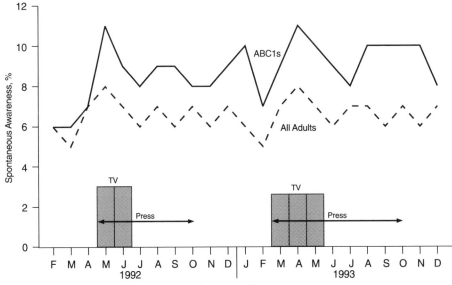

Figure 10. *Spontaneous awareness of The Co-operative Bank amongst ABC1s*
Source: NOP

Brand Predisposition

Ad hoc surveys were conducted pre and post each advertising campaign which monitored predisposition to do business with The Co-operative Bank.

On a national basis predisposition to bank with The Co-operative Bank increased by 50%, from 22% to 33%, over the campaign period 1992-1993.

The most significant increases in predisposition were apparent in the TV regions after each burst of activity in 1992 and 1993, with a fall back during the interim period.

However, a less marked upward trend was also apparent in the non TV advertising regions suggesting that the press support did have an effect, particularly in 1992, when the press activity was heavier.

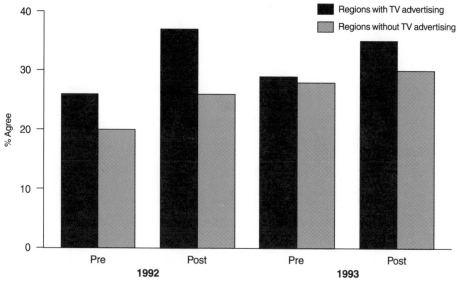

Figure 11. *Agreement that The Co-operative Bank is "A bank I would do business with"*
Source: NOP

On this measure, also, the increases in predisposition were led by the core target audience of ABC1s.

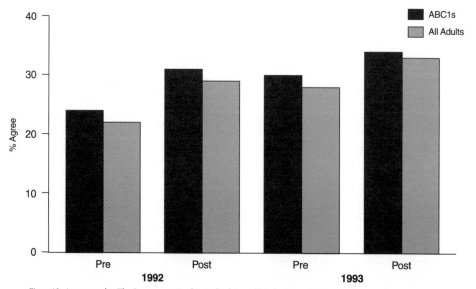

Figure 12. *Agreement that The Co-operative Bank is "A bank I would do business with" by ABC1s*
Source: NOP

WAS IT WORTH IT?

Over the period May 1992 to December 1993 The Co-operative Bank spent £1,800,000 advertising its ethical positioning.

Over the same period of time:

— the financial losses experienced in 1991 were overturned and a significant return to profitability achieved;
— there was a dramatic increase in balances in a time of low inflation and difficult economic circumstances;
— there was an increase in current account openings;
— there was a decrease in current account closures;
— a better quality of customer was recruited providing better cross-sell opportunities;
— new opportunities in the personal banking sector were facilitated; a student package was launched in January 1994 due to popular demand;
— new opportunities in the corporate banking sector were facilitated; specifically in the Education, Charity and Health sectors;
— predisposition to bank with The Co-operative Bank rose by 50%;
— staff morale was boosted and the Bank's ability to recruit motivated staff enhanced.

Confidentiality rules prevent us from revealing the precise level of return to The Co-operative Bank in financial terms but their Company Report & Accounts for 1993 reveals the upturn in the Bank's fortunes in 1992 and 1993.

TABLE 12: THE CO-OPERATIVE BANK'S RESULTS 1990-1993

	1990 £'000s	1991 £'000s	1992 £'000s	1993 £'000s
Deposits	2,621,121	2,437,853	2,707,105	2,982,944
Profit/(loss) before tax	(14,872)	(5,972)	9,845	17,789

Source: Company Report & Accounts, 1993

We do not claim that advertising was 100% responsible for these results but we hope that we have demonstrated that it was a major contributor and the driving force behind all the other promotional activities undertaken.

CONCLUSIONS

In 1991 The Co-operative Bank's market share was declining, its customer profile was becoming increasingly downmarket and its competitors were spending millions promoting themselves to the public.

The Bank could not afford the advertising spend required to fight head-on with the competition so instead a unique advertising strategy was developed for the Bank which enabled it to outflank them.

The real key to the ethical positioning that was developed was that it was something that the Bank owned already but it just wasn't being expressed in the right way to the general public. Advertising served to access a core truth about the Bank and deliver it in a relevant and motivating way.

The identification of a niche target audience and careful media targeting then enabled the message to be delivered cost effectively.

This paper has demonstrated the increases in awareness and predisposition generated towards The Co-operative Bank via the advertising campaign and the key role it performed in overturning the 1991 decline and returning the Bank to profitability.

The Bank recognise the valuable brand platform that has been established and are committed to building upon it via advertising support in 1994. To this end two new commercials promoting the Bank's ethical proposition were produced this Spring.

16

"A Widget We Have Got"

How advertising helped John Smith's Bitter to break into an established market

INTRODUCTION

John Smith's Bitter, owned by Courage Ltd, has been brewed in Tadcaster, Yorkshire since 1758. The brand has had an illustrious career, and is popular with bitter drinkers nationwide. Until October 1993 the brand was available in draught form in pubs (the 'on-trade'), and in cans for the take-home market (the 'off-trade'). This case study will follow the launch of John Smith's Draught In Can – an off-trade variant that more closely resembles the on-trade product in terms of quality and taste delivery than does the previously existing canned product.

BACKGROUND

In 1990 John Smith's Bitter was riding high in the canned bitter market. For thirteen years the brand had maintained its number one position, always managing to keep one step ahead of its main competitor in the off-trade, Stones Bitter.

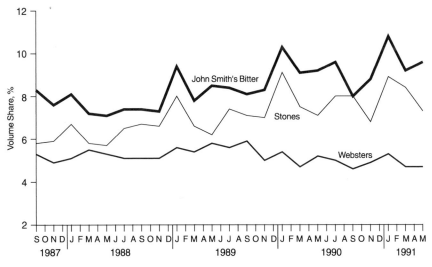

Figure 1. *John Smith's vs competitors – GB off-trade bitters*
Source: Stats MR

From such a position of strength it can be a temptation to rest on one's laurels, particularly in a sector characterised by a distinct lack of innovation. It seemed that all Courage needed to do was to maintain product quality and marketing activity and consumers would continue to buy canned John Smith's.

This is not to say that the brand did not face a certain problem also faced by the rest of the canned bitter market. An historical problem of the sector had been that the canned products bore little resemblance to their on-trade counterparts, drinkers often claiming canned bitter products to be gassy, 'tinny' and a poor comparison to 'real' pub bitter. Indeed, in 1990 only eighteen percent of on-trade bitter drinkers actually claimed to have drunk bitter from cans during the previous week (PAS Drinks Market Monitor).

This long-term problem for the sector was exacerbated in the late 1980s by the 'arrival' of a plethora of packaged lager brands. These products tended to be stronger in alcohol content, most were of very high quality in taste terms and, in addition, were surrounded by a sense of newsworthiness long absent in the beer market. Further, being generally of foreign origin, they were imbued with a sense of intrigue and 'sexiness'. Drinkers of both bitter and lager could easily find themselves seduced by these new, usually bottled, foreign lagers.

It was clear that in the off-trade, both standard strength bitters and standard strength lagers could suffer at the hands of these 'better' products. Something had to be done against what was described by Vincent Kelly, MD of Carlsberg-Tetley, as "the unstoppable tide of continental lager".

A NEW MARKET

In early 1991, something was done. Unfortunately for Courage, this something would have even more dramatic repercussions for John Smith's within the take-home bitter sector.

April 1991 saw the launch of a new type of canned bitter. With the aid of a small, in-can device (keeping a small amount of beer or CO_2 under pressure until the can is opened then releasing it with a 'surge'), these products were able to replicate both the look and quality of draught bitter. This seemed to be exactly what the bitter-drinker was looking for, judging by the success of both Boddingtons Draught from Whitbread and Draught Guinness Bitter – the two spearhead brands of what was a valuable new sector of the beer market.

These two brands took the bitter market by storm. Not only were they totally innovative in product format, but each had a degree of newsworthiness about it beyond this. Guinness, whilst a famous brand in itself, had never existed before as bitter. Boddingtons, although a well-respected bitter name, had formerly been largely restricted in availability to its North-West England heartland.

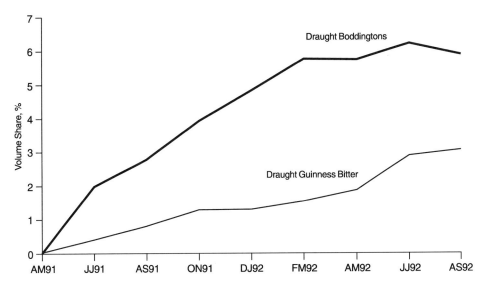

Figure 2. *The first draught-in-can bitters – All GB off-trade bitter*
Source: Stats MR

By 1992 the off-trade bitter market was beginning to change. The draught bitter consumer could now be content with the quality of the take home product and previous rejecters appeared to be at long last drinking bitter from a can:

TABLE 1: WHAT ON-TRADE BITTER DRINKERS DRINK AT HOME
Base: 7-Day Penetration

	December 1990	December 1991	December 1992
Packaged Bitter	18	18	20

Source: PAS Drinks Market Monitor

As the *Independent Grocer* put it:

"Bitter is going through a born again revival with the advent of draught in a can".

The consumer may well have been very happy. Courage were quite understandably not. Although overall volume in the bitter market was increasing, many canned bitter brands were beginning to suffer in the wake of these new products. John Smith's itself began to lose share and volume (see Figure 3).

As the long-time brand leader, John Smith's obviously had a lot to lose. Consumers were becoming ever more interested in this new technology and, more importantly, in its results. An article from *Supermarketing* in 1992 states the situation in no uncertain terms:

"Thirteen could prove to be unlucky for John Smith's Bitter. The leading bitter brand is now that age, and enters what will be some turbulent teenage years with youngsters Draught Boddingtons and Guinness Draught Bitter breathing down its neck".

There seemed to be only one option; Courage needed to develop its own draught in can product. This was no easy task. While the new draught in can products continued to gain ground, Courage was faced with the time-consuming technological headache of creating its own unique in-can device.

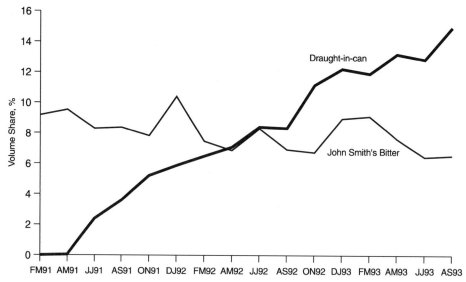

Figure 3. *Draught-in-can impact on John Smith's – All GB off-trade bitter*
Source: Stats MR

THE EVALUATION TASK

We will concentrate on a set of three commercials supporting 'John Smith's Draught In Can' throughout November and December 1993.

Specifically we will endeavour to show that what we shall term the 'widget advertising' has:

i)   Assisted John Smith's to rapidly gain a significant share in this market without having recourse to the novelty or newsworthiness value of draught in can technology.
ii) Enabled John Smith's to grow more strongly than its traditional off-trade rival, Stones Bitter, which launched into this sector of the market at the same time.
iii) Has had a positive effect not only on the specific brand variant advertised, but on the John Smith's brand as a whole.

THE LAUNCH OF JOHN SMITH'S DRAUGHT IN CAN

Not until October 1993, two and a half years after the emergence of the draught-in-can sector, did Courage feel that it could successfully supply John Smith's in a can that was as good as its on-trade product. Having overcome the technological barrier to entry, however, Courage now faced an even greater obstacle – an established, consumer franchise for the *existing* brands, which by then had 15% volume share, and almost 24% value share, of *all canned bitter* (see Figure 4).

Boddingtons Draught and Draught Guinness Bitter had bedded in and, to make matters worse, had been joined in this rapidly developing sector by several other well-known and respected brands such as Theakstons, Marstons Pedigree, Castle Eden and others from the Whitbread stable.

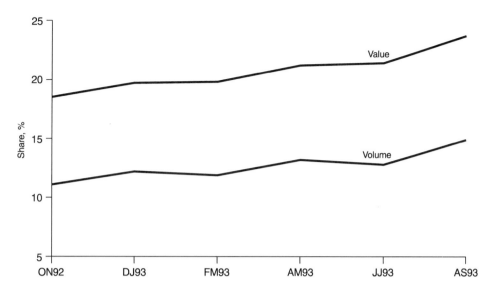

Figure 4. *Draught-in-can share – All GB off-trade bitters*
Source: Stats MR

It was clear to Courage and BMP that we would not be launching anything particularly 'newsworthy' in a market sense. Given the proliferation of brands in this, by now, well-known sector there was a distinct danger that the John Smith's variant might gain little attention.

Thus, there was a clear role for advertising. Something beyond simply being available on shelf would be needed to break us into this market.

We knew we already had a popular TV campaign for the John Smith's brand in the 'No Nonsense' commercials featuring the comedian Jack Dee. The campaign had already been aired nationally and people were familiar with the format – important to us, as our need to 'catch up quickly' meant our draught in can product had to be launched nationally and gain awareness rapidly.

We decided to use the existing campaign, believing it likely to be the most significant 'edge' we would have over the other players.

The 'No Nonsense' campaign worked to a very simple model:

Using a brand spokesman whose attitude is quintessentially that of our target audience – contemptuous of gimmickry and anything that gets in the way of his enjoyment of his pint – the 'No Nonsense' campaign demonstrates an understanding of and affinity with the contemporary bitter drinker.

ADVERTISING JOHN SMITH'S DRAUGHT IN CAN WITH 'NO NONSENSE'

It was very important that not only did we communicate that we now *had* a 'widget', but that there was a good reason for it, this being that John Smith's Draught In Can was a high quality beer due its performance. Our model changed accordingly:

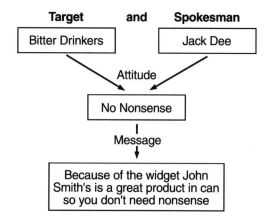

Our decision to use 'No Nonsense' was reinforced by the fact whatever creative vehicle we used, it would necessarily have to do a job for the whole John Smith's brand, not just for the new canned variant. Thus, our objectives were as follows:

Marketing

— To achieve volume levels consonant with being a significant player in this market by January 1994.
— To continue to support the draught brand in the on-trade.

Advertising

— Announce the launch of John Smith's Draught In Can.
— Communicate that this product tastes "just like John Smith's in the pub".

Another concern was that the launch of John Smith's Draught In Can, an ostensibly better product, could harm our current standard can which was to be left on sale. We saw no way, however, in which our advertising could actively promote the extant canned John Smith's without confusing the message we wished to communicate. We did, though, feel that the use of the familiar vehicle would go some way in rewarding loyalists of the standard can (some of whom we had to assume would never switch – particularly given the price premium of the draught in can product) with the type of advertising we knew they enjoyed.

TARGETING

The advertising was targeted against 18-35 year old bitter drinkers. As heavier drinkers, this was essential if John Smith's Draught In Can was to become a large brand quickly.

THE 'WIDGET ADVERTISING'

Within the existing campaign BMP created three commercials: 'Dancing Ladybirds' (40"), 'Penguins' (40") and 'Sad' (10") broke in November 1993 and ran for eight weeks following the launch of the new product in early October.

MEDIA

TV was chosen as the primary medium for two reasons:

i) Because of the need to 'catch up' quickly with the other draught in can brands.
ii) To appear credible in relation to other beer brands during the highly competitive run up to Christmas.

National advertising was dictated by the necessity of supporting our overall national brand and not just the launch of our new variant.

We also used 48-sheet posters outside supermarkets.

TABLE 2: MEDIA PLAN, 1993

	November	December	Total
Television			
ITV/C4: Network excl. Scotland, Ulster, BSkyB	450 TVRs Dancing Ladybirds	280 TVRs Penguins/Sad 2:1	730 TVRs
Cost	£1.763m	£0.607m	£2.370m
Male 18-34 Coverage & frequency	90 @ 8.1		
Outdoor			
200 Stores – 48-sheets	<———— 400 sites ————>		£0.140m

'DANCING LADYBIRDS'

After a hundred years, you can now enjoy John Smith's Draught in a can. It's got a widget for that 'just served by the landlord' taste.

Oh, I'm not doing this.
Don't you like the beer?
I like the beer – it's just not my material.

I'm sorry but I'm not prepared to compromise my hard man of comedy image – I mean why should I?
(A bag of money is put on table)

(Jack sings) Widget, it's got a widget,...

... a lovely widget, a widget it has got.

'SAD'

Have you ever wondered how the little widget thing in new John Smith's Draught actually works?
Then you're very sad.

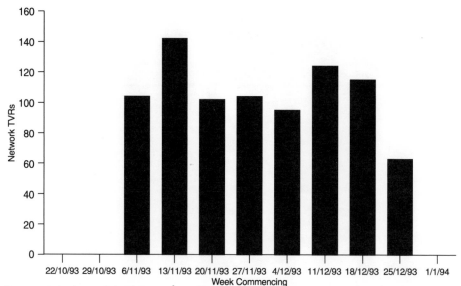

Figure 5. *John Smith's Draught launch campaign – Actual weekly TVRs*
Source: Media Register

RESULTS

John Smith's Draught In Can quickly reached sales levels in line with our objective of becoming a significant player in the market.

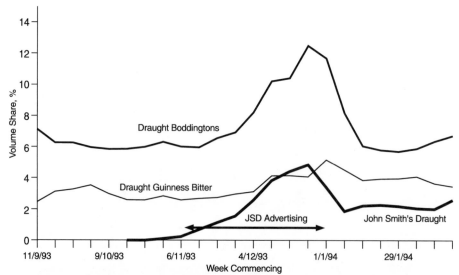

Figure 6. *John Smith's Draught at launch – All GB off-trade*
Source: Scantrack

(It will be noticed that all three brands lose share in the first weeks of January. This is an annual occurrence for 'big name' beer brands and results from artificially inflated share levels around Christmas as 'light users' come into the market and purchase the big brand names, and by regular bitter consumers trading up as a 'treat'.)

Not only did John Smith's Draught In Can achieve sales levels close to those of Guinness Draught Bitter, it achieved them very quickly, as shown by the comparison of sales and rate of sale of the three brands in the weeks following their respective launches.

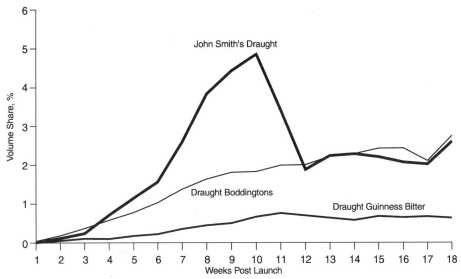

Figure 7. *Draught-in-can brands launch – All GB off-trade bitter*
Source: Scantrack

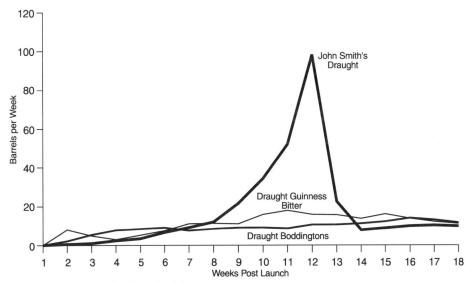

Figure 8. *Rate-of-sale at launch – All GB off-trade bitter*
Source: Scantrack

Although the above *does* demonstrate the rapidity with which John Smith's Draught In Can reached significant share levels in this sector, too many other factors (such as media spend and usage) call for caution in interpreting these data as evidence of a superior performance to Boddingtons or Guinness.

'Claimed usage' figures would further appear to support our contention that John Smith's Draught In Can had become a significant player in the market, with 10% of 18-34 year old bitter drinkers claiming to drink it nowadays, and another 8% claiming they would consider trying it (Admonitor January 1994).

This picture becomes even more satisfying when we consider our other marketing objective, ie the need to continue to support our on-trade franchise. If we look at the performance of John Smith's in the on-trade since our widget advertising we see a very positive picture compared to the same period in the previous year, despite a seven pence per pint price increase year on year leaving us more expensive than our principle competitors.

TABLE 3: JOHN SMITH'S ON-TRADE PERFORMANCE

	D/J 93	D/J 94
Volume (barrels)	106,950	117,040
Volume share (%)	6.9	7.6
Rate of sale (barrels per month)	4.0	4.0

Source: Stats MR

These volume gains are partially due to increased distribution but John Smith's consistent rate-of-sale would suggest that, despite the off-trade focus of the advertising, the on-trade product has continued to perform well.

As with John Smith's Draught In Can, we have seen increases throughout the advertised period in 'claimed usage' figures for the on-trade also:

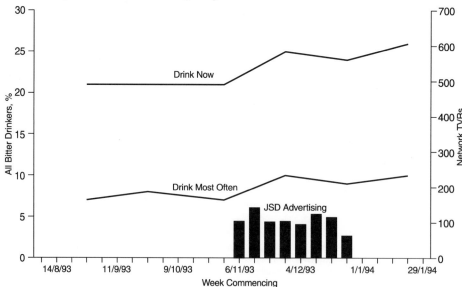

Figure 9. *John Smith's claimed usage – GB on-trade*
Source: Admonitor/Media Register

Having seen from this section that Courage has met its primary business objectives of:

i)   Establishing John Smith's Draught In Can as a significant player in the draught in can sector.

ii) Of maintaining John Smith's in the on-trade.

We now turn to the role of the advertising in that success.

THE EFFECT OF THE 'WIDGET ADVERTISING'

Firstly, it is clear that the advertising was an immediate hit with consumers. Marketing's annual survey of Bitters and Stouts demonstrates the immediacy with which the campaign hit home:

TABLE 4: TOP 10 BITTERS & STOUTS

	Brand	Agency/Buyer	Prompted Recall (%)
1	John Smith's Bitter	BMP DDB Needham	55
2	Guinness	Ogilvy & Mather	55
3	Guinness Draught	Ogilvy & Mather	49
4	McEwan's Export	Collett Dickenson Pearce	43
5	Tetley Bitter	Saatchi & Saatchi	43
6	Boddingtons	Bartle Bogle Hegarty	41
7	Murphy's Stout	Bartle Bogle Hegarty	34
8	Tennent's Special	The Leith Agency	29
9	Stones Bitter	BSB Dorland	24
10	Beamish	Young & Rubicam	23

Source: Marketing

Significant increases in brand and advertising awareness showed the campaign was being seen, remembered, and associated with the brand:

TABLE 5: JOHN SMITH'S DRAUGHT LAUNCH ADVERTISING

	October '93 (pre-advertising) %	January '94 (post-advertising) %
Spontaneous (overall) Brand awareness	39	43
Spontaneous TV ad awareness	22	41
Total ad awareness	44	65

Base: 18-34 year old male bitter drinkers

Source: Admonitor

Within only three months, more young bitter drinkers were aware of John Smith's in-can device than were aware of those of Boddingtons or Guinness:

TABLE 6: BRANDS AVAILABLE WITH AN IN-CAN DEVICE
Percentage Agreeing

	October '93 (pre-advertising) %	January '94 (post-advertising) %
John Smith's	2	59
Boddingtons	40	56
Guinness Draught Bitter	35	47

Base: 18-34 year old male bitter drinkers

Source: Admonitor

The can's presence in-store will have contributed to this, as it indicates the presence of a 'caskpour' device. However, quantitative and qualitative data indicate that a significant part of this knowledge must be coming from the 'widget' advertising.

The main communication of the advertising was John Smith's possession of 'a widget':

TABLE 7: PROMPTED ADVERTISING MESSAGE
Percentage Agreeing

	Dancing Ladybirds %	Penguins %	Sad %
Now available with a widget	74 (n = 149)	59 (n = 122)	41 (n = 64)

Base: 18-34 year old male bitter drinkers who recognise ad

Source: Admonitor, January 1994

The word 'widget' was, in fact, only ever mentioned in our advertising.

Qualitative research demonstrated to us that not only was our advertising very salient, but that it had provided a consumer friendly term for the 'in-can device'.

"Everyone talks about the one with the widget."

"It started the name 'widget' going – you'd never heard of it before."

18-34 year old male bitter drinkers who recognise ad
BMP Qualitative, February 1994

It is clear now that John Smith's Bitter has come to own the previously industry-only term, 'widget'. It was not until Jack Dee spoke the word in our advertising that the device had been given a truly consumer-friendly name.

Two years later the term is applied across all draught in can products, as indicated by The Sun's headline, "It's The War Of The Widgets" in January 1994. An informal, 'mystery-shopper' survey of off-licence managers in London provides further evidence for our advertising's success in providing the generic name for the sector. In response to the question, "Which bitter has a widget?", the answer was never only John Smith's, but also other draught in can brands that had never laid claim to the term:

"Three types with a widget in it, definitely John Smith's, or Boddingtons or Worthingtons."

"There are quite a few with widgets, but John Smith's is the one that advertises it."

"There's lots of them now, Guinness, Boddingtons and the one that actually calls it a widget, John Smith's with Jack Dee."

From the above evidence we would strongly contend that the high awareness levels of John Smith's Draught In Can were largely due to the 'widget' advertising and not simply to the presence of the brand in-store. This is reinforced by the fact that only 9.5% of the sample claimed Marstons Pedigree to contain a draught in can device despite comparable distribution levels to John Smith's Draught In Can.

Further, and very importantly, it is clear that consumers were not just associating the word 'widget' with John Smith's, but were understanding the product quality benefit of the device:

TABLE 8: PROMPTED ADVERTISING MESSAGE
Percentage Agreeing

	Dancing Ladybirds %	Penguins %	Sad %
Tastes as good as at the pub	38	34	19
It's a good quality bitter	20	20	25
	(n=149)	(n=122)	(n=64)

Base: 18-34 year old male bitter drinkers who recognise ad

Source: Admonitor, January 1994

'FREE PR'

The media constantly referred to the advertising. We welcomed the deluge of positive attention it was receiving and, although impossible to calculate the discrete effect on sales of the myriad press and TV references, it *is* possible to assert that all of the brand's free PR was generated directly from the advertising:

The Tabloids

"His (Jack Dee's) widget ditty and dance routine with the giant ladybirds have persuaded tipplers to drink gallons of the ale."

Daily Star

"The widget song, with dancing ladybird girls, is so popular it may be released as a single!"

The Sun

And the more restrained broadsheets

"Does it sell? No one's providing convincing evidence, but it certainly generates the tabloid column inches."

The Independent on Sunday

"No longer referred to as Deadpan Comic Jack Dee, he has become Jack Dee, star of John Smith's hilarious 'widget' TV ads."

The Sunday Times

The campaign was also honoured by the use of the 'widget song' in a TV sketch lampooning the Chancellor of the Exchequer (Rory Bremner taking liberties with the lyrics to tell us that the Minister has "got a budget"). It seemed that the media was taking every opportunity to talk about the campaign, the Daily Mirror seeking out a little boy actually named Andrew Frederick *Widget* Crane, to report that:

"(he) stares transfixed at the screen when the John Smith's adverts come on... he thinks someone is calling him".

We have shown that John Smith's Draught In Can has achieved volume levels in line with its objectives. We have further demonstrated that the advertising has proved to be hugely popular with consumers, generating awareness of the brand to the levels of its major rivals. We have also shown how the advertising has created much free publicity for the brand.

It remains for us to demonstrate that the success of John Smith's Draught In Can is largely attributable to its 'widget advertising' by elimination of other factors that may have contributed to this success.

ELIMINATION OF OTHER FACTORS AS CAUSAL IN THE SUCCESS OF JOHN SMITH'S DRAUGHT IN CAN

Seasonality

The launch period of John Smith's Draught In Can covered the traditionally heavy beer consumption period of Christmas, when the John Smith's standard product habitually sees an uplift in volume. This makes it very difficult to eliminate seasonality entirely although we do not believe that it can have been overwhelmingly important, given that the volume uplift of John Smith's Draught In Can is more than double that normally experienced by the standard can at this time of year.

Cannibalisation

John Smith's Draught In Can could have grown rapidly had it been allowed to replace sales of the standard product. In fact the standard can has not suffered. Volume sales of the standard can were identical over the Christmas 1993 period to those in the previous year and this was not the result of market growth or opportunistic pricing. Volume share remained unchanged whilst value share rose, prompted by an increase in price relative to the market average. Thus, cannibalisation of the standard can by the new variant can not be regarded as a causal factor in its success.

TABLE 9: AVERAGE PRICES – NOVEMBER 1993-JANUARY 1994

	Index (Total Off-Trade = 100)
John Smith's standard	108
Total off-trade bitters (including DIC brands)	100

Source: Scantrack

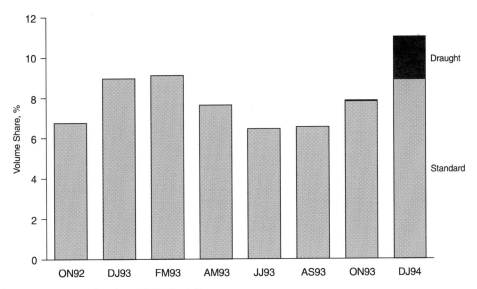

Figure 10. *John Smith's volume share – All GB off-trade bitter*
Source: Stats MR

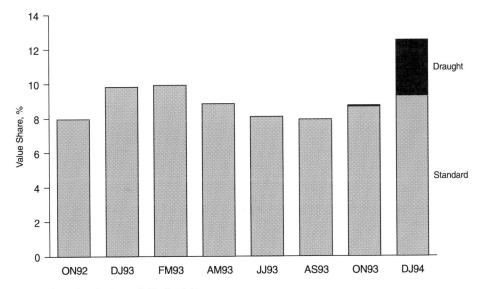

Figure 11. *John Smith's value share – All GB off-trade bitter*
Source: Stats MR

Distribution

There are two issues involved in discounting a distribution effect, one involving the standard can and one the draught in can product itself. The standard brand could have maintained its sales base by gaining distribution on the back of John Smith's Draught In Can. The draught in can product, however, generated no new distribution, only being stocked in outlets which already sold the standard product.

Distribution is undeniably key to the success of any launch. The success of John Smith's Draught In Can could therefore have been purely the result of obtaining distribution levels superior to earlier entrants. Comparison with Marston's Pedigree (selected as having similar distribution levels and already a year old by Christmas 1993) shows, however, just how much better John Smith's did on a comparable distribution base and that distribution alone could not have been responsible for the brand's success.

TABLE 10: DISTRIBUTION AND SHARE DURING LAUNCH
6 November 1993-31 December 1993

	John Smith's Draught In Can	Marston's Pedigree
Volume share (%)	2.4	0.9
Distribution (%)	72	71

Note: John Smith's average distribution once distribution stabilised.

Source: Scantrack

Price

Throughout the launch period John Smith's Draught In Can was at a higher average price than Draught Boddingtons and Guinness Draught Bitter. Thus price can not be considered as a differential factor in the brand's success.

TABLE 11: AVERAGE PRICES
November 1993-January 1994

	Index (John Smith's Draught In Can = 100)
John Smith's Draught In Can	100
Boddingtons Draught	97
Draught Guinness Bitter	94

Source: Scantrack

The 'Famous Brand' Effect

It is necessary to eliminate as causal the notion that a 'famous brand' prior to the advent of the draught in can sector would only have had to launch such a variant to achieve success similar to that of John Smith's Draught In Can.

This is a very difficult task given that we had no non-advertised areas. However, we can eliminate the 'famous brand' effect with recourse to what is, for the purposes of this paper at least, a fortuitous coincidence.

Unbeknown to us during our advertising development, Bass had been developing its own version of 'the widget' for use in a draught in can version of Stones Bitter – John Smith's traditional rival in the off-trade sector. Further, Stones was launched as a draught in can product simultaneously to John Smith's. However, Stones did not enjoy initial success comparable to that of John Smith's at a national level.

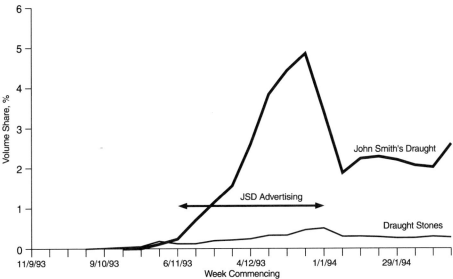

Figure 12. *Comparative launches –John Smith's Draught vs Draught Stones: All GB off-trade bitter*
Source: Scantrack

The above clearly shows John Smith's to have achieved significantly greater success within the draught in can sector than that of its previously major off-trade rival.

To attribute this entirely to advertising, however, would be unfair, given that Stones launched nationally, but only *advertised* in Granada and Yorkshire.

TABLE 12: STONES AND JOHN SMITH'S MEDIA BREAKDOWN
Yorkshire & Granada, 1993

		October	November	December	Total TVRs
Stones	Yorkshire	—	390	132	522
	Granada	2	271	40	313
John Smith's	Yorkshire	—	422	399	821
	Granada	—	387	487	874

A clearer picture of the brands' relative performances can be obtained by comparing 'share per point of distribution' (thereby 'controlling' for the effect of different roll-out patterns at launch).

Figure 13 shows quite conclusively that John Smith's performance has far exceeded that of Stones.

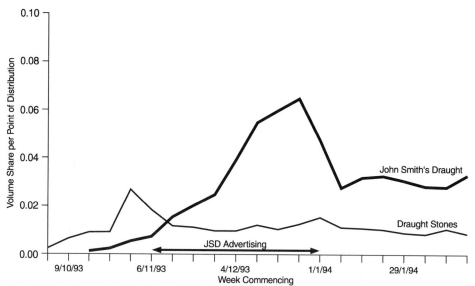

Figure 13. Volume share per point of distribution – All GB off-trade bitter
Source: Scantrack

Looking at tracking data for Yorkshire and Granada, we see that John Smith's has clearly outperformed Stones in these regions on key dimensions:

TABLE 13: JOHN SMITH'S DRAUGHT IN CAN LAUNCH ADVERTISING
Yorkshire & Granada

		October '93 (pre-advertising) %	January '94 (post-advertising) %
Spontaneous (Overall) Brand Awareness:	John Smith's	46	54
	Stones	51	53
Spontaneous TV Ad Awareness:	John Smith's	16	35
	Stone	21	14
Total Advertising Awareness:	John Smith's	34	56
	Stones	38	37

Base: All Yorkshire/Granada male bitter drinkers (sample-size too small to allow breakdown by age)

Source: Admonitor

TABLE 14: BRANDS AVAILABLE WITH AN IN-CAN DEVICE: PERCENTAGE AGREEING
Yorkshire & Granada

	October '93 (pre-advertising) %	January '94 (post-advertising) %
John Smith's	1	50
Stones	5	12

Base: All Yorkshire/Granada male bitter drinkers

Source: Admonitor

The above evidence allows us to reasonably discount the effect of being a 'famous brand' as a factor in the successful launch of John Smith's Draught In Can and throws further into relief the role of the 'widget advertising' in the success of the brand nationally.

RETURN ON INVESTMENT

Given that our advertising focused on the off-trade, it is to the off-trade we look primarily when evaluating our performance in terms of profitability.

Courage are, understandably, reluctant to disclose actual profit figures. That said, a straightforward comparison of total John Smith's off-trade value sales during the 1993 Christmas period with the previous year shows a 42% increase. Such a dramatic year-on-year change is not uncommon with small brands starting from a small sales base: however, given John Smith's stature within off-trade bitter, this clearly represents a substantial increase in revenue in the short term. Ideally, we would like to quantify advertising's contribution to this increase by econometric analysis. However, product launches are notoriously difficult to model and, at the time of writing, there was insufficient data to allow us to do so.

We can take a more long term perspective. In contrast to Stones, who did not support their new draught product with national advertising, John Smith's is now firmly established in the fastest growing and most profitable off-trade bitter sector, the value of which is expected to exceed £50 million in 1994. The brand is therefore in a position to take financial advantage of that growth.

SUMMARY

In conclusion we would contend that all of our original objectives for the 'widget advertising' have been met:

i) John Smith's Draught In Can has been successfully launched into an existing sector of the bitter market, despite the simultaneous launch of a major off-trade competitor.

ii) The brand enjoys high levels of awareness and consumers understand that John Smith's Draught In Can tastes "just like John Smith's in the pub".

iii) The brand as a whole appears to have benefited from our 'widget advertising' ie the off-trade standard product has been maintained and the on-trade product has seen volume uplifts over the advertised period.

In addition to the fulfilment of these objectives the advertising seems to have provided us with a bonus. The word 'widget' is now common consumer parlance and is used liberally in the press to refer to any of the draught in can products. It is also inextricably linked to the John Smith's brand (and to Jack Dee, who is reportedly often heckled as "the midget with the widget" at his shows). Thus, not only have we created advertising that worked for the brand, we have created a property for John Smith's that can be exploited in the future.

17

How Advertising Helped Strepsils to Grab a Market by the Throat?

INTRODUCTION

This is the account of how distinctive creative advertising successfully re-positioned Strepsils with dramatic sales results in an increasingly competitive market. We will demonstrate how the advertising worked upon consumers in an unusual way: by not being liked. We will show that this way of working was intrinsic to its success and, therefore, fundamental to the brand's growth.

Over The Counter Medicines and the Throat Remedy Market

The government embarked upon a strategy of cutting the costs of the public provision of healthcare during the 1980s. This was achieved by increasing prescription prices and by relaxing constraints on where medicines could be sold[1]. At the same time, there was an increasing consumer awareness of, and interest in, healthcare. The net result of these political and social factors was significantly increased spending on health through the over the counter medicine (OTC) market in the late 1980s, and also increased competition.

The throat remedy market exhibited all these trends: a growing market, new products, rising adspend and broader channels of distribution including drugstores, grocery and CTNs[2].

STREPSILS: A BRIEF HISTORY

Strepsils was the first licensed throat remedy, launched in 1958. It was positioned as a specialist sore throat treatment and therefore marketed as 'medicine for sore throats'.

The product formulation remains unchanged. The Strepsils lozenge is a hard-boiled sugar lozenge containing two 'active' ingredients which work by mildly treating the painful symptoms of a sore throat.

The Strepsils range has been extended over time and now consists of four variants[3]. Each product has the same lozenge format, and the same 'actives'. Strepsils has a reputation as being pleasant tasting. The overall benefit of the brand

---

1. All medicines have to be licensed by The Department of Health. Medicines are licensed as Prescription Only Medicines (POMs), Pharmacy only (Ps), or as General Sales List (GSLs). The licence dictates where the product can be sold, by whom, and how it can be displayed.

2. A note on definitions. CTNs is the abbreviation given to confectioners, tobacconists and newsagents. Drugstores are outlets such as Superdrug which sell OTC medicines and toiletries, but do not have a registered pharmacist on the premises, and therefore cannot sell 'P' registered products.

3. The range now consists of: Original (the original!), Honey and Lemon (launched 1970), Vitamin C (launched 1985), and Menthol and Eucalyptus (launched 1990).

can be expressed as: the effective and palatable medicine that both soothes and treats a sore throat.

Theoretically, Strepsils was in a good position to take advantage of the opportunity presented by the market growth. It was the first throat remedy, it was the largest of the non-confectionery brands, and it had strong brand awareness.

THE PROBLEM

In practice, however, the prognosis for Strepsils was not quite so good. Increased competition had created a very segmented market during the 1980s, divided into four sectors (Figure 1):

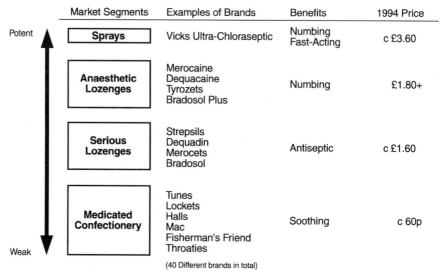

Figure 1. *Sore throat remedies*

The serious lozenge sector, in particular, was coming under concerted attack. From below: with the incursion of the medicated confectionery brands challenging for distribution in the serious lozenge pharmacy heartland. From the side: with the rise of own label. From above: with the growth of the anaesthetic lozenges and the OTC launch of the spray format (Vicks Chloraseptic). The whole serious lozenge sector was being squeezed.

Strepsils was especially vulnerable. In a piece of qualitative work conducted at this time, Strepsils was described merely as a "dependable soother". (Source: Jones Rhodes Associates, 1990.) This implied that Strepsils was rather old-fashioned and not as effective as other brands on the market. This perception was reflected in the usage data. Strepsils started to come adrift from the other serious lozenges and move closer to the medicated confectionery brands (Figure 2).

To make matters worse, Strepsils was more expensive than other serious lozenges such as Dequadin and Merocets, its closest competitors.

Strepsils had grown in recent years, mainly due to market growth, extra distribution through grocery, and the sales of new variants (especially Vitamin C). However, the first indication of a fundamental problem could be seen at the heart

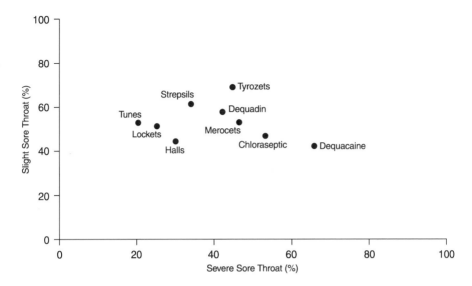

Figure 2. *Reasons for usage*
Base: *All used last 6 months*
Source: RSGB (Winter 1990/91)

of the brand. The long established core variants (Original and Honey/Lemon) were declining in share in Strepsils' traditional chemists heartland, as Figure 3 shows:

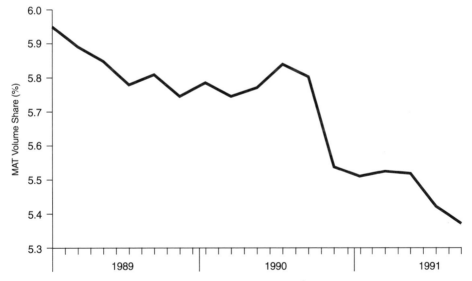

Figure 3. *Old Strepsils variants – Original and Honey/Lemon volume share*
Base: *GB Chemists*
Source: Nielsen

Signs of a greater future sales deterioration were also becoming visible in 'softer' awareness and usage data (Table l):

TABLE 1: STREPSILS AWARENESS AND USAGE AT THE END OF THE 1980s

Tracking points (Post):	'87/'88 %	'88/'89 %	'89/'90 %
Brand Awareness			
Spontaneous	30	26	24
Prompted	82	80	79
Usage			
Used in last 6 months	10	9	9

Base: All adults

Source: RSGB

Strepsils clearly needed to react as soon as possible, to stop a real decline occurring.

THE SOLUTION

A brand and product review showed the way forward. This revealed that consumers did not have an accurate picture of Strepsils product qualities. Strepsils was already an effective medicine, and always had been. It contains two medical 'active' ingredients: Dichlorobenzyl alcohol and Amylmetacresol, which was not widely known. A review of past Strepsils advertising revealed the reason for this lack of knowledge: Strepsils advertising had tended not to communicate these medical credentials but had traded upon the brand's heritage. This needed to be put right.

THE MARKETING OBJECTIVE

Therefore, the marketing objective was to create a more effective image for Strepsils and reposition the brand, thereby increasing Strepsils sales and share of the market. The solution to the marketing objective *seemed* beguilingly simple: use advertising to tell consumers about the brand's treatment credentials. Therefore, the following creative brief was developed:

The Creative Brief

Advertising Objectives
— To challenge consumers to re-evaluate Strepsils as an effective sore throat medicine, so that they buy Strepsils instead of medicated confectionery, other serious lozenges and anaesthetic lozenges.

Advertising Strategy
— By making Strepsils more top-of-mind again.
— By focusing on the effectiveness of Strepsils.
— (And retaining the quality of 'soothing' associated with Strepsils currently.)

Target Market
— All adults who suffer from a sore throat and use sore throat remedies.

Proposition
— Strepsils attacks the bacteria that can cause even the most severe sore throats.

Support
— Strepsils contains *active* anti-bacterial ingredients: Dichlorobenzyl alcohol and Amylmetacresol which treat the inflammation of a sore throat.
— Strepsils also soothes, as everyone knows.

Guidelines
— We know that people do not perceive Strepsils to be effective – they must be forced to re-evaluate. We must prevent the brand from being perceived as less effective and therefore more old fashioned than the many other products now on offer.

THE CREATIVE DEVELOPMENT OF THE ADVERTISING

However, the OTC market is highly regulated and controlled[4], and we immediately ran into a problem with these regulations because the proposition was regarded as an overclaim. The permitted revised proposition was much softer:

Revised Proposition – Strepsils relieves the pain of a sore throat

The problem this gave us was fundamental. How could we challenge consumers to re-evaluate Strepsils, when we couldn't make a claim which was intrinsically challenging?

The creative idea itself was the way around this problem. It allowed us to make our point forcefully, within the legal restrictions. How was it developed?

We observed that advertising for sore throat remedies tended to focus on trying to get sore throat sufferers to identify with a person suffering from a sore throat rather than with the symptoms or feelings associated with it. We decided that this represented an opportunity and we set out to understand the feelings associated with a sore throat. In research, consumers made it clear that their feelings towards sore throats were extremely strong. The pain/discomfort of not being able to swallow was the major feeling:

"Even a crumb feels like you're swallowing a boulder, you can hardly get it down."

The Qualitative Consultancy, 1989

THE ADVERTISING

The creative team's inspiration came from taking the observation made in research about pain and discomfort and dramatising it as a fear of swallowing.

They created two complementary ads (30 second TV scripts) called 'Celery' and 'Baguette'. The fear of swallowing was executed through visual metaphors. In

---

4. The product licence which each pharmaceutical product is granted dictates where the product can be sold (ie pharmacy or grocery) and also defines what product claims can be made. Crookes Healthcare, like most healthcare companies, also voluntarily subscribe to The Proprietary Association of Great Britain (PAGB) code of ethics which includes guidelines for the advertising and promoting of OTC medicines to consumers.

'CELERY'

SFX:

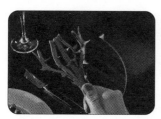  

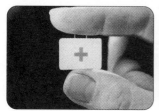  

MVO: Strepsils. First aid for sore throats

'Celery', a stick of celery transformed into thorns to visualise the feeling of a painful sore throat. In 'Baguette', a french baguette transformed into a wood log. The soothing action of Strepsils was visualised using another metaphor: the lozenge changed into a small first aid box. The suspenseful music, unusual casting and black and white film gave the adverts an eerie, mini horror film quality which was unusual and discomfiting. The endline was: "Strepsils. First aid for sore throats".

THE MEDIA STRATEGY

Sore throat suffering is very seasonal, because it is closely correlated to the incidence of colds and flu.

The season lasts from around October to March every year and all the throat remedy brands expend their marketing efforts in this period. Therefore, it is important to build awareness of message rapidly. This meant that TV advertising was the natural medium.

Usage of throat remedies tends to be slightly up-market (as is usage of all OTC products). Therefore, we targeted all adult ABC1s, and aimed for programmes which maximised their conversion. The two executions in the campaign were rotated equally. 'Celery' and 'Baguette' first went on air in January 1991. The campaign has, therefore, run every winter for four consecutive seasons. The spend per each burst is shown in Figure 4. The total expenditure on the campaign was £4.1m.

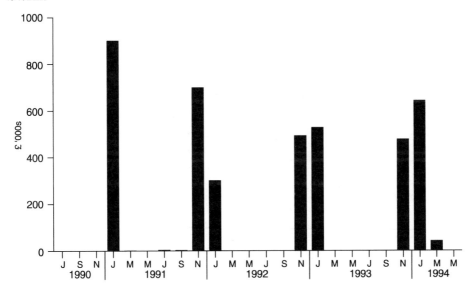

Figure 4. *Strepsils adspend – 'Celery' and 'Baguette'*
Source: Register-MEAL

'BAGUETTE'

SFX:

  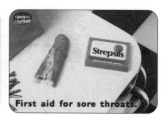

MVO: Strepsils. First aid for sore throats

OTHER ELEMENTS OF THE MARKETING MIX

The promotion of OTC medicines directly to the consumer is cautioned against in the PAGB code of practice. Crookes Healthcare have only promoted the brand to the pharmacy trade. They offer margin incentives for levels of stock and margin incentives for the displaying of the full Strepsils range.

RESULTS

Definitions

We will be looking at sales and share results in the GB chemists and grocery market (in Nielsen). The definition of this market is the sum of pharmacies, drugstores and grocers. Together, they account for 70% of Strepsils volume. The remaining 30% is made up of Boots The Chemists volume (23%), and CTNs (7%). Boots do not allow Nielsen to monitor their sales. Crookes Healthcare do not buy CTNs data. The GB chemists and grocery market is, therefore, the best available representative snapshot of the total market.

The Results

The sales and share results were far more dramatic than we had expected.

Strepsils Volume

Despite the fact that the throat remedy market volume was static, Strepsils volume increased dramatically, as Figure 5 shows:

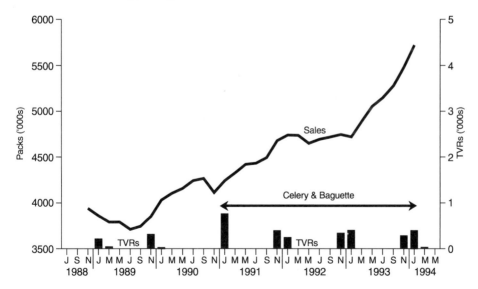

Figure 5. *Strepsils MAT volume – GB Grocers and Chemists*
Source: Nielsen

This was an increase of 33% in the period of 'Celery' and 'Baguette' (1993 vs 1990).

Strepsils Volume Share

As a result, Strepsils grew share by 33% (Figure 6):

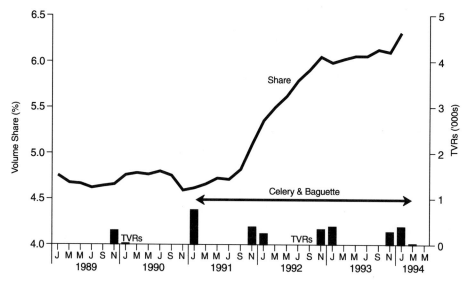

Figure 6. *Strepsils MAT volume share – GB Grocers and Chemists*

Strepsils Value

Whilst market value grew by a healthy 28%, Strepsils value grew by a massive 66% (1993 vs 1990).

Strepsils Value Share

As a result, Strepsils value share grew by 30%.

Therefore, the marketing objective of growth was met, and dramatically exceeded.

SIGNS OF THE EFFECT OF ADVERTISING

Advertising Awareness and Brand Awareness

The advertising was definitely noticed. Following the first burst of 'Celery' and 'Baguette' advertising awareness and brand awareness were boosted by five percentage points, each (Table 2):

TABLE 2: TOTAL STREPSILS AWARENESS

Tracking Points:	'Pre'	'Post'			
	1990	'90/'91	'91/'92	'92/'93	'93/'94
	%	%	%	%	%
Advertising awareness	12	17	13	21	16
Brand awareness	79	84	83	85	82

Base: All adults

Source: RSGB

This suggests that the advertising was *probably* responsible for the brand effect. Both awareness measures follow a similar pattern: an initial rise followed by a fall, a rise and a further fall. This is a consequence of the levels of TVRs delivered each year (Table 3):

TABLE 3: STREPSILS TVRs

Year to April:	1991	1992	1993	1994	Total (Since Jan 1991)
TVRs	762	643	743	716	2,864

Source: MEAL/Media Register

It is important to note that although the awareness figures rise and fall, they are maintained throughout this period at a higher level than achieved by previous advertising.

Main Impressions from the Advertising

Definitive proof of the effect of advertising comes when we look at what the advertising communicated. 'Celery' and 'Baguette' clearly communicated one dominant thought: the proposition. This contrasts with the communication of previous advertising (Table 4):

TABLE 4: MAIN IMPRESSIONS FROM STREPSILS ADVERTISING

	<— 'Steelworker'—>			<— 'Celery' & 'Baguette' —>			
Tracking Points: (Post)	'88/'89 %	'89/'90 %		'90/'91 %	'91/'92 %	'92/'93 %	'93/'94 %
(Ranked order of most mention)							
They're good for you/your throat	29	27	Strepsils relieves sore throats 45		46	50	53
Strepsils are comforting	7	13					
That you should buy Strepsils	6	4					
	⇓ Unfocused				⇓ Very focused		

Base: All Adults

Source: RGSB

This is clear independent evidence that the advertising communicated the benefit of effectiveness which we will see in the next section became much more associated with Strepsils over the advertised period.

Brand Image

Our marketing objective was to re-position Strepsils as an effective sore throat medicine. Achievement of this objective was to be measured against two brand image measures on the advertising tracking study: 'effective' and 'having active ingredients'.

Both had recently declined as a consequence of the previous advertising strategy. The following figures (Figures 7 and 8) show that this objective was dramatically achieved:

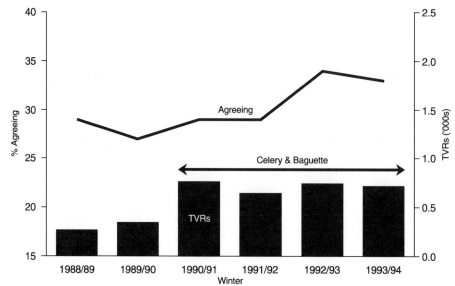

Figure 7. *Strepsils brand image – "Effective"*
Base: *All adults*
Source: RSGB Tracking (Post Stage)

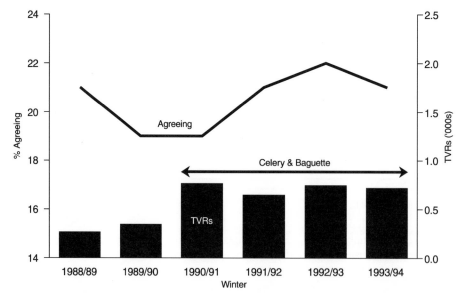

Figure 8. *Strepsils brand image – "Active Ingredients"*
Base: *All adults*
Source: RSGB Tracking (Post Stage)

We also wanted to retain Strepsils' soothing credentials. In fact, we significantly enhanced this aspect of the brand's offering (Figure 9):

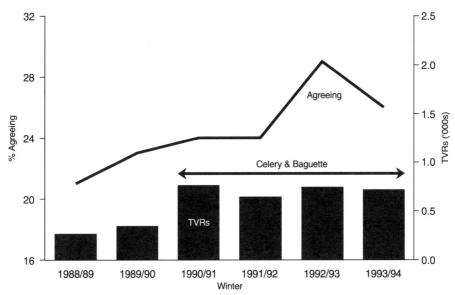

Figure 9. *Strepsils brand image – "Soothing"*
Base: *All adults*
Source: RSGB Tracking (Post Stage)

We must conclude that since these benefits were as communicated in the advertising then the advertising played the key role in leading consumers to re-think what Strepsils offered them: in effect to re-evaluate the brand.

The only alternative hypothesis is that because more people were buying Strepsils this altered the brand image, rather than advertising creating a re-evaluation which then lead to increased purchase. We do not believe this could be true because the *only* image dimensions which changed significantly were those we have reported on above. Each of these image statements were very closely related to the advertising content and message. Other image statements which were not related to the content of the advertising did not shift significantly. They would have been expected to rise if the improved image was caused *simply* by greater goodwill as a result of a large consumer franchise (Table 5):

TABLE 5: STREPSILS BRAND IMAGE – OTHER MEASURES

	<———— 'Celery' & 'Baguette' ————>				
Tracking Points: (Post)	'89/'90 %	'90/'91 %	'91/'92 %	'92/'93 %	'93/'94 %
Image Statements Modern	–	11	13	14	11
Recommended by chemists	22	22	22	22	21

Base: All adults

Source: RGSB

Clearly, the advertising objective of challenging consumers to re-evaluate Strepsils on the grounds of an enhancement of its effectiveness *through advertising* has been met. We will now go on to prove that this re-evaluation lead to the sales uplift by looking at how advertising changed behaviour.

Linking the Advertising to the Use of the Product

The first two bursts of 'Celery' and 'Baguette' activity were accompanied by an increase in penetration (+3 percentage points; TGI 1990-1991) and by an increase in usage as Table 6 shows:

TABLE 6: STREPSILS USAGE

	<'Steelworker'>			<— 'Celery' & 'Baguette' —>			
Tracking points: (Post)	'87/'88 %	'88/'89 %	'89/'90 %	'90/'91 %	'91/'92 %	'92/'93 %	'93/'94 %
Used in last 6 months	10	9	9	12	12	12	12
Ever used	34	32	32	43	43	43	44

Base: All adults

Source: RSGB

Of course, just because usage increased at the same time as the advertising does not prove that the increase was advertising driven. However, we have also achieved changed usage and behaviour which does imply an advertising effect.

The advertising set out to create a more effective image for Strepsils. The potential implications of this re-positioning in terms of changing use were: firstly, Strepsils being used by more consumers for more severe sore throats. Secondly, as a consequence of the brand's treatment credentials being strengthened, more consumers using *only* Strepsils to treat a sore throat rather than a range of products. Both hypotheses were clearly proved and correlated with advertising activity. First, changed usage (Figure 10):

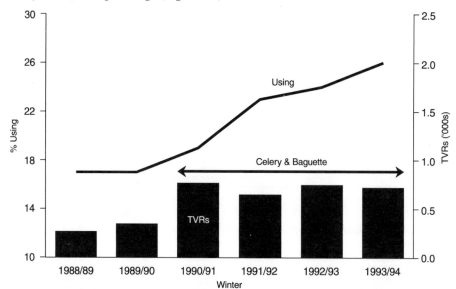

Figure 10. *Percentage using Strepsils – Most often for a severe sore throat*
Base: *All adults who have used Strepsils*
Source: RSGB Tracking (Post Stage)

Again this is not a consequence of increased penetration. This is proved by contrast with the marginal percentage changes in all adults using Strepsils "most often for a slight sore throat" (Table 7):

TABLE 7: STREPSILS USED MOST OFTEN FOR A SLIGHT SORE THROAT

Tracking Points: (Post)	'89/'90 %	'90/'91 %	'91/'92 %	'92/'93 %	'93/'94 %
Used most often	16	18	17	18	19

Base: All adults who have personally used Strepsils

Source: RSGB

Quite simply, slight sore throat usage is not a consequence of the repositioning of the brand.

In summary, severe sore throat usage increased much more than slight sore throat usage reflecting the intended shift of Strepsils towards the more serious, effective end of the market.

In so doing, we have also secured a more valuable kind of user. 28% of Strepsils users are loyalists (Source: TGI). This represents a significant achievement in turning back the tide of consumer promiscuity afflicting the serious brands in the market. The average percentage of users who are loyalists in the serious sector has declined from 27% in 1989 to under 20% in 1993. (Source: TGI)[5]. Therefore, Strepsils bucked a trend and proved the second hypothesis of changed behaviour (Table 8):

TABLE 8: STREPSILS LOYALISTS

					<— 'Celery' & 'Baguette' —>	
TGI Publication Dates*: 1987 %	1988 %	1989 %	1990 %	1991 %	1992 %	1993 %
23	22	23	22	23	26	28

Base: All Strepsils users

Note: * TGI collects data from April of the year previous to publication to March of the year of publication. Therefore, 'Celery' and 'Baguette' activity is first covered by TGI 1992 (April 1991 to March 1992). TGI 1994 had not been published at the time of this analysis.

Source: TGI

The rating of Strepsils as 'value for money' has increased during the period of 'Celery' and 'Baguette' advertising. Because this is contrary to the brand's real price movement and to its price movement relative to the market it is probably a strong side-effect of the communication of changed usage. In other words, although the brand has become more expensive, it has also become much more valued as there has been a marked change in what the brand is seen to offer (Figure 11):

---

5. This has-been calculated from TGI data using the serious brands covered in that survey: Strepsils, Merocets, Bradosol, Tyrozets and Dequadin.

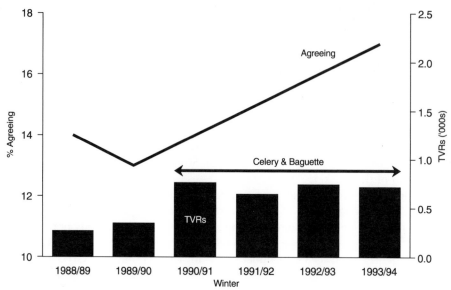

Figure 11. *Strepsils brand image – "Value for money"*
Base: *All adults*
Source: RSGB Tracking (Post Stage)

HOW THE ADVERTISING WORKED

We have evidence suggesting that 'Celery' and 'Baguette' worked upon consumers in a somewhat unusual way. This is suggested by the apparently contradictory conclusions of the qualitative pre-test:

> "Although the creative idea was *widely condemned*, the research indicates that it has *tremendous potential for the brand*... it positions Strepsils precisely as a serious sore throat remedy that will relieve rather than cure the condition."
>
> The Qualitative Consultancy, 1990

The same kind of observations were made throughout the campaign. On the one hand, the post-advertising tracking studies told us that the ads clearly communicated the required proposition. On the other, however, what also comes over consistently is that the ads are not particularly liked as can be seen from Table 9:

TABLE 9:   FEELINGS ABOUT 'CELERY' AND 'BAGUETTE'

Tracking Points: (Post)	'90/'91 %	'91/'92 %	'92/'93 %	'93/'94 %
"I liked it"	8	12	14	12
No likes	48	42	40	33

Base: All adults aware of Strepsils advertising

Source: RSGB

The conclusion to be drawn from this is that the advertising did not need to be liked to work. In fact, we believe that the overall discomforting feel of the advertising was a critical factor in the its success. The reason for this goes back to our advertising objective: the need to *challenge* consumers to cause re-evaluation.

By not being liked the advertising worked as a 'shock tactic', fracturing the traditional and cosy image of Strepsils, thereby causing re-evaluation:

> "The lack of emotional warmth was widely regarded as dissonant to current perceptions of Strepsils imagery... Rather than being misunderstood or misinterpreted, the advertisements seemed to reinforce a differentiation between Strepsils and sweetie brands [ie medicated confectionery]."
>
> Expressions Research, 1993

If the ads had been truly popular and likeable Strepsils existing image as a 'dependable soother' would have been nurtured rather than challenged.

THE STORY SO FAR

We have shown that the brand met its marketing objectives. We have provided evidence which strongly suggests that advertising was the prime mover in achieving these goals, and we have presented evidence which directly links the advertising with real changes in attitude and behaviour. In order to prove further that advertising *caused* the improved sales performance of the brand and strengthened it for future development we will now eliminate the possible effect of other variables, and examine the performance of the brand on a regional basis. We will also put a value to the contribution of advertising.

ELIMINATING OTHER VARIABLES

Population and demographic changes

This is unlikely. Population and demographic changes have been too slow to yield the dramatic changes we have observed in three years.

Weather

Weather has no direct effect on the market, although it does affect rates of illness somewhat as can be seen below.

Incidence of colds and flu

Since 1990, the average number of flu cases has fallen, but colds have been on the increase. When the rates of illness are high, the more serious medical products do tend to benefit disproportionately to the rest of the market. Therefore, it is plausible that Strepsils share gain might be partly due to rising rates of illness. There are two pieces of evidence that illness is no more than a partial effect.

Firstly, prior to the new campaign there does seem to be a much stronger relationship between Strepsils share and the rates of illness (MATs January 1989 to January 1991), than there is after the launch of 'Celery' and 'Baguette'. From January 1991, therefore, Strepsils share growth is much higher than one would expect given the rates of illness (Figure 12):

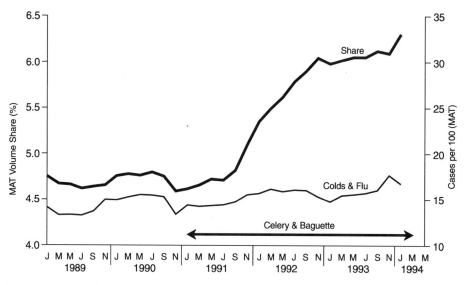

Figure 12. *Strepsils market share vs cases of colds & flu*
Sources: Nielsen, OPCS

Secondly, if Strepsils was gaining from higher rates of illness, one would expect Strepsils closest competitors, Dequadin and Merocets, which are similar in terms of efficacy, price and distribution to have gained too. Yet they lost share (–24%, –20% respectively in value terms, 1993 vs 1990).

Could the growth have been due to general market growth?

The market was virtually static in volume terms over this period. The market did grow by 28% in value terms, but Strepsils grew more than twice as fast as this (by 66%).

Did the market become less competitive?

The market in fact became even more competitive. As a result of several product launches[6] the number of competing brands/variants in the average store increased during the campaign period by 9%. None of Strepsils' major competitors suffered distribution problems. It would also be wrong to suggest that the market became 'quieter', and therefore that Strepsils could reclaim some of its past pre-eminence by default. On the contrary, almost £21m has been spent by the other throat remedy brands on advertising since January 1991, for example.

Strepsils price relative to the competition

Strepsils price per pack rose by 12% in real terms between January 1991 and January 1994. There have been no pack size increases which could have mitigated the impact of this effect upon consumers. More importantly, Strepsils' price has also increased relative to the market by 7% (Figure 13):

---

6. Mac Extra was launched in 1989, Vicks Ultrachloraseptic in 1991 (strictly speaking, the relaunch of Chloraseptic in a better format), Halls Soothers (1992), Bradosol Plus (1992), and a new Fox's medicated sweet (1993). Merocets and Merocaine (anaesthetic lozenges) were re-packaged and re-launched. Private label took more of a hold in both chemists and grocery.

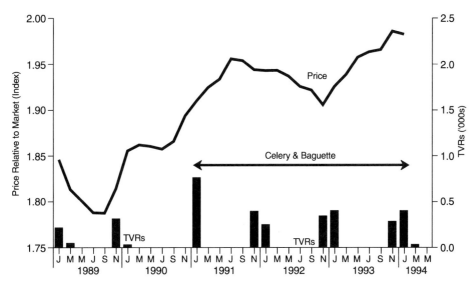

Figure 13. *Strepsils relative price (MAT basis, GB Chemists)*
Source: Nielsen

Clearly therefore, Strepsils' share growth has been earned, not bought.

Packaging

Strepsils packaging was re-designed in October 1990. However, competitors were quick to copy it[7] so the benefits to Strepsils would have been short-lived. Putting aside the competitive reaction, any effects of the new pack on sales are likely to have been fairly short-term anyway, yet sales continued to grow over the full three-year period of the campaign.

Promotions

There were no consumer promotions. Trade promotions were aimed at getting increased distribution for the brand and the variants. The following sections show, however, that the sales uplift did not come principally from distribution or from increased stocking, or from more variants being stocked.

Distribution

Strepsils distribution has increased by 12.8% (percentage change: 1993 vs 1990). However, the percentage increase in volume was more than two and a half times as large as the percentage increase in distribution. Furthermore, Strepsils sales and share increased in chemists too (+15% volume, +9% volume share), despite the fact that distribution there was static. We have calculated that 40% of the sales uplift *did* come from distribution gains, but by far the majority of the growth (60%) was driven by extra Rate of Sale (ROS). Without ROS (ie with distribution growth

---

7. The culprits: The Merrell Dow range of serious and anaesthetic lozenges (Merocets, Merovit, Merocaine), and Lloyds (the worst offender), Superdrug and Unichem, amongst the private label products.

only) volume sales to January/February 1994 would have been 4.8m packs, instead of 5.7m packs as achieved.

Increased Stocking

Looking at Strepsils' share of stocks in GB chemists (the outlets where trade promotions were concentrated) it is clear that in the period of the campaign market share growth resulted in stock share growth, not vice versa (Figure 14):

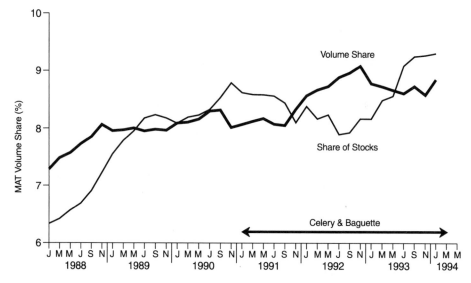

Figure 14. *Strepsils share of stocks – MATs, GB Chemists*
Source: Nielsen

This suggests that increased stocking did not create the growth we have seen.

Variants

No new Strepsils variants have been launched since 1990. In this period the average number of Strepsils variants stocked has decreased by –0.2%, while the number of variants of other brands has increased by almost 9% (1993 vs 1990). In GB chemists, Strepsils' situation was even worse, the number of Strepsils variants stocked decreasing by almost 4%. Another way to eliminate the impact of new variants is to look at the two oldest variants (Original and Honey/Lemon) which have had almost 100% distribution in chemists since at least 1982. Their volume share in chemists was declining steeply in the late 1980s. Yet their share of market in that sector has risen by 7.3% since the new campaign began (Figure 15):

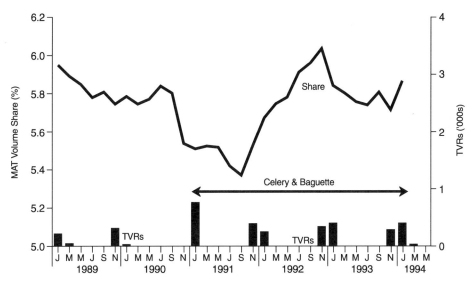

Figure 15. *Old Strepsils variants – Original and Honey/Lemon MAT share (GB Chemists)*
Source: Nielsen

This is a significant achievement in its own right.

Is there any direct evidence that it was advertising?

There are two good pieces of evidence. Firstly, there is a very strong relationship between advertising activity and share gain. Strepsils' share increased immediately each time the ads went on air (Figure 16):

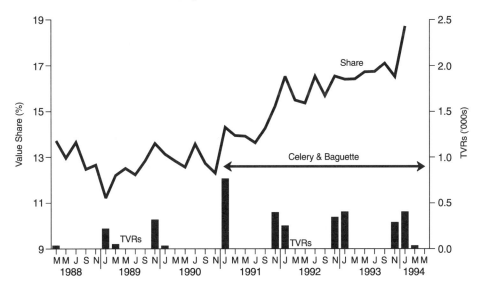

Figure 16. *Strepsils value share vs ads – (Grocers and Chemists)*
Sources: Nielsen, BARB

There is very close correlation (highly statistically significant) between share and cumulative exposure to the new ads (Figure 17):

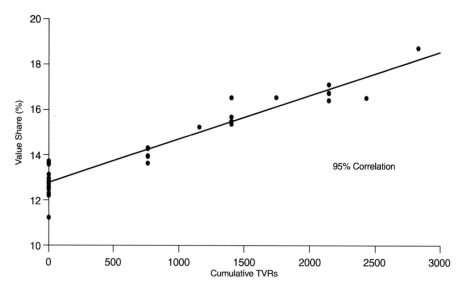

Figure 17. *Strepsils share vs cumulative exposure to new advertising campaign*
Sources: *Nielsen (Grocers & Chemists), BARB*

It appears that the ads ratchet share up each time they run.

The second piece of evidence is that between 1991 and 1993 (the longest period for which consistent regional data is available) the regions that saw the fastest growth were those that had the biggest increase in TVRs[9] (Figure 18):

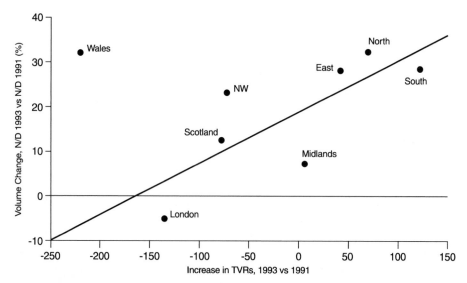

Figure 18. *Strepsils sales growth vs ads – GB Chemists by region*
Source: *Nielsen*

---

9. The anomaly of the Wales result in Figure 18 can be explained by very high 'Out of Stocks Forward' (OSF) percentages for this region, for all Strepsils variants, as reported by Nielsen (N/D 1991). This means that Strepsils had a very low level of stock in the forward selling area of Welsh chemists. Therefore, the volume uplift, N/D 1993 vs N/D 1991 is in reality less dramatic than it appears. By N/D 1993 this OSF problem had been corrected.

By contrast, Strepsils' closest competitors (Dequadin and Merocets) received virtually no advertising support during the period under consideration. Both declined in sales and share terms.

THE CONTRIBUTION OF THE ADVERTISING

We know from our analysis that three factors have driven Strepsils' revenue up between 1990 and 1993. The first is general market growth. The market grew by 28.2% in value terms. All else being equal, one would have expected Strepsils sales value to have grown roughly in line with the market.

The second factor is distribution. Strepsils distribution increased by 12.8%. For most brands in most markets, sales value is roughly proportional to sterling weighted distribution, so we would have expected distribution to have added an extra 13% to Strepsils sales, on top of the 28% gained from general market growth, which gives a total of 45%.[10]

But Strepsils revenue increased by 66.2% over the period in question, so some growth is left unaccounted for. The only other factor that could have been responsible is advertising. So, the new advertising must have boosted sales by 15%[10] above the level that would otherwise have been achieved.

Another way of looking at this is to say that:

Sales Value = (Market Value) x (Distribution) x (Other Factors)

Re-arranging this equation, we can produce a measure of the contribution of the 'other factors' to sales:

Other Factors = (Sales Value)/(Market Value) x (Distribution)

This measure is plotted in Figure 19. As can be seen, the contribution of the other factors has increased by 15% since 1990. But our analysis has shown that the only 'other factor' was advertising, so the quantity in Figure 19 is really a measure of the contribution of the advertising to sales. The chart suggests that advertising boosted sales by about 15% above their underlying level.

Advertising expenditure, on the other hand, fell over the same period (Figure 20).

So the new advertising increased revenue without advertising costs increasing, and so must have increased the profitability of the brand. Confidentiality prevents us from revealing actual profit figures but we can reveal that Strepsils was a profitable brand in the late 1980s. We can conclude from the above that Strepsils is now more profitable.

---

10. Percentage increases cannot simply be added. The figures are obtained as follows:
    112.8% x 128.2% = 144.6%
    114.9% = 166.2%/144.6%

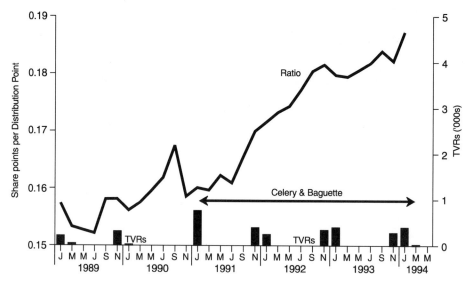

Figure 19. *'Effectiveness ratio' – Value share / Distribution*
Source: Nielsen

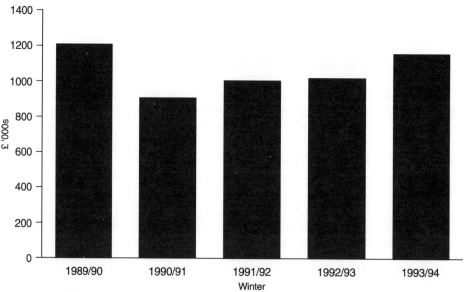

Figure 20. *Strepsils adspend*
Source: Register-MEAL

CONCLUSION

We believe that this case history demonstrates the critical role a particular advertising campaign played in re-positioning Strepsils, thereby rescuing the brand from a precarious position in a dynamic market and delivering dramatic sales and revenue growth.

The distinctive approach of the advertising was the vital ingredient.

Anything less powerful and distinctive than 'Celery' and 'Baguette' would have meant that the familiar, rather cosy brand image of Strepsils would have taken over once again. The brand would still be merely a one-dimensional 'dependable soother', rather than the rounded effective sore throat medicine which treats and soothes, which it is today.

18

Health Education Board for Scotland

Smoking: Sticks and Carrots

INTRODUCTION

The Health Education Board for Scotland (HEBS) has to tackle a wide range of priority health issues, a reflection of Scotland's poor record in the health league of the Western world.

Because so many of Scotland's health problems are highest in C2DE socio-economic groups, HEBS pays special attention to encouraging attitudinal and behavioural change in this population segment.

Smoking remains the largest single cause of preventable illness and death in Scotland with over 10,600 smoking-related deaths each year.

For its anti-smoking programme this sets the organisation the difficult task of trying to persuade the heaviest regular smokers to change their ways.

This paper deals with the effects of advertising by HEBS, aimed at reducing the prevalence of smoking among adults in Scotland by employing a new "carrot and stick" advertising approach and setting up a free telephone helpline ('Smokeline').

HEBS aims in its adult anti-smoking marketing were to:

— remind smokers of the consequences of smoking;
— motivate those who smoke to give up smoking;
— contribute to a reduction in smoking prevalence.

To encourage regular smokers to quit the habit, HEBS had to acknowledge the real difficulty smokers face in coping with actual and anticipated consequences of smoking cessation.

To quit demands both individual willpower and a helping hand, which is why HEBS provided 'Smokeline'.

PREVALANCE OF SMOKING

The prevalence of smoking among adults is in gradual long term decline, as shown by data from the Government's General Household Survey (GHS). The rate of decline in smoking among adults in Scotland is similar to that of GB as a whole, averaging just under 0.8% per year over the last 18 years. However, the overall prevalence of smoking among Scottish adults has remained at a higher level than nationally.

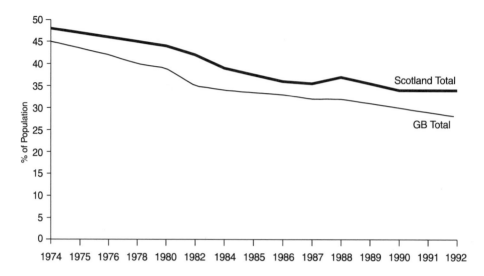

Figure 1. *Prevalence of cigarette smoking (Scotland vs GB)*
Source: General Household Survey

It is assumed that without significant intervention the Scottish smoking problem will remain relatively worse than the UK problem for the rest of this century.

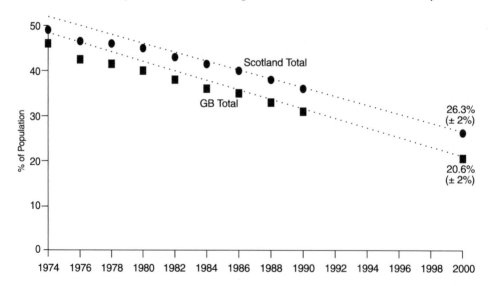

Figure 2. *Projected trend in prevalence of cigarette smoking (Scotland vs GB)*
Source: General Household Survey

A NEW SOLUTION TO AN OLD PROBLEM

The Old Problem

For over 20 years there has been widespread anti-smoking advertising and publicity in the British mass media. As a result, there has been no shortage of information on the health problems associated with smoking. Most smokers are now highly informed of the risks, and the social pressure not to smoke is increasing gradually. Nevertheless, HEBS faced an uphill struggle in its efforts to tackle the most difficult segment of the smoking population.

There are a disproportionate number of smokers in the C2DE bracket, and they also tend to be heavier smokers, as demonstrated by findings from a survey of the smoking population in Scotland.

TABLE 1: C2DE SMOKING BIAS IN SCOTLAND

Social Class	% of Scottish Population 1991	% of Scottish Smokers Oct 1992	Index
ABC1	39	24	61
C2	24	31	129
DE	38	45	118

Source: 1991 JICNARS/RSL Marketing Data Book; System Three Scotland

TABLE 2: SMOKING POPULATION BY SOCIAL CLASS AND CONSUMPTION

Social Class	All Smokers %	Heavy Smokers Index	Moderate Smokers Index	Light Smokers Index
ABC1	24	70	87	154
C2	31	103	103	80
DE	45	100	102	77

Source: System Three Scotland

Research evidence suggests that avoidance, denial and resistance to even attempting to quit are defence mechanisms commonly found among regular smokers.

The following findings from the qualitative research commissioned by HEBS illustrate the initial barriers to achieving any change in attitude, let alone behaviour:

"You're as likely to get cancer from other things"

"When your number's up you'll go anyway"

"There's few enough pleasures in life"

"Cancer is dormant in people anyway"

"You can still get ill even if you don't smoke"

"I'm not a heavy smoker so it's not an issue"

"They are still selling them"

"We've all got to die"

C2DE regular smokers

"In many cases almost nothing, they felt, could amend their smoking behaviour because it was so entrenched and they felt either powerless or unmotivated to change.

Many/majority had experience of death via cancer, yet this had little effect on their smoking behaviour. We observed some fatalistic acceptance of a long term health risk without really being able to deal with the implications.

Those who are keen and willing to quit are under no illusion as to the nature of the task."

"It's hell when you try – real misery"

C2DE Smoker

Strategic Research Group, July 1992
(Sample: C2DE regular smokers)

The resource required to quit by smokers is most commonly believed to be individual willpower. Smokers wishing to quit generally said they would get round to doing so in their own way and in their own time.

In the face of such stonewalling resistance, and accepting the view that kicking the habit has to be self-initiated, the health education debate about the best approach to foster change in this damaging behaviour remains unresolved. Conventional wisdom suggests that the main alternative routes are the stick and carrot.

In the 1970s the stick approach, focusing on the negative aspects of damage done to one's health predominated, whereas in the 1980s the focus shifted to concentrating on positive views of the benefits to individuals resulting from the adoption of healthier behaviours.

A seminal research paper, published in Scotland in 1980, contrasted positive versus negative approaches in advertising[1] (extract given in Appendix). It was stated that a negative route creates anxiety and thus heightens a rejection of messages, whereas the use of humour relaxes the recipient and is more likely to lead to acceptance of the message.

To set the advertising context for the 1990s, HEBS commissioned extensive qualitative research among C2DE smokers in order to test contrasting concepts for advertising: a humorous, positive tone of voice, on the one hand, and a hard hitting warning of the health hazards associated with smoking, on the other.

On the basis of the research findings, HEBS concluded that the purpose of advertising was not to impart knowledge of the benefits of stopping smoking. Nor was the issue about one tone of voice being intrinsically superior to another.

Smokers strongly rejected the concepts based on humour. These were felt to trivialise what to them was a serious matter.

Those who wanted to quit sought empathy and practical help. Information and confrontation were not enough.

It appeared that, the heavier the smoking, the greater was the difficulty of changing behaviour.

---

1. Defence-inducing Advertising. D S Leathar, Advertising Research Unit, University of Strathclyde, Glasgow

A New Solution

From the qualitative research we developed a picture of the complexity of the quitting process. Smokers go through a number of stages, from building desire, making an announcement, choosing one's method to quit, summoning willpower, making an attempt, quitting and (sometimes) relapsing back to smoking again.

A review of existing literature on the subject allowed us to understand in more detail how quitting works.

A paper published in 1983 of results from a quantitative study of adult smokers who had recently changed their smoking behaviour of their own volition identified five stages and ten processes of change.

TABLE 3: STAGES AND PROCESSES OF QUITTING SMOKING

STAGES: Precontemplation ⇒ Contemplation ⇒ Action ⇒ Maintenance ⇒ Relapse

PROCESSES	Exemplifying Attitude
Consciousness Raising	"I look for information related to smoking"
Self-Liberation	"I tell myself I am able to quit smoking if I want to"
Social-Liberation	"I notice that public places have sections set aside for non-smokers"
Self-Re-evaluation	"My depending on cigarettes makes me feel disappointed in myself"
Environmental Re-evaluation	"I stop to think that smoking is polluting the environment"
Counter-Conditioning	"I do something else instead of smoking when I need to relax"
Stimulus Control	"I remove things from my place of work that remind me of smoking"
Reinforcement Management	"I am rewarded by others if I don't smoke"
Dramatic Relief	"Warnings about health hazards of smoking move me emotionally"
Helping Relationships	"I have someone who listens when I need to talk about my smoking"

Base: Sample of 872 adults recently attempting to quit smoking

Source: Prochaska & DiClemente, USA 1983

Our new solution to the problem was not to use either a carrot or the stick, but to combine approaches by focusing on both the 'Dramatic Relief' and 'Helping Relationships' factors within the quitting process.

The chosen strategy was twin-pronged, combining hard hitting messages on the health risks of continuing to smoke, together with the proffering of an aid to quitting via 'Smokeline'.

ADVERTISING

The Advertising Plan was laid out as follows:

Advertising Objectives

— To increase desire to quit smoking.
— To create awareness of the 'Smokeline'.
— To generate response to the 'Smokeline'.

Advertising Strategy

— Twin-pronged: Stick and Carrot.
— By raising consciousness of the consequences of continuing to smoke using hard hitting realism of the foreshortening of life, and...
— By offering help with the process of quitting via the 'Smokeline'.

Role of Advertising

— To acknowledge smokers feelings about the problem and act as an empathetic enabler.

Advertising Execution

HEBS used a mix of media.

Broadcast television utilised twinned commercials to create the combined carrot and stick approach. The buying strategy of topping and tailing commercial breaks heightened this effect.

Posters were another stick to maintain a hard hitting message on the consequences of continuing to smoke.

'Smokeline', a free telephone helpline operated 12 hours a day by trained counsellors of Network Scotland, was launched and promoted initially solely through this advertising.

A booklet was available free only through the 'Smokeline' to adult callers entitled 'You Can Stop Smoking'. The 'Smokeline' was only publicised through advertising.

The television ran in three bursts using three commercials.

'Hospital' is a 50 second commercial portraying a realistic hospital scene where a mother, ill in bed, pleads with her visiting son to promise never to take up smoking.

'Presenter' is a 20 second commercial of a woman talking to camera, presenting the 'You Can Stop Smoking' booklet and announcing the 'Smokeline' phone number and explaining that someone like her will be on the end of the line to talk to.

'Terminal' is a 30 second commercial which realistically portrays a terminally ill man talking to camera of his regret at not seeing his family grow up and his fervent desire that he had quit smoking.

48 sheet posters appeared in December '92 and March/April '93.

'PRESENTER'

FVO: If you want to quit smoking get this guide.

It's full of great advice from ex-smokers on how you can give up for good.

We'll send you a copy free if you call the Smokeline right now on 0800 84 84 84.

'Course if you want to just chat about stopping, call this same number any time and you'll get someone like me on the line. Come on, you can do it, and we can help.

'TERMINAL'

MAN: ... he took me into a room and told me how long I had to go ... I could'nae really take it in ... I mean, I don't think of myself as old ...

I want tae see my son's wee boy grow up ... I want tae be with my lassie on her wedding day ... *(he apologises to the camera crew as he breaks down)*

... I'm sorry ... I'm not ready to die ... I always wanted tae stop smoking ...
(fade sound)

FVO: If you want to stop smoking, or you want someone you care about to stop, phone the Smokeline on 0800 84 84 84.

48-SHEET 'SMOKELINE' POSTERS

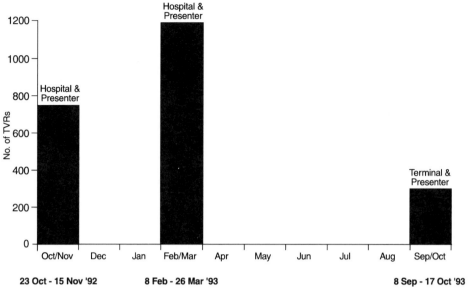

Figure 3. *Television bursts*

TABLE 4: CONSOLIDATED MEDIA PLAN
September 1992 - October 1993

	Sept 1992	Oct	Nov	Dec	Jan 1993	Feb	Mar	Apr	May	June	July	Aug	Sept	Oct
TV		▬	▬		▬	▬	▬					▬	▬	
Posters				▬		▬	▬						▬	

Source: The Media Shop, Glasgow

HEBS was careful not to have advertising presented as any kind of substitute for willpower. It was not acknowledged that giving up was difficult and smokers were encouraged to do so with a helping hand – hence the campaign strapline "You can do it. We can help".

One of the factors underlying smokers' propensity to deny, avoid and reject health messages is dismissing the idea of "healthy do gooders telling me what to do".

Therefore the casting was important in lending the commercials a style of being for "people like us" smokers.

The empathetic counsellor in 'Presenter' gave an impression of the kind of person who would be on the end of the line when you call the 'Smokeline'. She was meant to look like an ex-smoker herself, who could fully understand the problems face by people trying to stop.

THE EFFECTS

Introduction

The effects can be categorised in four areas:

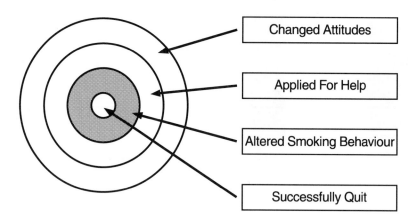

Figure 4. *Bull's eye*
Source: HEBS

This diagram illustrates the dynamic stages of change towards the bull's eye of quitting.

Positive effects attributable to advertising in *any* of these four areas would be a claim for success. This advertising campaign can lay claim to effects in *all four* areas.

A monitoring programme was devised to measure the telephone response to advertising, attitude shifts amongst smokers, the level of smoking in the general population and change in the smoking behaviour of callers to 'Smokeline' over a year (by means of a one year follow-up or panel study).

Data continues to be gathered, but the cut off point for this paper is taken to be one year since the start of the campaign.

TABLE 5: THE MONITORING PROGRAMME

Activity	Description	Oct 1992	Nov	Dec	Jan 1993	Feb	Mar	Apr	May	Jun	Jul	Aug	Sep	Oct
Research	Network Scotland (1 in 10 sample of 'Smokeline' callers)	▨	▨	▨	▨	▨	▨	▨	▨	▨	▨	▨	▨	▨
	Network Scotland Telephone Panel Study revisited 3 times (3 random samples from 1 in 10 callers to 'Smokeline')	▨			▨										
	System 3 Scottish Health Survey	▨					▨								
	RUHBC CATI Monitoring of Smoking Trends in General Population	▨	▨	▨	▨	▨	▨	▨	▨						
Advertising	Posters			▬			▬								
	TV	▬		▬		▬	▬							▬	

Source: HEBS

Applying for Help by Calls to 'Smokeline' and Booklet 'Sales'

During the first year (23 October 1992 - 21 October 1993) there were 129,717 interactive calls logged at 'Smokeline'. This is an average of nearly 2,500 a week.

A call is considered to be interactive when a counsellor offers information, as opposed to hoaxes, being cut off, or no information exchanged (non-interactive calls).

There were 110,230 lost calls over the year, over half of which were in the first few weeks, due to a shortage of lines following the unforeseen extraordinary demand. Original estimates of the number of lines and on-line counsellors required proved to be well out, with the number of lines having to be doubled and more counsellors put on in the second week to cope with demand.

The original estimates were based on response levels to other helpline services including 'Quitline', which had been set up in England as part of an advertised anti-smoking campaign.

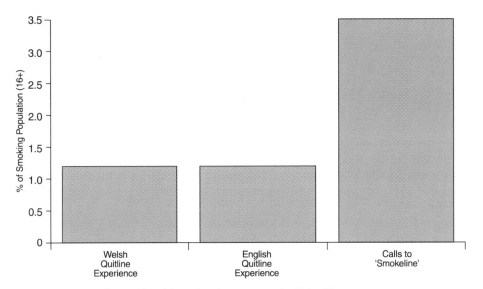

Figure 5. *The relative performance of 'Smokeline' in first advertising quarter (Oct '92-Dec '92)*
Source: *Network Scotland, Health Authorities*

Compared to the general population in Scotland, 'Smokeline' callers were significantly more likely to be renters than owner/occupiers. This is evidence of the successful targeting of the helpline at smokers in the lower socio-economic groups.

TABLE 6: PROFILE OF CALLERS TO SMOKELINE
BY TYPE OF HOUSING TENURE

	Index
Owner occupier	90
Council/Private rented	118

Sample: 1 in 10 callers to 'Smokeline'

Source: Network Scotland

The direct correlation between TV advertising and response is evident with clear boosted response with each burst of advertising.

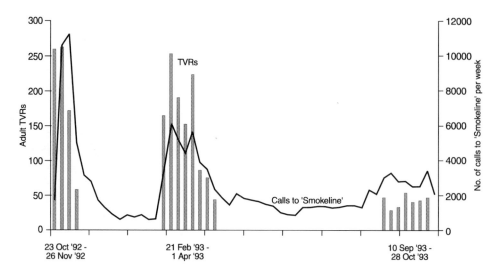

Figure 6. *Adult TVRs for HEBS 'Smokeline' advertising vs telephone response*
Source: Network Scotland; The Media Shop, Glasgow

The average weekly interactive call rate when TV advertising was running compared to when there was none is 4,340 versus 1,520.

Adjusting the number of calls to exclude those from children (the booklet was not given out to under 16 year olds), non-smokers and repeat calls, it is estimated that 84,000 (6%) of regular adult smokers in Scotland made genuine contact with 'Smokeline' in its first year.

The booklet had to be reprinted after only four months. 79,013 booklets were given out over the year, reaching 5.6% of all Scottish adult smokers.

Changing Attitudes

Within six months of the launch of 'Smokeline' there was an increase in smokers' desire to quit, with 20% claiming to be desperate or very much wanting to quit in March 1993 (compared to 17% in September 1992). In the same survey we have seen a decline in the weight of smoking, with smokers claiming to have cut down on how much they smoke (see Figure 7).

We know from the panel study that the lower the level of smoking, the greater the likelihood of successful quitting. Cutting down is a positive move along the path which leads to the bull's eye of quitting.

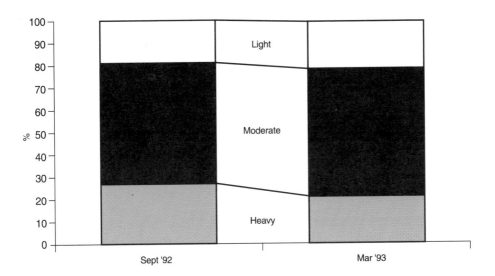

Figure 7. *Change in weight of smoking*
Sample: 603 smokers, 16-45 years
Source: System Three Scotland

Changing behaviour of 'Smokeline' callers

In order to measure changed behaviour, HEBS created a panel study among callers to 'Smokeline'. Three random samples, each of 300+ adults, were recruited at different times and subsequently interviewed by telephone at 3 weeks, 6 months and a year after calling 'Smokeline'.

The survey measured whether the respondents still smoked at the time of each telephone interview and what proportion of the period they had been non-smokers.

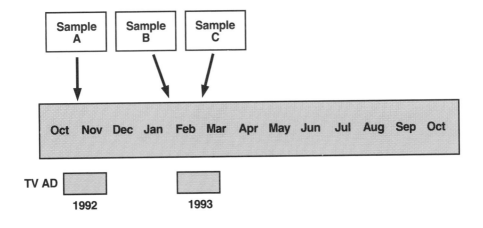

Figure 8. *Sampling recruitment versus advertising exposure*

TABLE 7: QUIT RATES OF SMOKELINE CALLERS

Smoking Behaviour at Sample Point	At 3 Weeks *(819 Smokers) %	At 1 Year *(599 Smokers) %
Non-smoker	21.6	24.0
Still smoker but reduced consumption	23.3	0.0
Moved to a lower tar brand	0.2	2.5
Quit at some point but restarted	25.5	60.6
No change in behaviour	29.3	12.5

Note: *Sample sizes vary due to panel sample attrition.

Source: Research Unit in Health and Behavioural Change (RUHBC)

A year after the initial call to 'Smokeline' nearly one in four of the original smokers were non-smokers, and only 12.5% claimed no change in their smoking behaviour.

The three sub samples from this panel study were recruited at different times and therefore exposed to different amounts of advertising as the campaign progressed. There is clear evidence that quit rates improved with increasing advertising exposure: the sample which was recruited latest (C) had the best quit rate, while the sample recruited in the first week of the campaign (A) has the worst quit rate.

TABLE 8: QUITTING RATES IMPROVE WITH ADVERTISING EXPOSURE

Sample Recruitment	Quit at 3 Weeks %
A October '92	15.8
B January '93	23.8
C February '93	25.4

Source: RUHBC

Sample C had been exposed to most advertising at their 3 week follow-up interview.

The only direct comparison we have for these data is from a study of quitting among respondents to National No Smoking Day which measured changed behaviour and quitting 3 months after calling their helpline. The 'Smokeline' response was significantly better than that reported for National No Smoking Day (see Figure 9).

Taking the quitting rate of 24% after a year from the panel study and applying it to the estimated number of regular adult smokers calling the 'Smokeline' (84,000), gives an estimate of successful quitters to be 20,160.

Applying these data to the universe of 1.4 million smokers would mean a 1.4% reduction in adult smoking prevalence in Scotland directly linked to 'Smokeline' over one year. This figure needs to be compared to a 'natural smoking decay rate' as shown by the General Household Survey of 0.8% per year. The difference between these two percentages (1.4% − 0.8% = 0.6% or 8,400 smokers) represents the impact on smokers' quitting behaviours attributable to 'Smokeline' alone.

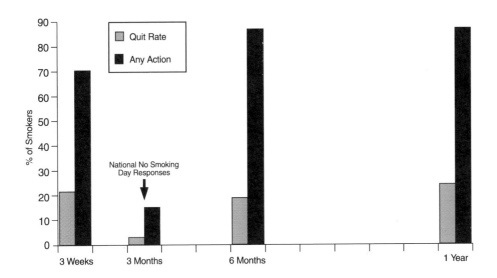

Figure 9. *Panel smoking status over time*
Sample: 300+ adults (1 in 10 universe)
Source: Network Scotland, National No Smoking Day, RUHBC

DISCOUNTING OTHER FACTORS

There are a number of factors other than advertising which could feasibly have caused this increase in quitting or decrease in smoking levels, including the price, distribution, and marketing of cigarettes and smoking cessation aid products.

Cigarette Advertising

HEBS spent £654,300 on TV and print advertising compared to an estimated £5.6 million by tobacco companies on above the line advertising.

During the period of this campaign there was a high profile launch on posters of new advertising for Scotland's brand leader in cigarettes, high tar Embassy Regal, known as the 'Reg' campaign.

There has been no change in distribution of tobacco products in the timespan of this advertising campaign.

Pricing

The Chancellor's Budget put 6.5% on the price of cigarettes in March 1993.

We do not have a regular monitor of the price of cigarettes but any change in price should be put in to a context of long term trends. Over the past 30 years the real price of cigarettes (relative to earnings) has been in significant decline. But change over the past decade has been almost imperceptible.

TABLE 9: REDUCING THE REAL PRICE OF CIGARETTE RELATIVE TO EARNINGS

Year	Income %
1961	1.4
1971	0.9
1981	0.8
1991	0.7

Source: Hansard, 11.3.91

Cessation Products

In tune with the long term decline in popularity of smoking, cessation products are now being marketed to help those wishing to quit (eg patches containing nicotine released through the skin).

We have not tried to assess their overall level of impact on the Scottish market but wish to point out that their advertising presence does not appear to correlate with use of 'Smokeline'.

Nicorette was the only product advertising during HEBS's launch of 'Smokeline', whilst total cessation advertising remained at a relatively constant level before and after 'Smokeline' was launched.

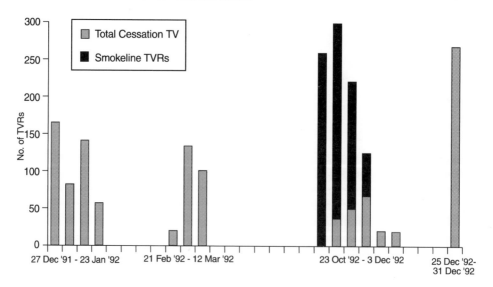

Figure 10. *Quitting aids advertised*
Source: The Media Shop, Glasgow

CONCLUSION

HEBS employed a new twin-pronged advertising strategy and approach in their anti-smoking advertising – the 'carrot and the stick'.

The carrot was the proffering of help to pave the way to quitting smoking. The stick was a realistic reminder of the years of life lost due to smoking.

Smokers' attitudes changed with an increasing desire to quit.

Smokers' behaviour changed with a lowering of consumption and more quitting than one could expect from long term 'natural' trends.

HEBS's 'Smokeline' generated an unprecedented response, requiring double the number of lines to be put on after only a week. Discounting false calls, children's calls and repeat calls, 'Smokeline' reached 84,000, or 6%, of regular smokers.

Analysis based on a year long panel study reveals a 1.4% reduction in adult smoking prevalence directly attributable to 'Smokeline'. This figure needs to be put in the context of the likely average yearly reduction (derived from government data) of 0.8%, ie. the level of quitting is 75% more than would be expected naturally.

This was achieved with an advertising spend of £650,000 whilst tobacco company above the line spends ran at an estimated £5.3 million.

Perhaps the real benefit of this advertising is the life years gained by quitters as a result of advertising, the value of which to them, their families and friends is inestimable.

The IPA Effectiveness Awards set out to isolate the case for advertising as having increased profitability for advertisers.

Setting a price and return on advertising investment is difficult for anti-smoking.

A review of existing sources[2] allows us to estimate costs to the NHS in Scotland as follows:

TABLE 10: ESTIMATED COSTS TO THE NHS IN SCOTLAND

Smoking Related Illnesses	£ Million
In patient costs	73
Primary care (GP) consultations	14
Prescriptions for tobacco related diseases	5
Outpatient costs	21
Total	**113**

2. Bostock Y (ed.) *The Smoking Epidemic: counting the cost in Scotland.* Action on Smoking and Health Scotland and Health Education Board for Scotland. Edinburgh, 1991.

General Register Office for Scotland. 1989. Annual report 1988. HMSO. Edinburgh, 1989.

Royal College of Physicians. *Smoking or health: follow up report of the Royal College of Physicians.* Pitman Publishing: London, 1983.

Confederation of British Industry/PERCOM. *Too much time out.* 1993

Marmaldy AA, Pearce DW. 'The social costs of tobacco smoking'. *British Journal of Addictions.* 84: 1139-1150, 1989.

Amos A, Hillhouse A, Alexander H, Sheehy C. *Tobacco use in Scotland: a review of literature and research.* Edinburgh: Action on Smoking and health Scotland, 1991.

O'Connor M and Pollock D. *November 1993 budget tobacco taxation.* 1993.

Furthermore, in 1991 the then Secretary of State for Health estimated (for the UK as a whole) 50 million working days lost due to smoking related illness at a likely cost of £2,200 – £3,200 million. This represents an estimated £220+ million to the Scottish economy.

With 1.4 million adult smokers in Scotland the cost is therefore conservatively put at £238 per smoker. This is £333m (NHS + 'working days lost' costs) divided by 1.4m adult smokers. The saving to the Scottish economy through an incremental reduction in smokers in year one of the campaign is 1.4% (our calculated reduction) less 0.8% (natural decay) which is 0.6%.

The cost saving is £238 x 8,400 new quitters = £1,999,200. The 'profit' is thus £1,999,200 less £654,000 = £1.35m.

APPENDIX: ARU RESEARCH CONCLUSIONS

DEFENCE-INDUCING ADVERTISING*
by D S Leathar, Advertising Research Unit, University of Strathclyde, Glasgow.

SUMMARY

This paper discussed the research applied to the development of the Scottish Health Education Group's publicity material, and outlines the two major problems incurred. The first is that, unlike much of product advertising, most health publicity is negative. Although benefits are projected, they are to be obtained by avoiding something negative, which is enjoyable, instead of achieving something positive in addition to what is already done. As a result, much health publicity induces anxiety, which in turn creates defensiveness. This defensiveness can be observed methodologically, for example in behaviour in a group discussion situation, as well as in response to content, as in the perceptual defensiveness shown by smokers to a highly negative, deeply threatening advertisement.

The second problem encountered is that health publicity often projects a distinctive class tone, and can lead to its being regarded as official Establishment material telling people what they should and should not do. It is thus often criticised as failing to identify with the life-style and problems of its audience, particularly working class groups whose values of immediacy and certainty conflict with the longterm probabilistic nature of the message that is presented.

Two major conceptual approaches are discussed which have recently been adopted to try to overcome these problems. Both are illustrated by case histories. The first is the projection of positive images, whereby the negative aspect of a concept is toned down and positive attributes enhanced, by surrounding the messages with images leaving behind attractive, and hopefully motivating, impressions. The second is the use of humour, where theoretical analysis shows that its use, though logically counterproductive, can in fact aid the communication of social messages without defensiveness. The paper concludes by outlining some of the likely trends over the next decade, in both theoretical research and practical application.

* Main text of a paper presented at a meeting of the Institute of Health Education "Improving Dental Health in Scotland" held on 8th October 1980. The paper was first presented at the XXIII ESOMAR Congress, Monte Carlo, Monaco, September 1980: "Taking Stock: What have we learned and where are we going?".
Permission to reprint this paper was given by ESOMAR, Wamberg 37, 1083 CW Amsterdam, The Netherlands.

19
National Dairy Council
The riddle of twin peaks –
or how a new way of looking at the data has
helped us to develop our campaign to
encourage kids to drink milk

INTRODUCTION

This is a paper about how we have managed to gain new insights into the way a campaign works by looking at our data in a new way: by focussing on how behaviour (children's milk drinking) responds to increased exposure of each execution (cumulative TVRs). This led us to discover an interesting new phenomenon which we have dubbed 'Twin Peaks'.

Since BMP took over the National Dairy Council's advertising in 1989, we have run a specific campaign to encourage children to drink more milk. This campaign has now been running for five years, and over time we have developed and aired four executions. Our advertising, as we shall demonstrate, has been extremely successful. We have seen a sustained 12% increase in drinking over the past five years, which in turn has generated an extra £23 million for the NDC. The advertising has paid for itself nearly three times over.

BACKGROUND

BMP took over the National Dairy Council's advertising in 1989. Since then, encouraging children to drink milk has been a consistent and discrete part of our overall campaign to increase milk sales.

The previous campaigns ('Geldof' – 1988 and 'Lotta Bottle' – 1982-87) had tried to target everybody by positioning milk as essential for a healthy lifestyle.

Why did we set out to encourage milk drinking?

Milk drinking is the only *use* of milk that can effectively be targeted by advertising.

It's a discretionary activity that isn't dependent on a desire for other products (like wanting a cup of tea). Secondly, it isn't supported by other manufacturers (eg Cereals). Finally, it symbolises milk as a whole: its purity and wholesomeness (source: BMP Qualitative 1988). As such it could have a positive influence on milk's image.

What was happening to milk drinking?

Total household milk sales had fallen by 8% between 1979 and 1988. Per capita milk drinking had, by comparison, fallen by 30%. While children aged 2-15 made up 20% of the population, they accounted for 50% of total milk drunk. (Source: OPCS, NDS.)

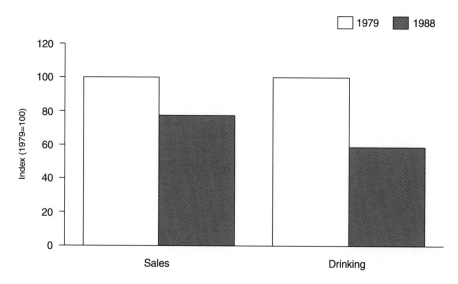

Figure 1. *Milk sales vs per capita milk drinking*
Source: MMB, NDS

(Note: From now we will express milk drinking and other drinks in terms of units (⅓ pint) per capita per day which takes account of fluctuations in the child population.)

While children's milk drinking was declining, their consumption of other soft drinks, particularly fizzy drinks, had increased (see Figure 2).

The Opportunity

We wanted to try and encourage children to drink more milk instead of other soft drinks. At the time, children were drinking around 600 million pints of milk a year. (This equated roughly to the total UK consumption of Coca Cola, source: NDS.) In addition, the child population was forecast to grow by 5% over the next 5 years. This was, potentially, a very worthwhile opportunity for advertising.

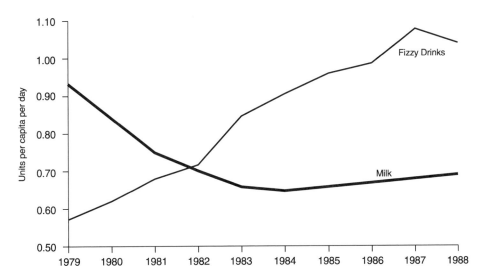

Figure 2. *Milk vs Fizzy drinks consumption*
Source: NDS

The Target

Our target in its broadest sense was children aged 2 to 15.

Our children's campaign began in April 1989. Since then, we have developed and aired four executions.

HOW DID WE DEVELOP THE KIDS' DRINKING STRATEGY?

Qualitative research with children indicated the following:

Milk is unique: both a food and a drink rolled into one. On a physical level, it's refreshing and nourishing. Emotionally, it's nurturing and caring. (Source: BMP Qualitative 1988.)

At it's heart, milk is good for you.

However, kids tend not to like things that are good for you. Because they don't believe they'll grow old they don't feel driven to eat healthily to prolong their life span. Healthy foods tend not to score too well on taste either. They prefer sweets and biscuits to brown bread and vegetables.

Milk is also seen as rather 'goody goody'. It's one of those things that mums tell their kids to drink.

We needed to overturn milk's worthy, dull and 'mumsy' image and make milk drinking something kids would find admirable.

On the surface, milk's core qualities were unappealing to children. However, there was one potential area we could exploit. Milk was regarded as something that helps kids to grow up strong, fit and healthy. And sport embodied exactly these benefits of milk. It's something boys and girls of all ages aspire to, whether it's playing in the school football team, admiring particular sports stars or having the right brand of trainers.

By linking milk with sporting success, we could appeal directly to children's aspirations.

The Creative Brief

Target Audience: Children aged 5 to 15

Objective: To persuade children to drink more milk

Strategy: To make milk's healthy properties admirable to children by linking them with sporting success

The Executions

'Rivals', a wry observation of the way children inter-react, and a sister execution, 'Tennis' were developed to this brief. They began running together from April 1989.

The Media Plan

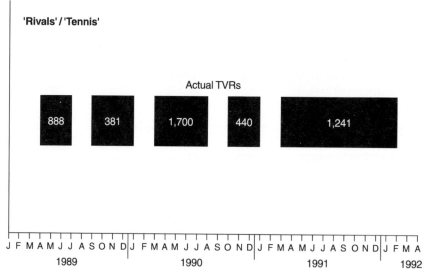

Figure 3. *Media plan*

How did 'Rivals'/'Tennis' work?

Qualitative research revealed that our advertising, in particular 'Rivals', seemed to have touched a nerve with children.

'Rivals' very quickly became kids' favourite advertising. They thought it was hilarious. In groups, they would give us a perfect rendition of the ad, with every line and nuance of the accent correct, and then fall about laughing. "Exactly" and "Accrington Stanley, who are they?" became playground catchphrases.

'RIVALS'

BOY 1: Got any lemonade?
BOY 2: If you want.

BOY 1: Milk! Ugh.

BOY 2: It's what Ian Rush drinks.

BOY 2: And he said, if I don't drink lots of milk, when I grow up, I'll only be good enough to play for 'Accrington Stanley'.

BOY 1: 'Accrington Stanley', who are they?
BOY 2: Exactly.

Kids had begun to copy the ad to the extent that it had entered playground culture and become a craze.

On one level, there were aspects of 'Rivals' that kids got involved with and copied. But on another, it tapped into their deeper aspirations: being successful at sport, but also being witty, independent and popular. The characters in 'Rivals' seemed to reflect exactly the sort of people children wanted to be.

'Tennis' worked in a similar way to Rivals. It appealed more to girls, who weren't into football. However, overall, 'Tennis' seemed to lack some of the qualities that made 'Rivals' such a playground favourite.

Refining the strategy: Exploiting 'playground culture'

The key task for our milk advertising was to get it into 'playground culture'. This meant, in practice, giving kids things they could copy and tapping into their aspirations. So the way in which "Rivals" worked served as a model for developing future kids' advertising.

At this point, we decided to refine our targeting for a number of reasons.

Creatively, it was unrealistic to suppose that we could hope to influence all kids: from 5 (infant school pupil) to 15 years (young adult) with one execution.

Older kids are the key soft drinks consumers. Also, we'd observed in qualitative research that older kids were more likely than younger kids to regard milk as a dowdy, 'mumsy' drink.

By targeting older kids, we hypothesized that we might be able to exploit the 'copying' mechanism further. Younger children might copy their older brothers and sisters.

Summary Creative Brief

Target: Children aged 10 -15 (and their younger brothers and sisters)

Reward: Other kids would admire me if they saw me drinking milk

Strategy: Get milk into 'playground culture': create a craze
  — catchphrases, humour, songs to copy
  — tap into their aspirations (sporting and personal)

The Executions

'Linford' began running in July 1990. It featured top sprinter Linford Christie.

'Cool for Cats' followed in March 1992. This blended humour, a catchy song, ('Cool for Cats' by Squeeze) with a startling new animation technique. 'Match of the Day', a sister execution to 'Cool for Cats' came on air in March 1993.

'COOL FOR CATS'

Song 'Cool for Cats' by Squeeze

Me mother's down the bingo
and me old man's out of town

They said that I could party
so I called me mates around

I spot a little diamond in a corner
on her own, the lads all try it on

but end up with their fuses blown
And then she eyes me bottle
in a way that I condone

So while the party's raving
I step in with same old chat
And let her share me pint of milk
because it's Cool for Cats

The Media Plan

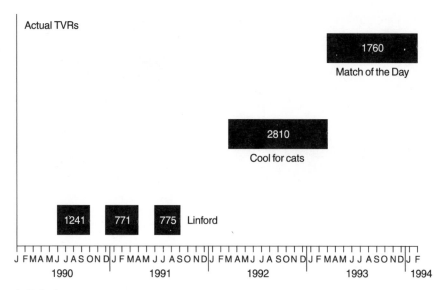

Figure 4. *Media plan*

How did these ads work?

We discovered from qualitative research that these ads entered 'playground culture' in much the way we'd hoped.

'Linford', for example, was particularly popular with older boys for whom he was a hero. The ad also tapped into the emerging craze for athletics and athletics gear, especially trainers.

> "The Linford Christie one is my favourite milk advert. He's pretty cool."
>
> Boy aged 15, BMP Qualitative 1991

'Cool for Cats', on the other hand entered playground culture in another way. The new animation technique we used was a real playground conversation piece.

> "We were trying to work out how they did those fruit machine eyes ."
>
> Girl aged 14, BMP Qualitative 1992

In addition, the song became very popular.

> "Now when it comes on, I sing it and my little sister dances to it"
>
> Girl aged 12, BMP Qualitative 1992

THE BIG PICTURE. WHAT HAPPENED TO DRINKING?

We had aimed to increase the amount of milk drunk by 2 to 15 year olds. Since our advertising has been on air, we have seen a 12% increase in drinking vs the comparable pre campaign period.

We will go on to show that this is the result of our advertising.

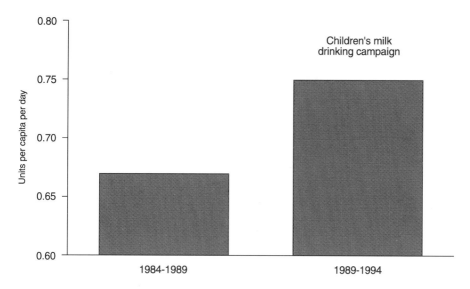

Figure 5. *Milk drinking: 2-15 year olds*
Source: NDS

ISOLATING THE ADVERTISING EFFECT

Awareness and Image

We have positive evidence to suggest that the image of milk improved over the period of our advertising.

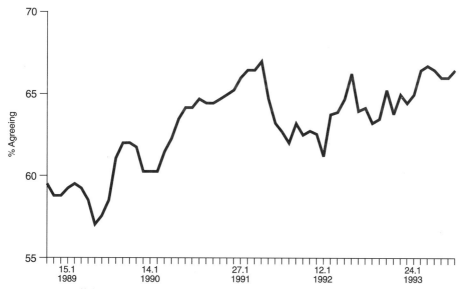

Figure 6. *Percentage of kids agreeing: "It's important that kids should drink milk"*
Source: Millward Brown

In addition, our tracking study confirms our qualitative findings that the ads were well recalled, well loved, and saying the right things about milk.

TABLE 1: TRACKING STUDY RESULTS

	Geldof	Rivals	Linford	Cool for Cats	Match of the Day
	%	%	%	%	%
Prompted Recognition	81	96	92	95	87
Prompted Attitudes					
"I enjoy watching it"	43	53	54	64	65
"Sticks in your mind"	39	47	55	57	34
Spontaneous communication					
"Milk is cool"	–	–	–	30	12
"Makes you healthy"	11	28	28	8	38
"Gives you energy"	18	16	36	–	41
"Good for you"	30	40	31	30	29

Source: Post campaign Millward Brown 3/91, 3/93, 10/93

Eliminating other factors

We have shown that when our advertising was on air, children's milk drinking increased. We shall now show that it was only the advertising which could have caused this.

The increase was confined to children

Adult milk drinking levels remained constant. This would therefore suggest that the increases seen among children were not part of some more general trend.

TABLE 2: ADULT MILK DRINKING

Average units per person per day	1988	1989	1990	1991	1992	1993
Adults (>16 years old)	0.15	0.14	0.15	0.14	0.14	0.15

Source: NDS

Temperature effect

There is evidence to suggest that a fall in temperature has a small positive effect on milk drinking: (probably explained by children switching out of milk into other soft drinks when it's hot). However, over the period of our advertising, the average temperature was 0.2 degrees higher than the pre campaign period.

TABLE 3: AVERAGE TEMPERATURES

	'85-'89	'90-'93
Average temperature (°C)	10.0	10.2

Source: MET Office

The real price of milk rose

An econometric model of the total milk market, constructed by MMD estimates that for every 1% increase in the real price of milk a corresponding decrease of 2.4% occurs in milk sales. The real price of milk rose over the period 1989 to 1993

Child population

Child population did indeed increase by 5% between 1989 and 1993, (source: OPCS) but our data source measures milk drinking in units per capita.

School milk volume has been declining

School milk drinking is included in our measure of drinking (NDS), and accounts for around 20% of all milk consumed by kids. However, its importance has declined as fewer schools provide milk for their pupils.

TABLE 4: SCHOOL MILK VOLUME

	1985-1988	1989-1993
School milk volume (millions litres)	96	79

Source: MMB, MAFF

There have been no other major campaigns encouraging kids to drink milk

Our other big campaigns have focussed on
— Milk *purchasing*: 'Milkman' campaign (see below)
— Adult milk drinking

Throughout the late 1980s and early 1990s there has been a small, consistent spend on other milk drinks targeted at children. The bulk (£1.2 million) of this has been for branded flavoured milk drinks such as Aero and Mars. However, the measure of drinking we have used is the amount of milk drunk neat. The MMB's Milk Can received a lower level of support (£0.5 million)

TABLE 5: MEDIA EXPENDITURE ON 'OTHER MILK' PRODUCTS AIMED AT KIDS

	1987 £'000s	1988 £'000s	1989 £'000s	1990 £'000s	1991 £'000s	1992 £'000s	1993 £'000s
Mars Milk	91.8	356.4	464.7	–	–	–	–
Aero Milk	–	–	–	–	65.9	196.5	–
Milk Can (MMB)	–	–	48.5	415.8	–	–	–
Other	–	–	–	–	–	–	–

Source: Media Register

The effect of 'Daybreak'

Our 'Milkman' advertising began in April 1991. It aimed to encourage housewives to remain loyal to their milkman and order extra from him. (See 1992 IPA ad effectiveness paper 'Milkman Relaunch'.) Interestingly, and quite unexpectedly our ad, 'Daybreak', appeared to have an effect on children's milk drinking.

On reflection, we can understand why this should have happened. 'Daybreak' had a new animation technique, the dancing bottles, and a catchphrase, 'empties!': all the elements that would allow it to enter playground culture.

However, our milkman advertising contributed in only a small way to the overall increase in milk drinking. Firstly, drinking had increased with the advent of 'Rivals'/'Tennis' two years before the milkman advertising began. Secondly, it behaves much like the other children's executions as we shall see. The milkman advertising has not caused a sustained uplift in children's drinking.

We can isolate the effect of 'Daybreak'. We will show how this is done later.

A DEEPER UNDERSTANDING OF THE CAMPAIGN

We have shown that our advertising works by starting crazes. However, this raises further questions. How does the craze mechanism work? How can we predict when a craze will end? We can shed light on some of these issues by looking at the data in a new way.

A closer examination of the data

There seemed to be a faint relationship between the introduction of new ads and peaks in drinking: as new executions are introduced, drinking increases and then falls away. So we formed a hypothesis, that this effect was the result of impact and then wear out of our ads.

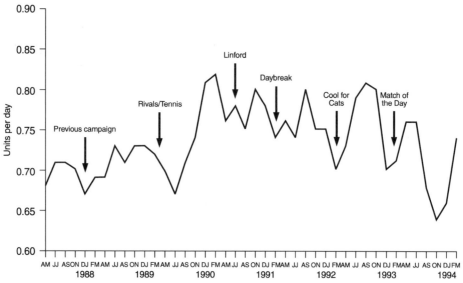

Figure 7. *Children's milk drinking aged 2-15*
Source: NDS

To put our hypothesis to the test, we needed to look at how drinking responded to the levels of exposure of each execution. So for the period over which each execution ran, we plotted each of our bi-monthly data points against the corresponding bi-monthly cumulative TVRs. (Rather as you might look at how advertising awareness responds to TVR levels.) We ended up with 4 graphs. (Note: Because 'Rivals' and 'Tennis' ran together we have treated them as one execution.)

When we did this a consistent pattern emerged which was highly unusual, but was also, as we shall see, highly significant.

At the time it seemed appropriate to dub this the 'Twin Peaks' phenomenon!

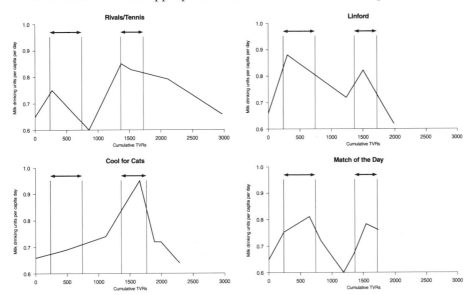

Figure 8. *Milk drinking vs TVRs by execution*
Source: NDS, BARB

The 'Twin Peaks' effect

The 'Twin Peaks' graphs revealed two interesting things. First, it appeared that there were wear in/wear out effects going on for each execution

— 'Rivals'/'Tennis', 'Linford', 'Match of the Day' exhibit a double wear in/wear out pattern
— 'Cool for Cats' behaves differently, with a single wear in/wear out.

Secondly, the peaks in drinking for each execution fell into two narrow bands (illustrated on the graphs) around 500 and 1,500 TVRs. This suggested that there might be a relationship between TVRs and drinking.

We will later show that from the 'Twin Peaks' graphs alone, we can estimate the size of the effect for each execution and the campaign as a whole.

Unravelling the mystery of 'Twin Peaks'

Our 'Twin Peaks' plots revealed that somehow our advertising was having a double wear in/wear out effect. The question was, what could possibly explain this effect?

We can show that the probability of producing these graphs by chance is 0.01. This was unlikely to be a freak event!

The way we had plotted our graphs (using cumulative TVRs) meant that we had smoothed out media flighting effects. The effect could not, therefore, have been the result of the timing and weights of media used.

Neither could 'Twin Peaks' be explained by seasonality. Our executions had started running at different times of the year. When we look at the drinking data for each execution on a calendar basis, no consistent relationship emerges.

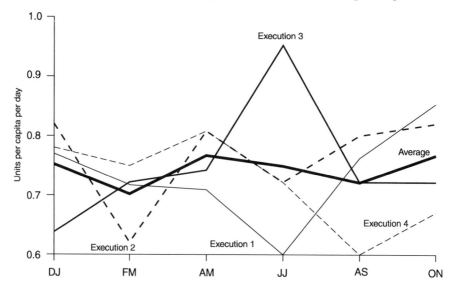

Figure 9.   *Children's milk drinking by bi-month*
Source: NDS

The Mystery Revealed!

We split our drinking data into two age bands, 2-9 year olds and 10-15 year olds. At this point, because base sizes became low, we aggregated our bi-monthly data to get a combined plot for 'Rivals'/'Tennis', 'Linford' and 'Match of the Day'. What we discovered was that **drinking among older children rose before drinking among younger children.** (See Figure 10.)

This lag between older children's response to the advertising, and younger children's could explain the 'Twin Peaks' effect.

What about 'Cool for Cats'?

Here, drinking rises among older children and younger children at the same rate. We believe that this is because 'Cool for Cats' was aired at a much higher initial weight than the other executions. (See Table 6.)

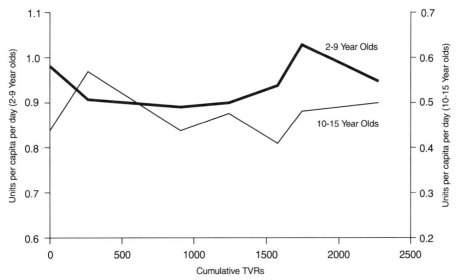

Figure 10. *Milk dringing by age group*
Note: *Aggregated 'Rivals', 'Linford' and 'Match of the Day'*
Source: NDS

TABLE 6: INITIAL ADVERTISING WEIGHTS

	Initial TVRs
Cool for Cats	474
Rivals/Tennis	254
Linford	306
Match of the Day	234

Source: BARB

'Daybreak'

Interestingly, when we plot bi-monthly drinking data against cumulative TVRs for the milkman ad 'Daybreak' we see a 'Twin Peaks' effect. (See Figure 11.)

This is not the result of 10-15s responding earlier to our advertising: it is, in this instance, explained by 5-9 year olds responding more quickly than 2-4s! (See Figure 12.)

Two Playgrounds

We can now explain why we see the 'Twin Peaks' phenomenon. Our qualitative research showed that our ads entered 'playground culture'.

The reason we saw a difference in the rate of response of drinking to our advertising among different age groups was because our ad was being picked up in two separate playgrounds.

We hypothesized that the craze started in the senior school playground and then filtered down to the junior playground by way of younger brothers and sisters.

Anecdotally, this seemed plausible. In groups, older children would often talk about how crazes would pass from their peer group to the younger age group.

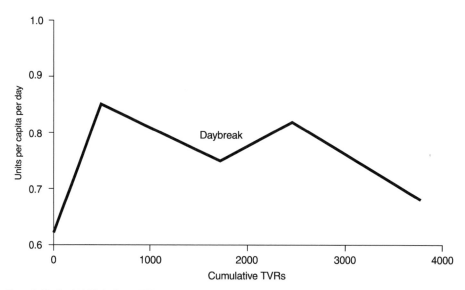

Figure 11. *'Daybreak': Milk drinking vs TVRs*
Source: NDS

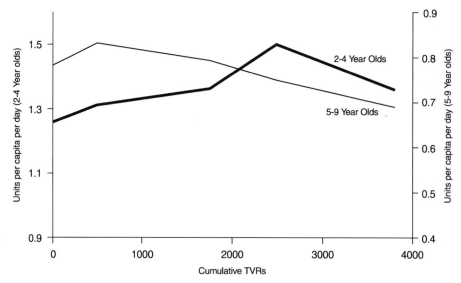

Figure 12. *'Daybreak': Milk drinking vs TVRs by age group (2-4s vs 5-9s)*
Source: NDS

"We used to like 'New Kids… (on the Block)'. The only people who like them now are people like my sister, and she's six!"

Girl aged 13, BMP Qualitative 1992

"My little brother really annoys me. He's always trying to copy me on my BMX"

Boy aged 12, BMP Qualitative 1992

Furthermore, given that TGI estimates that only 36% of senior school kids have younger brothers or sisters at junior school, there is only relatively limited mixing between the two playgrounds. It seemed likely that there would be a lag before younger children 'adopted' the advertising.

IMPLICATIONS FOR OUR STRATEGY

This finding has a number of implications for the way we approach our advertising.

How kids use advertising

Kids are very prone to crazes. They live in a world where social acceptance is very important. All sorts of things from their everyday experiences of life form a kind of social currency: from pop music and fashion through to TV programmes and adverts.

Kids copy things they admire and in their social world, this escalates into a craze.

But because kids are always seeking out new experiences, and continually trying to assimilate trends from the adult world, crazes are short lived. This means that novelty is crucial. (We can see this from the response in drinking as each new execution is aired.)

The implications of the way kids use advertising are broadly twofold. Firstly, in a creative sense, because we compete against the likes of Sega, Tango and Peperami, we will continue to need advertising that's original, distinctive and well loved. (It is interesting to note that our tracking study shows that our advertising has become progressively more enjoyable.)

Secondly, we need to try and predict and, if possible, avoid wear out.

A theory of wear out

Measuring/predicting wear out

The way in which kids use advertising suggests that there should be a rapid rise in milk drinking, followed by an almost equally rapid tailing off. (Our 'Twin Peaks' graphs confirm this.)

Measuring and predicting wear out have been difficult. Our ads exhibit 'extreme' wear out: behaviour is affected before our tracking study reveals any changes in awareness or attitudes to the advertising.

This has meant that in trying to predict wear out, we have come to rely on more sensitive techniques such as qualitative research to probe in more depth attitudes to our advertising.

Maximising returns

Since our ads exhibit 'extreme' wear out, we need to refresh our campaign continually to make sure that increases in drinking are sustained.

The 'Twin Peaks' graphs have given us a rule of thumb: that after an execution has had around 2,000 TVRs, we begin to see diminishing returns.

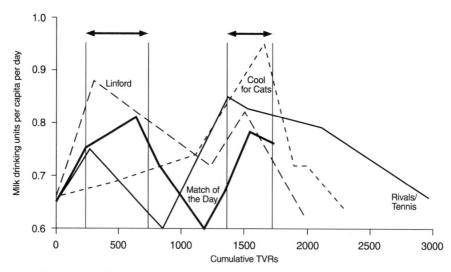

Figure 13. *Milk drinking vs TVRs by execution*
Source: NDS, BARB

In order to maximise our returns, therefore, we need to replace executions every 2,000 TVRs or so.

Targeting

The 'Twin Peaks' graphs have provided us with quantitative evidence that crazes pass from older children to younger children because young children copy their older brothers and sisters.

Hence, we are able to target the older end of the age spectrum in both creative and media terms.

A SUMMARY OF THE EVIDENCE

Milk drinking among 2 to 15 year olds has increased over the past 5 years.

We have shown that this could only have been caused by our advertising: we have eliminated any other possible contributory factors.

In addition, our qualitative research, and awareness and image data, suggests that our ads worked much as we'd planned: by entering playground culture and creating crazes

The 'Twin Peaks' phenomenon has given us further evidence that peaks in drinking correlate with the advent of new executions: (the effect is not produced by randomness). It has also provided quantitative confirmation that the craze starts among older children and then passes to younger children.

EVALUATION OF THE CAMPAIGN

1. Average amount drunk by 2-15 year olds: units per person per day:

   Pre advertising: April '84-March '89   0.67
   Post advertising: April '89-March '94   0.75

   Children's drinking increased by 12% over this period. We have shown nothing else could have caused this increase.

2. Over April '85 to March '89 the average total amount drunk by kids was approximately:

10.7 billion pints per year	(total average household milk volume, source: MMB)
x 0.112	(percentage of milk drunk neat source: Taylor Nelson)
x 0.5	(percentage of milk consumed by 2-15s, source: NDS)
= 600 million pints per year	

3. The total extra milk consumed as a result of our advertising was:

600 million pints per year	(see 2 above)
x 5 years	(April '89-March '94)
x 0.12	(percentage increase in kids' milk drinking: see 1 above)
= 350 million pints	

4) An estimate of the profit per pint is 10p:

   Total profit generated by advertising   = 350 million x 0.10
                                                      = £35 million.

Total expenditure on this advertising was approximately £12 million (media and production).

The advertising paid for itself nearly three times over.

We need to take account of the effect of 'Daybreak'. We can do this through our alternative evaluation of the campaign using only the 'Twin Peaks' graphs.

An alternative evaluation of the campaign

We can estimate the effect of our advertising by adding up the area under each of the 'Twin Peaks' graphs.

Calculating the effect

Taking our base level drinking figure to be the level of drinking at 0 TVRs, we can calculate the average increment for each execution.

TABLE 7: AVERAGE DRINKING INCREASE BY EXECUTION

Execution	Base Drinking Level Units	Average Increase Units
Rivals/Tennis	0.65	0.09
Linford	0.66	0.09
Cool for Cats	0.69	0.05
Match of the Day	0.64	0.08
Daybreak	0.62	0.07

To get to the average amount of milk consumed per execution in pints, we need to do the following calculation.

Average increase

x   no. of days over which campaign on air – (NDS measures drinking per day)

x   no. of children in population = 8 million (OPCS: England & Wales) – (NDS measures drinking per capita)

/3   NDS measures consumption in units ($\frac{1}{3}$ of a pint).

TABLE 8: EXTRA MILK DRUNK DUE TO ADVERTISING

Execution	Average Increase Units	Campaign Duration Days	Extra Milk Million Pints
Rivals/Tennis	0.09	420	100
Linford	0.09	240	57
Cool for Cats	0.05	360	48
Match of the Day	0.08	420	90
Daybreak	0.07	300	56
Total			351

Evaluating the effect of the campaign in this way gives a very similar result.

Subtracting the contribution made by 'Daybreak' of 56 million pints, our children's executions have contributed 294 million extra pints. This equates to a total profit of:

294 x 0.10
= £29.4 million.

SUMMARY

We have demonstrated that our children's campaign has been responsible for a sustained 12% increase in children's milk drinking. As a result we have generated £35 million profit for the NDC on a total spend of £12 million, a total extra profit of £23 million. The advertising has paid for itself almost three times over.

We set out with the objective of making milk drinking admirable to children. To do this we needed to create advertising that would start a craze and enter playground culture. We have seen that all the executions we have aired to date have, in their own way, achieved this.

We were left with some fundamental issues as to how the campaign actually worked, and how best to manage the strategy. Our discovery of the 'Twin Peaks' phenomenon has helped us address some of these issues. It has helped us gain a better understanding of the way our ads are used, which will allow us to refine our strategy for the future.

'Twin Peaks' demonstrates that the key to gaining new insights into advertising strategy can often lie in unexpected places. The data traditionally used to evaluate a campaign has, in this case provided us with new learning as to how it actually works.

CONCLUSIONS

The learning we have developed on our children's campaign has some obvious parallels with other markets and implications for the future.

The way in which older and younger children react to our advertising is broadly analogous with other markets in which products find favour initially with a group of 'early adopters' and then with the mainstream (eg fashion, 'rave culture').

This phenomenon seems bound up with the way trends are consumed, with groups of people continually striving to be on the leading edge. It also demonstrates the power of the craze, which once started, takes on a life of its own and passes, 'virus like' from one group of people to another (in our case, from older to younger siblings). The craze dies out as people become 'immune' to it.

We would expect to see this phenomenon at work in many other markets: in fact any where a product's image/values have social currency (eg beer, hi-fi).

APPENDIX

It is statistically very unlikely that the peaks observed are due to random statistical fluctuations. Even if random factors did introduce large movements in the data, they would, (if truly random), be as likely to produce troughs as peaks. The probability of an outlier producing a peak would be 0.5 and hence the probability of finding 7 peaks in succession would be $(0.5)^7 = 0.008$, ie less than 1%. The peaks are thus almost certainly due to some causal factor(s).

20

How the Awareness of the Symptoms of Diabetes was Increased

BACKGROUND

This is a peculiar case history in that its conception was in a hospital clinic.

In 1991 Jeremy Prescot, Managing Director of Kilmartin Baker, was visiting Charing Cross Hospital for his annual check-up – he, himself, has diabetes. He became involved in long discussions with Dr Dev Singh and Dr Peter Wise who were both concerned by the late diagnosis of non-insulin dependent diabetes.

What is Diabetes?

Diabetes is a common disorder of the body where there is too much sugar in the bloodstream. There are two types of diabetes, insulin dependent and non-insulin dependent. Non-insulin dependent is the most common, is estimated to represent 90% of all those with diabetes and is controlled by diet or diet and tablets.

Charing Cross Hospital Research

Dr Singh and Dr Wise had recently concluded two research studies of their own. Firstly they had analysed 100 consecutively newly-diagnosed patients who had non-insulin dependent diabetes. Only 39% of these patients had reported major symptoms to the referring doctor. After completing a symptom enquiry form, 80% actually recognised some symptoms.

Additionally, a number of patients did not see a doctor until major complications had set in – one or two had contracted gangrene which led to amputations. Yet when questioned they recognised that they had had the symptoms of diabetes for many years.

The second study consisted of street interviews in Hammersmith and Fulham. Of 480 people interviewed 48% were unable to name a single symptom of diabetes and only 4% were able to name the important combination of thirst and polyuria (going to the loo a lot). These findings were in fact in close agreement with the only other study (from North America) of public knowledge of diabetes and diabetes symptoms.[1]

The doctor's research had established that many sufferers did not recognise the symptoms of diabetes and therefore failed to consult their GPs. Since diabetes is a

---

1. Michielutte, R, Diseker RA, Stafford CL, Carr P. Knowledge of diabetes and glaucoma in a rural North Carolina community. *Journal Community Health* 1984 4:269-280.

common disorder affecting 1 million people in the UK, this level of ignorance was disturbing as late diagnosis can result in major complications such as blindness and gangrene leading to limb amputation.

Jointly the doctors and Jeremy Prescot approached the British Diabetic Association with a comprehensive presentation which set out the problem (ie, the ignorance about the symptoms of diabetes) and provided a carefully considered solution which was to carry out a symptoms awareness advertising campaign.

Relevance to the British Diabetic Association

Such a campaign was extremely relevant to the aims of the BDA, because they are concerned with the welfare and care of people with diabetes as well as funding research aiming to prevent and eventually cure diabetes. It was believed that this campaign could be a very public demonstration of what the Association stood for and that it would work well alongside a general awareness and fundraising campaign.

The British Diabetic Association recognised that.

THE TEST CAMPAIGN

Choice of Test Areas

The test areas for the campaign became self-selecting as the doctors wanted to set up detailed monitoring systems of new patients with non-insulin dependent diabetes. This relied upon the voluntary participation of GPs and hospital clinics and the doctors believed they had the necessary contacts in Wolverhampton and Basingstoke. Coincidentally this provided two very different areas in socio-demographic terms, and was a useful contrast for research.

CREATIVE STRATEGY

Non-insulin dependent diabetes can affect anybody at any time. The symptoms are easily identifiable – tiredness, increased urination, thirst, blurred vision, sudden weight loss and genital irritation. The problem was how to communicate them effectively without causing anxiety. It was very important that we did not panic thousands of people into rushing in to see their GP simply because they were run down.

Target Audience

The primary target audience was non-diagnosed diabetics, they probably do not realise they have a medical problem ("it's not me").

However, our media target market was really *all adults* because we didn't only want to reach potential diabetics but also their family and friends. Some people who had some of the symptoms may avoid going to the doctor because they were scared of the consequences. Yet if their families and friends also recognised the symptoms they were showing, they may encourage them to take action.

Advertising Strategy

To make the target audience aware of:

1. *The Symptoms:* Tiredness, having to drink a lot, numerous visits to the loo, blurred vision, sudden weight loss, genital irritation.

2. *The Possible Diagnosis:* Plus the reassurance that it's easily controllable.

Tone of Voice

Optimistic. It was our contention that traditional public health awareness campaigns tended by their very nature either to be frightening or lecturing (and sometimes both).

As getting diabetes was nobody's fault we had an immediate factual advantage – we weren't trying to get people to give up something or change their habits. However, we did decide against any kind of scare-mongering about the possible consequences of failing to act if the symptoms were recognised. We wanted to end on a positive note. Action could be taken if you had diabetes and the condition was controllable. Additionally, throughout the process of creative development we had to ensure that we did not alienate the 1 million existing people with diabetes.

MEDIA STRATEGY

Media Objectives

— To maximise coverage of all adults.

— To achieve a level of coverage and frequency that could be replicated on a national basis.

— To limit media exposure to within the two test towns so that monitoring could be more effective.

The Media Choice

4-sheet posters and local press were selected because they provided the best possible discrete coverage of all adults living in Basingstoke and Wolverhampton at a cost level that could be replicated on a national basis.

The advantage of 4-sheets is that they do not discriminate against any sector of the community as they are seen by motorists and pedestrians alike (it was important to ensure that we reached older people who may not drive).

Local press was considered to be an effective support medium which provided potential 100% household penetration using a combination of paid-for and free distribution titles. 25cms x 4cols spaces were chosen because this size was considered to be the most cost-effective – it ensured that the advertisements stood out from other local press advertisements and provided a certain degree of page dominance.

If you're tired, rundown, thirsty- it may not be a tonic you need.

You could be suffering from a form of diabetes.
Ask your own doctor for a test – diagnosis and simple treatment
could quickly restore your old sparkle.

BRITISH DIABETIC ASSOCIATION
10 QUEEN ANNE STREET, LONDON W1M 0BD. REG. CHARITY No. 215199.

Weight of Advertising

It was important to mount a campaign that could be replicated on a national basis at an affordable level (the British Diabetic Association's annual advertising budget being limited). We constructed a medium weight campaign that ran on a continuous basis for ten weeks.

Budget

Media and production for the test campaign was £25,500.

Media Plan

TABLE 1: MEDIA PLAN

	July w/c	August w/c	September w/c
Basingstoke			
Basingstoke Gazette Series	13,20	3,17,31	14
25 x 4-sheet sites in shopping precincts & high street locations	13	————————	20
Wolverhampton			
Wolverhampton Express & Star	13,20	3,17,31	14
Wolverhampton Chronicle	13,27	10,24	7,14
64 x 4-sheet sites in shopping precincts & high street locations	13	————————	20

THE RESEARCH PROGRAMME

The doctors were particularly anxious to set up the research so that the samples were robust enough to withstand the statistical rigours of the medical profession. In this they were successful as the campaign results have recently been reported in the *British Medical Journal*.[2]

1,000 street interviews were conducted (500 in each location) at both pre and post stages. Pre-advertising interviewing was conducted between 15 June to 3 July and the post stage between 21 September to 9 October. The advertising ran from 13 July to 20 September. The sample was representative of the adult population in each location and was conducted by Business Planning and Research International – an independent research organisation.

---

2. Effect of advertising on awareness of symptoms of diabetes among the general public: The British Diabetic Association Study. Baldev M. Singh, senior registrar, Peter H. Wise, consultant Department of Endocrinology Charing Cross Hospital. *British Medical Journal* Volume 308.

'SYMPTOMS II'

If you suffer from the following symptoms,

☐ thirst ☐ passing excessive urine
☐ tiredness ☐ weight loss
☐ blurred vision ☐ genital irritation

don't

You could be suffering from a form of diabetes.
Ask your own doctor for a test – diagnosis and simple treatment
could quickly restore your old sparkle.

BRITISH DIABETIC ASSOCIATION
10 QUEEN ANNE STREET, LONDON W1M 0BD. REG. CHARITY No. 215199.

RESEARCH RESULTS

Introduction

In reporting the research results we have restricted ourselves to unprompted scores as these provide the purest form of measurement.

TABLE 2: KNOWLEDGE OF ANY SYMPTOMS OF DIABETES (UNPROMPTED)

	Pre (Base 1000) %	Post (Base 1000) %
No knowledge	55	39

The level of ignorance of any symptom was substantially reduced.

TABLE 3: KNOWLEDGE OF SPECIFIC SYMPTOMS (UNPROMPTED)

	Pre (Base 1000) %	Post (Base 1000) %
Increased thirst	25	41
Tiredness	18	37
Blurred vision	15	14
Increased urination	7	10
Weight loss	8	9
Genital irritation	1	2

The campaign was particularly successful in increasing awareness of two of the major symptoms of diabetes.

TABLE 4: UNPROMPTED AWARENESS OF DIABETES ADVERTISING

	Pre (Base 1000) %	Post (Base1000) %
No	88	57
Yes	10	41
Don't know	2	2

Unprompted awareness quadrupled over the campaign period. Specific recall was also monitored. At the pre-stage the majority of what advertising recall there was related to the old, long running 'Shadow of Diabetes' campaign.

TABLE 5: POST STAGE – UNPROMPTED ADVERTISING RECALL

	(Base 406) %
'If you suffer'	58
'If you're tired'	35
Mother and child	5
Shadow of diabetes	3
Other	4
Can't remember	11

The symptoms campaign dominated recall at the post stage.

There was equal weight given to the two symptoms creative executions, so it would appear that the simple list approach was more effective. Concurrently the BDA were running a new national awareness/fundraising campaign on 4-sheets, 16-sheets and in the national press. This campaign 'Mother and Child', achieved 5% recall among those claiming awareness of diabetes advertising.

There can be no doubt that the symptoms advertising campaign caused the change in awareness previously monitored.

TABLE 6: WHERE SYMPTOMS ADVERTISEMENTS SEEN

	(Base 324)
	%
Poster	71
National newspaper	22
Local paper	17
On transport	7
TV/Radio	3
Others	7
Can't remember	4

Over 70% of those recalling symptoms advertisements correctly attributed posters as the medium, while a further 17% mentioned local newspapers. We believe there was a blurring of distinction between national and local newspapers.

IMPACT ON NEW PRESENTATION OF PATIENTS WITH DIABETES

During the 10 weeks before and during advertising, 43 general practices monitored the numbers of their patients who specifically requested tests to exclude diabetes. Compared with the pre-advertising phase there was a 71% increase in such presentations during the advertising phase (99 vs 58). The numbers of new patients with non-insulin dependent diabetes that resulted similarly increased by 70% (17 vs 10).

CONCLUSIONS

The test campaign proved that it was possible to educate the public and increase their knowledge of the symptoms of diabetes. Although the number of patients covered by the general practice monitoring was small, it is not hard to calculate the positive impact if this scale of response was replicated nationally.

We believe the advertising awareness figures themselves are quite remarkable considering TV was not used. Unlike public health campaigns (anti-smoking, heart disease etc) the BDA campaign did not seek to shock, it sought to inform – a very pure form of advertising.

THE NEXT STEP

After much soul-searching and attempts to convince the Department of Health to contribute towards the national roll-out, the BDA has decided to put the majority of its 1994 fund-raising budget behind the campaign.[3]

3. Diabetes puts education first. *Campaign*, 6 May 1994.

Index